THE POLITICS OF THE VATICAN

PETER NICHOLS

THE POLITICS
OF
THE VATICAN

FREDERICK A. PRAEGER, *Publishers*
New York • Washington • London

FREDERICK A. PRAEGER, PUBLISHERS
111 Fourth Avenue, New York, N.Y. 10003, U.S.A.
77-79 Charlotte Street, London W.1, England

Published in the United States of America in 1968
by Frederick A. Praeger, Inc., Publishers

© 1968 Peter Nichols

All rights reserved

Library of Congress Catalog Card Number: 68-11321

Printed in the United States of America

TO MY FATHER AND MOTHER

Contents

		page
	Introduction	ix
1	STAND AND UNFOLD	1
2	BELOW GOD AND ABOVE MAN	9

Persecution and Favour · Toleration and Riches · Conservatism and Success · Priests and Politics · Primacy of Rome · Authority and Unity · Seeking a Protector · Foreshadowing of Future Empire · New Empire Established · German Emperors · Gregory VII and the Investiture Controversy · Innocent III and the Papal Zenith · System Undermined · Greatness Withered

3	DIVERSITY AND ADVERSITY	74

Clash with the Modern World · Rerum Novarum and the Lateran Pacts · Pius XII and the End of Isolation

4	THE MASTER KEYS	107

John XXIII · Paul VI

5	WHERE PETER IS	131

Pope and Cardinals · The Curia

| 6 | WALLS OF THE VATICAN | 173 |
| 7 | TO TREAT WITH THE DEVIL | 195 |

Democracy and Communism · Italian Politics · Poland and Wyszynski · Mindszenty and Beran · Goodness and Peace · New Nations · Old Catholic Countries

| 8 | GUESTS AT THE BANQUET | 266 |

CONTENTS

9 LIGHT THE WEARY VESSEL 290
The Ecumenical Council · Curia and Progress · Bishops and their Powers · The Ecumenical Approach · The Modern World

10 ALONE ONCE MORE 323

11 EVEN FROM WITHIN 359

Index 361

ILLUSTRATIONS

following page 86

I Constantine

II Charlemagne

III Innocent III

IV Precursors of the Modern Papacy

following page 118

V Pius XII; John XXIII

VI Paul VI; Cardinal Browne and Cardinal Ottaviani

VII Cardinal Wyszynski; Cardinal Beran

VIII Cardinal Döpfner; Cardinal Bea

Introduction

IN a world largely distributed among the specialists, the work of a foreign correspondent still calls for knowledge of quite a number of subjects. For some years now, the Vatican has been one of mine. This period included the whole preparation and proceedings of the Second Vatican Council. I have attempted to look at the Vatican, its inner life and its policies, in what seems to me the best, though not the only, way for a correspondent to approach his subject, large or small: with sympathy and respect, whatever his private views may be (and I am far from being a Roman Catholic), applying constructive criticism and using, directly or indirectly, what he knows about other things to help explain.

This survey ranges from Constantine to Paul VI, entering on the way the fields of many specialists. I have not given a bibliography because the more interesting elements in the books are those owed to personal observation. This is not to say that I had no preparation for dealing with an immense subject which must, to be understood, be shown in its historical setting. That I have confidence about the facts in the earlier part of the book is due to the kindness of Canon J. N. D. Kelley D.D., the Principal of St Edmund Hall, Oxford, who consented to read and advise on the first two chapters. The views and treatment are, of course, entirely my own.

My thanks are due in a hundred places, not least to Mrs Julian Vranek for dealing so well with the proofs. In particular, I want to say that I was grateful to the former editor of *The Times*, Sir William Haley, who generously used his dispensing power to allow me to write a book at all.

Rome, October 1967   P.N.

I
Stand and Unfold

THE Vatican dazzles, slips and slides. It can be firmly, satisfactorily, grasped only by a mind which, in the last resort, has the reinforcing clamp of faith. Then it holds still, is neatly powerful, like the Almighty depicted in a precise mosaic; or ornate and triumphal, like the stance of a baroque pope in marble.

Taking a steady look at the Papacy with no such aid—and what a labour that entails, what effort to be fair—is much the same as attempting an intent gaze at a distant hill-town in the hot Italian sun. Reason tells you that the place is substantial enough. Built on rock, quite obviously—what else could it be built on?—and in such a way that the builders over the centuries have left plenty of margin for doubt as to where the rock ends and all that superstructure begins. The shimmer of heat from the rock excites the whole construction into a confused motion of detail, making it difficult to determine the precise shape of each part. Even the most sceptical mind must be impressed by the grandeur—the enormity, if you like—of the spiritual claims emanating from that rock-palace, that joining of the natural with the man-made, at once mysterious and hugely serviceable. This is no ordinary hill. For its inhabitants and, formally, for about five hundred million people throughout the world, the Vatican hill is the seat of Christ's Vicar on earth. The unique fascination of such a claim reflects on the fascination of the policies devised there and applied from so lofty a spiritual height.

To judge these policies is not simple. Anyone can approve or disapprove of some features of them: such as the giving by ecclesiastical authorities of explicit instructions to an Italian peasant about which political party should have the benefit of the theoretically free exercise of his democratic right to vote. In this sort of case, the individual observer's attitude would depend on whether he thought that worse evils than clericalism were threatening, or whether, whatever the other threats, priestly participation in politics should *ipso facto* be condemned. But an intelligent appraisal of the Vatican and its policies requires an understanding of the formative influences of the past as well as of the conditioning factors of the present. The late leader of the Italian Communist Party, Palmiro Togliatti, described the pontificate of Pope John XXIII as the end of the age of Constantine. If his conclusion, like so many conclusions about the Vatican, is open to question, he was certainly right in placing the roots of the Vatican's political power in the tired soil of the fading Empire of the West. Constantine must loom largely over any discussion of Vatican policies. Indeed, a good case can be made out to show that Togliatti exaggerated in speaking of the end of the age of Constantine. There is still a lot of the Constantinian in the Vatican's character and outlook.

More than at any other time in modern history, the Papacy is now making its spiritual voice heard in international affairs. In the course of a few short years, mainly during two pontificates, the Holy See has evolved quite detailed views on such problems as the proper approach to the underdeveloped areas of the world, and to communism; has won the goodwill of many hitherto indifferent to or suspicious of the Roman Church and its head; has sought through the methods of secular diplomacy to bring about a settlement in Vietnam. The present pontiff has broken long tradition by travelling outside Italy to distant parts of the world like India and New York, places indescribably remote from the atmosphere of the Vatican. The hills around Rome are as far as many a worthy prelate ventures from his office and lodging, and only then when the heat of summer forces him to seek cooler surroundings. Popes may, as Paul VI did without success, plan to take a jet aircraft to a communist country (the Polish government refused the Holy Father a visa); yet the actual life of the Vatican is mentally very circumscribed and still does not tally with the determination of John XXIII and his successor to force a break from its narcissist provincialism and look out to the world at large.

This determination explains why the Second Vatican Council— the greatest religious event so far witnessed in this century— should have issued an entire document, and a lengthy one at that, dealing specifically with such contemporary problems as the validity of the nuclear deterrent, and the need to find succour for hungry nations. It also explains the insistence on the less intransigent approach to communism that has recently been adopted to replace the policy—so deep-set in the post-war years as to seem immemorial and immortal—of anathemas against the communist East from a spiritual authority which could be relied on to strike at the enemies of the West. The ideological war against communism had been joined with a good deal of religious fervour, but only—to be just to Pius XII, who became identified with it— after some hesitation and under provocation. The policy of condemnations was abandoned under John XXIII, except in so far as the official teachings of communism were concerned. The change was made with a striking forthrightness.

Today, two tendencies, a 'hard' and a 'soft', have become combined in an attitude typical of the Vatican: equivocal yet arguably logical. This attitude serves ecclesiastical purposes very well as a policy. Many argue its logic—always in spiritual terms, of course —as well as its potential effectiveness as a display of political common sense. Others distrust it. But two things are plain. The Roman Church wants to be once again in the midst of the world: 'almost', as Paul VI said in closing the Ecumenical Council, 'to run after it in its rapid and continuous change'. This is a fundamental innovation after the century or so in which the Papacy has sat brooding, uncommunicative except to its own, in the ruin of its temporal domain. The second is more daunting. Where reasons for and against are being heard—and this is one of the results of the Council's debates and their aftermath—the automatic acceptability fades of texts hammered out with seemingly supernatural force in some remote place, and brought down from the mountain. Once the process of argument becomes normative, the sense of remoteness goes. This is what is now happening at the Vatican. Some call it a wind of change, if they happen to like it; those who dislike it call it a crisis of authority.

The men in the Vatican are devising policies after the manner of men elsewhere, seeking to look after their own or, in fairer words, seeking to protect the inheritance left to them. An outlook of this kind has been part of political thinking there since the early Church had to protect the tombs of St Peter and St Paul from the barbarians, to safeguard its spiritual prerogatives against the pretensions of the later Roman emperors.

To be just, another consideration must be borne in mind which is deeply felt by progressive prelates: the fresh realisation that, if the Church is to be true to the Gospel, a principal function must be to serve the world, not only to save souls and not just to protect this inheritance. Christ Himself said: 'I am among you as one who serves'.* In other words, Christianity cannot be practised in isolation from the world.

Looked at in these ways, the policies devised by the Vatican are 'political' only as a secondary consideration. That is how 'involvement in the world' is officially explained at the Vatican. The aim is the well-being of the Church; the saving of souls; the freedom to teach and to practise the one true religion as revealed by Christ and entrusted to the successors of St Peter. Thus, or in some such terms as these, runs the argument, looking after the Church is to look after the interests of humanity. The world being what it is (in a word, worldly), a spiritual authority must be made effective by temporal means, and methods of this world must be kept in regular use to safeguard human hopes for the next.

*   *   *

Look up from St Peter's Square. There on the third floor is the window of the quite modest, but very pleasant and airy, study in which the pontiff works. It is big. The window looks down on the colonnaded embrace of the great square. John was apt to take

* Luke *xxii* 27.

away the rather impersonal effect of the papal study by having around him gifts presented by Venetian friends. He had been patriarch of Venice before his election, and the outward signs of that pastorate were the huge, somewhat incongruous, chandelier of Murano glass hanging from the centre of the ceiling, and a crib containing glass figurines. Paul VI has given it a rather more austere impression. The whole papal apartment is now rather dully neutral in tone, with shades of grey predominating. Heads were nodded knowingly when the colour-scheme was first made known. Of course, after John of Venice, Paul of Milan would appear to be an austere man: very thin, a Cassius-type, more calculating than emotional. That was but one of the many wrong ideas which seem to have grown up around Paul. Above the study is the roof-garden he commissioned: a structure so weighty that cracks in the walls of the old palace have been ascribed to it. As colourful and elaborate in design as could be devised, it is clearly not the retreat of a cold, insensitive man. It is, however, a retreat. John was wont to move about the sacred enclave of palaces and garden with almost embarrassing freedom. Paul more often paces his roof-garden than the formal walks below. Not Cassius, then, but perhaps Hamlet?—a Hamlet grappling with his feelings and his sense of duty? Some see him as such, but his dilemma is perhaps less one of inner doubts as of listening too readily to the fears of others.

Behind the papal study, as one looks from the square, lies the hallowed maze of the Sacred Apostolic Palaces, and between the pope and the basilica is the Secretariat of State. Here advisers and administrators contribute to decisions that, in theory, come from an absolute monarch, the last of Europe's crowned heads in full enjoyment of *plenitudo potestatis*. Yet he is more, much more, than even an absolute monarch because of the spiritual authority surrounding the papal throne. The pronouncements of its occupant may vary from the formally occasional to the bindingly infallible. Their operative force depends, first, on the degree of solemnity which the pope himself attaches to them; secondly, on the degree of solemnity which later theologians and canonists decide can be proved to be attached to what a given pope said, or can be proved to be not attached to what he said. Since popes were declared infallible in faith and morals in 1870—an innovation (or confirmation, to be thoroughly faithful to the spirit of the dogma's promulgation) condemned by many non-Catholics* as impossibly authoritarian—popes have spoken, written and in other ways pronounced on a great many aspects of faith and morals: including, one might add because of its special importance today, the great condemnation of birth-control. But many a learned prelate will argue energetically, with relief, that no papal pronouncement since 1870 can be unquestionably accorded the respect and honour due to the utterance of an infallible teacher. Exception from this would have to be made in regard to Pius XII's grotesque promulgation on the doctrine of the Bodily Assumption of the Virgin Mary: a course that many people tried to dissuade him from adopting, and that many more would have advised against had they been consulted. As it is, save for some vague acceptance of the doctrine as good for the morale of the faithful, not a few prelates are no more inclined to accept it for themselves than they were before Pius proclaimed it *ex cathedra*. There is a lot in the Holy See that is neither black nor white. There is perhaps something symbolic in Paul's new colour scheme of grey and beige.

The atmosphere of the Vatican can be consolingly human. Men make their careers there just as men make careers in other spheres: by hard work, by devotion to duty and to the interests of the enterprise, by the help of a patron, by being ready with the right advice at the right time. They have their personal victories and defeats, their quarrels, their nervous breakdowns; sometimes their scandals. It is the environment they work in that makes them seem different in kind, not just degree, from other administrators. The ceremonial can be exhilarating. At times, it seems a trifle tawdry. Those old ostrich plumes, which used until recently to be carried by retainers as the portable throne was borne into the basilica, looked like props from the first-night of *Aïda*. These guards and courtiers with halberds, cloaks, ruffles, rings and swords, seem set to boom out the opening lines of one of those

---

*Condemned by an important minority of Catholics at the time, such as Döllinger and the 'Old Catholics', who refused to accept the dogma of Infallibility.

old-fashioned Shakespearian productions when the players were actually dressed in Elizabethan costumes.

> Who's there?
> Nay, answer me: stand, and unfold
> Thyself . . .

But no, it still is not Elsinore; it is just that there is the warmth and unreal reality of the theatre here, seen and felt from close to the lights.

With the majesty is mixed an impression of homeliness as well as holiness. The elderly gentlemen taking their part in the ceremonial have an earthy way with them, like old bachelors everywhere. They wipe their noses noisily as they go through the mysteries. Popes themselves are apt to talk in a rather elaborately sonorous way which can be less regal than stiffly fussy in its phraseology. It is packed with stock phrases, stilted expressions and conventions. The moving moments are usually those when, for a second or so, the personality of the pontiff— the man himself, his anxieties, his urgent wish to communicate a certain thought— is able to force its way through the protective vestments of language. Paul, oddly enough for some people, perhaps, does this more often than did John. The opaque phrases suddenly glow, like sunlight through thick old amber; and we know that the pope is moved.

The great prelates remain curiously human. Because of this, the scene around them can lose quite quickly its remote formality. A wait in the antechamber for a private audience is rewarding as much for this as for any other reason. Certainly, the feeling of authority is tangible. It is not much impaired by the sanctimonious texture of the red damask which is an inseparable part of ecclesiastical furniture and fittings. The feeling is not to be ascribed simply to the effect of the frescoed chambers, the gilt, the uniformed chamberlains and the guards ablaze in breastplates and helmets that reflect the colours of the painted ceilings. Its origin is in the mere awareness of all the spiritual authority surrounding the man at work a room or two away. The effect of waiting in a chamber containing a throne of stone from the original St

Peter's, built by Constantine with such exquisite care to reverence the awesome sanctity of the site, must deeply impress all but the most unbreathing of dead souls. The pomp begins to appear purely circumstantial. The mind is lifted in awe at the sacred dignity of the place.

It is quickly brought back to earth when a massive member of the Noble Guard comes forward, sweeps off his plumed helmet, supports it in white-gloved hands and ventures the smiling reminder that we last met in the Bank of Italy, where he works in the governor's office. ('I take my turn at this when the Holy Father is giving an audience.') Or when a harassed official comes up to a visitor with the plea 'if you could put in a good word with the Holy Father for a bigger office... you know our difficulties...' It can all be disarmingly human.

2
Below God and Above Man

To speak of politics and religion might seem much like speaking of the profane and the sacred in the same breath. So it is; and so it is not. There is no distinction in the Vatican's official view. Both must be talked about because the Vatican—to say this does it no injustice—has profane as well as sacred claims. The Vatican's political involvement is not a passing aberration, product of immediate circumstances, but is consequent on an outlook formed in the early centuries of its life. Though it may profess to be unpolitical, it has often been under attack for having a direct hand in politics, and no doubt it will be attacked again on this ground. The Holy See has been accused of subtle scheming, of weaving alliances favourable to its interests, of darkening the ways of simpler men by ecclesiastical mysteries, authority and expediency. It has been charged—by Napoleon among others—with deliberately confusing spiritual authority with political aims. What business did popes have in rivalling emperors, undermining kings and queens, leading their armies personally into battle; or, for that matter, what business do they have in pronouncing on Vietnam and on disarmament, and on the problems of the underdeveloped nations?

The answer for the outsider, seeking to peer with strained sight through the agitated detail to the rock beneath, can be put simply enough. The popes have almost infinite pretensions, though they do not always try to act on them. They are representing Christ and are chosen to do so—this the devout must accept—by the aid of the Holy Spirit's operation through that strange institution of improvised dignity known as the Conclave. The Church of which the pope is the visible head is the instrument of the Divine Will on earth. Most Christians would share the view that the Divine Will, as expressed in the Gospel, had far-reaching implications for human society. Thus, the final aim cannot be political; but to protect and foster that final aim, some political methods are needed. And, of course, by entering the field in this way, the popes must inevitably see their semi-divinity hedged. It is the hedging which requires the explanation. Divinity, even semi-divinity, if seen to be such requires no such assistance. Plausible explanations cannot be applied to issues of faith. With the nature of the hedging, though, the ground becomes clearer, because reasons must be put forward to explain what it is and how it came about.

The two principal reasons go far back into history. They form the leading themes of the Papacy's policies as these have evolved through the centuries. Whatever the evolution, its policies return to the same original constants. The first is the fact that the Church, early in its career, became the official religion of the Roman Empire and then the heir to the mystique of that Empire. Constantine enthroned the visible Church (making it thereby much more visible) alongside the temporal power of the Empire. Then he departed from Rome, preferring to make his capital at Byzantium. Hence, the spiritual pastorate of the senior patriarch of the Church was left to fend for itself politically at the confused times of the establishment of the new barbarian kingdoms. Inevitably, the Papacy partook not only of the imperial mystique but of some imperial functions as well. What, after all, was the title of Supreme Pontiff—*pontifex maximus*—if not the pagan title of the chief priest in Rome, and one which the popes did not regularly adopt until the fifth century, long after Tertullian had applied it to them satirically? It was a title continued by Constantine and his immediate successors. Gratian (c. 374) and Theodosius I were the first of the emperors to decline it.

The second reason follows logically from the first. In the eighth century, as part of the business of recruiting a strong ruler to help wield the secular power (in the name of religion, naturally), at a time of confusion and lawlessness, the popes obtained a principality for themselves. Theirs was no longer purely a spiritual authority, even a spiritual authority that could and did lay claim to primacy of honour over the wielder of the temporal sword. The popes became princes. They were to have the same problems as other secular rulers in conducting the defence and enlargement of their dominions—no longer simply as a means of protecting the places where St Peter and St Paul met their deaths, but to give themselves, as they argued then and ever after, temporal independence for the full play of their spiritual power.

They learned early the habits of sovereignty, first by being close to the greatest sovereign power in the Western world—the Roman Empire—and then by having territories and goods. It was not altogether the fault of the Roman Church that it should so soon find political matters of rather absorbing interest. When observing the grandeur of papal ceremonies, the busy industry of the Vatican's departments of state, the leading place the pope's representatives take in many of the diplomatic corps throughout the world, the lavish importance which some prelates attach to themselves: the impulse comes to demand in Christ's name a return to the simplicity of the faith in its early days. It is often forgotten how short those days were. Not only that: how exotically elaborate the courtly life of the late Roman Empire had become by the time the secular power was looking—paradoxically and yet logically enough—to the comparatively simple faith of Christianity to assist it in the business of preserving the imperial tradition. From the day when the apostles went forth to preach the Gospel, it was only ten times the life-span of Christ Himself before Christianity was installed by Constantine as part of the governmental system, and endowed by him with gifts of a lavishness which no Christian would have dreamed of in his dreams nor, one hopes, have prayed for in his prayers. This accounts for many of the outward signs of that formalised theocracy which was the court of Constantine and which the Vatican remains. A good deal of its decoration is baroque. The soaring convolutions of an exultantly religious classical revival are its perfect ornament. But this does not conceal the fact that its real spirit is of the late imperial court, Byzantine, in effect.

The period of the change from paganism to Christianity as the official religion of the Empire, the turn of the third and the early fourth centuries, has more than once been compared with our own era. Spiritually and psychologically, it was a difficult period. Uneasiness was apparent: a kind of spiritual exhaustion. The standards that had brought the Roman Empire to an unprecedented power seemed no longer to bring success or satisfaction. A world was running down. Spirits were disturbed; bad dreams were a sign of the times as much as a bad economy. The after-glow of late paganism was no longer the light of the sun-god around whom Emperor Aurelian (270–5) attempted to create a form of religious unity: a spiritual defence akin to the physical walls this emperor had built around Rome to protect it from the barbarians.

The uncertainties in the pagan world both enhanced the well-knit, confident attitude of the Christian communities spread about the Empire, and also stimulated popular resentment against them, so that a persecuting emperor found little difficulty in gaining public support for attacks either on the Christian hierarchy or on the Christians as a body. Their self-sufficiency and discipline were resented. Moreover, they became sharpened and hardened, not demoralised, by sporadic persecutions. This treatment effectively limited doctrinal disputes among them of the kind that would arise when times were easier. Many were willing to die for the faith. The butchery on the one side and the will to death of some of the martyrs belonged to a sick age. Heroism was certainly among them; at the same time, their morality was shrewd. They were aware that organised help for each other carried out the Scriptural injunctions, made life agreeable, and might well smooth the way to a more agreeable after-life. It was one of the great grumbles of Emperor Julian (361–3)—the nephew of Constantine who attempted with his apostasy to undo his uncle's work by bringing back paganism—that the Christians were so much better at looking after each other than was any set of pagans. He was annoyed by it; he also scorned it, as he did other facets of

Christianity. But he had to face the fact that his intellectualised paganism—his 'modernistic conservatism', so to say—was no alternative to Constantine's decision to base the new imperial structure on the spiritual foundation offered by Christianity.

Paradoxically, it was to be the Christians, not the pagan revivalists with all the rich toleration of their pantheon, who tapped the age-old springs of religion. Pagans proved notably incapable of absorbing into their religion elements of Christianity in the way that Christians were to borrow pagan feasts, customs and images —in some cases beliefs. There are still muddles to be found, in countries such as Italy, of pagan survivals mixed up with Catholic teaching: incantations, for example, which pass in two phrases from the sun to the crucifixion, comparing the dawn with the resurrected sun-god. The pagans had little to compare with the Christian voracity in digesting other people's high days and holidays. One notable attempt was made by Alexander Severus (222–235), who included Christ in the lesser pantheon, at the same time apparently allowing existing anti-Christian legislation quietly to become a dead letter. This was an ingenious attempt at a solution; an attempt to absorb this tiresome new faith and lose it in the web of the traditional gods. It was a complete misjudgment of what Christianity was about. His measures, moreover, were only temporary. In the late Empire, there were only two serious attempts at refurbishing the weaknesses of Roman society. They were carried out by Diocletian and by Constantine. Both were to have profound effects on Christianity. The experiments in ruling carried out by these two totally different personalities may be regarded as the pillars of what was later to become the temple of established Christianity. The first persecuted the Christians and was the last of the great persecutors. The second took up the Christian cause and was its first and greatest benefactor.

PERSECUTION AND FAVOUR

Diocletian (284–305) approached the problems of the failing Empire by introducing a more thorough-going style of theocracy than had been seen before in Rome. He drew on the Persian example for an experiment in semi-oriental rule. This attempt at reinvigorating the state logically led to persecution of the Christians, though Diocletian only arrived at the inevitability of the conclusion quite late in his reign. This Dalmatian soldier, who had made his way—the child of poor parents—to the highest place in the world through the army and a formidable organising brain, was nothing if not logical. To strengthen his absolute monarchy, he kept all power to himself as a semi-divine ruler, making his own person sacred and his palace the divine house. For much of his reign, the Christians were left in peace under an agreement issued in 260. But a little more than two years before his abdication, he published a series of edicts—three in all—against them and, in spite of having a Christian wife and a Christian daughter, brought to an end a period of about half a century of tranquillity. Their buildings were destroyed. Their sacred books were burnt, their treasures confiscated, and all of them called upon to offer sacrifices or be punished by penalties of increasing scale, the last being death.

Whatever may be thought of Diocletian's conduct—and he is understandably the villain for Christian historians and a somewhat unattractive character for anyone who has suffered from a sergeant major—he was a strong-minded man, and his campaign was carried out with the energy of a crusade, something yet to be seen in Europe. At Antioch, one of the apostolic centres of Christianity and a see in which, according to the Acts of the Apostles, the followers of Christ were first known as Christians, a pagan statue was said to have called for their expulsion, and they were deprived of all legal rights. The persecution was widespread, though it did not reach every province of the Empire.

Constantine (313–24) sought to undo much of Diocletian's system.* He did not, however, dispense with all of the elaborate court ceremonial introduced by Diocletian. Hence, even when the Empire became officially Christian, courtiers were forced to prostrate themselves in the sacred presence of the emperor. This habit is still followed at some ceremonies in the papal court and at

* Constantine became 'Caesar' in 306 and 'Augustus' in 308, after Maximinus's death in 313. Licinus was also Augustus until 324, after which date Constantine was sole emperor.

private meetings; kissing the pontiff's right foot—the sacred foot —is a custom in the same tradition. (It is a beguiling thought that the pope's summer residence at Castelgandolfo is built on the site of Diocletian's suburban palace.) Of incomparably greater importance, however, from the point of view of politics than any heritage of courtly manners is the political effect of Constantine's decision to bring Christianity into a ruling partnership. Put briefly, his contribution to organised Christianity was that, by moving the principal capital of the Empire eastward to Byzantium, he bequeathed in the East what was to be a Christian State-Church while leaving to the Latin Church in Rome the problem of finding a state with which to share its destiny. From this derives the constant problem of Church–State relations in Western Christendom.

In the space of a generation, Christianity was to be first the victim, savagely mauled, of Diocletian's attempt at reorganising the Empire and then, suddenly—and as it appeared to some contemporary Christians, miraculously—the favoured adjutant of the new imperial system. Rendering unto Caesar what was Caesar's became a problem—the very idea itself was novel—of dimensions which no early Christians could have envisaged. A later Church, with its greater experience of moving in the world, might have found some formula by which Christians could have given the emperors before Constantine what they wanted while preserving what the Church required. This would have saved Christianity from the nearly—not quite—mortal encumbrance of the state's favour. The Papacy was later to become skilled at this type of negotiation, and it still shows its talent in modern conditions.

The sacred nature of the imperial dignity of the pre-Christian emperors was fundamentally different from the Christian idea of God, except in certain outward externals of worship. They could in no sense be regarded as rival divinities. Nor could the Christian God, however much one wanted to cut Him down to the scale of other divinities, be demoted to being merely an equal. Alexander Severus failed to understand that the two approaches to the sacred had practically nothing in common. Christians were, on the whole, content to be loyal subjects; their revolutionary religious message did not suggest to them an overturning of the apparatus of pagan rule. They had, even so, certain crucial reservations. Tertullian, recalling St Peter's advice in 1 Peter ii 13–17, put their problem in these terms:

> As regards the honours due to kings and emperors, we hold it as a tradition to remain in due obedience to magistrates and princes according to the command of the Apostle; but we hold this tradition to be binding within the limits of that discipline by which we are separated from all idolatry.

That was reasonable doctrine for individuals and small, scattered communities. Once it became adopted by a powerful theocracy, it meant tension, the standing on one's dignity, and more martyrs. The basic problem of loyalty to a spiritual authority and to a temporal power was inherent in such a doctrine of the civil obligation of Christians. The Church, after all, had inherited not only the Christian message but was also to inherit the imperial tradition and some of the imperial institutions. Though popes were to give the title of emperor to others—to Franks, to Germans—it was Rome which retained the imperial manner. This is the essence of the clash between temporal and spiritual, and of the equally complicated relationship between Papacy and nations. The Church itself, having failed in spite of sporadic efforts to make its permanent peace with the earlier emperors, fogged the issue still more in later history by its position over the choice and anointing of medieval emperors. The blessing and crowning by the Supreme Pontiff were seen as endowing the Church's endorsement of the civil power with an aura of the supernatural. The popes were borrowing what was, in fact, a barbarian custom to give that touch of a sacred character to kingship which they had earlier refused to see in the Roman emperors. As far as their Christian subjects were concerned, the emperors could claim this property only after Christianity had become the official religion of the Empire. The one real distinction was that the Church retained the right to criticise the conduct of kings and emperors, whether anointed or not, and even to overthrow them if necessary.

The cry of two loyalties has been addressed to Catholics through the ages, and civil powers have been disciplined or upbraided by the Holy See. The present age has its fine examples. 'As Polish citizens', said Wladyslaw Gomulka of the Polish hierarchy, 'the Church leaders are temporally in our country; but spiritually, in accordance with the canonical decrees of the Church, they are in the Vatican.' The reply was equally timeless. Cardinal Wyszynski, the Polish primate, said: 'I tell you, you Caesars, you will bow down before God and serve only Him.'

Having suffered persecution, the Christians of the late Empire were then to face the equally staggering problem of a friendly Caesar. While maintaining the formalities surrounding a semi-sacred presence, Constantine covered his spiritual allies with a wealth and favour they had not known before. They were to have property and land. An ecclesiastical body seldom wears its wealth well, though it often disposes of it shrewdly from the point of view of financial gain. The Papacy's present industrial holdings, many of which are in Italy, still touch off controversy; and still, after all these centuries, there are people ready to be shocked to mark such indications of the Church's wealth as emerge from the secrecy with which these matters are surrounded.

No one can possibly give an exact account of Constantine's motives; and it might disturb some devout minds if one could. It is simpler to explain what he did than what he aspired to do. He took his throne with the Monogram of Christ upon the shields of his soldiers.* The symbols of Christianity thereupon stood at the centre of power, proudly surmounting the final confusion of paganism, just as the Cross to this day stands amid the ruins of the Colosseum. In Byzantium, Constantine was soon looked upon as the thirteenth Apostle. This is not just the 'wisdom of the East' brought face to face with a powerful monarch. Other people, with no theocratic propensities, have attributed to him a religious conviction that was positively Christian, aimed as a matter of policy to religious ends. The view of a sceptical rationalism is that he simply saw the advantages of Christianity for his own plans as emperor. 'The sublime theory of the Gospel', Gibbon wrote, 'had

---

* The 'sign' in Constantine's famous affirmation, *In Hoc Signo Vinces*, was not the Cross but the sacred Monogram, known as the *labarum*—☧, i.e. the Greek letters *x* (ch) and *p* (rh) combined, the first letters of Χριστός.

made a much fainter impression on the heart than on the understanding of Constantine himself.' Certainly he did well, as far as his personal position was concerned, by advancing from the old imperial status of a god to being God's Vicar on earth. Modern scholarship now generally accepts that he was a religious man and that his Christianity, which developed in him by stages, was sincere. Though he began by identifying Christ with his original sun-god, he probably went on to accept—if idiosyncratically—much of the faith which had proved so useful to him, seeing himself as Christ's representative on earth. Portrayals of him certainly make him *look* as if religion would have impressed him. The massive stone head on the Capitol is not that of a cynic; though, as it was made for a church, it could hardly have represented him in a cynical mood. It is as hard to grasp the religious motivation of a rather mystical emperor as it is to judge the politics of a pope. The problem is the same; and there is a similarity between Constantine's use of religion and the papal use of political power.

TOLERATION AND RICHES

In a mood of exultation, sacred dreams and helpful visions, Constantine reached the imperial throne. His approach to Christianity had two phases: first toleration and then an embrace. His shadow lay heavily on the Church until this present century; and both these aspects of his handling of religion are still relevant in their effect on the Vatican's policies. Of the two, the first is more interesting, and potentially far more valuable.

By the Edict of Milan issued in 313 (not, as it happens, in Milan), Constantine and his colleague Licinius completed the revocation of the laws against the Christians and introduced a principle of general toleration. Depending on the importance one attaches to Christianity, it can be seen as a step forward to the toleration envisaged by nineteenth-century liberalism, or a return to the easier, self-confident days of the Antonines. In fact, the removal of disabilities from the Christians was simply the conclusion of a process already in being. Diocletian's policy was an admitted failure. Many Christian lives had been lost, but the religion itself had not been eliminated; and all along there were Christians who continued firmly to reject Diocletian's attempt to settle the relationship between the temporal and spiritual powers by sanctifying the monarchy under the patronage of Jove and Hercules. Massacres, even in a morally listless age, were regarded by many non-Christians as a corrupting influence on civil life. There was, too, the belief that every man should have some sort of religion; by the destruction of their buildings, Christians were being deprived of the opportunity of the due practice of their faith. The experiment in repression, moreover, collapsed as much through the failure of the system at the centre as through the resilience of many of the Christians. Diocletian abdicated in 305. The Sacred College, the highest body in his administrative apparatus (and a name later to be taken by the cardinals of the Church*), had broken into factions. Six years later, the edicts of persecution were withdrawn.

On this point, then, Constantine was at first merely carrying out the policy, already begun, of letting the Christians have their place in the Empire instead of seeking to destroy them. His second object was to try to rally the surviving elements in the classical tradition of Roman rule which had been superseded, after its virtual decay, by Diocletian's oriental style of kingship. The Edict of Milan applied to Christians and non-Christians alike. It guaranteed the right of anyone to profess Christianity, removing all legal disabilities, and provided for the restitution of lands and buildings confiscated during the persecutions, including those already disposed of by grant to other parties. It undertook to compensate those willing to surrender such properties voluntarily. The Edict asserted that no man should be prevented from discharging the obligations of his religion. The liberties guaranteed to Christians were extended to other faiths. Hence, it established the neutrality of the state in religious matters, eschewing persecution of anyone, and making amends to those who had suffered.

To the *homme moyen sensuel* of the day, Constantine's Edict must have appeared to look back to the easier times—the 'good old days' for the nostalgic polytheist—of tolerant paganism, when all this talk of the nature of deity was kept decently in hand. To the

* Just as *Curia* is derived from the place in which the Roman Senate met.

Christian, it should have been as much as could properly be hoped for. To any observer at the time not greatly interested in the fortunes of any one faith, it must have appeared a repudiation of Diocletian's mistakes and a first attempt at basing a political society on free partnership between civil and religious authorities, with each side mutually respecting the other. To a modern observer, it seems an idea closely prefiguring the idea of 'a Free Church in a Free State', or the religious neutrality as envisaged, for instance, in the American Constitution. No such point of toleration—toleration of the state by the Christian Church, and toleration of other religions by both—was to be reached again until 21 September 1965, when the Vatican Council gave its general approval to a draft declaration on religious liberty which remarkably resembled Constantine's great decree. In the intervening centuries there were examples of productive partnerships between Church and state but not, as a rule, accompanied by toleration.

The present age is irreligious. In the Western world, it no longer matters for advancement or for social acceptance to declare oneself a Christian. Not being a Christian is held to be as natural as being one. This is one of the reasons why the Christian denominations, including the Roman Church, have been forced into shifting their ground. There are exceptions, of course, to the freedom now accorded not to call oneself Christian. In confessional states, it is still advisable for many people to behave as if they are among 'the faithful'. In Italy, there are still employers who want some sort of assurance about a prospective worker from the local priest. The obtaining of this assurance about himself is likely to place an obligation on the worker to abide by the Church's rulings, at least in outward conduct: voting for the Catholic party, for example, and not joining a left-wing trade union. On balance, however, this type of exception proves the modern rule: the criterion is now materialistic. But that does not mean that a religious man is at any disadvantage. Indifference provides tolerance more quickly than does faith or reason. No statues speak these days to call the crowds back to their faith, pagan or Christian. Plaster madonnas cry now and again, and stones miraculously turn blood-red where the head of a martyr was once placed. But the real tensions are past. So it must have seemed in 313. The persecutions were over. What more, then, could purveyors of the truth require than freedom to accept that truth, practise its tenets and carry it to others? The reason for being a Christian was because one believed in Christ. What other reason need there be?

All this was to change. Constantine was to show that he was not neutral, thereby inaugurating that long era from which, as Togliatti noted, we are only now emerging. The Edict of Milan was superseded by a new policy. Only the Christian Church was to receive the imperial favour. Though his private morality was to show shocking lapses as the years went by (including implication in the murder of his own son), Constantine's insistence on Christianity knew no such interruptions. The Edict of Milan had recognised the Church as a corporation that could own property. Eight years after its promulgation, he granted permission to his subjects to leave their private fortunes to the Church. He ordained that a regular allowance of corn be put aside in each city for the Church's charitable work. In Rome itself, he gave land and built churches, not least the first St Peter's. Constantine set an example of pious generosity to be followed by his subjects. The pleasures of plenty and the dangers of opulence became part of the experience of prelates.

While bishops increased their style of living to meet the dignity of office in great sees, there were some who detected the threat to the proper practice of a religion based on conduct and morality, and which had such simple beginnings. St Hilary of Poitiers, for instance, described Constantius—the son of Constantine who eventually gained control of both parts of the Empire—as an insinuating enemy 'who does not condemn to life but enriches to death; who, instead of thrusting men into the liberty of prison, honours them in the slavery of the palace; . . . who does not cut off the head with the sword but slays the soul with gold'. Wealth and palaces are a long step from Tertullian's presentation of the early Christians as people drawn largely from the lower classes. He approved of their simplicity: 'I address thee, simple and rude and unlettered and untaught, such as they have thee who have thee only: that very thing pure and entire, of the road, the street, the workshop.' It is an even longer step to involvement in public disputes, as the Vatican has lately been involved, over whether it is justified in refusing to pay the normal dividend-tax on its Italian holdings. The argument of its critics is not so much that it is improper for a religious body to have tax remission (after all, most Western countries make remission in the case of charitable and cultural bodies) as that the Vatican refuses to publish any account of its financial dealings. The argument of its supporters is that such reticence is defensible, both on the ground that the Holy See does good works with its money, and also because, given its enormous prestige among faithful and non-believer alike, publication of details of the Vatican's investments could exercise undue influence on public opinion in favour of the enterprises with which it is financially associated. The call for more simplicity, particularly in the dress and conduct of higher prelates, was frequently raised during the Vatican Council. The pope made some suggestions for less splendour in the dress of cardinals, but the effect was slight. Ecclesiastical tailors were not to be put off by mere regulations. The sheer bulk of vested interests settled on the Vatican is formidable in itself. Becoming aware of these was an educating experience for bishops from genuinely poor dioceses.

It did not matter to Constantine that Christians at the beginning of his reign, though widespread, still represented a comparatively small part of the population of the whole Empire—just as practising believers now represent a dwindling proportion of the population of what is known hopefully as the Christian West. Cohesion and quality mattered to him; cohesion and quality matter now. One of the principal reasons why the Roman Church held its Ecumenical Council, and one of the principal stimulants of the ecumenical movement as a whole, has been the thought that religion is failing, that in an irreligious age something must be done to bring back freshness to Christianity, to bring the methods of the Roman Church more up to date and all Christian groups nearer to unity. Christ's prayer that all might be one is even more exigent in an age when all are by no means Christian even if they live in the nominally Christian parts of the world. Constantine was dealing with a tired state, summoning the freshness of the one religion effective for the purpose—a religion in which he probably grew to believe—to redress the balance of the failing civil structure. The Church's problem in the twentieth century is the opposite. It is religion that is failing for many people. Civil governments are vigorous, self-asserting and at times persecuting. John XXIII recognised as much in his encyclical *Mater et Magistra*, which allows an extraordinary amount of responsibility in purely civic questions to the state. For this reason alone it would have been historic.

Sadly, but probably with truth, one can say that Christianity— whether Catholic, Protestant or Episcopalian—has developed its modern doctrines on the limits of the civil power as a direct consequence of the weakening of its own power. For the millennium and a half of alliance with political power, the course on which Constantine set it, the Church did not scruple to apply its truth by force and by persecution: the force of its ally, the state. The Roman Church was the direct imperial heir and so, by comparison with other Christian bodies, abided longer by these methods. The truth that truth will out was a long time in appearing, concealed for so long beneath the alternative view that only by rooting out error can the truth be kept pure and splendid. When the Second Vatican Council approved the principle of religious liberty, it was careful to deny to the civil authorities any rights in the matter of directing religious life, though by that time—under John's guidance—the Church had accepted a growing amount of state participation in other fields, such as social security. As far as religion was concerned, the state was to foster it, but not take a promoting hand one way or the other.

Even in the mid-twentieth century, the very idea of religious liberty can cause a lot of fears. Perhaps this reflects something of Constantine's own feelings when, after issuing his Edict on religious neutrality, he then showed so patently his preference for Christianity. If there is freedom of conscience, surely this implies —so the opponents of it argued in the Council—that all beliefs are placed on the same level, that error deserves as much respect as truth. This is something too difficult to digest, whether by conservative cardinals of the Roman Curia or by simple people brought up to suppose that they are in a superior situation to non-Catholics. This is why the final version of the Council's document on religious liberty contains references added at a late moment reiterating the Roman Church's claim to be the one true Church. Constantine may or may not have believed in the same thing. He would certainly have seen the virtue of avoiding what ecclesiastics call 'indifferentism': a very bad word meaning the habit of mind that puts religions on an equal basis. He could not afford the luxury of neutrality; some prelates are still convinced that they cannot do so yet.

CONSERVATISM AND SUCCESS

The Roman Church has survived all this time for reasons which can be ascribed to political acumen, good fortune, or the will of God. Certainly it is not for the contribution which the Church has made to political evolution. Its first political task—that of preserving what it could of the imperial ideal and administration—was conservative. So, more or less, it has remained. The change may be coming now, but the indications are not yet sure enough for us to aver that change *will* come. It is having to deal more with changing conditions. It feels it cannot remain the same. That is why the Second Vatican Council was called. The Roman Church, nevertheless, likes to retain a good deal of the imperial tradition in dealing with the modern world; just as Constantine for a time issued coins with a Christian insignia on one side and Apollo on the other.* It has never been easy for the Church to assimilate the idea of nations. It is trying these days to come to grips with the developing countries of Asia and Africa rather in the way it was forced to come to grips with the invading nations of barbarians. And it was only the last Council which laid down the structure of national episcopal conferences and adopted the principle of making over to them a number of issues of local or regional interest, instead of keeping everything centralised in Rome.

It is only proper that the sun should shine when a pontiff moves

* After 325, the solar device and references to the Unconquered Sun disappear, to be replaced by Christian symbols.

among the crowds. Sometimes it does. It is a reminder of Apollo's long hold on the mind of the first Christian emperor. Not that paganism stood much chance. There was still to come Julian's attempt to turn back to the old gods, but his was a misguided form of conservatism, a doomed effort. 'The exact balance of the two religions continued but a moment; and the piercing eye of ambition and avarice soon discovered that the profession of Christianity might contribute to the interest of the present, as well as of a future, life'—Gibbon again. It is a fair comment but only a partial report. Other reasons for Christianity's success were indicative of its destiny. The enemy was weak and divided. Neoplatonism, for example, continued to be taught by pagans at Athens, where Julian studied, until 529, but it had lost its vitality. The accumulation of cults had become disturbing. Christianity required little more than faith. It was a point which taxed educated pagans. It still does. 'There is nothing in your philosophy', Julian complained, 'but the one word "believe".' Marcus Aurelius had earlier thought much the same. Vitality and an invitation to believe must have seemed extremely attractive to people torn by spiritual, social and economic doubts. In the words of a modern scholar, Professor E. R. Dodds, who examined the conflict between Christianity and paganism in his Wiles lectures for 1962-3: 'It lifted the burden of freedom from the shoulders of the individual; one irrevocable choice and the road to salvation was clear. Pagan critics might mock at Christian intolerance but in an age of anxiety any "totalist" creed exerts a powerful attraction; one has only to think of the appeal of communism to many bewildered minds of our own day.' The parallel between the appeal of early Christianity and communism, or between the methods of the Roman Church and those of the communists, has often been made. It can very soon be driven too hard. There is a difference in quality between doing things so that society may be organised fairly on this earth, and doing things with the next world in mind. The difference is even more pronounced when the theory of building up treasure in heaven brings a fatalistic attitude of doing very little to make this life better for everybody. It is along this line of attack that the Vatican is frequently assailed. It is an outlook reinforcing an original conservatism. The essence of John XXIII's new teaching —and this has been overlooked—is that he accepted the benefits offered in modern life by a well-organised state, and he did not discount communism as a system which could bring such benefits.

By 313, the way was set for the great spread of Christianity. The heroic part which that religion would play in maintaining and developing Western civilisation ('we are not civilisation', Paul VI has said, 'but we are the promoters of it') was implicit in it from the beginning of its civic acceptability. So was the socially broad but intolerably exclusive stamp which it would place for centuries on that culture: the necessity for the next sixteen hundred years or so of being a Christian of some kind or another. And so was the effect—never to be measured, but substantial—of constant teaching, generation by generation, of the virtues of humility, goodness, charity and hope. It is on the accretion of its taught morality, whatever the political circumstances and misdemeanours, that the Church's continued existence is based, and nothing depends so completely from it as the political activities of the Vatican, because it is supposed to have before it the spiritual aim of clearing the ground so that the teaching may go on, or be taken elsewhere. Who can answer the final question of what effect all that teaching throughout all those years has had?

PRIESTS AND POLITICS

The strength of Constantine was his vigorous appeal to the urge for unity, for a visible head in the midst of imposed order. His weakness was that he did not understand priests. He failed to see that unity to them was necessarily a doctrinal unity, argued out and then in one way or another ascribed to divine guidance. The result was that Christianity experienced the heights of its power and the depths of its tribulations, both immediate and potential, before a generation had passed after Constantine's accession. Two types of priest emerged in consequence. One consisted of those who were aghast at the preponderance of the civil power over the spiritual power, and believed it should be diminished. The second were the ecclesiastical politicians.

BELOW GOD AND ABOVE MAN

The influence of prelates of the first type was crucial in the early years of the Church. By constantly reminding Constantine and his successors that they were in the Church, not controlling it from above, such prelates prevented the new monarchy from settling into the absolutist theocracy that the Eastern Empire was to become. St Hilary has already been mentioned. There was also Hosius, the firm-minded bishop of Cordoba, who told Constantius II, the effective Augustus of the West as well as of the East between 351 and 361, that he should not dictate to the clergy about ecclesiastical matters 'but rather learn from us'. Constantine's successor went a long way in demanding that his authority be paramount in Church as well as state: a total claim beyond any to be expounded by papal theorists on the pope's behalf (though the practical import of Innocent III's notion of papal power at its medieval apogee was to come close to it). 'My will must be considered binding' was Constantius's formulation of his attitude. It would have been bad enough had he been a right-thinking Catholic, but his Christianity was, in Western eyes, perilously akin to Arianism.* Hosius replied to this that, as the clergy do not arrogate to themselves the imperial authority, 'you likewise have no power in the ministry of holy things'. St Ambrose was similarly to discipline Emperor Theodosius I (379–95). Hilary, Hosius and Ambrose: these were voices that would sound through the centuries.

There would also sound the voices of such ecclesiastical politicians as Eusebius of Caesarea, first of so long a priestly line. Eusebius was close to Constantine in the formulation of day-to-day policy. He regarded the sudden glory come to the Church as a clear sign of God's hand at work. He was the type of prelate—the

---

* The West was almost wholly pro-Nicene and had no trouble under Constans (337–50). The East, however, except for Egypt, was in different degrees anti-Nicene. Constantius II, with his effective power-base in the East, followed broadly the line of his bishops and tried to extend their policy to the West when his authority was widened to include it. Hence, his attempt to unify the two halves of the Empire on the basis of a creed which seemed to the West so watered down as to be virtually Arian. Constantius II was not strictly an Arian, nor were most of the Eastern bishops. They were certainly anti-Nicene (i.e., anti-*homoousion*), but the description of them as 'Arian' is a Western smear.

Christian prototype on this scale—who saw the temporal authority as the instrument of the divine will. Once in the hands of a Christian prince, temporal power was scarcely distinguishable from the divine. Under God, the emperor; but mere mortals would have been hard pressed to detect much difference in practical terms between the two authorities. Eusebius wrote a life of Constantine which may be excessively flattering for anyone with the slightest doubts about the precise, divine inspiration of the emperor's actions, but it sums up the great extent of political sycophancy already reached by exponents of a still comparatively early Christian Church. 'The God of all, the governor of the whole universe, by His own will appointed Constantine, the descendant of so renowned a parent, to be prince and sovereign; so that, while others have been raised to this distinction by the choice of their fellows, he is unique as the one man to whose elevation no mortal may boast of having contributed.' It is clear that, for some Christians, favour was a more effective foe than persecution. The resilience and steadfastness of faith shown in Diocletian's day—to say nothing of Christ's own views on what should be rendered to Caesar—could be quite quickly undermined. Greatness was to come, but only after Rome had shaped the form which it would take. The cost was in simplicity.

Ecclesiastical history being what it is, then and now, with its own system of balances and compensations, the kind of view held by Eusebius was partly corrected by such men as Ambrose, Hilary and Hosius. Their insisting with great resolution on the limits of the royal power meant that the Church went forward with two great traditions of differing conduct towards lay authority. In one manifestation, the Church could side with the ruler, flatter him, praise him and hope that, in return, he might give something that the Church required; in adhering to the second tradition, it could take for granted what was required by the faith and at the same time keep the temporal authority severely in its place. Both still exist. Both are regarded as Christian.

Somewhere between the two traditions there grew the concept of the pope's unique position, and with it the primacy of Rome among the sees of apostolic foundation.

PRIMACY OF ROME

The original strength of the bishop of Rome's position depended on two things. He regarded himself, with some justification (but not enough to satisfy everybody), as the successor to St Peter, assuming at his election the leading place St Peter is believed to have enjoyed among the apostles. (Most scholars would agree that Peter was the leader of the twelve apostles; non-Roman Catholics would argue that his position of primacy was personal, not 'institutional'.) And secondly, there was the fact that Rome was the capital of the civilised world. There is much to show that Rome was regarded as the outstanding Christian see long before Christianity became the state religion. It was the seat of the inheritors and guardians of the *locus Petri*: the physical place where Peter had completed his ministry and, as tradition relates, died a martyr's death inverted on a cross in Nero's circus by the Mons Vaticanus. The subsequent martyrdom of Paul gave Rome its association with the two great missioners of Christ: an association which counted for much in the first two or three centuries of the Christian era, though the mystique of Peter came to predominate. Within thirty years of Peter's death, St Clement—who was probably the third in the accepted line of succession to the apostle—wrote his famous letter to the Corinthians (c. A.D. 96) which expressed the authority he saw attached to the see of Rome. St Clement spoke in explicit terms. He was intervening in the name of Rome in a dispute within the Church at Corinth, where some presbyters had been deposed. His epistle was a call to repentance; pointing out that God required due order in all things, he demanded the reinstatement of the deposed presbyters and obedience to superior authority. The tone is commanding:

> It is to you, the authors of this sedition, that I now turn. Submit to the priests and accept punishment as a penance. Learn to live in submission and cast off vain words and haughty speech dictated by idle presumption.

One may feel that his own presumption was far from idle. A little later, he makes even clearer the nature of the authority he feels is his:

> If one of you should not obey what Jesus has spoken through Us, let him know he commits a grave sin and lays himself open to dire peril ... You will give Us great joy if, by obeying what We have written in the Holy Ghost, you cast off the unrighteous vehemence of your anger, according to the admonitions which We have expressed in this letter in favour of peace and concord.

St Clement adds that the apostles appointed bishops and deacons in every place, and it was they who carried out the task of giving directions as to how the ministry should perpetuate itself.

The special status of the bishops of Rome is, therefore, of very early origin, and it was to survive what appeared to be deadly humiliations. Yet it was not until the eleventh century that they established firmly in the Latin Church their sole right to the title of 'pope', which is derived from the Greek word meaning 'father'. For long it was the common property of the great patriarchs of Constantinople, Antioch and Alexandria, and also of senior bishops in the Latin Church. But gradually it became particularly associated with the see of Rome, and in 998 the archbishop of Milan was rebuked for having himself addressed as 'pope'. At the Lateran Council of 1073, Gregory VII forbad its use by any bishop save the bishop of Rome.

Whatever one's view of papal authority and papal claims, it would require an utterly impervious scepticism to move through the legends and traditions without accepting any part of them. The first Christian emperor built the first St Peter's in the place where tradition had it that Peter was buried. He built it in such a way as to show clearly that, in his day, the site was a sacred place for Christians. Modern excavations under the high altar have revealed what appears to be the Constantinian memorial to Peter, which may or may not have contained his remains. The final proof to satisfy all reasonable minds that here was the actual tomb has not been produced. One lady professor claimed in two books to have solved the matter completely by inspecting the bones and other remains found on the site. The Vatican itself—misguidedly in the opinion of most scholars—appeared later to endorse her findings by announcing the content of her second book on the subject in a press release. In fact, no official endorsement has been given and fully convincing evidence has yet to catch up with the swifter steps of faith.

There can be no arguing with the evidence that Constantine put his builders to immense pains in order to place his basilica in a particular position by the Vatican Hill. They excavated part of the base of the hill to take the apse, filling in a number of pagan tombs in order to site the five-aisled church precisely where the emperor wanted it. From that time, the basilica and its successor have been taken by the faithful to mark the apostle's tomb. Its physical proximity to the site of St Peter's death and burial has aroused awe and fascination throughout the centuries. So strong is the mystique of Rome's locality that it was a major factor in ending the 'Avignon Captivity' in the fourteenth century, bringing the Papacy back to Rome. The arrangement with France (Avignon itself was papal property) seems to have been sensible and satisfactory, even though it too clearly showed the Papacy's subjection to France. In a way, it was rather like the present arrangement between the tiny Vatican state and the Italian state. But Avignon was not Rome; it did not have the mystique of St Peter. And so (for this reason among others) the popes returned to the turmoil and violence of medieval Rome.

Familiarity, one would think, should breed at least a lessening of the effect of this awe and fascination. Yet, however many times one goes to St Peter's to see the pope give his general audience, it is still an impressive moment when he speaks of the tomb of his predecessor beneath the altar by which he is sitting. Paul VI is particularly impressive at such times, perhaps because he, more than his recent predecessors, has felt the need to emphasise frequently the origins of his authority.

No place, and no office, can command so great an aura. There have been disputes and anti-popes, schisms, scandals, vice and bloodshed, but not a break in the line—at least, no break that could not eventually be mended. Moreover, a man treated in a semi-divine manner will assume the outward attributes of semi-divinity, whether or not they were there before, concealed from view. Thousands and thousands of times the papal choirs have intoned the *Tu Es Petrus* to reigning pontiffs: centuries of intoxicating invocation, triumphant and sweet. How could they not be dignified? How could they not be awesome?

There was no more regal performance in terms of majesty and heightened feeling than Paul VI's entry into St Peter's on 5 October 1965, immediately after driving from the airport on his return from New York. He walked with a forceful step along the entire length of the great nave while two thousand or so bishops attending the Council cheered the first pope in history to go to the New World. He was tired, almost overcome with emotion and extraordinarily dignified. No one, however great a man he be in the world's affairs, can stand unawed in the presence of the modern pontiff. When President Kennedy visited the Vatican in July 1963, there entered within the sacred apostolic walls a man who carried with him not only the dignity and power of the American presidency—the aura, one might almost say, of the modern Emperor of the West—but also the personal *savoir-faire* and force of character acknowledged with respect by immense numbers of people throughout the world. Yet, along with his entourage, he looked to be shifting uneasily in the antechambers. The new frontier seemed very new indeed. Kennedy's unease on this occasion is not explicable solely by the fact that, as a Catholic, he would naturally be moved by humble awe at the thought of approaching the spiritual father of his Church. In March 1966, when Dr Michael Ramsey, archbishop of Canterbury, was welcomed by the pope preparatory to their famous meeting in the Sistine Chapel, the chief prelate of the Anglican communion was observed to be overwhelmingly moved. The *Tu Es Petrus* is assuredly a triumphant anthem, a conditioning sound over the centuries. It stirs heart and mind together. What, one wonders, might it have done to the heart and mind of Peter?

BELOW GOD AND ABOVE MAN

AUTHORITY AND UNITY

St Irenaeus,* in his writings *Against Heresies*, said of the Roman Church:

> By its tradition and by its faith announced to men, which have been transmitted to us by the succession of bishops, we confound all those who in any way by caprice or vainglory or by blindness and perversity of will gather where they ought not. For to this Church, on account of its special position of leadership, it is necessary that every church, that is the faithful from all sides, should resort, in which the tradition from the apostles has always been preserved by those that are from all parts.

To the emperors, the problem was different. So it is with any civil authority which has close relations with the ecclesiastical authorities. Given an ecclesiastical or doctrinal dispute, Constantine was less interested in the precise way it was settled than that it should be settled, so that everyone could agree on what to believe and believe it. Ecclesiastical unity was not the same thing as that spiritual unity for the Empire which he had had in mind when he called in the support of Christianity. He did not understand the priestly concern for establishing right doctrine and for rejecting misreadings of the faith, in whatever direction the interests of unity might appear to lie. The two views are curiously in contrast, and sum up what was to be one of the fundamental preoccupations of the Church in its future dealings with the state. Becket explored the field as thoroughly as anyone, but the ground was already quite well turned in Constantine's own dealings with the heresies known as Donatism and, in its earlier stages, Arianism.

The Donatists, product of a changing and uncertain age, were African Christians whose complaint was that the incumbent of the see of Carthage was unacceptable to them. They argued that the bishop who had consecrated him in 311—Felix of Aptunga—had betrayed the faith during the persecutions of Diocletian by handing over the sacred books to imperial agents. They set up a

---

* A native of Asia Minor, St Irenaeus became bishop of Lyons and the first of the great Catholic theologians. He died about the year 200.

bishop of their own, Marjorinus, who was succeeded in the see in 315 by Donatus. The supporters of Donatus had an unpleasant shock. They found that they could not enjoy reparations or imperial benefactions from Constantine's liberal hand because these were going to the official bishop, not to their man. They therefore appealed to the emperor. Their proposal was that their dispute be put to the judgment of the bishops of Gaul on the grounds of the likely impartiality of those bishops, since Gaul had not been touched by Diocletian's persecution. Constantine's reply was to refer the matter to the bishop of Rome, at that time Miltiades (311–14), himself an African by birth.

The dispute was a matter of discipline as well as of fact because it involved the problem of whether a bishop in a state of sin could validly administer a sacrament. Its more practical aspect is one which has returned rather forcibly to trouble the Church in our contemporary conditions. How far can priests go in seeking compromises with the civil authorities? While the swing from Diocletian to Constantine was the most extreme case in Christian history, it is not alone in raising this problem. John XXIII, for instance, when he was nuncio in Paris at the time of the liberation in 1944–5, was faced with the demands of many patriotic Frenchmen for the removal of those bishops who had become too closely involved with Pétain's regime. Of even greater difficulty is the question of priests who may have gone too far in compromising themselves with communist regimes. In seeking agreements with communist governments, the Vatican must naturally appoint priests to carry out an agreement who enjoy its trust but are also acceptable to the civil authorities. Martyrdom is not wanted. Cardinal Mindszenty of Hungary, a hero to Catholics in the earlier post-war years, in now rather a nuisance. Even Cardinal Wyszynski of Poland is affected by the change in attitude at the Vatican. The decision to attempt a more flexible attitude towards the communists has renewed the problems raised by the Donatists on what is potentially the largest scale since the days of the Late Empire.

The emperor, in making over the Donatist controversy to the pope, at the same time proposed that three bishops from Gaul sit with the bishop of Rome in judgment. The pope added fourteen Italian bishops to this commission, making of the affair the beginnings of a council. The decision went against the Donatists, the pope gave sentence, and Constantine felt that the trouble was now over. The basis for a return to unity had been found, and that, to his mind, was the main issue. He reckoned without the persistence of prelates involved in dispute. The Donatists refused to accept the decision. Constantine gathered in Council at Arles bishops from Italy, Africa, Spain, Gaul and Britain. The earlier decision was reaffirmed. The Donatists appealed to the emperor again: a move which, though perhaps satisfying to his pride, must have been wearisome to his patience. 'The judgment of bishops', he said in a letter to the Council of Arles after its decision had been made known, 'ought to be regarded as if the Lord Himself were sitting in judgment.' Nevertheless, he took the matter out of the bishops' hands and gave judgment himself. He upheld the verdict of Rome and of the Council. The Donatists thereafter were to continue as a schismatic group, occasionally suffering theological attack and other, more direct, forms of coercion, until the Church in Africa was destroyed by the Arabs in the seventh and eighth centuries. But long before their destruction, ecclesiastical authority had won the struggle against them, though in a way which must have left sections of clerical opinion uneasy about the manner in which the imperial power had been deployed.

Equally heavy-handed with the Arians, the emperor was less successful. The teaching of Arius (apparently a Libyan born in the middle of the third century) was the principal heresy among a number denying the true divinity of Christ. Arius gained respect by his ascetic ways and the force of his personality; his teaching had an intrinsic attraction because it took to their logical conclusion a whole set of ideas prevalent in Eastern Christendom ascribing full divinity only to God the Father. His views gained wide currency in that they also had something in common with intellectual paganism. He taught that the Son of God was not eternal but created by the Father from nothing, as an instrument for the redemption of the world; He was not therefore God by nature, having had the dignity of Son of God bestowed on Him by God. Christ was neither 'very God' nor 'very man' but, through the Holy Spirit, was a link between the two: a phenomenon close to the 'intermediate being' of neoplatonism. The doctrine was condemned by Arius's bishop but it continued to spread. Constantine was as concerned as ever for the religious unity of his empire. In a characteristic gesture, he sent Hosius of Cordoba to Alexandria, pointing out that he had just defeated Licinius and, having thereby removed one cause of disunity, wished now to do the same in the religious field. In 325, the year after his defeat of Licinius, he summoned the Council of Nicaea, the first General Council of the Church to be recognised as fully ecumenical.

The Council of Nicaea condemned Arius, but its definition of the Church's views on the Trinity was unhappily chosen. In the Greek text of the Council's statement of faith, the relationship of Son to Father was expressed in the technical term *homoousis*; the Roman equivalent, long accepted in the West, is 'consubstantial'.* *Homoousis* was suspect in most of the East because it was unscriptural and seemed to involve a confounding of the natures of Father and Son. It is possible also that it had been earlier condemned in connection with a different heresy. All save Arius himself and two Egyptian bishops at the Council accepted the *homoousis* formulation, but the nuances of difference between it and 'consubstantial' were to create difficulties which the Arians were able to exploit.

Constantine was present at Nicaea and took part in the Council's debates. His aim was to obtain a decision, and he made it plain that he favoured the controversial form *homoousis*. Yet he declared: 'I myself received the exposition of the truth'. Some of the bishops, however, had been induced to join the majority only because of the emperor's insistence on agreement. He sought to make the minority acquiesce in the decision of the majority. This has to be seen as something more than a typical expression of Constantine's outlook. It is still the aim at General Councils. A consensus was the desired conclusion—largely achieved—at the

* Or, as rendered in the Eucharist of the Anglican Church, 'being of one substance'.

Second Vatican Council. Paul VI was so anxious to try to win over the conservative minority that he peremptorily added passages to some of the more forward-looking documents which substantially reduced their freshness and value.

After Nicaea, Constantine adopted a not dissimilar tactic. Realising the strength of the opposition to the *homoousion* in the East, he was content that the bishops should formally accept the Nicene creed, without inquiring too closely into the interpretation they put upon it. The result of his attempt at a consensus was that he made it possible for Arius to be restored to communion, while Athanasius (the principal opponent of Arius), refusing to acquiesce in any dilution of Nicene doctrine, was banished to Trèves.

Constantine received baptism only on his deathbed. Clothed in the white of innocence, perhaps aware of his unique distinction in having been honoured as a pagan deity at the same time as being acclaimed a Christian saint, he was admitted into the fold of Christ at the hands of the bishop of Nicomedia, an Arian.

Of the emperor's three sons who achieved the imperial dignity, Constantius II inherited the East and naturally espoused the anti-Nicene, even Arianising, policies which most bishops there favoured. Constantine II, the eldest, and Constans took over the West; but almost at once they fell out, and Constantine was killed in battle against his brother. Constans, pro-Nicene like most of the West, was assassinated in 350. Thereupon Constantius moved West, defeated the usurper Magnentius in 351 and took control of the Western Empire. His diluted theology—Nicene doctrine watered down by near-Arian infusions—could now move westward. In a sense, from the point of view of ultimate Christian unity, this was not a bad thing. The regional complication had been removed, even if at the price of impugning the strict Catholic orthodoxy of Western Europe. There was now less danger, paradoxically as it may seem, of the East's forcing its leaning towards Arianism to the point of schism, imposing on a theological discussion a purely geographical factor of division. The death of Constantius in 361, and the pagan inter-regnum of Julian (361–363), effectively ended the alliance of imperial power with an anti-Nicene, near-Arian Christology. Rejected by the popes, it gradually diminished among the indigenous Christians of the West.* When Theodosius I became Augustus of the East in 379, he was baptised by a Catholic bishop. He followed this with an edict, promulgated at Thessalonica on 27 February 380, which sternly called all Christians to Catholic orthodoxy.

> We desire that all peoples who fall beneath the sway of our imperial clemency should profess the faith which we believe to have been communicated by the Apostle Peter to the Romans and maintained in its traditional form to the present day, the faith which is observed likewise by the Pontiff Damasus and by Peter of Alexandria, a man of apostolic sanctity; to wit, that, according to apostolic discipline and evangelical teaching, we should believe in one deity, the Sacred trinity of Father, Son and Holy Spirit to be worshipped in equal majesty; and we require that those who follow this rule of faith should embrace the name of Catholic Christians, adjudging all others madmen and ordering them to be designated as heretics.

The standard of Catholic orthodoxy was thus the see of Rome. In 381, the Council of Constantinople confirmed the Nicene Creed. Though originally representative only of the East, this Council was declared fully ecumenical when its decrees were accepted by the West in the sixth century.

The protracted doctrinal struggle, unedifying and unseemly to the lay mind, and possible on this scale because of the security which the Church enjoyed, seemed settled in a way which prevented a split between the Eastern and Western branches of Christian civilisation. The split was to come later. After Byzantium became Constantinople and the seat of Empire, the city was given 'precedence of honour' as a patriarchate after Rome itself. This move, in effect, demoted Alexandria and Antioch, both of which, like Rome but unlike Constantinople, based their claims to precedence on their apostolic foundation, Antioch looking back to the presence there of Peter, and Alexandria to Mark. Unless one

---

* Its revival in the West was to come from the incursion of Germanic peoples from the fifth century onwards.

admits the inadmissible position of Constantine as the thirteenth apostle, Constantinople had no claim to precedence except for the fact that it had become the civil and administrative capital of the Empire. It was a capital that would continue in prosperity long after Rome had declined, for it was the economic centre of the Eastern Empire in a way that Rome never was of the Western. The manner of its obtaining a spiritual precedence was sign enough that the Church would become deeply involved with the state and be inevitably caught up in the later secular rivalry between Rome and Constantinople. Though the schism did not come formally until 1054, it was a long foreshadowed and natural development—however unnatural schism in the Christian Church is usually made out to be.

SEEKING A PROTECTOR

In the East, the Empire prospered, with the Church closely involved in it. In the West, the Empire disintegrated, and the popes were left to make what they could of relations with the new peoples invading and settling the Italian peninsula and the westernmost provinces of the old Roman *imperium*.

The popes had advantages. The Church was well endowed. It was respected, for the pontiff was the most eminent dignitary in Rome after the departure of the emperor. In its hierarchy, the Church possessed Western Europe's one reserve of trained and educated men able to handle administration, continuing by the very clothes they wore* and the way they cut their hair the traditions of Rome in its greatness. These new peoples with whom they would have to deal were simple at heart, for all their pugnacious strength. With these advantages, the Papacy prepared to fulfil a function which was the reverse of the Constantinian medal. Instead of being chosen by the prince to help support the secular power, the Church was about to choose for itself the political ally which it needed to complement its spiritual authority.

---

* Those clothes which only now are being discarded for everyday use, following the Second Vatican Council's decision formally allowing priests to wear trousers and jackets.

Yet, with all its advantages, it lacked security. In seeking to supplement this essential lack, the popes laid the foundation of medieval political society and, quite incidentally, began the process which was to lead to the full realisation, centuries later, of their own ambitions as rulers. They reached their heights from a low level, beginning with a shattered empire around them, abandoned by their protector.

Some contemporaries saw the papal situation not so sympathetically. Long before Gibbon, the Church was being blamed for the collapse of the greatest empire the world had ever seen, for having been party to 'the triumph of barbarism and religion'. Four centuries before Alaric's sack of Rome in 410, Virgil had pronounced the Roman realm of his time to be the high point of human civilisation. By 413, St Augustine had risen to 'refute those who, contending that the Christian religion was responsible for the overthrow of Rome, began to blaspheme the true God with even more than their habitual bitterness and virulence'. He was arguing the claims of the city of God against those of the city of men.

Rome was to become both, and to be once more the centre of an empire, through the conversion to Catholic Christianity in 496 of Clovis, king of the Salian Franks. However, there was not much reason at the time to suppose that the conversion of this personally unpleasant man was to be decisive for the future. The Franks were to become 'the eldest daughter of the Church', yet the Ostrogoths under Theodoric (493–526) appeared in most ways to be far more suitable as allies of the Papacy. But Theodoric was Arian, not Catholic. To be an Arian was a political misfortune that befell a number of the barbarian tribes whose conversion to Christianity was at the hand of missionaries of that heretical persuasion. To Rome, this was a grievous lapse at the very moment of their baptism; yet simple barbarians could hardly be expected to enter straight into, far less resolve, a devious christological argument that had sundered Christendom's greatest doctors. Politically, the Arian kingdoms in the West were to be short-lived; and Clovis as a Catholic had the ideal argument for destroying his natural adversaries: a holy war.

FORESHADOWING OF FUTURE EMPIRE

When Gregory the Great became pope in 590, the breakdown of order in the Eastern Empire, and its consequent powerlessness to protect Italy against the Lombards, was a dismaying spectacle. The Papacy had been left to deal with administration—and with invaders. St Leo, in the mid-fifth century, negotiated with the barbarians and was given the credit for persuading Attila to withdraw beyond the Danube and also for limiting, later on, the depredations of the Vandals in Rome itself. But what could be done appeared to be very little, as Gregory's pessimism shows. He compared Rome to a ship battered by the tempest to the point of foundering. The horrors of war were around him: 'When We consider the way in which other men have died, We find a solace in reflecting on the form of death that threatens us.'

More ill-fortune was to come. In the seventh century, the Arabs conquered Byzantine Africa. The African Church, the pride of Latin Christianity, vanished. The Muslims went on to invade Spain and southern France, where they were only halted at Poitiers by Charles Martel. They still commanded all but the northern shore of the Mediterranean. Constantinople could send no help to Rome. Catholic Christianity had Islam to the south of it as well as to the east, and barbarians to the north. The old unity of Latin Europe as a Mediterranean-based civilisation had broken. The Eastern emperors were forced to devote most of their energies to fighting the Arabs, a people which had found its strength in the identification of religious and territorial expansion under the stimulus of the teachings of Mohammed. The political sundering of the old Empire was followed by religious dissension between Rome and Constantinople. The great controversy over images broke out with their condemnation by Leo the Isaurian in his imperial edict of 726; images were declared to be idols and their destruction ordered. Rome denounced this iconoclasticism and gave what moral aid and comfort it could to Leo's opponents in the Eastern Empire.

The new political entity in the West took shape over two centuries. For all his tribulations, Gregory the Great (590–604) had a leading part in the process. He animated the morale of the Church and the Roman people in a dark hour. He put the finances of the Holy See in good order. He also dispatched Augustine and his companions to England in 596—which may not have looked like a political act, but its effect was to be no less political than religious. The Church in England was given an imperial mark. Celtic Christianity, which had been ready to accept local variations and countenance 'national' characteristics in its looser ideas of Church government, was now overborne by a Church that was consciously supranational and a direct foundation of the Roman pontiff. Within less than four generations, in 716, a luminary of the young English Church, St Boniface, was dispatched to convert the pagan Germans. The German Church he established and hallowed by his martyrdom was like the English Church; it was directly dependent from the pontiff. For these new, northern Christians, there was no question about what a pope could or could not do. He was accepted as what he claimed to be: the Vicar of Christ. With the widening of this new basis for papal prestige and authority, there could be less and less validity in the concept of the pope's subordination to the emperor in Constantinople, especially as the latter could not defend Rome against the Lombards. Between the mid-sixth and mid-eighth centuries, these latest of the barbarian incursors—Arians like the Ostrogoths they supplanted—had achieved supremacy in Italy, harrying the remaining outposts of the Byzantine presence in the peninsula, and threatening with extinction the very centre of Catholicism. In 751, the Lombards destroyed the clinging remnant in the West of the Eastern Empire, overcoming the Exarchate of Ravenna, seat of the emperor's representative.

The preliminary clearing of the stage was brisk and logical, as if history itself were bringing some help to a process which would give Europe a new face—and the Papacy its old political troubles in a new form. The conversion of Clovis to Catholicism was the start to the shifting of the scenery. It gave the Frankish leader the will and the pretext to fight the Arian Visigoths of Gaul in what might reasonably be called the first of the purely political holy wars. On beginning his campaign against them in 507, he is reputed to have said: 'Verily, it grieves my soul that these Arians should hold a part of Gaul; with God's help, let us go and conquer them and take their territories.' Like Constantine, Clovis found religion a useful auxiliary to his armies and the Cross an auspicious symbol on his soldiers' shields. Born a pagan, he became a militant Catholic; this fact was decisive for the fortunes of Europe and of his own house: the Merovingian dynasty founded by his grandfather Merovech. By his conquests, Clovis built up a new Catholic polity in Europe. He could hardly have foreseen the outcome of his ambitions and ruthlessness; the agent of the transformation of Europe was to be the Papacy, beleaguered in the midst of the confusion around the tombs of the apostles.

All these elements in the process came together around 750. The relief afforded to the Papacy by the intervention of the first Catholic king of the Franks proved short-lived, for the Merovingian dynasty after Clovis's death first fell into savage internecine conflict and then into degeneracy of will and vigour. By the end of the seventh century, the Lombards—yet another Arian Germanic people—had become the chief power in Italy; under Liutprand (712-44) they erased the last centres of Byzantinian authority in the peninsula. Pope Gregory III (731-41) tried to obtain the help of Charles Martel, the Frankish leader, against the Lombards, but he failed, despite the dispatch of a special embassy to confer on the effective ruler of the Franks the keys of the apostolic tombs. The attempt at a new alliance with the Franks, premature with Charles Martel, was to be successful with his son Pepin the Short, who succeeded his father as *de facto* ruler of the Franks in 741. He was 'mayor of the palace', not king. The Merovingian royal house was enfeebled and an object of scorn. In 751 Pepin obtained the approval of Pope Zacharias (shortly before the pontiff's death in that same year) for setting aside the last descendant of Merovech and Clovis. The intermediary between the pope and the usurping king was St Boniface, the West Saxon prelate and future martyr-patron of the German Church. He anointed Pepin at the coronation service, using the religious rite that, under ecclesiastical fostering, had taken root among the Anglo-Saxons in Britain and the Visigoths in Spain, but was until then unknown among the Franks. Sanctified by the holy chrism, France's kings were now to be kings indeed, partaking of a dignity at once imperial and religious. It was a precious boon for a usurper of the crown: a powerful sanction against the ousting of his descendants, thus divinely endorsed. By lending his authority to the removal of the heir of Clovis and to the crowning of the energetic Pepin, Zacharias nominated the champion the Papacy needed and established a firm precedent for future papal essays in *realpolitik*.

Stephen II (752–7)* renewed the anointing and received the desired *quid pro quo* on his visit to Pepin in 754. The pope asked for the Frankish king's help against the Lombards. This was the first time that a pope had travelled north of the Alps, and the first occasion of a pope's taking the initiative in a political negotiation of international import. It was an auspicious beginning to the Papacy's new role. Western Europe would soon have its own emperor; even sooner, the Papacy would become a great temporal sovereignty. Pepin agreed to attack the Lombards. He defeated them in 755 and again in 756, giving to the pope the recovered territories of the Exarchate of Ravenna and other former Byzantinian possessions in Italy, together with the duchies of Spoleto and Benevento. Between them, the pope and king disposed of territories nominally belonging to the Eastern emperor. Significantly, from this time onward, Rome ceased to date official documents according to the regnal years observed in Constantinople, and popes hereafter struck their own coins.

Of immense importance for the future was the fact that the popes now had a great temporality. The Papacy had already acquired large possessions ever since Constantine began his munificence to the Church. The papal endowment had been put in such good order by Gregory the Great that his successors could fairly be described as the strongest financial power in Europe. They also had capable men to administer their possessions: the only sovereigns in Western Europe with properly trained adminis-

---

* Sometimes styled Stephen III. Zacharias's immediate successor, who took the title of Stephen II, died unconsecrated four days after his election in 752.

trators at their disposal. What had been an estate became a principality after the alliance with Pepin, a principality that would endure until 1870, and would continue, symbolically, in our day as the sovereign enclave of the Vatican City.

NEW EMPIRE ESTABLISHED

The effect was immediately felt, and might have been a warning for all future popes. The papal principality was highly vulnerable and still needed to be defended, for the Lombards, though defeated, were not crushed and were intent on recovering their former possessions at the earliest opportunity. Paul I (757-67) strengthened the bond between the Franks and the Papacy by confirming Pepin a Roman patrician. All the same, this dignity carried nothing specific in terms of rights and duties. By Pepin's death in 768, the precise status and powers of the Church's champion had still not been determined. The continuing Lombard threat was to resolve the matter. Pepin's son Charles, soon known as Charlemagne, was to be crowned emperor by Leo III (795-816) at that famous ceremony on Christmas Day 800 when, after Mass in St Peter's, an apparently startled and by no means acquiescent king found himself saluted as 'Emperor of the West'.

Leo III not only crowned and saluted him as emperor; the pope went down on his knees, 'adoring' the new imperial authority in Byzantine fashion. A new political force now made its appearance as a component in the devising of a new Europe. The pope claimed authority for his action, not by virtue of any lordship of Rome, but as representative of St Peter. There were few, if any, in the West to assert against this the Constantinian concept of sacred and secular relationships, and to protest, in the name of Rome and the imperial system, against this bland mixing of two quite different ideas. Charlemagne was given the old imperial title and the old imperial gestures of respect; but he had received them from Heaven through the pope's good offices. For all that Leo III knelt before the first head of the new Western Empire, it would not prove difficult for his successors to affirm that the Church was very far from being subordinate to the temporal power.

Whatever Leo himself had in mind when he pressed the crown on Charlemagne's head, he had taken the most decisive step yet of any pope in giving the Papacy a promoting hand in the shaping of European history. Wittingly or unwittingly, he had begun the development which would raise the Holy See to the heights of its medieval power: its flowering as a fully fledged and powerful theocracy, with the destinies of kings and emperors at its beck and call. This he had done by offering a share in St Peter's authority to a vigorous monarch, sturdy, loyal, mystical, and rather simple. For all his intellectual interests, Charlemagne was, at the time of his coronation, illiterate. This did not mean, however, that he would be content to allow the pope a real primacy in their partnership.

Charlemagne (800–14) did not attempt to behave like the old Roman emperors, though he seems to have had some of Constantine's enthusiasm for theological discussion. The pretended connection in his title with the old empire was of more use to the pope than to him. It still had cultural and spiritual value because of its associations, but it would scarcely have made a deep impression on a man who thought more in terms of action. He had, after all, carved out his own empire and defeated his own enemies; that his enemies were frequently the enemies of the Church gave a kind of moral sanction to Frankish expansion. He fought religious wars against the heathen Saxons and against the Arabs. He destroyed the Avars, that Asiatic race of robbers who were terrorising eastern Europe, and thereby restored Christianity to the Danubian provinces. But his destruction of the Lombards was a different sort of religious war. It was done at the behest of the Papacy and was undertaken specifically to save the physical centre of the Church from the menace of invasion.

Once again, Church and state were to be mingled because Charles was himself of a theocratic turn of mind and regarded himself as governor of the Church as well as of the state, holding the two swords of spiritual and temporal authority. In making his political decision Leo III had certainly not intended to hand over the Church to a new political master, reducing it once again to Byzantine subordination. Presumably one reason why the pope revived the old title was because the powers of the Frankish king had in some way to be limited. The imperial relationship embodied a tradition of mutual checks, and gave unbridled authority to neither side. The popes would regard their own power as superior because authority, in their reading of the question of authority, was theirs to give, not to bargain over.

There is little reason to wonder why Charlemagne was surprised and not particularly happy about the sudden offer of the imperial crown. It did not, in effect, give him more than he already had. He did not, like Constantine or Pepin, require the reinforcement which Christian partnership could give. His family had already exploited that factor fully enough by having its assumption of the Frankish throne made good by the novelty of unction. He had a high view of his own authority. Its foundation was not in the traditions of late imperial Rome but in that of the Bible and the writings of St Augustine. He was advised on these intellectual problems of authority by Alcuin, the Yorkshireman who became abbot of Tours, and to whom he constantly turned for guidance on religious and educational matters after their meeting at Parma in 781. They decided that the authority of the Frankish king was of a higher kind than that of the Roman emperor, whom they looked on—even the Christian lord of Byzantium—as representative of the earthly kingdom, whereas Charlemagne had the superior dignity of ruler and guide of God's people. Theirs was a more mystical concept of imperial authority. Alcuin maintained that there were three supreme powers in the world: the Papacy in Rome, the Empire in Constantinople and the royal authority of Charlemagne; and of these the third was the highest because Charlemagne had been specifically appointed by Christ to lead the Christian people. Charlemagne himself told Leo III in a letter that the emperor (*sc.* in the West) was 'the representative of God who has to protect and govern all the members of God'; he is 'lord and father, king and priest, leader and guide of all Christians'. This was not simply a revival of the Roman Empire of the West. Like Constantine, Charlemagne had his apologists willing to place his authority on a unique pinnacle; Cathulf maintained that the king stood in the place of God over all his people, for whom he had to account at the Last Day, while the bishop stood in the second place as the representative of Christ only. The difference between the two empires is distinct; the Roman Empire was an ancient society which, at a given moment, changed from paganism to Christianity; the other was Christian in its origin. As a result of this Carolingian theory, in combination with the Carolingian practice of using clerics in governmental service, the state became more clerical and the Church more secular.

The administration of Charlemagne's realm was largely in the hands of priests. This is a factor of crucial, and unhappy, importance. The past cannot always justly be invoked against the modern Vatican, but the Holy See's attitude sometimes makes such an indictment inevitable. The habit of telling temporal authorities, from rulers down to quite minor officials, how to run their affairs came early to the Church. Pupils can never be admitted to having overtaken their master. In this renewing by the revived Empire of the old imperial system of priest-administrators can be traced the origin of the rather arrogant forms which ecclesiastical intervention in civil matters is still inclined to take.

Indeed, the Carolingian Empire, if anything, made an even more systematic use of prelates as civil officials than had the Constantinian Empire. Bishops shared equally with the lay nobility the local administration of the 300 counties which formed Charlemagne's administrative framework. Government itself depended to a large extent on the prelates of the Chancery and of the Royal Chapel. This latter institution began as a group of ecclesiastics whose duty was to guard the cloak of St Martin of Tours, patron saint of the Frankish kingdom.* Later, the Royal Chapel took over a good deal of the secular administration. It also functioned as a kind of synod of the Frankish clergy. Its arch-chaplain was a close adviser of the monarch and a great dignitary of the realm. Local administration was controlled by a body of royal officers, the *missi dominici*, who toured the counties to inspect the functioning of local administration 'to the end that they diligently inquire

* St Martin had excellent credentials to be the saint of the Franks. Born the son of a pagan, probably in 335, he served in the Roman army until, on cutting his cloak in two to share it with a beggar, he had a vision of Christ which led to his baptism. When visiting Milan, he was expelled by its Arian bishop.

if any man complain of injustice done to him by others'. The more important of such missions were entrusted to churchmen. This function was rooted in the superiority of the clerics' education and in the greater steadfastness of religious institutions in times of trouble. It was they who, in the dark days after the collapse of Roman authority, had kept the wheels of organised life turning and, in preserving much of Western culture, had provided personnel for administrative posts in the new kingdoms converted to Christianity. The barbarians were simple and unlettered; their religious instructors were neither.

The sad simplicity of the Frankish strain of religious devotion is touchingly expressed in a poem which Charlemagne wrote for the tomb of Pope Hadrian I:

> ... these verses I, Charles, wrote weeping for the death of the father. You were my sweet love, whom I now mourn, O father. Remember me; my thoughts will follow you ever. You are now with Christ in the Kingdom of Heaven. The clergy and people loved you with great affection; you were the love of all, O best of pastors. I desire, O illustrious man, that our names and titles be joined here: Hadrian and Charles, I king, you father.

It is hardly sophisticated. It has the early medieval simplicity. Charlemagne sent it, finished on its square of black marble of Tours, where St Martin had been bishop, to be placed on the tomb in the atrium of the basilica built by Constantine. In the old St Peter's it would, in terms of space and association, have brought together these two emperors who were the great twin formative promoters of organised Christianity. It can now be found—perhaps of little interest to the casual visitor—inside the portico of the present St Peter's. It is a reminder, expressed in words of lachrymose lyricism, of that strange alliance of pope and emperor which was the foundation of medieval Europe. For this reminder, the tablet is worth the visitor's pause before he presses through the doors of the basilica to behold the sumptuous triumph, to sense the rather hectic air of exultation which the present St Peter's conveys in its architecture and decoration. Constantine would probably have felt happy in such a basilica, and would certainly have understood its meaning. Charles probably would not, though very likely happily overwhelmed by it all. The massive head of Constantine (part of an immense statue) on the Capitol Hill is one of the survivals of antiquity on a scale comparable with St Peter's, and it is of Christian antiquity. It is easy to imagine it inside the basilica. The sun which pours through the golden glass of the window of the apse, with its representation of the Holy Spirit, would have made that first Christian emperor—who seems, for a time, to have identified Christ with the Unconquered Sun—feel very much in the right place.

The Papacy's advance towards the highest place in Europe was no simple matter of constant progress. Before they achieved the heights, popes were exiled and murdered; some were thoroughly bad in character. They lived amid disorders, and these were never more violent than at times of papal elections. Indeed, on that famous day in the year 800, Leo III had come back to Rome with Charlemagne after having been bodily attacked by members of the factious Roman families who had realised already that the possessions of the Church made the Papacy, in temporal terms, an office well worth the having. The advance to a real principality had sharpened this acquisitiveness. It is ironical that the foundation of the medieval empire should have been laid when the man whom the pope chose to be emperor had come to Rome to settle a local affair of squabbling and violence; ironical that the pope, arbiter of the imperial crown, should only just have escaped the manhandling of the mob. Perhaps this partly explains why Leo III ascribed to St Peter his authority for disposing of the crown, and not to any pretended overlordship of Rome. That tradition has been followed. Modern papal diplomacy is looked upon by the devout Roman Catholic as possessing a purely spiritual authority: that held by Christ's Vicar as successor to the leading apostle.

The Papacy had seen the problem of the Lombards removed by the Frankish intervention. It still had to maintain its position between the two emperors—the Frankish and the Byzantinian—and at the same time protect its own territories, to say nothing of the person of the pope, in the violent atmosphere of ninth-century

Rome. With the waning of Carolingian energies, as was quickly the case after Charlemagne's death, the Papacy in consequence increased its monarchical character in a way which neither Pepin nor Charlemagne would have intended. If subjection of the Byzantine type to a too-powerful emperor was inimical to it, as bad—and, in some ways, worse—was a powerless emperor in the West. Leo III had exercised his power of offering the crown to his own candidate when he sealed the Frankish alliance by a coronation. It was natural that his successors should want to find another potential protector when, by the late ninth century, the Carolingian Empire had grown ineffectual, largely as a result of Charlemagne's conservatism in abiding by the Frankish custom of dividing territories on the death of a king among the surviving sons. Pope Hadrian III decreed in 884 that in future the emperor must come from the Italian peninsula. Presumably he had in mind a protector who would look after the defence of Rome but not be so powerful as seriously to challenge the superiority of the pope's position. His proposed solution, however, made matters worse. There was no one with sufficient authority in Italy to guarantee the physical and moral integrity of the Holy See. The most striking contribution of the Roman and Italian families was to be the local humiliation of the Papacy. It was the object of violence and intrigue. In half a century, the average pontifical reign was less than three years. Some of the pontiffs were debauched. A strong hand was needed, not only to provide the Papacy with temporal force, but also to give it protection against itself, as well as against the Roman environment which was scarcely offering a salubrious frame to the activities of Christ's Vicar.

It was in these circumstances that the Saxon, Otto the Great, came to Rome and was crowned in 962 in St Peter's. Unlike the Franks, the German emperors would prove strong enough to retain their empire.

GERMAN EMPERORS

The need felt by the Church for a temporal protector was once again to make a deep impress on European history. The Germans had less to offer, on the face of it, than the Franks. Unlike Charlemagne's, their realm did not include most of Western Europe; and, unlike the Byzantine emperor, the German had no unified state firmly under control, no secure centre of administration—while the Western Church was far from subject to the civil power. Again, on the face of it, a German as emperor made little sense of the retention of Rome as the spiritual heart of Europe. It had never made much sense in strictly Christian terms. A semi-oriental religion had first been drawn out of its geographical context because St Peter went to Rome, and then divested of its primitive characteristics by being made the religion of a failing state. Yet the necessities of the Papacy, if not the logical imperatives of Christianity, had consolidated, and were to continue to strengthen, the position of Rome as the centre of Christendom. The popes could not look eastward for their protector: too exigent in their sovereign claims to be tolerable to the Papacy's sense of its spiritual integrity, the Byzantine emperors after Justinian were also too weak to be serviceable to its need for security. By engaging first the Franks and then the Germans, the Holy See kept the western and northern regions of Europe bound to the attraction of Rome, which logically could only be the capital of a Mediterranean empire. In this sense, the popes made Rome eternal. It was inconvenient, inappropriate, turbulent, and with a bad climate; yet despite all this, Rome retained its prestige. German emperors and Roman popes were ill-assorted partners but, without the German connection, Roman Christianity might have moved back to a static, fully Mediterranean type of religious culture, and the pope have become a shadowy figure, revered perhaps but ineffectual. The Germans, moreover, diminished—if they could not wholly abolish—the papal servitude to local Roman families. The northern connection provided a means for reinvigorating the Church.

It is unfair to say that Europe's northerners are less liable to corruption than its southerners, but they are certainly more vigorous, less inclined to sink into fatalism. At the Second Vatican Council, it was the prelates from northern and north-western Europe—and particularly the theologians they brought to advise them—who set the pace for introducing fresh ideas. The Germans, the Dutch, the Belgians and the French provided bishops who were explicit in their demands and clear about what they wanted; and what they wanted was a liberalisation of Roman Catholic attitudes and institutions. There were no Italian figures who could be measured with their northern colleagues as far as a liberal approach was concerned. There are liberal Italian bishops but, on the whole, they kept quiet at the Council. There are also many conservative bishops who, on the whole, did not keep quiet. The Italians still boast that their country has produced no heresy. The northern Europeans have; yet, albeit breaking Christian unity in the sixteenth century, they have also produced valuable stimulants for Christendom. The price of freedom is higher than Italian ecclesiastical consciousness is willing to pay. Not paying it is likely to prove in the end a more expensive business, as the sixteenth-century revolt showed and as the bitterness towards the Curia revealed at the Second Vatican Council seems to confirm. The Reformation as much as anything else was a revolt against Italian handling of the Church.

In the tenth century, a somewhat similar feeling—but avoiding a break in Christian unity—brought northern help in setting the throne of St Peter in order once more. The Saxon emperors achieved this by accepting a more direct responsibility than their predecessors of the revived Empire for what happened in Rome. On several occasions they went to Rome to see that a worthy man was made pope, and their choices naturally tended to be northerners. Yet northern religious reform and northern imperial authority were unlikely to lead in the same direction. Strengthening the Papacy by purifying it meant that its renewed strength would clash with the emperor's temporal claims. The quarrel would be re-enacted over which of them had precedence: the emperor claiming his authority from God, the pope claiming to be Christ's Vicar on earth. The inevitable interplay of personal and institutional factors quickened the two sets of claims.

So did two other factors which were destined to shape the policies of the popes. In the first place, the papal principality, rich enough to be tempting, was too weak to defend itself. Secondly, prelates, and particularly in Germany, controlled much of the civil administration. The popes are not specifically to be blamed for this situation, which was to have an unfortunate effect on priestly behaviour in the future. As we have seen, the practice was introduced strictly as a matter of policy by the Carolingians, not by the popes. A good deal that is regrettable and seems to need sweeping away has accrued around the Vatican. It has collected history in something like the same way that a light attracts fish. One means of getting rid of the stinking fish that this process had accumulated around St Peter's barque would be to turn off the light—which is precisely what the popes cannot do. It is some such formulation of the problem as this which weighs heavily on Paul VI.

Arguably, the German kings would have done better to refuse the imperial crown. Certainly, the acceptance of it by Otto I, known as 'the Great' (962–73), brought prestige to Germany and to its monarchy. More important, it strengthened the German people's links with the Mediterranean world and so confirmed them as an element in the mixed tradition of European culture. Yet this—as some historians, not all of them Germans, would argue—was not an unmixed blessing, for it distracted the German emperors from following the immediate interests of their own people, delaying the process of national unification which was at work in England and France. Their involvement in Italian affairs also occurred at a time when the Germans were expanding to the east, moving across central Europe to those sparsely populated plains which have so profoundly operated on the German imagination. They were safe to the west. France was increasingly embroiled with England after the Norman Conquest. The pull southward was a distinct wrenching of the logic of German policy both from a natural, eastward expansion and from internal cohesion. This latter was hindered, not helped, by the prestige of the imperial crown, with its concomitant clerical and secular tensions between Germany and Italy, and within Germany itself. The monarchy remained elective: a weakening factor from which the French and the English had freed themselves. It suited the Papacy to keep it so and to sustain, when this seemed needful to its policy, the rights of the German princely nobility against the central power of the monarchy. A solid dynastic tradition, securely passing from one generation to another, would have given imperial authority too great an advantage over the Papacy, which itself was, and remains, elective. A temporal power with inherent weaknesses, a strong emperor but a simple and respectful man—these would be the ideals of the Papacy. While its imperial heritage taught it how to deal with emergent, young, recently converted nations, it could never grasp a more mature national spirit.

On the whole, the German emperors were not more pretentious than their Carolingian predecessors. The alliance of Papacy with the Frankish kings had been understood—in Rome at least, where it is perfectly illustrated in a mosaic at the Lateran—as a partnership in which both sides took their authority from St Peter, but in which the pope had the most intimate contact with the source of authority, being Peter's successor and holder of the keys to the Kingdom. Some danger must have been felt in the papal palaces when Otto III (983-1002) established himself in Rome, on the Aventine hill, and adopted surviving Byzantine fashions of dress and conduct—a danger because fashions in dress could imply fashions in politico-religious ideas. The Byzantine emperors regarded themselves quite differently from the Franks; they were the heirs of classical Rome as well as of Constantine, implicitly claiming an authority going back to a time before Christian saints were heard of, or Christ Himself for that matter. In any event, Otto III's attempt at a Byzantinian imperial revival came to very little. He was faced with rebellion in Rome itself and died amidst the total ruin of his ambitions. A fascinating figure he remains, though, sitting there with dreams of glory, a Saxon in semi-oriental garb, unaware that the idea of Empire, like its centre of gravity, could not again be Byzantine and eastern and classical. The popes had seen to that. The emperor's clothes really did not exist.

The revival of papal prestige under the earlier German emperors was part of a conscious attempt to raise the moral level of the Papacy at one of its lowest moments. Otto the Great's insistence on reasonably worthy priests in the chair of St Peter was maintained by his successors. At the Synod of Sutri in 1046, Henry III deposed two, perhaps even three, popes, and then used his authority to bring about the successive elections of four popes, of whom all were either Germans or imperial subjects of other race; and all of them were good men. They were, directly or indirectly, responsible for the arrival in Rome of the ideas about reform and spiritual renewal associated with the Cluniac movement.

The monastery of Cluny, near Macon in Burgundy, was founded in 910 by William the Pious, duke of Anjou. Almost immediately, it began to stimulate a whole new movement of monastic reform. Essentially, this movement represented a return to a highly spiritual form of the religious life, based on a strict observance of the Benedictine rule and with great emphasis on personal devotion and on freedom from lay influence in the day-to-day life of the monk. This latter it achieved principally by a reorganisation of the monastic economy and eventually by a shrewd development of conventual finances. With its high concern for the integrity of the devotional life and of the priestly function, the Cluniac movement increasingly came to regard any form of lay jurisdiction over the clergy as an intolerable offence to God. The period of Cluny's highest influence was in the eleventh and twelfth centuries. The future Pope Gregory VII was a prominent Cluniac, and this powerfully shaped his outlook on the priestly office and on such reforms as suppression of simony and the condemnation of married clergy in favour of comprehensive priestly celibacy. Cluny and its daughter foundations represent an important example of the Church's frequent searching for spiritual renewal. No less significant is the association of this search with clerical pretensions.

GREGORY VII AND THE INVESTITURE CONTROVERSY

In 991, just twenty-nine years after Otto I was summoned to Rome to receive the imperial crown and protect the moral as well as the physical resources of the Papacy, the French bishops were shrugging off the Holy See as spiritually bankrupt. Speaking of John XIII (955–64) and of Boniface VII (974, 984–5, an 'anti-pope'), they asked at the Council of Saint-Basle de Verzy: 'Is it to such monsters, swollen with their ignominy and devoid of all knowledge, human or divine, that the innumerable priests of God throughout the world who are distinguished by their knowledge and virtue should lawfully be submitted?' In 1073, the Sacred College of Cardinals—some fourteen years after it had received the right of electing popes—chose a Cluniac, Cardinal Hildebrand, who took the style of Gregory VII (1073-85). He was to come as near as any pope would to presiding over a revolution inspired by a genuine rethinking of the Papacy's status as a religious institution.

There have not been many periods in the history of the Papacy when revolution from within can be said to have occurred. One such period is that between the election of John XXIII and the early years of the present pontificate. Gregory VII, it must be said, far outpaced both of these modern popes; but in doing so he brought war and a struggle with the emperors that was to outlive his reign. He himself was to die in exile. What he did was probably of more significance in its immediate and long-term effects than the work of any other single pope, and the revolution he sought to apply to the world of his day is the one genuine precedent for what John and Paul in our day have tried to do, though they have been without the resources which an age of faith can lend to the spiritual leader of Christendom. Neither the same respect for religion nor the acknowledged leadership of the Roman pontiff as was operative in Gregory VII's day exists today. The driving forces in the Church, moreover, are slower moving, less titanic.

Rationally considered, Gregory VII was behaving as a pope—any pope—should behave. He was seeking, with great ability and devotion, to live up to the claims of his office. His work was astonishing in two respects: for itself, and for the fact that it was indeed revolutionary. This quintessential pontiff was not typical: he was, in the phrase used by Caspar, editor of his letters, *der grosse Anfänger*, the great innovator. It seemed natural that, when men found themselves enchanted by John XXIII's attempt to bring a more spiritual Church closer to the contemporary world, the comparison should be with Hildebrand. For the first time for centuries, the Papacy is thinking seriously again in terms of international organisation, not something 'Holy', nor necessarily 'Roman', like the old Empire, decked in its ponderous garments of divinely favoured kingship. But there is in the Vatican's contemporary policies something of the same idea: the idea that men should be governed through an all-embracing body, containing spiritual and political elements. The problem today is how a spiritual authority can be brought to bear on the full complement of nations. The visit of Paul VI to the United Nations in New York is the most striking instance of this feeling that governments must be made aware of what a great spiritual leader expects of them. When Paul published his encyclical on the problems of underdeveloped nations, in March 1967, it was made clear at the Vatican that he envisaged himself as representing the conscience of the world. If governments do not customarily come to him for advice he, following the contemporary revolution within the Church—the movement to look outward instead of inward, which was the effect of John XXIII's reign—must go out and speak to them. Behind such an action as addressing the United Nations is the historical authority of an office which was capable, at its greatest moments, of asserting itself against the emperor, whoever he was, to claim the senior partnership in the clumsy structure of the Empire which was the organisation so long destined, for good or for bad, to embody the medieval state.

One of Gregory VII's principal aims was to establish the correct priorities within the medieval state on the basis of Christian teaching. To him this meant that the Papacy must come first, and with it the Church; there could be no lay hand in ecclesiastical affairs. The Church should overcome its distrust of the world and its tendency towards withdrawal. To him, the idea that the priest's place was apart from affairs, in contemplation, had no validity. The world was to be converted by the priesthood. In order that they be fit to do it, celibacy was imposed and strict morality severely enjoined. There can be no doubt that he was right in the context of the historical development of the Church. He had the immense advantage of a world which attached great importance to the religious element in the structure of society. It was the strongest influence in most men's minds.

The Hildebrandine doctrine threatened the emperor with loss of control over the administrative pillars of his German kingdom, the bishops. He was not being denied their backing; he was being denied a free hand in their choice as well as threatened with a concept of priesthood quite irrelevant to their functions in the imperial administration. Since the days of Charlemagne, it had been established imperial policy to confer favours on bishops in return for the loyal administration of the territories under their authority and for their handling of crucial posts in government. Otto I had advanced this system until it had become an essential part of his rule. What was the point of being Holy Roman Emperor if the holy men of the Roman Church did not provide the necessary support in dealing with his temporal responsibilities; those same holy men who were urging him to be a powerful prince in the service of Christ and His religion? He had given up a good deal to become emperor. The honour overstrained the resources of his kingdom: a factor that was to have a lasting effect on German history. He faced constant challenges from his nobles. The only way whereby his rule as the leading monarch of Christendom could have effect would be for him to have control of the appointment of bishops. Lay rulers, great and small, had endowed the Church; lay authority had been sought, and given, for the Church's mission. In return for this, the Church had offered its leading prelates to aid the secular power in its mission. Without the right of episcopal appointment, the emperor—and with him all Christian princes and governors—might well find that the monarch's munificence, and trust, would be going to men on whom he could not rely. He would be seeking to administer without control over his 'civil service'.

But, for the pope, prelates were priests, sacred persons charged with sacred functions. However much it might be God's Will that they should exercise secular authority in the Christian state, that authority was spiritually based; they were men of God, doing His Will under obedience to His Vicar. To admit lay control of episcopal appointment was profanation of sacred things. Such a control, once admitted, would imperil the whole priesthood, for in countless benefices and parishes throughout Western Europe lay persons—counts, barons and mere lords of a manor—were claiming, and exercising, the right to appoint clerics. *Quis custodiet ipsos custodes?* Was the whole Church to be parcelled out as fiefs of courtiers and warriors, of venal and worldly men whom it was the priest's duty to instruct and, where necessary, admonish? For the pope, lay investiture meant the imperilling both of the cure of souls and of the Papacy's control over its agents in every country. By lay analogy, it, too, would be losing command of its 'civil service'.

These opposing positions are the substance of the conflict—the investiture controversy—which gave its name to the whole field of quarrelling between the two heads of medieval society. The controversy was at its height from the accession of Gregory VII in 1073 to the Council of Worms in 1122. Lay investiture had already received papal condemnation in 1059. Gregory repeated the condemnation in 1075. He was not opposed to the imperial idea or to individual emperors as such, some of whom were pious men who did much to improve the Church. He was simply against lay control of any branch of ecclesiastical affairs—or of ecclesiastics—as something wrong in itself. The open challenge came in his conflict with Emperor Henry IV (1084–1106). The Papacy had failed in England to force William the Conqueror to accept its views on lay investiture, but Gregory did not excommunicate him because William was compliant in applying other papal decrees and was forwarding the English Church's conformity with continental, particularly Cluniac, usage. In France, despite the opposition of Philip I, he managed to renew the whole episcopate. He felt strong enough in Germany to threaten Henry IV with deposition. Henry's response was to declare the pope deposed. Gregory retaliated by deposing the emperor and excommunicating him. A few years earlier, the Papacy had appeared to count for little and emperors had had to fight their way to Rome in order to ensure the election of an honest man as Vicar of Christ. Now, faced with rebellion at home, Henry was the one to be humiliated. In 1077, he was forced to make the bitter winter journey to Canossa, where he did penance before the pope and received absolution.

Gregory did not finally win. He was to die in exile. But he had made his point of insisting on the Church's freedom from the lay power. He had made his attempt at behaving in a manner appropriate to the claims of his office. Only the Church was divine, and the Church itself was united with the pope 'whose name alone could be uttered in the churches and whose feet all kings should kiss'. It is remarkable, when one looks at the extent of the papal claims, that so few pontiffs have been so uncompromising; but then, few could be expected to have to such a degree the combination which Hildebrand possessed of moral fervour, energy and diplomatic skill. He did not hesitate to support the emperor's enemies at home, and he picked his ground with great care before coming to the ultimate challenge, never hesitating to use all the weapons in the papal armoury: excommunication of rulers, their deposition and the freeing of subjects from their allegiance.

Lay investiture was only one aspect, though the most dramatic, of the conflict between the civil and ecclesiastical power for precedence in the medieval state. It was settled, more than a generation after Gregory VII's death in 1085, by a compromise agreement in 1122. The emperor relinquished the right to invest with ring and staff but continued to bestow temporalities. He received the homage of bishops in Germany before their consecration and in other parts of the Empire after six months. The emperors were allowed a certain influence in German episcopal elections. Basically, they were the opposite of anti-clerical; they wanted their clerical helpers to continue taking a hand in administration: exactly what is now meant by clericalism.

The compromise agreement by which the investitures controversy was settled in 1122 was the Concordat of Worms. It was the first of all concordats: a type of agreement which was to become common in papal diplomacy, and still is, for establishing the rights of the Church in its dealings with the civil power. The dispute still has its vague echoes. The Second Vatican Council asked all temporal rulers voluntarily to surrender existing privileges in such matters as the choosing of bishops, so that the Church's affairs need have no formal vestiges of lay interference.

INNOCENT III AND THE PAPAL ZENITH

The peak of papal power was reached by Innocent III (1198–1216). A Roman patrician trained in canon law, he was elected pope while still not in priestly orders. (It is still the canonists, incidentally, rather than theologians or scripturists, who command many of the most influential places at the Vatican.) Like others before him, he placed the Papacy in his theories far above any other authority; in practice, moreover, he brought this theory to a brief but perfect reality.

He was aided by his own amazing will-power and by the fact that the Empire was suffering one of its periods of feebleness. He was the first to use the title of Vicar of Christ. ('No king can reign rightly unless he devoutly serves Christ's Vicar.') He put no limits to the claims of his office in exercising authority over secular affairs. He was, he believed, like Melchizedek, prince, priest, king, uniting in his own person the fullness of all power and authority. The scriptural text of his sermon on the day of his consecration was that he had been 'set over the nations and over the kingdoms to pluck up and to break down, to destroy and to overthrow, to build and to plant'. And that is what he did. He acted as judge among nations. As arbiter among the rivals for the imperial crown at the death of Henry IV in 1197, he laid down in the bull *Venerabilem* that the appointment of an emperor came within the papal authority, on the ground that the pope had assigned the Empire from the Greeks to the Franks. What had, in fact, been a political convenience now became a moral sanction. Who could deny it, after all? Innocent was doing only what many popes have talked about and what, in a strictly logical sense, history can be said to have imposed on them.

He forced John of England to recognise him as overlord, giving judgment between the king and his rebellious subjects.* He forced Louis VIII of France to be reconciled with his wife. He brought about the dreadful massacres accompanying the extinction of the Albigensian heresy in southern France. His crusade for the Holy Land, the Fourth Crusade, was diverted from harrying the infidel

* There is a fresco in the Vatican's Secret Archive showing John handing over the kingdom of England as a papal fief of Innocent and his successors. This submission was made in 1213, a moment of severe internal difficulties for the king. It was a humiliation akin to Henry IV's at Canossa. There is nothing in the Archive to suggest that Innocent, or any succeeding pope, ever gave England back.

to attacking Constantinople: an act which, though personally horrifying to Innocent and acquiesced in by him with great reluctance, was ultimately condoned in that it established (for a time, at least) the supremacy of Rome over the Orthodox Church.

When questioned over his intervention in the quarrel between his friend Stephen Langton, archbishop of Canterbury, and King John, Innocent III declared that he was not passing judgment on a fief but on a sin. Langton had been appointed archbishop by the pope in 1207; but, because of John's objections to him, he could not land in England until 1213. Langton sympathised with the barons, and it was probably he who suggested the form to be taken by Magna Carta. Innocent's remark about intervening morally, not politically, is a fine example of the dual outlook still found at the Vatican. There is no longer a serious claim, of course, to universal government—except in moral fields. These can be stretched a long way. It is how an Italian priest justifies the threat of hell-fire to a parishioner voting for the extreme left. The acceptance of limits after the experience—enjoyed once upon a time, however briefly—of true commanding, is a difficult process. And the heights from which the loftiest claims were made were of a giddy altitude: a point so high that the secular authorities were hardly visible at all. 'As the moon derives its light from the sun, to which it is inferior alike in quantity and quality, in position and in effect, so too the royal power derives the splendour of its dignity from the power of the pope.' So said Innocent III. 'Christ left to Peter', he also said, 'not only the Church but the world to govern.' He was judge of the world, 'set in the midst between God and man, below God and above man'.

As a reinforcement of these claims, the Papacy had its document, the *Donation of Constantine*, in which the emperor apparently conferred on Pope Sylvester I (314-35) the primacy over Antioch, Constantinople, Alexandria and Jerusalem, and domain over all Italy including Rome and the 'provinces, places, and *civitates* of the western regions'. The pope was made supreme judge of the clergy and was offered the imperial crown (which he refused). It all sounded too good to be true, as indeed it was; in the fifteenth century the Donation of Constantine was shown to be a forgery.

The pope by Innocent III's day did, in fact, rule over a large part of Italy; on that point, the Donation does not falsify the situation, even if it is false in asserting that Constantine made over temporal authority to the Papacy on leaving for his new capital. Innocent III completed the boundaries of the temporality and won recognition of them from the emperor as the Papal States. The frontiers of these states, as defined by Innocent and confirmed in 1201 by the emperor, ran across Italy from the Tyrrhenian coast to the Adriatic, then turned north as far as the Po. In geographical order, this belt of states consisted of the Patrimony of St Peter, a broad area between the Tyrrhenian and Rome; the duchy of Spoleto, including much of modern Umbria; the March of Ancona, which was continued northward along the Adriatic coast by the Romagna and the lands of the Countess Mathilda of Tuscany. These were a disputed gift left to the Papacy in 1102 by the noblewoman whose castle at Canossa was the scene of papal predominance over the emperor. Mathilda was in the line of benefactors whose gifts provided the popes with the basis of their principality: Constantine himself, followed by Pepin and Charlemagne. In 1052, Leo IX was granted Benevento by the emperor, and seven years later Nicholas III's investiture of the Norman Robert Guiscard established the papal claim to suzerainty over Sicily. The mere definition of boundaries was of itself a complete acknowledgment of the Holy See's sovereignty, because the emperors claimed a degree of authority over the Papal States as the temporal arm of Christian society. Frederick II, for instance, who was willing to confirm the borders (in 1213*), insisted on his right to appoint officials and raise money in the territories of the Church. Innocent worked hard to rid his administration of German officials. Emancipation from this tutelage came in 1279 from Rudolf of Habsburg, who renounced Italian ambitions.

The document styled the *Donation of Constantine* is first known to have been used shortly before Innocent III's time. Leo IX

---

* He confirmed that the Papal States consisted of 'all the land from Radicofani to Ceprano, the March of Ancona, the Duchy of Spoleto, the Land of the Countess Mathilda, the County of Bertinoro, the Exarchate of Ravenna, the Pentapolis, with the other lands lying adjacent to them'.

attached it to a letter in support of papal claims written in 1054 to Michael Cerularius, patriarch of Constantinople. It was the year of the breach between Eastern and Western Christendom. The patriarch was excommunicated. He replied with anathemas and an encyclical setting out the Byzantine case. These hostile exchanges were not to be withdrawn until 1965, when Paul VI and Patriarch Athenagoras agreed to take this step as a move towards better relations. What effect it had on the actual fate of Michael Cerularius, so long dead and so long excommunicate, is a point for the theologians to argue. At the time of the formal opening of the schism in the eleventh century, the papal intransigence showed the self-confidence of Rome. The spiritual authority, not temporal policy, was making the running. In the succeeding centuries, the search for an end to the schism was to become an exercise in shaping an ecclesiastical policy, a policy in other words easily distinguishable from the Papacy's share in the conduct of more normal international relations. The schism and the crusades are the principal examples of policies which are ecclesiastical in aim and character. A united Christendom, with its holy places once again in Christian hands, was a splendid enough ideal; it was also something that a secular power would not necessarily adopt as its own.

The one other comparable example of a properly ecclesiastical policy was the suppression of heresy. From the beginning of the Church's association with the temporal power, the purity of doctrine had been jealously guarded. So was the direct episcopal succession from the apostles, with the special place claimed for the successor to St Peter. Neither of these basic principles was to go unchallenged. Innocent III showed how a strong pope reacted to the menace of heresy in his insistence on the massacres of the Albigensians. The Albigensian heresy was the first of the four great historic instances, described by Macaulay, of the rise of the human intellect, as he put it, against the Church's yoke.* The Albigensians did so in no uncertain terms. They rejected the

---

* Macaulay's three other challenges are: the Avignon schism, accompanied by the heresies of Hus and Wycliffe; the Reformation; and the eighteenth-century Enlightenment.

sacraments, the doctrines of hell and the resurrection of the body. They claimed that the Catholic Church, by taking the New Testament allegories literally, was carrying out the work of the devil. Christ to them was an angel with a phantom body; he did not suffer, or rise from the dead. They condemned marriage and procreation, and by so doing pressed the Catholic Church into a closer definition of its own doctrine on marriage and birth-control. They insisted on a life of great austerity, rejecting the eating of meat, eggs, milk and other animal products.

They took their name from the town of Albi in southern France which was one of their centres, though they spread into northern Italy and the Rhineland. Their challenge to Rome was complete. They were contradicting the faith and at the same time disturbing the traditional ordering of society. Councils condemned them: at Rheims in 1148, at Verona in 1184, and at the Fourth Lateran Council in 1215. Catholic doctrine was newly defined in order to bring out their errors. Yet they made progress. The austere way of life of many of them apparently appealed to people grown tired of clerical laxity—and this, it may be noted, during the reign of the most successful of all the popes. Innocent III sent the Cistercians on missions to convert them, as well as St Dominic himself whose order, like that of St Francis, was established in this splendid pope's reign. They were unsuccessful. In 1208, a papal legate was assassinated. The pope decided on a crusade against these dangerous heretics. Its leader was Simon de Montfort, father of the leader of the English baronial opposition to Henry III. This repression was the beginning of the end of the Albigensians, though only later popes would see their final suppression. In 1223, Pope Gregory IX was in a position to send the Dominican Inquisition: another aspect of the activity of this comparatively new religious order. By the end of the fourteenth century the heresy had been extirpated. Rome has ever been aware of the seriousness of the menace from heretical puritanism.

SYSTEM UNDERMINED

Two factors would seem to have made the future triumph of

heresy inevitable, if partial. One was the gradual realisation, as nations emerged, that the preservation of doctrine in its strictly Roman form need not necessarily be of interest to a monarch: a change of outlook which was gradually to bring the Papacy deeper into pure politics. Unity of faith was still the ideal but it did not necessarily mean the unity of Rome. The second was the Church's own failure to devise a sensible constitution for conducting its affairs. The great lack was of some machinery whereby the papal power and the growing demands of men who looked to General Councils to take a part in ecclesiastical government could be brought together instead of clashing. The search for superiority, sacred and secular, brought three vast clashes during much of the time of the Papacy's greatest strength: the clash of Papacy and Empire; the clash of Papacy and the new nation states of England and France during their fruitless century of war; and the clash within the Church between the conciliar movement and the advocates of papal autocracy.

This last problem was studied and debated in a serene atmosphere at the Second Vatican Council for the first time since the Middle Ages. The sixteenth-century Council of Trent faced the Protestant revolt and, as a natural consequence, the centralising tendency in the Church was strengthened. The First Vatican Council of 1870 never got past the definition of papal supremacy because it was suspended after Italian troops took Rome from the pope. The recent Council settled down seriously to the problem of how the will of the subjects can be made effective in what is technically an absolute monarchy. Two of the answers were the founding or proper ordering of national conferences of bishops, and the formation of an international synod of bishops to meet in Rome to assist the pope when he calls for help or advice.

Councils and popes; popes and anti-popes; then heresy in alliance with ambitious rulers—these were the signs which gradually were to show that an institution with such astonishing qualities for sheer survival would not remain capable of keeping all its claims intact. Some Catholic apologists assert that the Church has constantly maintained its superiority to the civil power and has only appeared at times in the course of history to be in a subordinate position because, for the sake of peace and to avoid hurt to souls, it has tolerated usurpations. It is fairer to say that Papacy and Empire both demanded more than they could sustain.

The emperors, with one exception, had nothing more resilient on which to base their claims than the confused state of Germany. It was insufficient. Even when they had the loyal support of the secularised bishops and abbots, they were not lords of an efficiently functioning principality. Once they lost the full powers of investiture by the Concordat of Worms, they found that they had forfeited their most potent instrument for directly impressing their authority. Purely feudal complications added to their difficulties. Local magnates took a bigger hand in the choice of bishops, and the emperors a smaller one. The exception to the imperial norm after the Concordat of Worms was Frederick II (1215–46). He attempted to sustain the imperial title from his inherited realm of Sicily. Had he not followed so closely after the superb pontificate of Innocent III, whose ward he was as a boy; had he been able to hide his amazingly modern mind, his powerful cynicism, behind some more conformist exterior; had he realised, as other powerful emperors (such as Henry III) had done, that the imperial authority could not break its association with the Papacy without losing meaning—then his extraordinary reign might have left more lasting effects. But this is a long string of conditions; with only one unfulfilled, the result would probably have been what in fact it proved to be: the last brilliant blaze of the dying fire of a distinctively supersovereign imperial authority.

When it came to real achievement, these German emperors could not establish an ascendancy over the Papacy. It was to be the French and the English kings who, fifty years after Frederick II's death, were to accomplish this. They were to do so, not only because each ruled a strong nation, but also because the crown with them was not, like the imperial crown, elective or so entwined by the conflicting rights and responsibilities of the imperial theory. It is clear what political wisdom the popes had shown in giving their temporal partners the high-sounding but ambiguous, and theologically hedged, title of emperor, keeping the political power within the manageable proportions of a papal concept. This wisdom, however, was to be of small avail to them against the monarchy of a powerful nation-state. Boniface VIII (1294–1303) thought like Innocent III; and who would not, after all, in the same place? He insisted on the predominance of the spiritual authority. Intending to revive the splendour of a theocratic papacy, he expressed his views unabated in encyclicals to the French king. He went no further in words than his predecessors had done, and a good deal less far in achievement. It was the Papacy itself which in the meantime had dropped back.

France and England were the two countries with genuine political constitutions. Both of them ignored the papal bull *Clericis Laicos* of 25 February 1296, which prohibited laymen from imposing taxes on the clergy without the consent of the pope, annulled all dispensations which might earlier have been accorded on the point, and threatened transgressors with excommunication. Edward I regarded the bull as null and void. Philip the Fair showed how dangerous it could be for the pope to interfere in French affairs. He banned the export of money and of letters of credit across his borders, which seriously damaged the pope's highly developed financial system. Worse was to follow for Boniface. In 1297, he attempted to intervene in Edward's war against the Scots because the Scots had appealed to Rome against the attack. He addressed himself to the king. Edward referred the matter to Parliament and obtained an indignant statement against the pope's interference in what was, in fact (if a sad fact), a popular war. Philip saw the wisdom of this example. In order to involve his whole people in the quarrel with the pope, he summoned for the first time the full States-General: the body which centuries later was to proclaim the Rights of Man. The pope himself narrowly escaped death at the hands of a local rising led by the Colonna family and backed by the French. After the brief reign of Benedict XI (1303–5), the Frenchman Clement V (1305–16) was elected. From his time until 1377, the Papacy's recognition of French power was made quite apparent by its 'Babylonian captivity' in Avignon.

GREATNESS WITHERED

Politically, the Church now had its finest performances behind it. In the mid-thirteenth century, under Innocent III, it had reached a political maturity allowing it at last to present a picture of majesty which Constantine himself could not have rivalled. The old imperial capital was once again lit by a semi-divine ruler who remained faithful to many of the traditions of imperial Rome, using its language, using much of its law augmented by the Church's own canons, and enjoying the spiritual support of simpler, if highly sophisticated, Christians such as St Francis and St Clare—very much the type of Christian whom Constantine would have liked to see giving moral support to his throne. The crusades were naïve; the papal administrative structure was excellent.

As it fell back in performance, the Church had no body of men outside it, as the Romans had had the Christians, to whom it could turn for a renewal of its strength. It was forced to deal with rising nations led by ambitious kings, not rough, impressionable barbarians; and it had no touch with such nations because they did not belong to its imperial, and imperious, view of how life should be ordered. Its own administrative structure was efficient, sharpened particularly during the stay in Avignon (1305-77), but it lacked the political instrument for allowing the adoption of fresh ideas without impinging on the principle of monarchy. The result was that Protestantism, when it emerged, came as a revolt; it could, in Luther's phrase, do no other. It was obedience or revolt.

Reform set half the nations of Europe against the Papacy. The myth of the Empire had long since faded by the end of the fifteenth century, and Charles V, elected in 1519, was the last of the emperors to be crowned by the pope. The ceremony, performed in Bologna —not until 1530—was now without substance, for either party. Like the Empire, the Papacy could not maintain its all-embracing glories from the turbulent territories in which it functioned.* Whether the papal temporality is judged by the area which it

---

* The pope's territories, moreover, were unified only in so far as they looked to him as ruler. His title to them varied from place to place.

comprised, by the strategic position athwart Italy that was effectively to hold up for centuries any Italian political development on a national scale, by the long and unsavoury feuds of the great Roman families amid which this great institution bore out its destiny, or by the estimated 6,800 prostitutes working in Rome itself at the turn of the fifteenth century, the papal princedom has always tended to consort ill with the Papacy's spiritual claims.

The epitome of this is the pontificate of Julius II (1503–13), who devoted most of his energies to defending and enlarging the papal dominions and to beautifying Rome with the help of such incomparable artists as Michelangelo, Raphael and Bramante. It was a pontificate of warfare, diplomacy and a certain amount of sensible reform at the centre, such as the condemnation of any papal election brought about by simony. Julius built in the revived classical style of his time. It was almost as if this warrior and deadly enemy, not only of his predecessor on the throne—the Borgia pope, Alexander VI (1492–1503)—but also of any power threatening his states, had made the grand attempt single-handed to be the temporal power as well as the spiritual, raising the buildings to house pope-emperors and imperial popes. But the resources were absurdly small for any such ambition. When strained to their breaking point, the consequences were to be inestimable. To build the new St Peter's basilica, he authorised the sale of indulgences on an unprecedented scale. The scandal of this to the Christian conscience was acutest in Germany, where the papal 'confidence men' were at their most active. The outcome was Luther and his Ninety-Five theses.

The temporality takes its place among the catalogue of factors which have brought politics to the door of the Vatican: the sharing of power in Constantine's empire; the lonely position of a spiritual power bound, after the emperor's departure, to enter in political relations with the barbarians; the habit of power, and its deployment for so long towards cultural inferiors; the emergence under Innocent III of a fully fledged theocracy with unlimited authority, accepted by all the civilised societies of the West; the financial acumen, shown for the first time at a high level by Gregory the

Great; the growth of an efficient ecclesiastical administration; the attempt to incite wars which could pass as holy, such as Charlemagne's attack on the Lombards and Saxons, the Albigensian holy war and the crusades against the Arab infidels; the need felt to discipline kings; the delight shown by a certain (but numerous) type of prelate to whom political power, quite frankly, gives pleasure.

* * *

There is little cause to wonder why the Vatican is such a dazzling institution; or why it contains within itself so much that arouses doubt. At the moment it is attempting a movement unthought of for centuries. It has thrown down the gauntlet to the contemporary world, emerging in a remarkable way under the last two or three pontiffs from the long withdrawal. As the recluse returns to the light of that bright and warming sun which has followed so much of its history, the exposure is proving painful, seemingly destructive of the old texture of the garments, of the dusty flesh. From the point of view of religion, it is a hard world to re-enter because religion is at a low moment. Yet it is easier for the fact that a new respect is there; more people than for many years wish the effort well.

Because of this good will, it perhaps matters less now, in this democratic age, that the Papacy is a completely autocratic body, with no pretensions to democracy (though some democratic Catholics try to make out that it is learning to practise democracy: a silly view which would falsify half its history), even though after the Second World War the democratic powers were pleased enough to have the help of its political influence. At the moment, there is a lot less pretence than twenty years ago about where the Vatican stands in international affairs. Its diplomacy can be disarmingly neutral. Its dealings with the problems of communism can simultaneously involve spiritual anathemas on all who practise it, and a sensibly flexible approach to negotiations with its representatives. It is ironical that the Vatican's conduct of its policy became identified in Protestant Europe with the teachings of Machiavelli—'base Machiavel'—whose real gospel was that

Christianity had shown itself as a failure in the field of politics and thus had to be replaced by other principles, or lack of them. For, whatever the Vatican does—and this again sets it shining brightly in a glaze of righteousness—is done in the name of the Kingdom of Heaven whose advance post, or rearguard, or simple representation, here on earth, it claims to be.

3
Diversity and Adversity

AT the time of the Reformation, when the papal position needed to be at its strongest, it was distracted by the pleasures of princes. It could not reply convincingly to the charges of the reformers. Once reformed itself, after the Council of Trent, the Papacy of the Counter-Reformation could expect to have the ear only of the Catholic faithful and, with it, the hatred of the Protestant rebels. Its opponents could not lightly have shattered Christian unity; their contempt for the embodiment of that unity, the former imperial Church which had placed unity so high in its essential requirements, was intense.

As politics, religion and nationalism were all mixed, the divisions went deep. The revival of the Papacy's spiritual prestige at the Counter-Reformation made it as fervid and enthrallingly conscious of its own triumph as the baroque architecture in St Peter's which so effectively expresses it. But national states and national rulers could now withstand the worst of the papal anathemas. Elizabeth of England was not the only ruler to survive conspiracies encouraged by papal policy, to defeat foreign forces advancing with papal support, to keep a throne despite the papal withdrawal of the subjects' obligation of loyalty to the monarch, and to have national poets represent the Roman Church as beautiful, perhaps, and beguiling, but corrupt and subtle and malicious. The false Duessa was there to ensnare the unwary knight, wearing all colours 'save the trew'. The spiritual strength accompanying the Counter-Reformation, for all its achievements, was insufficient to carry the Papacy through the abrasive process of rubbing shoulders with other benevolent despots. The secular approach to politics, which enlightened monarchs gradually adopted, left less and less space for the Papacy and for papal claims. The Enlightenment, as Macaulay pointed out, proved to be one of the most dangerous challenges that the Roman Church has ever had to face. By the close of the eighteenth century, the strength of rationalist humanism was to appear almost fatal for it.

At few times in its history could the Papacy have been seen to possess so little real power; not, perhaps, since it emerged from the Dark Ages, blood-boltered in a factious city. Instead of being heard, it was being told—not in the rough terms of civil strife, ambition and murder, for this was the eighteenth century—but it was none the less being told, even if politely. This is the real meaning of the suppression of the Jesuits by the Papacy in 1773, when Clement XIV (1769–74) was forced by political pressure from the Catholic monarchs of Europe to agree to the 'dissolution, extinction and utter oblivion' of the Society of Jesus. Such was the fate of the order which had won back for the popes so much of Catholic territories lost to the Reformation—Poland among them. That great depository of intellectual and pragmatic armament at the popes' disposal was to be forced out of existence.* Nine years later, Pius VI (1775–99) had to go to Vienna to meet Joseph II because the Habsburg emperor had refused a papal invitation to go to Rome to discuss his ecclesiastical policies, which were worrying the pope. It is a long way from Canossa when the pope has to seek out the emperor.

With the French Revolution's sweeping away Catholic institutions in France and in large parts of Europe, the Papacy appeared to be on the threshold of its burial chamber. Napoleon, though formally restoring the Church, showed it scant respect, making Pius VII (1800–23) his captive and not ceasing to remind the Holy

---

* The Jesuits were formally restored in 1814; and, in fact, the Society was never completely put down despite its disbandment. Under other names, Jesuit priests were to continue their educational and disciplinary work.

See that, like Philip the Fair or Charles V, he could imprison a pope at will. The pope won back his Italian states, taken from him by the French, as part of the settlement of Vienna in 1815. But he then lost them all again, this time finally, to the liberal forces of Italian political unity, the Risorgimento, which reached its climax in the taking of Rome in 1870. Ultimately, the Papacy was to gain in respect by these losses of its temporal power, but for many years it hated to admit as much.

CLASH WITH THE MODERN WORLD

For the Papacy, the modern world began in 1870. For both the Papacy and the world it was a bad beginning. With Rome lost, the popes retired inside the Vatican and remained there, voluntary prisoners, until 1929. During much of this period, pontiffs could not believe that the dreadful injustice of having been deprived of their states could possibly be lasting. They had had no wish for a nation in the Italian peninsula, a true national state. Throughout the centuries the Papacy had found the disunity of Italy more favourable to it than any single state could have been, and it had been in a position to ensure that no one else could impose unity. The 'prisoners of the Vatican' took it for granted that the Italian state, which had taken their possessions, would soon fall apart. From all points of view, it was a ramshackle affair; for the Holy See it was, in addition, anti-clerical. Its days would surely be numbered. As a matter of fact, they were; as things turned out, the popes were not so far wrong.

Few people by the end of the last century would have made the eighteenth-century mistake of supposing that the Papacy's days were numbered. Although politically discredited for a time in a large part of Europe, the Vatican was to show remarkable powers of recovery as revolutionary violence called in question the easy scepticism of the Enlightenment. In the reaction against Jacobinism and Bonapartist despotism, a wider sympathy was secured for the views of a confessedly conservative Church than had been possible before the Revolution. Its alliance with kings and its rejection of fervent pleas—like those of Lamennais—for a liberal and democratic Church at the head of a new spiritual revival, while these further antagonised progressive opinion, enhanced Catholicism's prestige among the disillusioned and the alarmed. The Papacy's position came to be endorsed by many in Europe who had hitherto been indifferent or even hostile to the Roman Church. The new respect shown for its political attitude was strengthened by certain of the intellectual revaluations of the Romantic movement. Notable in this field is the influence of Chateaubriand, the French writer and politician. He sought to refute the work of rationalist philosophers who had, directly or indirectly, undermined the Church and its tenets, and to unite Catholicism and Romanticism in an acceptable intellectual and moral theory. He argued that the Christian faith had been the great fount of art and civilisation in Europe, and that without the sustaining influence of this faith European culture and society would decay. Views such as his invigorated the Church's morale in the high period of liberalism, when the combination of radical political ideas and the transforming impact of the new technological and scientific revolution seemed likely to accomplish what philosophical rationalism had attempted: the sweeping away of Christianity as an intellectual system and as a social organisation.

This whole period of revolution and counter-revolution, which witnessed the dismemberment of the Papal States in three phases, produced at the same time surprising evidence of Catholic vigour and signs of a brighter future. Civil disabilities were removed from English Roman Catholics in 1829, at the behest of a generous-tempered liberalism. Catholicism was a popular, national force in the Polish and Belgian rebellions of the 1830s, and animated much of the Irish resistance to England. From the great immigration movement of the 1840s onwards, Catholicism in the United States began to grow apace. The Roman hierarchy was restored in England in 1850, and in Holland three years later.* Popular devotion

* Of great significance for the future development of papal authority was the strong tendency in the newly 'Romanised' countries for the faithful, clerical and lay alike, to regard devotion and obedience to the Pontiff as an absolutely binding rule of faith, admitting of no reservation. Prelates like Cardinal Manning in England were often to show themselves more curialist than the Curia.

was sustained by the definition in 1854 of the Immaculate Conception as a dogma of the faith, while the strength of traditional religion was intensified by the reports in 1858 alleging the appearance of the Madonna to children at Lourdes. This century, which had opened with the obsequies of a pope dead in exile and soon witnessed the imprisonment of his successor, both victims of militant French secularism and lay authoritarianism, was to see before its end the challenging dome of Sacré Coeur loom over 'infidel' Paris: the glittering white temple of a devotional revival that was specifically French. Even the Syllabus of Errors of 1864, which astounded moderate liberal opinion—particularly in Britain and America—by its condemnation of much of the best of contemporary thought (John Stuart Mill, for example, was listed as a writer inimical to faith and morals), even this is to be seen as a sign of vigour. The Roman Church was ceasing to be on the defensive, was asserting itself against the prevalent 'spirit of the age'. Even more important was the promulgation of the dogma of Papal Infallibility in 1870, shortly before catastrophe struck the pope's temporal power in the shape of Piedmontese soldiers marching into the Eternal City.

Pius IX (1846–78), whose reign witnessed these challenging assertions of Catholic doctrinal vigour, represents in his person and his acts the extraordinary resilience of Vatican conservatism. His election aroused great excitement among liberals and near-despair among reactionaries, for he made no disguise of his sympathies for the freeing of Italy from foreign control and for constitutionalism as opposed to arbitrary rule. Much was expected from him as a reforming pope. At last, it seemed, the Papacy would throw off the mantle of its history and apparel itself for the climate of the contemporary world. But the world's weather proved too blustery. The revolutions of 1848 alarmed him; the enormous difficulty of reforming the papal administration disheartened him; and he was embittered by the refusal of Italian nationalists to accept the idea of an Italy united in a kind of federation under the presidency of the Holy Father. Starting as the 'liberal pope', he became the archetype of shrewd papal conservatism, reaffirming tradition while enhancing the Church's authority by adding new canons of belief and devotion of a kind attractive to the mass of the faithful. *Aggiornamento* by adjustment to the world soon passed into a very different kind of *aggiornamento*: the insistence that the Church's relevance to the world lay in its renewing and advancing the doctrinal and disciplinary claims of the Roman faith and the Roman pontiff. Pius IX responded to a 'crisis of development' by a reassertion of authority. There have not been lacking voices, here and there amid the many applauding the *aggiornamento* initiated in our day by John XXIII, which suggest that the new 'liberal Papacy' may prove as disappointing to progressives inside and outside the Church as the pontificate of Pio Nono. Any satisfaction which troubled conservatives may feel at this possibility will be diminished by their awareness that the intellectual and moral climate in the Roman Church of Paul VI precludes adoption of the response of Pius IX to the situation of his day. The Vatican of the mid-twentieth century faces not only a 'crisis of development' but a veritable 'crisis of authority'.

The dogma of Papal Infallibility and its associated concept of Papal Supremacy were to have a profound effect on policy, though more in a direct than an indirect way. Many people, including Gladstone and Bismarck—otherwise at opposite poles of political philosophy—suspected the dogma of sanctioning a revival of papal claims to universal sovereignty. Pius IX tried to dispel these suspicions. On 20 July 1871, he explained to a group of Catholics gathered in audience that Infallibility had nothing to do with the right to depose sovereigns and to release subjects from their allegiance. This right had sometimes been exercised in extreme cases, he said, in the ages of faith when the pope was revered as the supreme judge of Christendom, and when his position as arbitrator among nations and between a people and its ruler was universally acknowledged. Its exercise was sanctioned both by prevailing public law and by the common consent of the nations. However, he went on: 'Our own times are quite changed, and only bad will can confuse two things so different: Infallibility in matters of revelation, and the right that the popes once exercised in virtue of their authority when the good of society required it.' Pius's distinction reflected hard reality. No pope, manifestly, could now claim the right to depose rulers. It would be as pointless as claiming to blow St Peter's down with a puff of rationalist logic. Even so natural a theocrat as Pius XII was to state publicly that the idea of the complete dependence of the temporal on the spiritual power was 'a medieval conception conditioned by the age'. This implies that he regarded it as a transitory historical concept; yet he, of all popes of the modern era, was most inclined to stride beyond the boundaries of the purely spiritual power, especially when local politics—one of his passions, particularly after 1945—was involved.

Accepting Pio Nono's disclaimer, there was at the time of the promulgation of the dogma of Infallibility some sound reason to suppose that politics were involved in the business. Gladstone and Bismarck may have given it an exaggerated interpretation, but they were not so wrong: just right the wrong way. Some of the promoters of the decree were moved by the need to enhance the prestige of a pope who politically was in trouble. Pius IX probably agreed to the placing of the subject on the agenda of the First Vatican Council (it was not among the original subjects for discussion in the preparatory phase); and the rushing of it through as a matter of urgency is ascribable to the same reason. Anything that could strengthen the pope's hand at this time of crisis was to be welcomed by the faithful; and what more strengthening than the affirmation by the Council of his Infallibility? Moreover, what more reasonable than its formal endorsement of a belief that could be argued as being a part of the traditional faith of Catholics, not a newfangled initiative? The reason for its elevating the pope in solitary splendour, with no reservations on his exercise of infallible power and with no balancing rights accorded to the episcopacy, is not simply to be found in the absolutist notions of curial officials and their supporters within the Church, though their influence was powerful. The arrival of Italian troops to take Rome disrupted the Council before the position of bishops and priests and other elements in the Church could be clearly determined in the context of the new dogma.

Across the Papacy's approach to the modern world yawned the gap opened between it and contemporary opinion at the time of the loss of the Papal States. It had misjudged the progress of liberalism and, despite the intellectual recovery of Catholicism, the Curia itself withdrew into a kind of resentful isolation, making occasional sorties to adjust its defences. Pius IX's successors were to make their accommodation with the Italian state, but only after more than half a century had passed and when liberalism had been replaced by fascism. In this sense, the popes of the Risorgimento and its aftermath were never to recognise the movement which took away their territories. Fascism was a different political animal. So is Christian Democracy, which has been the dominant political force in Italy since the Second World War, making of it a more or less confessional state where a cardinal's recommendation can make a career or break a politician almost as decisively as it could in the days of direct papal government.

From 1870 until 1929, when the agreements with Mussolini were signed, successive popes kept to the Vatican as voluntary prisoners. They held at arm's length the lay state that had usurped their direct rule and had imposed anti-clerical legislation on the country. They refused to allow Catholics to take part in its political or public life. The posture was not dignified and, indeed, could not be fully maintained. Among other things, it meant that the whole Roman Church was being seriously affected in its outlook by the Italian political situation which was so strongly operative on the attitudes of the popes and their advisers. A pope possessing real political insight might with dignity have taken advantage of his freedom from temporal possessions—something which no pope had experienced, and then only involuntarily, since the middle of the eighth century. Certainly, there were difficulties in dealing with the new state of Italy. Apart from the loss of the temporality, the Church could hardly let itself seem to be on friendly relations with a country officially anti-clerical. Yet, in fact, from the beginning of the movement for national unity, there had seldom been lacking ways and means—through individuals, through institutions and groups—whereby the effect of anti-clerical legislation could be softened. Pillaging the Church is an old custom and derives, as a rule, more from greed than from conviction. To lose ecclesiastical property at the hands of anti-clericals would scarcely be an obvious blessing to popes and prelates; but, in less obvious ways, it certainly was one, notably in the gradual increase of respect for their spiritual power. In practice, it was prestige, not astuteness, that was to maintain in the modern Papacy that mixture of spiritual and political authority which had sustained pontiffs throughout the centuries.

Perhaps we are enjoying in this matter the familiar advantage of hindsight. For over a thousand years, the Church had associated its exercise of the Christian mission, its very integrity, with the independence secured to the popes and great prelates by their possession of inalienable temporalities. After 1815, the pope was the only remaining prince-bishop in Europe. The only institutions comparable to the Papacy in temporal terms had been the ecclesiastical principalities of the Holy Roman Empire, and these were all abolished by the second decade of the nineteenth century. Their fate did not, understandably, incline the popes to shrug their shoulders at their own losses in enjoyment of the possibility of a rise in spiritual power as the accompaniment of the loss of the principality. The resentment was profound: a resentment not only at the thing in itself but at what one might call the psychological shock it gave to the morale of papal tradition. A striking characteristic of most popes is their concern to hand on to their successors an inheritance intact and unalienated. It is not only the keys, not just the splendour of the office. It is the body of doctrine; it is the attributes of office; it is also the possessions. Popes do not often give things away. There are exceptions, of course. Benedict XV, for instance, gave away what ready cash he could find to anyone who came asking his help in furthering some pious work or other, but the rule is to hold on to what is there. Paul VI is a case in point. Though in some ways a courageous innovator, he tries to give the impression that nothing is changing. In theory, this is not the same as holding on to physical possessions; in practice, the two things are close.

Through many centuries, the policies of the Church were in part determined by its temporal sovereignty; yet apologists constantly argued that the reason for the existence of the Papal States was to prevent other princes from determining papal policy, or impinging on its spiritual authority. The Papacy, it was argued, needed not only to have ground on which to function freely but also to be seen by the world as functioning freely. Pius IX in 1871, a year after he had lost his territorial patrimony, said to the French ambassador: 'All that I want is a small corner of earth where I am master. This is not to say that I would refuse my States if they were offered to me. But so long as I do not have this little corner of earth, I shall not be able to exercise in their fullness my spiritual functions.'

Advocates of a papal temporality have all along attempted to give the original 'donation' a place in the divine plan. The classic justification was made by Bossuet, the great French apologist of Catholicism in the seventeenth century. In his *Discours sur l'Unité de l'Église* (1681), he wrote:

> God, who desired that this Church, the common mother of all kingdoms, should not be dependent upon any one of them in temporal matters and that the See through which all the faithful should preserve their unity should be above all partisanship that the conflicting interests and jealousies might cause—God, I say, laid the foundations of this great plan through the instrumentality of Pepin and Charlemagne. As a felicitous consequence of their liberality, the Church, which in her chief is independent of all temporal powers, is in the position of exercising this Divine Power to rule souls more freely for the common good and under the common protection of the Christian kings, so that, holding upright in her hands the scale of justice, in the midst of so many empires so often enemies one with the other, she maintains unity in the whole body, sometimes by inflexible decrees and sometimes by wise compromises.

This is the theoretical argument, noble and shrewd. The practical effect of the temporality, however, was to inhibit rather than promote the Church's independence of 'conflicting interests and jealousies'. A princely ruler in an unruly Europe has to think of his frontiers and of his alliances; a purely spiritual ruler need have no such preoccupations. But when, from the days of Constantine onward, can it be said that the popes were ever spiritual figures only? At no time. Nobility and shrewdness intertwine curiously in Bossuet's rationale. He argues from a theory of the ideal character of the Papacy in the best of all possible circumstances to justify hard realism—'wise compromises'—in the normal course of events. Elect from all the nations, the Papacy as a temporal power claimed a divine brief to engage in purely political shifts and calculations in order to defend its temporality; and defence was interpreted, when circumstances admitted, to mean extension of territory and the contracting and breaking of diplomatic and military alliances. This tendency reached its height under the Renaissance popes. Given the situation of the Papacy as a temporal power, there is something to be said for their attempt to protect and strengthen their states, and perhaps rather more to be said for their efforts to restore to Rome its ancient grandeur with great edifices in the new classical style. Yet the motivation for this is hardly recognisable as spiritual. That worldliness should gain the upper hand, even in a nobly dedicated institution, is understandable from the human point of view, if not from that of the divine claims made on behalf of the papal institution. But, even if we regard the exuberant worldliness of the Renaissance popes as a transitory episode, this period represents a development, not an aberration, from a centuries-old norm. This norm—the involvement in power politics, and the governing influence of Italian considerations on papal policies at all levels—was to operate in the nineteenth century to set the Papacy in hostility to political liberalism in Europe. Far from rising above worldly circumstances, it became subjected to them. This was a high price to pay for those temporal possessions which were supposed to afford it spiritual freedom.

There were some anti-clericals and a number of liberals with religious convictions (like Massimo d'Azeglio, for example) who did not want Rome to be the Italian capital. They felt it a grave mistake to give Rome this predominance for sentimental and historical reasons while overlooking more realistic arguments. Later experience has borne out this minority view. Prime ministers of modern Italy have been heard to say in private that Rome is impossible as a seat of government. But its unique prestige made the choice of Rome inevitable for the Italians of the Risorgimento. It was, moreover, a challenge which the new lay state felt it must take, this acquisition of the most abrasive point in the general conflict between united Italy and the Papacy over the very existence of the Papal States. Their geographical position and papal interests had been major obstacles to unification. They had been there for centuries, straddling the peninsula and dividing the north, which gave the impetus to the movement for unity, from the south where feelings of belonging to an Italian entity were strong. Cavour, who shaped Italian unity, worked from the north southward; Garibaldi, the rough-hewn instrument for imposing unity, began his final effort in the south and worked northward.

Of the three stages in the loss of temporal power—the acquisition by Victor Emmanuel in 1859 and 1860 of the pope's territories in central Italy, the entry of his troops into Rome in 1870, and the Law of Guarantees of 13 May 1871—it is to the last we must properly look for an appreciation of what the new secular state envisaged as the basis of permanent relations between itself and the head of the universal Roman Church. The two previous stages, from the nationalist viewpoint, had been the logical and inevitable culmination of the Risorgimento. The Piedmontese government and its successor of united Italy—unwilling though Cavour had been to accede to the radical nationalists' demand for a *coup de force* against the pope's sovereignty—had in effect cut the Gordian knot of the Papacy's intertwined spiritual and temporal status by regarding it primarily as a secular power inimical to unity, just as Austria was. Now, having gained their victory, the king and his ministers had to tackle the problem of coming to permanent terms with a bitterly resentful spiritual force, national and international, which was determined to refuse recognition of its temporal loss. Someone had always come to its aid before, or been persuaded to come: Franks, Saxons, French. But not this time—at least, not until after the Second World War.

The Italian government hoped that the Law of Guarantees would solve the 'Roman question' once and for all. It was a notable effort; it did not, however, go so far as the Lateran Pacts of 1929, which set up the Vatican City as a sovereign state. The Law of

Guarantees governed ecclesiastical and state relations until then, though on the Vatican's side it was never recognised. The pope was to be deprived of his old sovereign rights, retaining possessions only of the Vatican and Lateran palaces and of the summer residence at Castelgandolfo. At the same time, he would be accorded all the honours due to a sovereign, including the rights of precedence conceded by Catholic rulers. The diplomatic corps accredited to the Holy See would be entitled to all the immunities and privileges granted to diplomatists accredited to the king of Italy. The pope would be allowed to maintain his armed forces (the Swiss Guard, the Palatine Guard, the Noble Guard) and his own telegraph office and diplomatic bag. He would be paid an annual allowance of 3,225,000 lire (worth approximately £150,000 in 1871) to cover specified expenses. Legally, he would not be arraignable under Italian penal law, even in respect of acts not immediately concerned with his ministry; on the other hand, those who attacked or wronged him would be liable to the same penalties as were prescribed for similar offences against the king.

These measures remained unilateral. Pius IX refused to accept them, considering the guarantee of independence insufficient and the degree of freedom too little to compensate for the loss of the principality. There was no assurance that the Italian state would not subsequently revoke the Law of Guarantees. Moreover, the state would have a dangerous financial hold over the Papacy.

Both sides behaved in a bad-tempered way. Until 1929, when Pius XI came to terms with Mussolini, the popes remained in the Vatican, refusing to compromise with the lay state. Though short of money, they rejected the annual allowances. They preferred to bide their time, and maintained a ban on political activities by Catholics in Italy. This ban cannot be justified except as a reprisal for the loss of the Papal States and for the anti-clericalism of these early Italian governments. Cavour, the commanding figure in the achievement of unity, was not a practising Catholic.* While unity

---

* He was, however, realist enough to send money to Rome to bribe the ecclesiastical authorities, using as his agent a Jesuit priest called Passaglia. At one time, Passaglia was in direct contact with Cardinal Antonelli, Pius IX's Secretary of State.

Paul Horne

PLATE I CONSTANTINE: head surviving from a colossus of the emperor, Capitoline Museum, Rome

PLATE II CHARLEMAGNE: Agostino Cornacchini's equestrian in St Peter's

Paul Horne

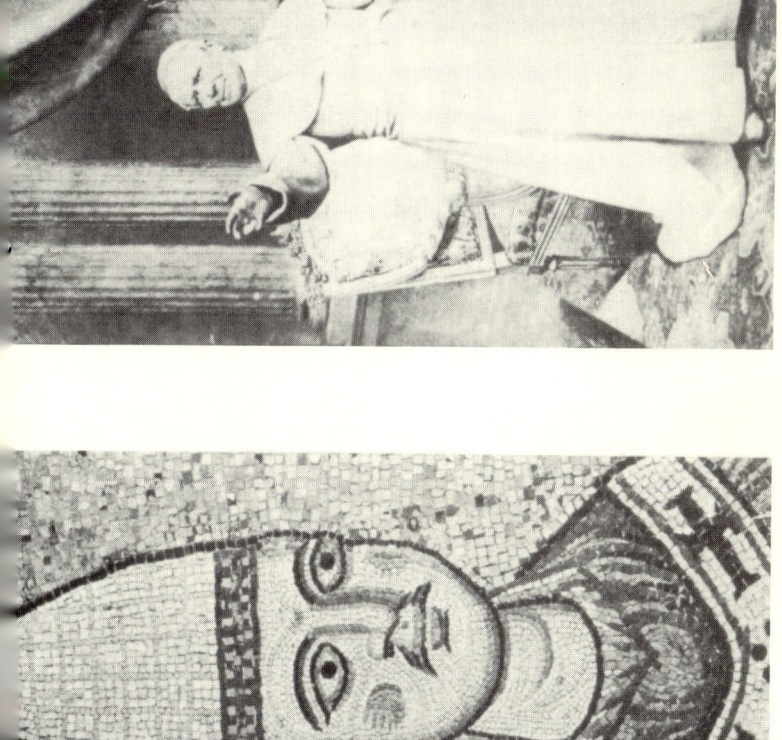

1 INNOCENT III (1198-1216): a contemporary portrait of the pope, part of a mosaic formerly in the apse of old St Peter's and now in the Museo di Roma

Oscar Savio

2 PIUS IX (1846-78): the first known photograph of a pope, c. 1860

Radio Times Hulton Picture Library

PLATE III

Radio Times Hulton Picture Library
1 LEO XIII (1878-1903)

Radio Times Hulton Picture Library
2 PIUS X (1903-14)

Radio Times Hulton Picture Library
3 BENEDICT XV (1914-22)

Radio Times Hulton Picture Library
4 PIUS XI (1922-39)

PLATE IV   Precursors of the Modern Papacy

was still to be achieved, he had dissolved the monasteries in Piedmont (describing the contemplative religious orders as 'useless and even harmful') and had abolished clerical privileges in law. In 1866, a measure was introduced against religious orders and congregations; 13,000 religious had already had their communities suppressed, and the new law affected a further 25,000. The Neapolitan concordat was unilaterally denounced by the state and, within scarcely six months of the creation of the united kingdom in 1861, sixty-six bishops had been arrested in the southern provinces alone. Don Bosco, the Piedmontese inspirer of technical education and founder of the Italian Salesians, was held for questioning. These events need to be borne in mind when assessing the difference in Italian life since the Christian Democrats came to power in 1948. The Vatican, probably, is not today stronger than the Italian government, but it is the strongest of the pressure groups which effectively ensure that the national government does not have a mind of its own. Apart from their anti-clericalism, these early Italian governments were responsible for keeping the Papacy away from the Hague conferences of 1899 and 1907, fearing that the question of the pope's temporality might be raised at these international meetings.

Events were to show that the papal attitude was the more farsighted. Temporal rule over a part of the Italian peninsula was to be replaced by control over Catholic political activities throughout the country. There were to be two stages in this 'repoliticisation' of the Papacy: the concordat with Mussolini in 1929, which set up the tiny sovereign state of the Vatican City, and—far more dramatic—the great victory of the Catholic political party in Italy, the Christian Democrats, after the Second World War. It was the first time that Catholic politicians had come to power since the country's unification. It was a vindication of the Papal policy towards Italy since the loss of temporality.

RERUM NOVARUM AND THE LATERAN PACTS

After the end of the long pontificate of Pius IX, the voluntary 'prisoners of the Vatican', though still beleaguered, began to look over the battlements to mark the course of events in the outside world. Leo XIII (1878–1903) inherited a Papacy so estranged from Italy that nationalist revolutionaries were planning to snatch Pius IX's body and throw it into the Tiber. The Holy See was regarded but lightly abroad. France was dominated politically by a Radical party whose anti-clerical left wing grew increasingly belligerent as the old century waned and French Catholicism staged its remarkable recovery. Germany was in the midst of Bismarck's struggle against the Roman Church, the *Kulturkampf*. In all countries of the Catholic tradition, liberals and socialists, however divided in their general programmes, were united in seeking to free individual electors and national institutions—particularly the educational system—from clerical influence. Leo saw the need to come to a parley with the menacing forces beyond the Vatican's walls. He had some success in his relations with the new imperial Germany, but little with republican France and none with monarcho-liberal Italy. The signing by Italy of the Triple Alliance with Austria-Hungary and Germany was a clear enough indication that the time was past when a great power could be besought to intervene on the pope's behalf to help him retrieve his temporality. Emperor Francis Joseph of Austro-Hungary, it is true, insisted on a formula aimed at assuring the pope that the three powers had made no engagement that could be taken as involving Vienna's recognition of the annexation of Rome. But as both Austria-Hungary and Germany agreed to defend Italy against France—the one country where it was just possible to conceive, given a shift in the internal balance of political forces, a rallying of support to the pope—the assurances of the descendant of the Holy Roman Emperors hardly changed the real situation.

Yet, if the great powers of Europe were either hostile or indifferent to papal irredentism, they themselves enjoyed little internal ease of mind. Far-reaching social changes were creating widespread unrest and even the strongest governments—democratic and authoritarian alike—were conscious of a grave domestic crisis. However belatedly, the prisoner in the Vatican perceived the opportunity for a papal excursion into the world outside. And not the opportunity only, but the urgency. Troubled by the economic and social problems of increasing industrialisation and by the growth of socialism in particular, the lay and clerical leaders of the Catholic faithful in the advanced countries of the Western world urgently required a new guidance from the Holy See. The most outstanding example of the Vatican's response to their appeal is the social teaching of Leo XIII.

His encyclical *Rerum Novarum*, issued on 15 May 1891, attempted a Catholic solution of the social problems of the time. Traditionalist in its view of society, it was none the less remarkably radical in its scope and intentions. Papal documents on social matters are inclined to sum up existing situations rather than provide a lead for the future. Leo at least made the attempt to analyse what the situation was, and in so doing provided a basis for Catholic thinking on the complex social problems of the modern age. *Rerum Novarum* laid down the principle that the worker had the right to a just wage sufficient to allow him and his family to live decently. Leo XIII stressed the Christian obligations of the employer, and denounced the selfish and materialistic practices which he attributed to '*laissez faire* liberalism'. In his endorsement of the humanitarian and socialist attack on capitalism, he gave papal sanction to that tradition of 'progressive Catholicism' which was to foster the growth of confessional trade unions on the Continent and ultimately of Catholic democratic political movements pledged to social reform.

He was hostile to modern trade unionism, however, and sought protection for the worker in a revival of something very akin to the medieval guilds. While censuring the abuse of economic power, he declared the right of private property to be 'by nature' and a principal distinction between man and the animal world. He gave a complete condemnation of class conflict:

> ... the great mistake ... is to accept the notion that class is naturally hostile to class, and that the wealthy and the working men are intended by nature to live in mutual conflict. So irrational and so false is this view that the direct contrary is the truth.

He rejected socialism because of its insistence on the class conflict and of its opposition to private property, 'working on the poor man's envy of the rich'. Leo's analysis of the social conditions of his time was shrewd and comprehensive:

> That the spirit of revolutionary change, which had so long been disturbing the nations of the world, should have passed beyond the sphere of politics and made its influence felt in the cognate sphere of practical economics is not surprising. The elements of the conflict now raging are unmistakable: in the vast expansion of industrial pursuits and the marvellous discoveries of science; in the changed relations between masters and workmen; in the enormous fortunes of some few individuals and the utter poverty of the masses; in the increased self-reliance and closer mutual combination of the working classes; as, also, finally, in the prevailing moral degeneracy.

It is patrician in tone, stamped more with home truths than anything so lofty as absolute truth, and it came half a century after the *Communist Manifesto*. Even so, it reveals an anxious awareness that what is happening in the world is something new and of a wholly different order from previous experience.

The danger from socialism was one of the reasons why the Papacy was gradually to withdraw its ban on allowing Catholics to take part in political life in Italy. Pius X (1903–14), worried by what he felt to be a threat from socialism, decided in June 1905 that Catholics should be allowed to stand for office in certain areas in order to oppose socialists. The total abolition of the ban came in 1919. In face of a greater danger, the liberal state was regarded as the minor evil. The pope who took the final step was Benedict XV (1914–22). He probably did so without misgivings. Apart from such eccentricities as a high regard (outlandish in Rome) for punctuality and the giving away of money (which he kept stuffed in the drawers of his desk; gifts of watches and sums for charity were frequent in his day), he took a more detached view of affairs than his predecessors. It is unfortunate that the overshadowing of his pontificate by the First World War prevented this extremely able man from doing more than hint at what he might have achieved as pope.

The development begun by Pius X's decision enabling Italian Catholics to participate in national politics led to a transformation of the Church's relations with the state in Italy. The liberal regime crumbled under attack from left and right extremists. The latter triumphed, and the establishment of the fascist regime in 1922 offered the Papacy the opportunity for a complete review of its relations with the lay state. The outcome was the Lateran Pacts of 1929 between Pius XI (1922–39) and Mussolini: a series of agreements embodying a concordat and a treaty. The treaty accorded the pope his little piece of ground in which he was to be master: the 100-odd acres of the Vatican City. Unlike the Law of Guarantees half a century earlier, it recognised the papal domain as independent and sovereign. This for the Papacy was the vital point. In return, it recognised the Italian state as the legal and moral embodiment of the Italian people, and acknowledged Rome as the state's capital city. The pope also received a financial settlement of some 1,500 million lire (about £20 million in 1929). Though less than the untouched sums that had accrued under the Law of Guarantees, this money was useful for building new administrative offices, and some of it was shrewdly invested.

The financial arrangements and the concordat accompanying the treaty gave full recognition to the unique place of the Church in Italian life. Catholicism was formally declared the official religion of the state. Religious ceremonies became sufficient in all civil effects. As marriage ceremonies in town halls were no longer required by law, electing to have a civil ceremony became a means of dissociating oneself from religion. The registry office could then be considered—and has been—as the refuge for an anti-clerical wanting to flaunt his distaste for religion. There was, however, to be no refuge in the Italian courts for those seeking a divorce; civil law maintained the principle of canon law in this respect. The proselytising work of Protestants was curtailed, and Catholic processions were protected. Harsh clauses were included for preserving the Church's control over its own ranks, such as the requirement that no defrocked or 'fallen' priest could be given any employment which would bring him into contact with the public.*

The treaty and concordat were favourable to the Church. They also set up the international arrangements by which the Vatican continues now to have its attributes as a sovereign power recognised and respected. Mussolini, in turn, could feel that there was now an end to the divisive effect of the Church on the state. He would be photographed kneeling before the statue of St Peter in the basilica, for all the world like any of the great emperors who had co-operated with the papacy since the Christian Empire began. Mussolini could afford generous terms. He was a dictator and could deal fairly easily with any encroachments from the other side. In fact, the main quarrels to come were precisely on this point of encroachments. They largely concerned the Catholic Action movement which was protected by the concordat.

Catholic Action is a movement that incurs the dislike of milder people than dictators. It began in the late 1860s as an organisation seeking to promote a Catholic communal life distinct from the life of secular society. Its fundamental motive was to provide a counter to the secularisation of public life under the early governments of united Italy. Catholic Action was given international encouragement by Pius XI's encyclical *Ubi Arcano* of December 1922, which promoted the activities of lay bodies dependent on the national hierarchies. Its outlook in Italy was conditioned by the principles of Pius IX's *Non Expedit*: the ban on Catholic political participation in the affairs of the nation. In a sense, then, it could claim to be strictly non-political since it adjured its members and the Catholic faithful as a whole to take no part in national politics.

---

* Protestant bodies in Italy find—no doubt to their own contentment and *amour propre*—that a certain proportion of the destitute who come to them for help consists of former priests unable to earn a living. What, after all, can they do when faced with a general ban on everything from teaching in schools to driving buses? According to the Waldensian authorities (the oldest of the Italian Protestant bodies), most of the former Catholic priests whom they help gave up their orders because of the political obligations imposed on them. (The Vatican recently has been less severe in applying this legislation to former priests.)

Mussolini intended that the organisation should remain isolated from political life. The concordat declared that:

> The state recognises the organisations dependent on Catholic Action in so far as they conduct their activities as the Holy See has laid down, unconnected with any political party and in immediate dependence on the hierarchy of the Church, for the realisation and diffusion of Catholic principles.

Catholic Action has separate sections for the various professions, for students, for boys and girls, and so on. The claim that it was always non-political is questionable. It is true that it took no part in national political affairs in the first half century or so of the new Italian state; but the decision not to participate was in itself a political act. Under a liberal regime, the pope, as a matter of principle, had kept Catholic Action clear of national politics. Under fascism, Italy became a one-party state, and the Church accepted, *faute de mieux*, a continuation of the organisation's non-political character as part of the general settlement with Mussolini. The movement was even more closely driven in upon itself. Even so, the fascist and the clerical view of what constituted political activity differed a good deal. Confronted by fascism's restrictionist interpretation, Catholic Action became increasingly resentful of what it considered to be intolerable curbs. Gradually, among some of its younger members, this resentment developed into antagonism to the regime itself. In 1931, Mussolini constrained Pius XI to curtail certain of the organisation's activities. During the later stages of the Second World War, some members of Catholic Action or of its component bodies took part in the resistance movement.

It became far more important at the end of the war. With the replacement of fascist rule by Christian Democracy, many of the men who became leading politicians were members of Catholic Action. Through this movement, they had gained training in organisation and administration, and had acquired experience of public affairs. Moreover, such men had the confidence of the Catholic hierarchy. This strengthened the Church's identification with the new government; at the same time, it gave the hierarchy a new opportunity for exerting political influence. With the heavy hand of fascism gone, the prelacy could be less cautious than hitherto in observing the distinction between political and spiritual matters. The 1929 concordat, however, was still operative; indeed, it was sanctioned anew by the post-war constitution of the state. To maintain the required abstention of Catholic Action, as such, from political activities, and yet to give the Church a freer hand in them, a theoretically separate and specifically political arm of Catholic Action was devised by Professor Luigi Gedda, a leading medical authority in Rome. This was the National Civic Committee, a body organising political committees of Catholics throughout the country. With the organisational strength and experienced personnel of Catholic Action behind them, these committees quickly grew to great influence. They are today an indispensable part of the Christian Democratic electioneering machine, with a notable influence in the choice of candidates for local and national elections.

At one time, feeling was strong at the Vatican that Catholic Action should replace the Christian Democrats. On 20 April 1952, the then Monsignor Montini dined with Emilio Bonomelli, manager of the papal villa at Castelgandolfo. Bonomelli asked him if the pope (Pius XII) and his advisers realised that the plan to impose a right-wing alliance on the Christian Democrats in Rome's municipal elections would break the party and the government. 'It is just what they want', Montini replied; 'they have done nothing but repeat for a long time now that the party is carrying us to ruin, and they think that Gedda and his Catholic Action is the only efficient force capable of replacing the party and standing up to communism.' The projected shotgun marriage between right-wing groups and Christian Democracy was (as we shall see later) frustrated by De Gasperi. Thereafter, Gedda was for some time under a cloud. He lost his post at the head of Catholic Action during John's pontificate, and for several years little was heard of him, except for his marriage to his secretary and the escape from a near-fatal mishap in a boat off Sicily. Paul VI partly rehabilitated him, but made it clear at the same time that Gedda's National Civic Committee and its affiliates, whose direction he had maintained, were to have limited functions.

A highly centralised body like Catholic Action, taking its instructions from the bishops, conflicts with the more modern Catholic concept of lay participation in religious life as something more personal and spiritual than mass meetings and exultant pressuring. 'You Italians', said a member of a French Catholic youth movement, 'when you have succeeded in organising a great meeting in the public square, believe you have testified to the truth.' Catholic Action was criticised at the Second Vatican Council on much the same lines. It is not limited to Italy, of course, but it is in Italy that it has its strongest effect. In wider terms, an organisation such as Catholic Action raises the crucial issue of Catholic exclusiveness. How much is gained, how much lost, by organising Catholics as Catholics with exclusively Catholic aims, regarding all others as outsiders? It is a stern distinction, and maybe a self-defeating one, to maintain through life, onward from the classroom, to sort children out from one another on a confessional basis: to be played with, perhaps; to be prayed with, no—only prayed for. And in the meantime, buy the Catholic papers, and no others; wherever possible, do business only with Catholics ...

PIUS XII AND THE END OF ISOLATION

Circumstances can completely change a seemingly unchangeable situation. The circumstantial change after the Second World War was that Italy's government passed to the confessional Catholic party, the Christian Democrats led by Alcide De Gasperi. Not only did the state cease to be abrasive, it also ceased to be strong towards the Church. The treaty negotiated with the Vatican on the behalf of a dictator was now inherited by a democratic republican state, controlled by a government acknowledged as representative of political Catholicism and, so far as could be seen after 1948, destined to rule the country for decades. Within little more than two generations of the papal humiliation of 1870, the tables had been turned on the lay state.

The Lateran Pacts were specifically re-endorsed in the new Italian constitution. The Vatican was no longer politically beleaguered, far from it; it was now a strongpoint of the nation's political life. The monarchy had gone, and so had the Fascist Party which had claimed to have recreated the Empire. The Papacy remained. It is easy, sometimes too easy, to make a direct connection between the loss of the Papal States and the deep interest which the Vatican has shown since 1945 in internal Italian politics. Even so, the habit of mind and the 'operational skills' developed by centuries of rule over a substantial part of the peninsula, combined with deep resentment at the loss of those states, must have quickened the response of many in the Curia to any opportunity for influencing affairs—and all the more so when faced with the prospect of exerting influence over the whole of Italy, not simply the old papal domain. And the advent of Christian Democracy brought the Papacy to the controlling centre of events.

The inheritor of this situation was Pius XII (1939–58). He is frequently misjudged and, indeed, is triply unfortunate. In the first place, it is always unfortunate to come at the end of an epoch; and he was the last pope to be brought up in the atmosphere of the Vatican as a threatened fortress. And then, it is also unfortunate to begin a process which your successors will take much further forward, so that it will look in retrospect as if one's death was the start of better things. This is very much the picture that has been presented of him, except by those—fewer in number but fervent in their views—who obstinately look on Pius XII as the greatest of the modern popes. Lastly, the rather forbidding Pius was succeeded by John XXIII, whose popularity throughout the world has had no modern parallel. John quite frequently appeared to dissociate himself specifically from the conduct and some aspects of the work of his immediate predecessor. Paul VI began his reign with so much goodwill simply because he undertook to carry on John's work—and also because, as Monsignor Montini, his disagreement with Pius XII's conduct of affairs had led to his being forced out of the Secretariat of State.

When his long pontificate of twenty years ended at Castelgondolfo in October 1958, Pius XII lay, a few hours after death, serene and almost childlike in expression. Young priests prayed at the foot of his iron bed. It was difficult to imagine less than the most profound rest for a man bearing such a quiet mask of death:

a blissful rest where there would be no wars to sadden those smiling lips with anguished appeals for peace; where no politics would be played, no constant stream of visitors beseeching words of wisdom on the intricate, specialised problems that concerned them. It was to be his own doctor who symbolically set the tone for the memorialising of the departed pontiff. Dr Galeazzi Lisi's experiments for preserving the body by a new method failed. Decomposition was obvious even before the lying-in-state in St Peter's was over, despite repeated efforts to give a more wholesome appearance to the decaying remains. Members of the Noble Guard are said to have fainted at their posts. The doctor went on to sell his medical diaries of the pope's last days to the press, with photographs, and called a press conference to explain his failure.

Too much has been written about John XXIII without pause for real assessment. Too little has been written about Paul VI which is not in the form of an assessment. This is because John brought men to him by his warmth and humility, while Paul is engaged in a more cautious attempt at bringing the Papacy out into the world: a process that invites assessment before assent. What is important is the fact that, together, they have raised the Papacy to a point of influence which, a matter of only a few years ago, might well have seemed unattainable.

Pius XII had his part in this development. When the bare truth is admitted, comparatively few people listened to what he said, least of all in the Vatican itself where the personal remoteness of his later years, among his canaries, the German housekeeper and a curious collection of friends (his doctor and Professor Gedda were among them), meant that decisions unwelcome to him could be avoided by curial officials, while unwelcome decisions by him—and his demand for greater freedom for biblical scholars is a case in point—could safely be ignored in Rome itself.

He was ascetic but loved crowds; even in the closing years of his pontificate, when he was withdrawn from day-to-day contact with the curial administration, he rejoiced in large gatherings. His predecessor, Pius XI, had begun the custom of receiving almost any visitor of note to Rome who cared to ask for an audience. Pius XII went radically forward from this. His interpretation of the visible Church's place in the modern world, so far as it touched the Papacy, was to show himself to as many people as possible. He inspired large gatherings with his strange quality of fanatical gentleness. He gave the impression of concentrated spirituality: the complete holy man. As he was carried into St Peter's on the portable throne, obviously excited by the cheering crowds, the tight, tense smile lighting up his thin face, it seemed as if he were weightless, as if the throne could fall away from under him and leave him suspended, in animation.

On 9 March 1958, a specially organised audience took place in St Peter's as a demonstration of loyalty to a pope who had recently expressed his sorrow, wrath and indignation at the sentencing of a bishop by a civil court.* General audiences are weekly occasions, but this one was meant specially to show solidarity with a hurt pontiff over the 'Prato verdict', who had cancelled the nineteenth anniversary celebration of his coronation because of the 'bitterness, grief and outrage to the Church' arising from the verdict. The occasion was thus described by *The Times*:

> A group of workers, estimated at about 40,000, thronged St Peter's this morning to give the Pope an ovation. Their enthusiastic show of loyalty was designed as an expression of popular sentiment towards him at a time when the Church in Italy is at the centre of controversy.
>
> Most of the great throng were Neapolitans, who are known for their love of spectacle and of uninhibited emotional display. The Pope's entry into the basilica at public audiences of this kind is always a dramatic moment, but the special circumstances gave an added effect today to the excitement as he was carried on the *sedia gestatoria* through the cheering crowd to his seat in front of the papal altar. His Holiness had just celebrated his eighty-

---

* On 24 February 1958, Monsignor Fiordello, bishop of Prato, was summoned to appear before a Florentine court to answer charges of libel and slander. He had denounced a couple who had married in a registry office as living 'in sinful concubinage'. The bishop refused to appear in court, claiming that he was answerable in the matter 'to my conscience as a bishop, to the Supreme Pontiff and to God'. He was found guilty (a verdict reversed on appeal).

second birthday and the nineteenth anniversary of his accession to the Papacy. There would have been a ceremony in St Peter's on Wednesday to mark the date of his coronation if he had not felt bound, after the announcement of the verdict against the bishop of Prato, to cancel the event.

The Vatican Radio described today's scene as an act of 'filial homage' to the Pope and of the faith and devotion of the Italian working classes. Brass bands and placards inscribed 'Long Live the Pope' heightened the impression of a popular demonstration. Speaking of conditions in Naples and the need there for more work and more houses, the Pope praised the exemplary worthiness of the Neapolitans in rejecting the temptations of materialism. . . .

It was all very much a reversion to the post-1870 atmosphere in which Pius XII had been reared. The ornate, proud splendour of St Peter's came into its own. So did Pius. The delicate, excited hands traced patterns as involved as those of the painted ceilings. The bands played and the crowds roared. It was a spectacle that one moment was shimmering throughout this greatest church in Christendom, rising to the top of Michelangelo's dome, and the next, as the pope was carried away, dissolving into marble, old brass instruments and several thousand Neapolitan workmen. This sort of transformation he could do magnificently.

In more private functions he could also be effective. There were few more entrancing sights, for instance, than to watch Pius XII addressing the Sacred College in a secret consistory. The vestments perfectly arranged; the pose, the expression, were those of a pope. Not of Pius; of a pope. At private audiences he had the habit of bowling over the sceptical visitor. There are many stories, such as that of the deep-dyed Protestant who, scarcely able to bring himself to go to the papal palaces at all, once in the pontiff's presence fell on his knees and kissed his hand. Pius had a brilliantly retentive memory and developed the ability to study the essentials of a specialised subject in a short time. He then produced his newly found knowledge to astonish members of expert congresses who soon adopted the habit of including a call on the pope in their programme if they happened, as many do, to be meeting in Rome.

He was a Roman of a not particularly distinguished family, despite the constant references to his 'nobility'. His parents were upper bourgeois, the mother extremely devout and at the same time extremely devoted to her son. The father was a Vatican lawyer, son of a senior civil servant in the papal administration. That was at the time when to be papalist as they were was looked on as being anti-Italian—rather like being a papist in England under Elizabeth I. Ardent patriots taunted Catholics about their lack of loyalty to the new state. This was the mental atmosphere into which he was born. He grew up in the period during which Catholics were not allowed to take part in Italian politics. It was the atmosphere of siege. It was deep in his mind. The universal Church was to have a narrow mental field at its centre.

As pope, he came to hate communism as a power in the world; as primate of Italy, he sought to break its grip at home. This is not altogether surprising, given the severe provocation he suffered in the form of widespread persecution of Catholic faithful. He ended by aligning the Vatican closely with the Western world against communism: a move away from the Church's traditional neutrality. It was to cost his successor a great deal of effort to re-establish neutrality, but it must be said for Pius that he went to much trouble to avoid any impression that the Church was involved in a spontaneous crusade against the Marxists. In his dealings with them he had remarkable patience, if not very remarkable foresight, and his ultimate revulsion took some time to rise to its peak.

The communists after the Second World War were not simply the modern version of the socialists who had frightened earlier popes. They were the perpetrators of a persecution of a kind which the Church had not known for centuries, perhaps never known before. The Church was not faced by a rival religion but by the widely disseminated idea that religion was a vicious folly. It is an easy, albeit mistaken, theory (though frequently advanced) that communism and Catholicism are much the same thing because both are authoritarian, well-disciplined, interested only in the final end and willing to apply their beliefs by force. This type of similarity is superficial and as wrong to make as the supposition that the two forces were destined from the beginning to be mortal enemies. Communism is not a religion in the same sense as Catholicism, though it may be as powerful a driving force for the individual as a religious belief. It is a religion only in the way that devotion to the Roman emperor and to the gods of the state was a religion. The Roman Church is authoritarian and can apply sanctions on its members to enforce their loyalty, but centuries of imperial behaviour cannot totally conceal an ideal higher than the authoritarianism by which it is expressed. The point about communism which John instinctively grasped was that its practice could be better than its theory: the opposite of the Church's own experience, since what the Church preaches is usually better than what it practises. John's optimistic outlook, so different from the fatalism of Pius, lent credibility to the expectation that the field for co-operation would increase, not diminish. Under him, the Church was engaged in putting its methods and worldly appearance in order at much the same time that communists were adapting their system to allow more flexibility. In Pius's time, the ugliness of that system was more apparent than the usefulness. Communism's anti-religious outlook was then rampant. In 1947, the Hungarian campaign against the Church had crippled Catholic activities and led to the arrest of Cardinal Mindszenty at the end of 1948. In that same year, the communists seized power in Czechoslovakia and promptly attacked the Church. The Chinese People's Republic was proclaimed in October 1949, and within the next eighteen months it launched a ferocious onslaught on Christianity.

The close attention which popes pay to Italian affairs often brings the criticism that special Italian conditions have too great an influence in shaping policy for the universal church. Pius XII has been frequently criticised on these lines. His regard for Italy was that of a paternalist dealing with recalcitrant children, who might frequently behave irresponsibly. The Pacelli family, even after the agreements with the Italian state of 1929, would still have been inclined to look on the Italian people as liable to be wrongheaded if not shown what to do. Look what they had done in 1870, after all. Fortunately, the family would have argued, the fascists had replaced the muddled anti-clericals and were at least in a position to enter a serious negotiation, though they could be tiresomely overbearing at times. Since the unification, popes had done what they could to control the situation by the ban on Catholic participation in Italian affairs, lifted only when it looked as if Marxism was likely to be even worse than liberalism.

It was in this domestic tradition and against this international background that, on 14 July 1949, the Holy Office issued its famous decree prescribing the punishment of excommunication for those who freely and consciously joined or collaborated with the communists or their allies. It was as bad to place an advertisement in the communist press as to vote for the Communist Party; in either case the sacraments would be denied. One Catholic historian, E. E. Hales, described Pius XII's decree as 'an effort to defend the West against the East'. That is one way of putting it. The decree certainly showed the Vatican as allied with one side in the great international struggle. Few people now would doubt that it was a mistake. Its exact effect cannot be judged. The aim of cutting down support of communism, especially in Italy, was not achieved. A decade and a half after its publication saw a quarter of the Italian electorate go to the polls and vote for the communists. The printed intimations hanging in the confessional boxes grew yellow and dusty, but legally they were still in effect. Cardinal Suhard,* the radical archbishop of Paris who died a month before the decree was issued, left in his *carnets spirituels* a comment applicable to the forthcoming measure: 'One does not win souls by excommunicating them, or annexing them by unreasonable means of coercion, even if this be done in the name of truth.' What he said was later to be recognised as true—notably at the sessions of the Second Vatican Council. Hurling anathemas was merely to blunt the main issue (an issue Pius never grasped) that the Church was destined before long to reduce the imperious side of its nature in an attempt to come nearer to the modern world, while communism would look increasingly less savage and more willing to compromise.

* Thought by some people to have had a deep influence on Montini, who had markedly radical views on social questions.

DIVERSITY AND ADVERSITY

To be fair, Pius could restrain his direct condemnations. There is no reference to communism in the index of the *Acta Apostolicæ Sedis* from the beginning of his reign to the Holy Office decree, though in fact Pius frequently referred to it by circumlocution, of which he was a master. All the same, though he may be exonerated from any charge of vulgar or unpremeditated anti-communism, it looked at times as if his policy would mean that the United States would gradually come to fulfil the old imperial role of temporal arm against the enemies of the Church, with the Vatican acting as spiritual vicar to the Western alliance. Pius never quite endorsed this interpretation, and he apparently had misgivings about the materialistic aspects of the American way of life. The point, however, was to be made strongly enough by Cardinal Ottaviani, then acting head of the Holy Office. During a visit to the United States in the early summer of 1959, Ottaviani said of the support extended to the Holy See by American Catholicism:

> . . . let me tell you that it resembles the role played by the emperors during the Middle Ages and, in more recent times, that of France. You are in a way the support, the help and the protector of the Church of Rome, and yet you do not constitute a threat or even a usurpation of power. Never was aid dispensed with so much disinterest. You have not yet produced sanctity, but you have certainly not stirred up heresy.

There is an unmistakable reference here to the immense amount of financial help provided for the Vatican by the Catholic Church in the United States.

Alongside Pius's dislike of American materialism, there are to be set his frequent assertions of the need for an efficient international organisation to safeguard peace, which suggests that he saw temporal help to be broader than American aid. Though in his day developments had been comparatively rapid in political relations between the United States and the Vatican, this was as much due to the marked growth of the Church in America as to that country's emergence in the role of Western champion. As Catholicism expanded in the United States, largely as a result of immigration, it proved itself unrivalled in loyalty to the Holy See. It closely followed the wishes of the Vatican and cherished the ties with Rome with more zeal than the older hierarchies. In this it seemed to resemble the Church built in England in the Dark Ages by Gregory the Great's initiative. It was both respectful and rich. That would help to account for Cardinal Ottaviani's favourable comparison with the medieval emperors. It was a long way from the visit, less than a century earlier, of Abraham Lincoln's special envoy, who was treated at the Vatican like some outlandish interloper. His mission was to suggest that the time had come for an American cardinal or two. Cardinal Antonelli, who received him as Secretary of State, was heard to mutter to the prelate-interpreter: 'The man is mad!' Not so mad, though, for the pope himself not to think seriously of the point made by the envoy. A decade or so after the visit, in 1875, the archbishop of New York became Cardinal MacCloskey, the first American member of the Sacred College. Pius IX came out of the encounter rather well; he went so far as to tell his Secretary of State that he wanted men of every race and tongue in the Sacred College. The day was to come, but not in his lifetime.

Pius XII, on the other hand, not only spoke about internationalising the Sacred College but went some way to carry out the intention. Given his indecisive nature, this was a still greater achievement. His great consistory of 1946 was the clearest indication of this policy. He created thirty-two cardinals: the highest number ever admitted in one list up to that time. Before that consistory, there were twenty-three Italian cardinals and fifteen of other nationalities. His new creations brought the respective totals to twenty-eight and forty-two. He had begun the process of breaking the Italian predominance in the College and the Italian monopoly of the papal throne. He did not follow it up. But that was not his way. In private he spoke of the possibility of a non-Italian pope. If one should be elected in the near future, it will be to Pius that a good deal of credit must be given for preparing the way.

He was also an innovator in other fields. He introduced liturgical changes, such as the evening mass for those who had spent a

DIVERSITY AND ADVERSITY

day in the country or at work, and a more logical sequence for the Easter observances, which set the course for the liturgical reforms accomplished at the Council. He spoke out strongly for allowing biblical scholars to employ modern methods of discovery and research: another aspiration of his which the Council's work would make more nearly a reality against the wishes of the conservative prelates of the Curia. His audiences were events which few people would have cared to miss if they had the chance to go to them. He was something more than the pope against whom his successors had to react in order to place themselves on terms with the modern world. Moreover, the Catholic Church's change of approach since Pius's death may change again. Too many people speak as if the Second Vatican Council has finally liberated the Roman Church from its awkward old ways. So far, it has brought more confusion than transformation: a point which is painfully—literally—obvious to Paul VI. Zealots of the cause of Pius XII are heard to maintain that John could have done nothing, nothing, had it not been for Pius.

It could also be said, however, that a pope who wished to do nothing could look back beyond John to Pius XII. A master with the crowds, a tense, withdrawn man whose body shook with the tonic excitement of a mass audience, Pius oddly misjudged the requirements of the day in the way of specific acts. Like the excommunication of communist supporters, his proclamation of the Bodily Assumption of the Virgin Mary was a misjudgment of effect. His early Roman background and his later isolation—combined perhaps with a desire to be identified with some great devotional development in Catholic doctrine—account for this insensitivity of touch. His reign ended in a kind of precise Byzantinism, formality for formality's sake, and generously touched with intrigue and decay. His isolation in this unreal atmosphere was also the reason for his indecisiveness in many matters, where he tended to flutter like a butterfly trying to make up its mind where to settle. The terrible picture of an introverted Papacy is drawn in the malicious memorial oration of Cardinal Tardini. The cardinal elaborates on the tiresome fussiness, the fastidiousness and affectation of a pontiff to whom the business of signing a paper involved elaborate cleaning of the nib with a special cloth, fresh discussions as to where the signature should appear, a careful delineation of the signature itself and, finally, a thorough cleaning of the nib again—'otherwise', Pius would say, 'the nib gets rusty and cannot be used any more'.

4
The Master Keys

It is all very well to make resounding claims. It is even better if there is somebody listening. To make more people listen means that much of the old exclusiveness must go. The great distinguishing feature of the reign of John XXIII was that the world wanted to hear him—the whole world, not just the Catholic Church. The principal feature of Paul VI's pontificate is that he intends the world to heed the Vatican and has gone to unprecedented lengths to make sure that it does.

Sure? Well, perhaps not quite. Certainty, the absence of doubt, is the setting for Rome's doctrinal truths and its proud authority. There, however, the certainty ends and the rest is a deceptive glow of glittering distortion, or indeed of plain surprises. Paul VI's reign has brought its share of both, and also disillusionment.

The Papacy, because of the enduring tradition of electing its monarch, passes rapidly from one man to another. The pontiffs are always, as far as modern times are concerned, mature in years and sometimes in experience: always in some way remarkable, and if they were not particularly distinctive at the beginning, the mere fact of being pope is inclined to make them so. They are also always apt after election to talk of papal predecessors, 'of blessed memory', in flattering terms which are meant to show the continuity through the line from St Peter to the pontiff who, two hundred and sixty or so popes later, is 'gloriously reigning'. But they are naturally different as human beings. This is what gives the Papacy its fascination. It can make all the difference in the world, this world (elsewhere one cannot vouch for), which cardinal is chosen by his fellows in the secrecy of the Conclave— or, to abide by the terminology of the subject, 'on whom the Holy Spirit alights'.

Sometimes a candidate is bound by the circumstances of his election to follow a certain course. Despite the real secrecy which surrounds the Conclave, only the most innocent would suppose that an election does not involve a good deal of subtle discussion, if not bargaining. At one time, negotiation was open and legitimate. When the conciliar movement was strong in the fifteenth century, the cardinals attempted to clip the wings of papal absolutism by exacting conditions from future popes in return for electing them. It was not until 1695 that Innocent XII, with his constitution *Ecclesiæ Catholicæ*, condemned these capitulations as simony. It remains that some of the Church's best popes were elected simoniacally; the series of pontiffs imposed by Otto I, for instance, which raised the Papacy from one of the lowest levels reached in its history. Simony may now be excluded but quite evidently the bargaining goes on; cardinals meet and talk as soon as a pope is dead, and before they enter the Conclave they take soundings among themselves as to what sort of man they should be looking for and, presumably, as to whether a particular individual would find a majority. Though fascinating, the machinery is in a way self-defeating. In view of the fact that, after comparatively few years, the Sacred College returns to the task of finding a new pope, the cardinals ought in theory to adjust and modify the policy of the Church in some detail by the choice of man whom they elect. It is a matter of judging the requirements and then agreeing on the man. There are, however, two imbalances in this gyrostabiliser for steering the Church. In the first place, the discussions in the Conclave are completely private. It is seldom possible, unless one is told in confidence by a cardinal who was present, to assess the degree of truth in the stories circulating about a Conclave. Hence, there is no public sanction on a newly elected pope. The second factor that cannot well be provided for is that a man is apt to change after election to the papal throne. He may suddenly start to have fresh ideas of his own, or reveal ideas that have been lying out of the sunlight of the previous pontiff's presence, in the shade of some mental niche.

John XXIII (1958–62) is one of the supreme examples of a man elected pope, after a somewhat mediocre career, who quickly asserted his remarkable personality, to become, long before his short reign was over, more popular than any other pope in the history of the Church. He determined to look out to the world. He knew that he would not be abashed or alarmed at what he saw because, better than most members of the Sacred College, he knew the world. He looked kindly on it. He may not have expected the world to look similarly on him, for he was a genuinely humble man, but he would have ascribed the extraordinary phenomenon of his popularity to God's will. When worried about his immense task, he used to comfort himself at night with the thought: 'But who governs the Church? You, or the Holy Spirit? Very well then, go to sleep Angelo.'

We have his own word for it that he did nothing to reach the Papacy. In his diary, he notes the graces bestowed on him, and the first is:

> ... to have accepted with simplicity the honour and the burden of the pontificate, with the joy of being able to say that I did nothing to obtain it, absolutely nothing; indeed, I was most careful and conscientious to avoid anything that might direct attention to myself. As the voting in the Conclave wavered to and fro, I rejoiced when I saw the chances of my being elected diminishing and the likelihood of others, in my opinion truly most worthy and venerable persons, being chosen.

The implication here, of course, is that other people had certainly been known to do something to obtain the pontificate.

It is often supposed that John XXIII agreed to take the thoroughly, if amusingly, traditionalist Monsignor Tardini as his Cardinal-Secretary of State before the seals were taken from the doors of the Conclave. There were, in fact, reasons other than pleasing the Curia and conservatism in general. Tardini had spent all of his life in the Curia and most of it in the Secretariat. As

Under-Secretary of Pius XII (who had no Cardinal-Secretary in his later years), Tardini grew to know the field thoroughly and controlled the Vatican's diplomatic machine. Its members were largely his appointees. There would have been little reason in dispensing with him unless the new pontiff intended to introduce radical changes in the personnel and methods of the diplomatic corps. Like Ernest Bevin, Pope John could have done so but he attempted no such thing. Moreover, the alternative to Tardini, and the man who had been his colleague for years at the Secretariat of State, was Monsignor Montini, archbishop of Milan. He would have been a difficult choice as Secretary, given his mysterious ejection from the department, following, apparently, a serious disagreement with both Pius and Tardini. It is certain that John intended no slight to Montini in appointing Tardini, for he undoubtedly regarded the archbishop of Milan as his successor in St Peter's chair. John may also have felt, in his compassionate way, that Tardini, too, had been harshly used by Pius, and that he deserved to be a cardinal at least, meriting more than retirement.

Though elderly, Tardini was very active. Some held that the original arrangement was to keep Tardini for a year, let him taste the full glory of office and then send him honourably away. Whatever John's idea on this matter may have been, Tardini had no intention of leaving once he had reached the Secretaryship, and, in fact, he died in office. He was wily, narrow, witty in his earthy Roman way, and knew everything of the world through official dispatches. (Personally, his direct experience of human affairs—like that of most members of the Curia—was limited; it took in the Vatican, the orphanage which he patronised, and practically nothing else.) His appointment was a mixture of policy, softheartedness and perspicacity. He was the first to hear of John's decision to call a Council and, to judge by his conduct, feared the project. He was also the first to give, formally and with no restraint, the fullest picture of the faults of Pius XII. Though he had his reward of office from John, he did not wish to let the world go uninformed of what he had suffered from the preceding pope as he laboured in the shadows. The catalogue of Pius's more exasperating habits was produced by Tardini in a discourse celebrating the first anniversary of that pontiff's death. Its tone was libellous.

Political pressure from temporal powers is felt, rightly, to have ended in 1903. During the Conclave of that year, the Austrians, wielding for the last time the power of veto claimed by the emperor, prevented the election to the Papacy of Cardinal Rampolla, Leo XIII's Secretary of State, who was thought in Vienna to be too close to the French. It was the last direct effect of the crowning of Charlemagne in the year 800. Moral pressure on a pope, in the real sense of the term, is quite another matter and can be immensely important in shaping a new pope's policy. The outstanding example in recent years is the election of Paul VI. An incident which happened on the night before Cardinal Montini's election touchingly illustrates the point. His votes were already sufficiently high for most people, including himself, to suppose that next day he would be pope. He was walking in one of the galleries of the Apostolic Palaces, looking disconsolate and worried as he paced this limited area in which the cardinals could take an evening stroll within the confines of their temporary captivity. Montini was among those who believed that his predecessor had had some special grace, a supernatural reinforcement of his personality. It is another way of saying that John's instincts in making judgments were uncannily right. One of his friends tried to cheer him up with something jocular: 'You have not far to go now!' It brought the anguished reply that the inheritance of John was a frightening burden. A fearful burden, certainly, especially for a natural worrier like Montini. He took it on loyally, often painfully pressing along paths to which his own nature and training would never have brought him. (It should never be forgotten of Paul VI that many of his best decisions are taken against everything which, by character and experience, he would be expected to represent.) Before the eve of his election, he had made up his mind that John's path had to be followed. On the eve itself, in that strange atmosphere of improvisation and inspiration that marks a Conclave, the necessity seemed even clearer.

Montini had one immense advantage which ought to have helped ease the moral pressure. Like no other pope in the Papacy's history, he came into an inheritance of world-wide goodwill. If there were great difficulties in following one of the most loved men in history, it was also certain that the new pontiff's performance would be watched with sympathy. This seems to be the part of his inheritance that Paul VI is least capable of either valuing at its fullest measure or handling in his own manner. It is here, nevertheless, that the real transformation of the Papacy in the twentieth century took place. It looked out on the world, and the world looked back with surprised interest.

JOHN XXIII

Examining the pontificate of John XXIII is like turning the earth of a piece of ground so well ploughed that nothing new can surely be revealed. Everybody thought they knew him. He is not really controversial, though some people have attempted to make him so. Yet turning the earth again has some purpose. Even after a vast number of attempts at disclosing the whole of John, there is always the chance that some new detail will come to the surface. Moreover, it keeps the ground fresh and John—with everything, from canonisation to a permanent place in left-wing folklore in reserve for his memory—needs the ground kept fresh around him.

One of the most attractive features of the Roman Church, and one of its great strengths, is that it has offered splendid careers to men of simple origins. As one looks at the cardinals when the Sacred College is present in full strength, one sees a cross-section of social types. Some are of rather grand family, like Cardinal Aloisi Masella; working class, like Cardinal Siri, whose father was porter in a block of residential flats in Genoa; peasant, like Cardinal Beran; scholarly, like Cardinal Bea. Simple conclusions cannot be drawn between a cardinal's origins and his standpoint in the contemporary Catholic debate. Siri is one of the most autocratic, formidable and reactionary members of the College, with the reputation of being difficult to like.* Bea, who might be expected

---

* In fact, he is an extremely engaging talker in private conversation; not spontaneous but frank, orderly and urgent in expressing his opinions.

to be overcautious and reserved in his views (a Jesuit, after all, and private confessor to Pius XII as well as a biblical scholar), is the most outspoken of all the cardinals over the need for better relations with other Christians, with whom he deals as head of the Vatican's Secretariat for Christian Unity.

Much has been made of the humble origins of Angelo Giuseppe Roncalli. He was born of a farmer's family near Bergamo, a part of Italy that has a reputation for being very Catholic. It has also had its social reformers. John XXIII in his young days served under a reforming bishop, Radini-Tedeschi, whose life he was later to write: one of a number of volumes from his hand which were of little interest to anyone until after his elevation to the Papacy. Yet it is a mistake to ascribe his goodness and simplicity directly to his peasant origins. (Frequently made, this mistake serves to sustain the accusations of John's critics, that he simplified truth through sentiment.) Roncalli preserved his simplicity by two methods. In the first place, he cultivated it. Secondly, his career, though bringing him finally to the Sacred College, was not particularly distinguished before his election. Most of his work was done out of Italy: in the Near East, in the Balkans, and then in France as nuncio. When Pius XII made him patriarch of Venice, there was no reason to suppose that his appointment to that (admittedly splendid) see was anything more than the close to the career of an obedient and faithful servant.

People who came into contact with him were impressed by his charm, his pleasant wit and his ability to deal with questions of the moment with dispatch. He had much common sense. He got on well with people, which was important for his work as apostolic delegate in Sofia, in Athens and in Constantinople, where he was among non-Catholics. It was a totally different atmosphere from that within the walls of the Vatican, where he could never—and did never—feel at home. His competence in settling differences was shown during his nunciate in Paris immediately after the Second World War. He had to deal with the unpleasant problem—reminiscent of that presented to Pope Miltiades by the Donatists—created by the demand that French bishops who had been collaborators should be removed from their sees. He cooled opinions into accepting a reasonable compromise. Not that he always avoided mistakes. The incident of the marriage of the Bulgarian King Boris in 1930 showed how capable he was of misjudging a situation. The king married a Catholic Italian princess in Assisi, having made the promise required by the Roman Church that the children would be baptised and educated as Catholics. Boris then had the ceremony repeated in the Orthodox cathedral in Sofia, and his daughter was baptised and brought up in the Orthodox Church. Pius XI was indignant, but Roncalli, who was in charge of the arrangements on the Catholic side, survived the trouble.

The most impressive feature of John's diary, *The Journal of a Soul*, is the extent to which it reveals the sheer hard work necessary for being simple in manner and outlook. This is something for which he is seldom given proper credit, yet it was the foundation of his life. He devotedly applied himself year after year to the task of retaining humility, right from the beginning when he was faced with the problem of any young son who has been able to leave his native town and receive a better education than any other member of his family. Pride and vanity, patronising reserve, a feeling of superiority—these come easily. He tried hard that they should not; and he went on trying throughout his life to be humble towards other men and towards his God. His God was very much a personal being. So were the angels and saints to whom he prayed, like the rather old-fashioned man of religion that he was.

His benevolence was an active quality, not simply the passive kindliness of an indulgent character. He could be stern with others, just as he was strict with himself. Once, for instance, when visiting English seminarists at their summer villa in the Alban Hills, he became cross at having Gilbert and Sullivan played to him. He would have preferred, he said, to have heard some devotional music. He disliked television and recommended his priests not to watch it. He was known in Venice to be strict with his priests, and throughout was firmly against all demands for a relaxation of the rule of celibacy, which he regarded as a voluntary sacrifice of great value. John was conservative in everything but goodness and simplicity; these he sought for with a revolutionary zeal.

THE MASTER KEYS

There was every reason for the Sacred College to suppose that, by electing him, they would enthrone a 'transitional pope' who would do nothing strikingly new, so that the problems left by Pius XII's personal rule could gradually be resolved behind the scenes until things were ready to pass into the hands of a more modern pope with a distinct policy. It seems also that the members of the Conclave who elected him had in mind a pope who would be less isolated from the world than Pius had been. Thus, while it is true to say that John was intended to be merely transitional, the choice of him did have in some of the cardinals' minds, at least, the basis for that *volte face* which he accomplished by turning the attention of the Church outward and attracting to it the sympathetic attention of the world at large. One of the strongest candidates was the Armenian Cardinal Agagianian, but some of his colleagues objected to him on the grounds that, after his long stay in the Curia, he had become more Roman than the Romans. Though he was non-Italian, his election could have meant a continuation of Pius XII's basically inward-looking approach to the office. For the same reason there were objections to the choice of Cardinal Aloisi Masella.

Roncalli also had the support of the French cardinals, who certainly were not looking for a perpetuation of the previous reign. They knew him from his days as nuncio in Paris, and respected him. As there was no serious French candidate for the pontificate, it seemed to them it would be well to have an Italian pope who was sympathetic towards the aspirations of the French hierarchy. The French cardinals, moreover, had the largest national group among the electors after the Italians. It was a sound compromise: the Italians would want an Italian pope, and the French a pope who shared something of the French outlook. His years in Venice had brought him into contact with a number of other cardinals because this famous see was a place frequently visited by great prelates. This, combined with his earlier diplomatic posts, meant that John had many points of contact with his colleagues in the Sacred College. According to his secretary, Monsignor Capovilla, who was in the Conclave with him, he was shown 'delicate attention' from the outset by a number of cardinals who clearly regarded him, as one round of voting passed to another, as the likely next occupant of the papal throne.* It was not just a question of a humble man surprisingly picked to hold the fort during the few remaining years left to him.

It is often a pity to dismiss warmly held popular beliefs as popular fallacies, but it is necessary to have clear in our minds what the circumstances were of John's election. Much of the sympathy he received was won because people were led to believe that he was elected by a basically conservative group who were looking for an old and harmless man to take over while they thought more deeply about what they needed to do. He then turns the tables on his electors and becomes a great innovator, to the chagrin of the disillusioned conservatives. There is a strand of truth in this version, but only a strand. There are indications that a number of curial cardinals—led by Tisserant, the French dean of the Sacred College—had accepted the point that the Church needed to have someone more closely aligned with the world at large. Hence their rejection of the candidatures of Aloisi Masella and Agagianian. If John was seen by many in the Conclave as a stop-gap in the sense of keeping the throne warm for a younger man (obviously Montini), he was also seen as a stop-gap in another sense: as a pontiff who would go some way towards closing the gap between the Church and the world.

In other words, John did have a limited brief for what he was to go on to do, though he transformed his brief into a text of great splendour. What he did with the limited commission he was charged with was rather akin to what Mozart did with Schikaneder's text of the *Magic Flute*: he did what he was asked to do, but so superbly that the authorship of the script was forgotten and the

* John apparently showed an abundance of delicacy in the way he cast his own vote. According to the account of the Conclave given by Vittorio Gorresio—the shrewdest of commentators on this period of papal affairs—he voted for Cardinal Valeri. Roncalli had replaced Valeri as nuncio to France after the war. Valeri had been accredited to the Vichy government, and de Gaulle asked that he be withdrawn. The request was met, and Roncalli arrived to sort out the problems left by the German occupation. The vote to Valeri was thus an expression of esteem for a colleague whom, under orders, he had supplanted.

elaboration of it by genius made it a high point in the story of humanity.

John should not be valued for the wrong reasons, but also he should not be undervalued. He was a great natural statesman. He was great by artifice, because he worked at it, and by instinct. It is understandable that his electors should not have appreciated these aspects of his character; most people have failed to do so even after witnessing his pontificate. He had shown remarkable obedience to Pius XII, exhibiting a thorough-going discipline in applying Pius's ideas on the place of the Church in Italian politics. He was outstandingly loyal. He was more besides, and not all of what he was to do as pope was to be completely against the ideas of his supporters in the Conclave. He did not know much about the Vatican itself, having spent so little of his career in Rome. Yet, at times during his career, to judge from his later performance, he must have sat back in Sofia or in Athens or in Venice, or wherever he was, and dreamed that most exotic of fancies: If I were pope . . .

His cult of simplicity and acceptance of the obligation of obedience counted more than the gnarled hands of his father and uncles in maintaining and developing a character that was later to have so profound an effect on the world. He worried much less than most people. What was done was done; what had to be done should be done; and what was to come could wait until morning. Once he had said his prayers, it seems that he was able to look forward to a new day with an open mind. An outstanding instance of this gift was his choice of Secretary of State after the death of Cardinal Tardini.

It is said that in the evening of the day on which Tardini was buried, the pope's secretary telephoned to Cardinal Cicognani, former apostolic delegate in the United States, asking him to call on the pope. The cardinal was not happy at having to turn out at that hour (John often kept late hours) but, given the circumstances, could hardly do otherwise than agree. John explained to him that, as the members of the Sacred College gathered for the late cardinal's funeral, he had looked at each of them to see which might be Tardini's successor. And he had decided on Cicognani. The latter demurred, pointing out that he was old, not in the best of health and would like some time to think about it. John apparently talked on about other subjects (he could always fill in the time talking when the situation demanded it, sometimes amusingly, sometimes to no great point; the idea that he was always an inspiring or entertaining man to talk with is wrong). He then pointed out that the cardinal had had time to think and, of course, would be accepting the post. And that was what Cicognani did.

The significance of the story lies not so much in the choice of the particular cardinal as in the fact that apparently John had not thought about the problem of a Secretary of State until Tardini was literally in his grave. 'No one', Cardinal Heenan has said, 'seemed less like a great thinker and planner than the Pope John who talked to me.' But, once he took up the matter, he settled it quickly and, from his point of view, satisfactorily. His most frequent visitor would now be a man of his own generation who, like himself, had been in the diplomatic service but with experience of a part of the world which John knew little about. He had grasped by that time, moreover, that the problem of reforming the Curia—the pope's executive arm—was one which would be beyond him, so that he did not require a vigorous innovator as his principal minister. The disadvantages in the appointment were only to come during the next reign. John was his own innovator; Paul VI was not. An energetic adviser to keep him moving through the most urgent issues, comforting him when the doubts began to come, spurring him on when the will to go forward was uppermost, giving him, above all, straightforward advice, would have helped Paul through the first years of his reign.

It is, incidentally, a habit among popes to leave reform of the Curia to a successor. Pius XII certainly saw what was wrong. With his intense papalist loyalty, which could have embraced the whole machinery of the Vatican, he would not take on himself the task of reforming the fortress. Instead, he ignored most of the members of the Curia and, at the same time, the problem itself. John did not feel able to tackle it; and Paul, with every reason to do so—both because of demands from the Ecumenical Council and because of the intrigues of which he was a victim—dislikes

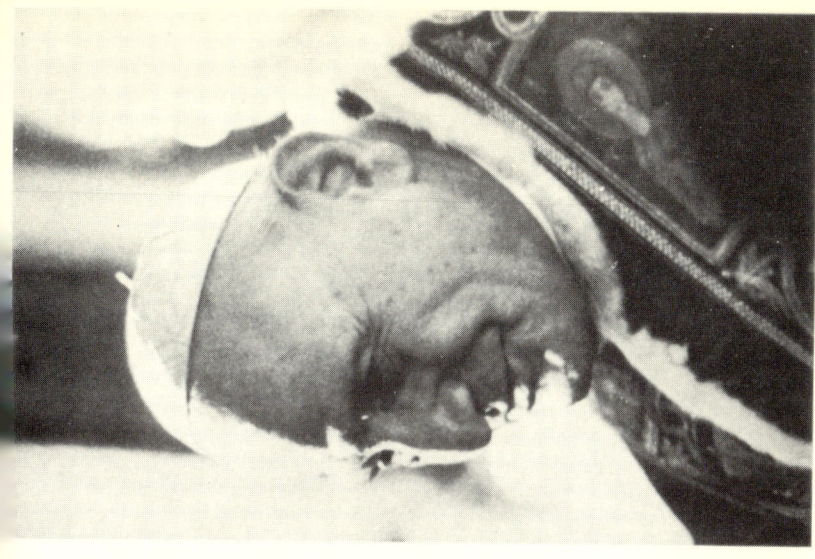

1 Pius XII (1939-58) *Mansell Collection, London*

2 John XXIII (1958-62) *Curtis Pepper*

Plate V

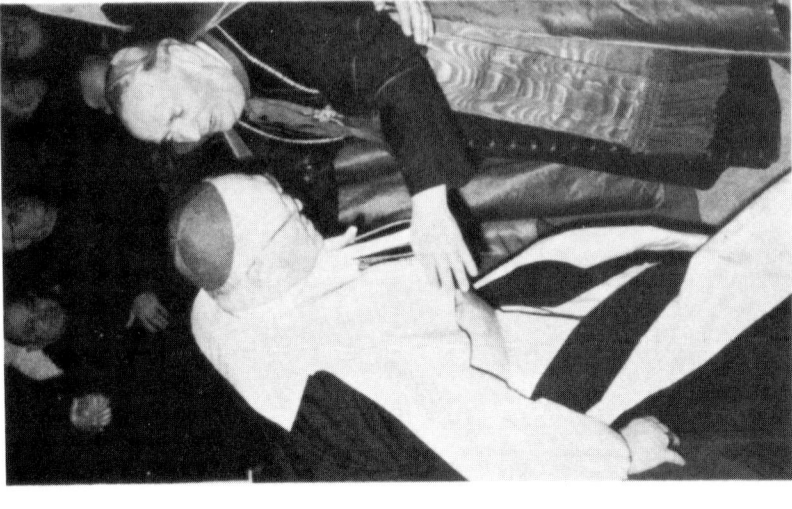

1 Paul VI

Curtis Pepper

2 Cardinal Browne (left) and Cardinal Ottaviani

Dufoto, Rome

Plate VI

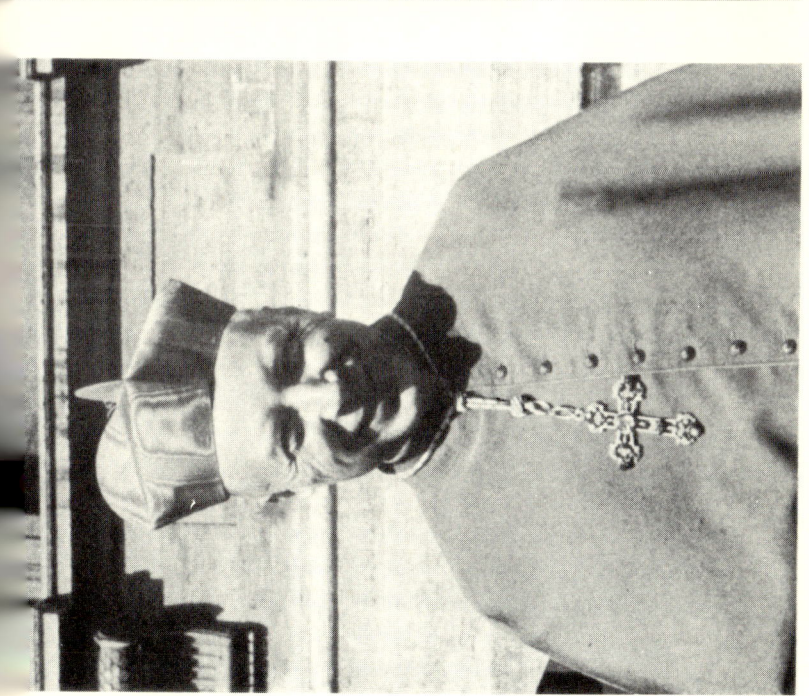

Curtis Pepper

Curtis Pepper

1 Cardinal Wyszynski   2 Cardinal Beran

Plate VII

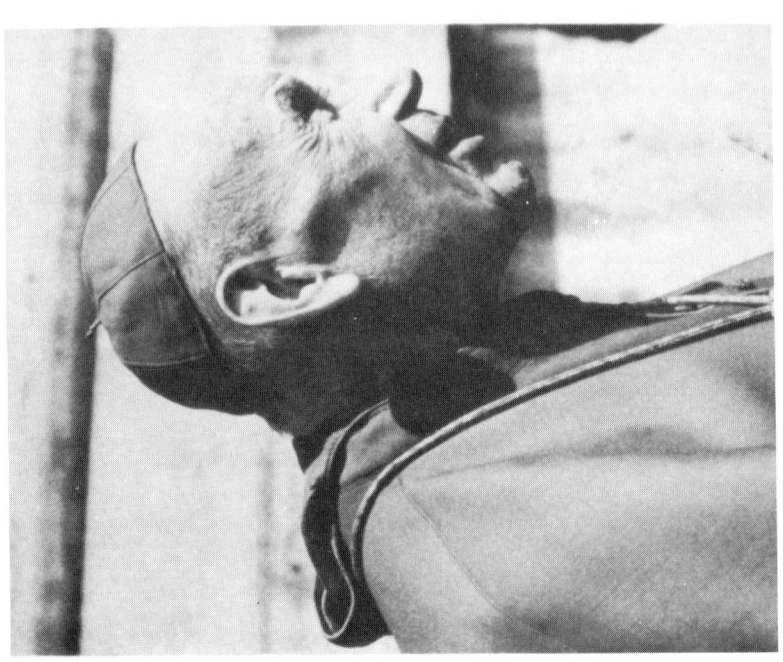

1 Cardinal Döpfner

Curtis Pepper

2 Cardinal Bea

Curtis Pepper

Plate VIII

giving an impression of carrying out retribution on his opponents. So the Curia escapes profound changes; the problem grows and, in this matter at least, every pope is transitional.

John's insistence on a spring-cleaned mind meant that he was natural in behaviour and quite liable to take rapid decisions of great magnitude, with no tormenting prelude of worry of the kind only too liable to afflict his immediate successor. With his constant efforts at remaining humble went his faith in being God's instrument. So long as he was sure that what he was doing was right—and this would be an instinctive judgment on his part—he ceased to have anxieties.

John's own description of how he came to call a Council—a momentous decision if ever there was one—is exactly in this line of mental behaviour. He was talking to Cardinal Tardini, he says, about the troubled state of the world and of the apparently hopeless clamourings for peace and justice. As he asked his Secretary of State what might be done, the words 'a Council' rose to his lips. In the shock of the inspired moment, Tardini replied: '*Si, si; un concilio.*' That was how it all began.

The Second Vatican Council was to be the greatest of the three main contributions of John's pontificate. It signified decisively the end of beleaguerment. It was the means of breaking through the sealed walls of curial conduct. It was also the means by which John involved the whole Church in his aspirations, for the future as well as his own lifetime. Having already resumed substantial contact with the modern world, the Church was about to take the process much further forward, and at the same time show the world that its intentions were serious by looking at itself with the object of changing what needed changing if it was to be able to go out into the world of today.

His second contribution was political. There was no good reason at the time of his election to suppose that John would have anything new to offer in the field of the Church's political behaviour, either international or purely Italian. The mould looked set. Pius XII, with his logical mind, had recognised that communism was anti-religious and, in particular, anti-Catholic. He had gradually come to the rational conclusion of outlawing it while allying himself with its international enemies. In Italy itself, Pius had taken a passionate interest in politics. It was said that no local election was too small for his concern; the detailed results were brought to him. He personally dealt with the minutiæ of policy. This intense regard—Pius seemed relaxed in nothing—for Italian affairs would have stimulated his interest in international affairs even if he had not already been absorbed in them before his election. His position was a tenable one. Quite apart from the mentality of a besieged fortress in which he had been brought up, he was influenced by a very particular factor. Italy, like Spain and Portugal, was a thoroughly Catholic country by tradition. All three countries had remained Catholic because the anti-liberal outlook of their hierarchies and past popes had managed to keep them so; or, as in the case of Italy, had recovered the state for Catholicism after an inter-regnum of liberalism. In Italy, the bishops still had a formidable hand in internal affairs.

John was not particularly concerned with Italian politics. He tried to withdraw the Church's direct hand in them. At the same time, unlike Pius, he did not see the world as divided between red and black. He saw it as a conglomeration of human beings, many of them confused, most of them wanting instinctively to find a way out of the confusion towards such general aims as peace in the world and a reasonable standard of living. Some were Catholics; many were not. Of those who were not, some formed part of atheist systems which the Church had condemned. Yet, to a great extent, the essential desires were the same. This being so, a given political system, though wrong, might yet produce good results. That was why he was the first pope to address all men of goodwill in an encyclical letter, instead of simply the Roman hierarchy. The style of approach was both warm and also, at times, distinctly fustian. It is hard to suppose that the detailed advice on how to administer farms, or the passages on social security in his encyclical of 1961 on social questions—*Mater et Magistra*—will go on being read for generations to come; but other passages will be. Their importance is that in them a pontiff was dealing in far greater detail and a much more straightforward manner than any other recent pope with subjects of immediate interest to ordinary people. John constantly referred to the work of Leo XIII. In fact, the *Mater et Magistra* was issued for the seventieth anniversary of the *Rerum Novarum*. It does not have the patrician eloquence of the earlier document, or the elegant abstractions of Pius XII's style. But it meant more to the world at large, all the more so because John XXIII was saying it.

This is his third great achievement. His reign was short: four and a half years. In his last months he was pitifully ill. But he had time enough to bring his humanity to play both upon problems and, perhaps more important, on people. Particularly in the second half of his pontificate, he seemed to bear a charmed life despite his advancing sickness. Perhaps he had learned by that time what he had to contend with in getting his wishes accepted in Rome. He would have said that he had prayed for guidance and received it. Others near him, and this included Montini, then archbishop of Milan, believed that he had received some form of special grace. Others thought that he was being rather forcefully advised. Whatever it was, the man had the secret of enthralling people in a manner completely different from his predecessor or his successor. When it comes down to it, ordinary men can seldom feel that they are being treated as ordinary men by the great leaders of the world. They are votes, mouths to feed, faithful or heretic, and many other things besides, but never ordinary human beings seeking justifiable aims. John was not a man who wanted to appear wise on all sorts of specialist subjects, as Pius XII had been, but he was seldom far wrong in his immediate judgments. His was an attraction owing little or nothing to the *mystique* attached to the office. That was why Romans, who are as cynical a people as any, found their lives turn unexpectedly grey when the old man lay dying.

An American bishop flew to see John XXIII on business important enough to have warranted a flight to Rome in order to seek the pope's own decision. He waited a very long time in the antechambers of the papal apartment. John was seldom punctual. He was inclined to talk and let his appointments go well over the prescribed time. The bishop was eventually received. Unlike his successor, John was no listener and was well into the flow of talk before any question of business could be raised. The pope wanted to know what the bishop's palace was like; more, he wanted to know whether it was near a certain road which he mentioned. He was glad to hear that it was, being rather worried, he said, about two Venetian emigrants who were living in that road in the city far away from their birthplace. They were unhappy and, partly because of this, surely, were going to be married in the near future in a registry office. The pope asked the bishop to find them, tell them that he had called to see the pope and that the pope sent his blessing for their marriage. The business in hand was then dealt with promptly. The bishop did as he was asked. He found the two Venetians in his diocese and brought them the pope's good wishes. They were so overcome that they wept.

In March 1963, Alexis Adzubei, Khrushchev's son-in-law and at that time editor of *Izvestia*, asked to be, and was, received by the pope. The encounter was of enormous importance. Even someone utterly ignorant of the international scene, who happened to be inside the Vatican that day, could not have avoided noting in its officials a dreadful state of nerves, fuss, apprehension and self-conscious efforts at behaving as if nothing unusual was happening, though desperately anxious to keep everybody away from the library door through which the Russian and his wife would later be going for the audience with the pope. The meeting took place immediately after John had been given the insignia of the Balzan Peace Prize, awarded by an international committee that included four Soviet representatives, all of whom voted for him. The ceremony was in one of the smaller throne-rooms of the papal apartment. The audience was there by invitation and consisted mainly of forty or so journalists. Adzubei and his wife were seated in the third or fourth row. In his speech of thanks for the award of the prize, the pope drew attention to the 'perfect supranational neutrality of the Church and her visible chief'. The point of his words at that moment could hardly have been made more clearly. Never once did he give any special attention to his Soviet guests. His composure was complete. Before going off to his study for the private meeting with Adzubei, he had a word for everyone. ('From Australia, you say? I doubt that I shall get that far! . . .) The explanation of why he received so important a communist was more than simply the 'perfect neutrality' of the Church. A man had asked to see him; the door could not be kept shut. No one so well as John was able to mingle so effectively politics and goodness.

The encounter brought many rumours. Perhaps Khrushchev himself would be the next to come: two sturdy peasants to decide the fate of the world. The appetites of the photographers grew huge at the prospect. Kennedy and Khrushchev would meet under John's chairmanship; Venice was to be the rendezvous. Under John's inspiration, they would surely reach agreement. Everybody wanted to do what John wanted—except his own great civil servants and courtiers, some of whom quite openly hated him.

Was there anything in such high-flying hopes? Probably very little that was substantial. But it was a remarkable moment, however long passed now into the limbo of old enchantments. What remains of it is a Papacy rather uneasily clinging to that 'perfect supranational neutrality' which Paul VI has tried to advance, and a method of dealing with communism outlined in the celebrated passages of the encyclical *Pacem in Terris* which John produced a few months before his death. He refused to condemn the communist system out of hand, seeing no reason why there should not be a collaboration with communists in certain fields. 'A false philosophy of the nature, origin and purpose of men and the world', should not be identified with an economic, social, cultural or political programme, 'even when such a programme draws its origin and inspiration from that philosophy.' He always regarded communism as false and wrong. He liked the idea of converting communists. But he applied his pragmatic attitude to its practice and found that its effects were not totally bad. One can well feel that such an attitude, more than just representing the Church's 'perfect neutrality', was the proper application of a Christian morality to the essential political problem of the age.

He tried to apply the same approach to Italian politics. The result was severe attacks on him in the conservative press. He was accused of having contributed to the rise in the communist vote in 1963 at the election which followed shortly after Adzubei's visit. It was argued that the idea of the pope hobnobbing with an eminent Russian communist persuaded large numbers of voters that the communists could not be so bad after all. When he was told that he had been accused of aiding domestic communists, he apparently wept. They did not understand, he said, what he was trying to do. Certainly they did not.

When he died there was nothing so grotesque as the circumstances that disfigured Pius's death. Unmistakable, however, as the old man lay dead, were the sense of relief among the members of the papal nobility—the 'black' aristocracy, who could not abide him—and the easy smiles of curial officials, who never had had his measure, as they all bustled through the stone corridors to view that strong face. It was now the colour of clay, expressionless, no sign left of the vitality which had moved so many people to look to him for a moral lead.

PAUL VI

On the morning of Paul's election, the sun shone. St Peter's Square was full. The crowd basked in warmth and in the confident knowledge that they were present at an historic event. The word had gone immediately around that the smoke from the chimney of the Sistine Chapel—more efficiently handled than at John's election—indicated that a pope had been elected. This is the central point in the life of Rome, the moment when everyone feels part of a great unbroken tradition, and the city itself smiles with a sort of laconic pride. Ordinarily, it is not a capital with the feeling of being a capital; at papal elections it once again comes close to being the centre of the world.

With the election of Giovanni Battista Montini in June 1963, it was exactly that. The announcement was made from the central balcony above the main entrance to St Peter's by Cardinal Ottaviani as head of the order of deacons of the Sacred College. He got no further than the Christian name before the roar of the crowd endorsed a popular election. There was no surprise about it, but the outcome of a papal election is never certain until that small figure appears on the balcony of the basilica to give the new pontiff's name. The representative in Rome of the archbishop of Canterbury ordered champagne as soon as the news was heard.

Most people were delighted. The new pope was liberal, or thought to be. John's work would be in safe hands, for this was the man who had publicly declared that John's road was the one to follow. As the wait grew longer, the crowd grew larger. Thousands of people were nervously expectant, restlessly content in awaiting the moment when they would actually see the new pope and be able to liberate their excitement by shouting, stamping and cheering, and finally falling down on their knees to receive the first blessing. He was a dignified figure in white as he stepped on to the balcony to acknowledge the applause. It was almost, somebody said, as if he had always been pope. He made his appearance shortly before midday on 21 June 1963. Only Romans with many generations of Roman blood could object to his northern birth, like an old woman who muttered: 'Montini . . . Siri . . . they are all Milanese to me.' (In fact, Siri was Genoese—for all the difference it would make to her.)

What sort of a man had been elected? Montini's career was already well known. He had spent practically half of his life in the Secretariat of State. In the later years of Pius XII's reign, when the pope had no Secretary of State, he had relied on Montini and Tardini to advise him. Of the two, Montini was regarded as the liberal influence, counter-balancing the narrow, curial mentality of his rival. Like Pius XII, whom he resembled physically and in gestures, he had not been a healthy child and had been closely cared for by his mother. He was a northerner, like John, but scarcely resembled him in any other way. At the time of his election he was sixty-five years of age.

His birth-place was Concesio, near Brescia. There were marked differences of background between Montini and Pacelli, and between Montini and John. He was not, like Pacelli, brought up in the tight ecclesiastical atmosphere of Rome; he was not, like John, of peasant origin. His family belonged to the higher middle class; it was a politically active Catholic family. His mind had a far more broadening background than Pacelli's had had. His father had been a member of Parliament and had sat in three legislatures, and had also edited the local newspaper, *Il Cittadino*. Strong though the family was in its Catholicism, talk in the house was by no means restricted to comings and goings at the Vatican. From an early age, the son would have been used to meeting his father's political friends. His brother went into active politics and became a Christian Democrat senator. One answer given at the time of Paul's election to the irritated question of why the pope always had to be an Italian, was that Montini was the first Italian to be elected pope, meaning the first man of an 'established' family to reach the papal throne since the achievement of national unity who did not feel in automatic opposition to the Italian state.

A great reader from early youth, his propensity for study has had two disadvantages. The first is that he is looked upon as an intellectual. For a limited class of people this is a recommendation, but generally in Italy an intellectual means a person of strictly circumscribed interests, especially when the intellect is Catholic in temper. John was freer for not being judged an intellectual. The second effect of his reputation for studiousness is that he has always been considered a rather cold person. To these disadvantages there was to be added another: John, who looked upon Montini as his natural successor, once described him as *amletico*—Hamlet-like. This was eagerly taken up by the press, though at the time it showed John's unfamiliarity with Hamlet rather than a just appreciation of Montini's character. What followed when he became pope was almost as if he wanted to justify his predecessor's appraisal. He listened to the advice of the Poloniuses of his court, to the gossip of the Rosencrantzes and Guildensterns. He publicly admitted his difficulties in making up his mind on so crucial an issue as birth-control. Soon the news was out that he was building a garden on the roof of his palace. Immediately he was imagined walking alone, too much alone, with anxiety to haunt him. The imaginative picture drawn by gossiping curialists and undiscriminating journalists proved soon enough to be a credible portrayal, though not a full picture.

Montini's clerical career was straightforward and successful. He studied privately for the priesthood, as Pius XII had done. In both cases, it was probably the mother who had a good deal to say in the matter, including some exaggeration of filial ill-health. He was ordained priest on 29 May 1920. For a summer he served as a parish curate, but in the autumn of the same year he went to Rome to study at the Gregorian University. From that moment, his destiny was set. He was recommended to Pius XI by Monsignor (later Cardinal) Pizzardo, and entered the academy for training ecclesiastical diplomatists. He was sent to a humble post at the nunciature in Warsaw, but the climate proved too much for him and he returned to Rome, where he was to work in the Secretariat of State until 1954, when he was appointed archbishop of Milan.

He was to all intents and purposes ejected from his post in the Secretariat. It is generally supposed that the cause was his differences with Tardini. Probably the principal factor was his social views, which were far more advanced than those of Pius and Tardini. A heavy silence still surrounds the whole affair, and no indication has ever been given of the personal conflicts involved. What seems indisputable, however, is that Montini and Tardini quarrelled sharply, and that Tardini was able to command the support of Pius. In any event, the nine years in Milan were the one period of Montini's life in which he could apply himself to pastoral work. It cannot be said that he made much of an impact there. The impression he gave was of a transitory stay—as if, so one Milanese remarked, he were already marked for higher things.

Pius XII did not make him a cardinal, although Milan is a see which by custom has a cardinal-archbishop. A man with Pius's close familiarity with, and taste for, formality would have realised that, in denying Montini his cardinal's hat, he was not only diminishing his stature in the see itself but was subjecting him to the frequent embarrassment of finding prelates whom he had previously outranked now senior to him in precedence. In the Vatican that would be important. In 1953, Pius held what was to be the last consistory of his reign for creating cardinals. In the course of it he announced that both Tardini and Montini, then still at his post in the Vatican, had declined to be made cardinals. It was a strange episode. One explanation given at the time was that Tardini refused because he feared that Montini, once having been made a cardinal, would become Secretary of State. By refusing, he virtually forced Montini to do the same thing. Whatever the explanation, the lack of the cardinal's hat put Montini's chances of being elected as Pius's immediate successor at a low level.

In theory, any Catholic male is eligible for election as pope, but a long tradition has it that popes are chosen from the ranks of the Sacred College. The voting slips in a papal election state: 'I choose Cardinal . . .' It was said that at the Conclave which saw John's election some of the Sacred College crossed out the word 'Cardinal' and entered the name of Monsignor Montini. Had he been elected as Pius's immediate successor, the history of the Vatican would have been radically different. Most people are agreed that Paul VI would not have called a Council. It was a French prelate who remarked that John could call a Council but could not have finished it; Paul could conclude a Council but would never, never have summoned one himself. Holy Ghost or not, it was thus providential that they should have been elected one after the other: the first a mildly surprising choice whose conduct was to be extremely surprising, and the second an heir apparent.

This is the extraordinary thing about Paul VI. He is not by nature an innovator. What he has done by way of innovation—and he has done a good deal, especially by his journeys—has been done against his rather cautious nature and training. Truly, he has looked every inch a great pope in his public *persona* from the moment of his election. He carries himself with dignity. Elegant in dress, he has the polish of the Italian upper middle class. When he was finally made a cardinal at John's first consistory, he headed the pope's list, and his carriage as he went to swear the oath beneath the red hat held above him in the ceremony in St Peter's was that of a practised ceremonialist. His movements and gestures are invariably polished. Of his physical attributes, it is only his rather grating voice that disappoints. Yet, in private, he is neither lofty in manner nor intellectual. He may have read a great number of books but he falls short of being a real intellect. He seems to be gentle, shy, affirming the power of his office but not altogether sure of himself. He is amazingly at ease with children. Unlike Pius XII, he is not a man for mass occasions, for all his dramatic dignity (and for all the massive size of the audiences which have become routine in his pontificate); unlike John XXIII, he does not give all of himself at every meeting. His mind, nevertheless, has a core of sensitivity. There is genuine goodness there. This came out clearly in his address to the United Nations. If nature had had its way, he would first have been an excellent parish priest and then a bishop. With Montini, nature did not have its way. From a youthful age he was marked for the bureaucracy, and then for great office.

On his election as pope, he had the responsibility, which seems to have been something of a nightmare to him, of following a pontiff whose reign was a phenomenon of popularity and instinctive good judgment. It was a reign which upset much of what Pius XII had left behind. Montini, curiously to some, evidently feels a loyalty to the master whom he served for so long. In a man of his temperament, the fact that Pius treated him badly would make him more inclined to insist on his duty of loyalty. It is fortunate for the Church that John opened the way for him. The present pope's tendency to see all sides of a question can be self-defeating as far as action is concerned. John left him with an Ecumenical Council to bring to conclusion; with the pledge to foster Christian unity; with a field in relations with the communist world which demanded further exploration; with a policy towards the underdeveloped countries which came near to aligning the Papacy with the non-aligned. John also left him with an administrative machine in Rome which urgently required reform. This was a fearsome inheritance for a man whose training and experience had been thoroughly traditional as well as largely gathered within the Curia itself.

Paul's first encyclical letter—*Ecclesiam Suam*, 1964—was incomparably more lucid than John's two great encyclicals. It expressed the heavy, and to him rather frightening, responsibility of being pope: a burdensome onus which John did not allow to overwhelm him.

We bear the responsibility of ruling the Church of Christ because We hold the office of bishop of Rome and consequently the office of successor to the blessed Apostle Peter, the bearer of the master keys to the Kingdom of God, the Vicar of the same Christ who made of him the Supreme Shepherd of His world-wide flock.

Sic omnes papæ; some people wondered why he had to labour the point. His purpose perhaps became clearer when he went on to express his sorrow that the papal throne should be looked on as an obstacle to unity:

> ... it distresses Us to see how We, the promoter of such reconciliation, are regarded by many of the separated brethren as being its stumbling block because of the primacy of honour and jurisdiction which Christ bestowed upon the Apostle Peter and which We have inherited from him. Do not some of them say that, if it were not for the primacy of the pope, the reunion of the separated Churches with the Catholic Church would be easy? We beg the separated brethren to consider the inconsistency of this position, not only in that, without the pope, the Catholic Church would no longer be Catholic, but also because, without the supreme, efficacious and decisive pastoral office of Peter, the unity of the Church of Christ would utterly collapse.

Yet he did not seek to protect this inheritance purely defensively or in isolation. He went to Palestine, the first pope ever to go back to the springs of the faith. He went to India, the first pope to carry the message of the Roman Church's determination to be heard by the younger nations. He went to New York, giving that blasé metropolis an historic day, and arousing real emotion at the United Nations by his appeal for an end to war.

The result is a world-wide interest in what the Vatican is doing, with far less suspicion than in the past about Rome's motives. Paul's difficulty, given his highly developed qualms about the direction in which the Church is going, is to use this new prestige of the Roman pontiff to the best, to everybody's best, advantage. 'The apostolic art', he said in his first encyclical, 'is a risky one.' Yet it would hardly profit a man in his position to have gained the ear of the whole world and lose the opportunity of speaking significantly to it.

5
Where Peter Is

THE Holy Spirit is much invoked for guidance in the conduct of the government of the Roman Church. *Veni Creator Spiritus* is a just and reasonable invocation, given the nature of the task which the Holy See believes itself destined to fulfil. Christ's representative can do no less than claim a spiritual authority deriving from supernatural assistance of a kind that knows no equal.

To apply that authority, he requires an administrative machine just as, to preserve its liberty of exercise, he needed a temporal principality, however small. He is an absolute ruler. His claim is immense but simple; the organs of government through which the Vatican functions are numerous and complicated. The invocations for divine aid rise daily from many quarters, august some of them, antiquated others; committees and offices, ceremonies and private meetings, ritual and discussion. 'Forgive the delay'—a fairly common apology in the antechambers—'the cardinal must see the Holy Father immediately to receive the Golden Rose which he is taking to Portugal and has no other time . . .' The painted ceilings are there for precisely this sort of thing: the rustle of silk and the portly response to bows as a swiftly moving member of the Sacred College hurries through the state apartments to receive that high-blown rose which he will then give to his chaplain to carry as they leave. But next it may be the turn of a prelate with urgent business in the field of foreign affairs to sweep past the courtiers, the halberds of the Swiss Guard and the still surviving accoutrements of a decorative absolutism long since passed away elsewhere in the West with the twilight of the princes.

Theoretically, it should be essential to distinguish the papal court from the real government of the Church, because in theory the first should represent the retinue of the pope as temporal sovereign, and the second the channels through which he executes his spiritual authority. In practice, it is no easier to distinguish between the two than it is to distinguish clearly between the temporal and the spiritual power. The same people quite frequently occupy positions both in the court and in the government of the Church. Seldom is anything abolished at the Vatican. Circumstances change, however, so that a particular office may rise and fall in importance over the years or centuries or may entirely change its function, which may come to have little to do with what is implied in its title.

The Pope's Cupbearer, for example, was a title held by Monsignor Loris Capovilla, created bishop of Chieti in July 1967. The title goes with his post as one of the Privy Chamberlains Participating: historically, the members of the papal household who 'participate' at the papal table. The Cupbearer of old lifted the pope's wine to his lips. This duty is no longer regarded as necessary, but the post is a useful, if overblown, way of giving a title to a prelate who is, in fact, a member of what might be called the papal private office. The post of Master of the Sacred Palace is medieval in origin, dating from the reign of Honorius III (1216–1227). He is the confidential theologian of the pope; or perhaps it is better to term him the official theologian to the Holy See, because popes—and Paul VI in particular—are inclined to look outside official ranks for theological advice. Potentially, it is an influential post and is always held by a Dominican. The present incumbent, Father Luigi Ciappi, is regarded as possessing less influence with the pope in theological matters than Monsignor Carlo Colombo, the pontiff's private adviser. Father Ciappi's predecessor was Father (now Cardinal) Michael Browne of the Irish Dominicans, who has a formidable book-learning and would almost certainly have been consulted with some frequency during his occupancy of the post. At the Council, he supplied the traditionalists with appropriate references from the schoolmen to back their arguments. He was strongly against the idea of episcopal collegiality.* Unlike many of the conservatives, Cardinal Browne was happy enough to talk at length about his reasons for opposing the views of the conciliar majority. What he said might be regarded by many as misguided; it was always deeply grounded in scholastic theology.

Many of the courtly titles are hereditary, such as that of the Superintendent of the Posts, which is retained by the Massimo family. Its incumbent has nothing to do with posts and telegraphs; the office originally was concerned with providing the coaches and horses and other travelling arrangements of the papal court. Similarly, the post of Master of the Sacred Hospice is traditionally filled by a member of the Ruspoli family. (The post is vacant at the moment, but not abolished.) The Master of the Sacred Hospice no longer carries out his original duties of seeing that pope and cardinals have proper supper and accommodation when they are away from the Apostolic Palaces. He still has his time-honoured place at solemn ceremonies, but his duties now are simply to welcome reigning sovereigns and heads of state, accompanying them to the apartment of the pontiff and later escorting them on the formal visit to the Cardinal-Secretary of State and to the basilica—taking a queen, if there is one, on his arm. Probably the most striking figure among lay officials at papal ceremonies is the Prince Assistant, standing on the right-hand side of the papal throne in his black velvet kneebreeches, with buckled shoes and sword. The holder of this dignity is traditionally drawn from the Colonna or the Orsini family.†

---

* One typically Roman comment on this controversy over whether the apostles acted as a college ascribes to Cardinal Ottaviani (who was decidedly averse to the idea that they did) the observation that the one occasion when they acted as a college was in the Garden of Gethsemane. He wryly cited the appropriate text: 'And they all fled'.

† The post became a Colonna preserve quite unexpectedly several years ago, when Prince Filippo Orsini was ejected after becoming publicly involved in a scandal with a British film actress. As a temporary expedient, members of the Torlonia family were brought in to share the privilege, which is too

This strange galaxy of mellowed privilege could be expatiated on at length. It is only a part of the Vatican's official life; yet, like the machinery for the ecclesiastical government, the court is able to resist reform. To pass from top to bottom of the system, through the overlapping temporal and spiritual strata, is like the odyssey of a raindrop falling through a dense growth of flowers from petal to leaf, and from thorn to stalk until it finishes in the brown earth.

POPE AND CARDINALS

The pope is absolute, and there is no legislature. He is advised, not constitutionally imposed upon, by lawmakers. Collective responsibility has scarcely existed, simply the pope's own responsibility as supreme head. That is the principal reason why rivalries among his advisers can become intense. It can be vital to have the pope's ear in order to introduce some measure disliked by another group, or to stop a project which, under the pressure of advice, the pope might accept. Paul VI has shown some awareness of this in his curial reform of 1967, which provides for periodic meetings of heads of departments.

His principal advisers are the cardinals. This function is theirs by long tradition. The term 'cardinal' is derived from the Latin word *cardo*, meaning a hinge. It is reasonable to say that the government of the Church turns on them. Too much, however, can be attached to a name which, in early Christian times, could be used to describe any priest permanently appointed to a church. Some authorities believe that the name was originally derived from the supposition that, once a priest was *incardinato*—hinged—to his parish church, it became the *cardo* of his life. Eventually the term 'cardinal' became confined to the clergy of Rome. The predecessors of these greatest of prelates belonged to three categories: the priests of the city's parish churches; the seven (later fourteen) district

taxing for one man. The Torlonias have no claims of birth and dignity comparable with those of the Orsini and Colonna families, but are very rich from banking. Representatives of the old papal nobility were worried lest a family of rich bankers should appeal to the upper middle-class, Lombard instincts of Paul VI, for the Montini family is also involved in banking. Another Roman prince was threatened with the loss of courtly office for appearing as a candidate in the list of the extreme right at a city election in Rome.

deacons whose business it was to care for the poor; and the bishops of certain sees near Rome known as the suburbicarian dioceses. All these last-mentioned were in easy reach of the city, and it was natural for the incumbents to be called on to advise the bishop of Rome, or to represent him at functions which he was not able or not willing to attend. These dioceses were, and still are: Ostia, Velletri, Albano, Palestrina, Sabina-Poggio-Mirteto, Frascati and Porto-Santa Rufina.

These three separate types of origin—deacons, priests and bishops—are preserved in the three orders into which the Sacred College of Cardinals is divided. By about 1150, the cardinals were formally organised in the Sacred College: the title Diocletian had given to the body of counsellors that replaced the Senate. (The Sacred College is sometimes referred to as the Senate of the Church, in the Canons as well as elsewhere.*) The idea that two of these orders—the cardinal-deacons and the cardinal-priests—were drawn from the Roman clergy is sustained in the custom by which cardinals of these two ranks are given the titles of churches in Rome, even if they have dioceses of their own. Cardinal Heenan, for instance, is not only archbishop of Westminster but has as his titular church in Rome the church of San Silvestro. The cardinal-bishops, the loftiest of the three ranks, still hold the seven suburbicarian dioceses. John XXIII introduced two changes. He insisted that every cardinal, whichever order in the College he belonged to, should be consecrated bishop. He also reduced the status of the suburbicarian dioceses to one of only the barest historical continuity. Until his pontificate, the seven cardinal-bishops had the cure as well as the title of these ancient sees, the Dean of the Sacred College always holding Ostia. In the last decade or so, these towns around Rome have become transformed into highly populated areas with the expansion of the capital. John decided that they needed active, resident bishops. Following his decision, received rather badly by some of the cardinals, he appointed resident bishops and left the cardinals with the mere title. In most cases, the change

* 'The Cardinals of the Holy Roman Church constitute the Senate of the Roman Pontiff and assist him as counsellors in the government of the Church', Code of Canon Law, Canon 230.

was probably justified. All the cardinal-bishops were working in the curia and most were well advanced in years. Cardinal Tisserant, the present Dean, was extremely upset at being deprived of the active running of his diocese of Ostia; unlike some of his colleagues, he had attended to the cure of it with notable energy.

To these three ranks, with their roots in the Roman past, Paul VI added three* of the patriarchs of the Eastern Churches in communion with Rome. By his *motu proprio* (*Ad Purpuratorum Patrum* of February 1965), he placed them immediately after the cardinal-bishops in rank. Though it may not seem so at first sight, it was an unimaginative decision because, historically and actually, the patriarchs are not directly involved in Rome's affairs and have quite different origins from those of the cardinals. It can, of course, be argued that, though they have, as patriarchs, no part in the election of the bishop of Rome and no membership of the Roman clergy, they are, as fellow-patriarchs of the pontiff, interested in who is elected 'patriarch of the West'. Hence, the logical solution—bearing in mind that the dignity of cardinal is not regarded as promotion by most of the Eastern patriarchs—would have been for them to be given a vote in papal elections without regular membership of the Sacred College.

Popes are now invariably chosen from the ranks of the Sacred College. The last pope never to have been a cardinal was Urban VI (1378–89): no heartening precedent because his election was followed by the Great Schism which lasted forty years. The exclusive right of the College to elect popes was confirmed by the Third Lateran Council in 1179. Before that date, Rome's bishops had been chosen by acclamation, by emperors, by insurrection or by designation of the predecessor. Whatever way was employed, it was frequently accompanied by violence. The idea of achieving an election by locking up the cardinals seems first to have occurred

---

* Making, in fact, four in all, because Cardinal Tappouni, patriarch of Antioch of the Syrians, had been made cardinal by Pius XII. (He was not fully representative of the Eastern-Rite communion, however, having been criticised by some of his colleagues.) The three patriarchs raised to the College by Paul are: Maximos IV Saigh, patriarch of Antioch of the Melchites; Paul Pierre Meouchi, patriarch of Antioch of the Maronites; and Stephanos I Sidarouss, patriarch of Alexandria of the Copts.

to impatient pilgrims in the early thirteenth century, and it became an institution in 1274 after one of the most famous conclaves in papal history. The College met at Viterbo where Clement IV (1265-8) had died. The opposing factions were well-balanced and could not agree on a candidate. Their formal sessions became rare; they banqueted and hunted. Some two years passed. The atmosphere was worsened by the sacrilegious murder of Henry of Cornwall. Faced by disorders, the cardinals returned to the palace. The local people were exasperated and kept them locked inside, cutting down the supply of food until they made up their minds; to encourage them the more, they removed the roof. Despite threats from the prelates within that this oppression of their eminences would incur the wrath of God, the populace continued in their view that hardship was a salutary inducement to decision-making. Nothing but bread and water was sent into the building. Violent rainstorms helped to bring about a decision, and a new pope emerged—two years, nine months and two days after the death of Clement. Three years later, the new pope, Gregory X (1271-76), with the experience of Viterbo to sustain him, promulgated a series of rules for future conclaves at the Second Council of Lyons. They were based on the principle which is still followed: that physical discomfort is an effective method of inducing inspiration.

Gregory X's rules were not quite so stringent as the conditions imposed at Viterbo, but they were severe enough. The cardinals were to wait ten days after the death of a pope in order to allow all of them to gather; they would then be locked inside the papal palace, each with a single servant, or two at most. No one would have access to them. No messages or letters could be sent to them under pain of excommunication. A few windows might be left open so that food could be passed to the cardinals. Three days after they had entered the Conclave, if no pontiff had been chosen, the supervisors reduced their food to one dish only, either lunch or dinner, for five days. Thereafter they went on to bread and water. They could receive no money from the papal treasury and were warned that, during the Conclave, they 'must entirely disregard their own affairs and have regard only for the common welfare of the Church'. Under pain of excommunication, none of the electors might make promises or in other ways attempt to convert the other cardinals to their own way of thinking about the election. 'Indeed, all pacts, agreements and obligations sealed with oaths are of no value, and whoever breaks them deserves praise, not the accusation of perjury.'

This decree, issued in July 1274 with the title *Ubi Periculum Maius*, was the first document to use the word 'Conclave' (meaning 'with a key') in connection with a papal election. It met opposition from the cardinals at first, and was not promulgated until some months after the Council of Lyons had dispersed.* The effectiveness of these rules is shown by the fact that Gregory's successor Innocent V (who ruled only a few months), was elected in a matter of hours. The regulations were not always followed, however, and were revoked after the three elections following the death of Gregory X. As an immediate result, the Conclave which elected Nicholas III (1277-80) lasted six months, as did that electing his successor, Martin IV (1281-5). The next pope, Nicholas IV (1288-1292), emerged after a year of deliberations, and his death was followed by an inter-regnum of twenty-seven months. Boniface VIII (1294-1303) reaffirmed Gregory's rules; his successor was elected in a day. They have not been scrupulously followed since then. The Conclave held at Carpentras in 1316 which eventually elected John XXII lasted two years, and the cardinals were certainly not living all that time on bread and water.

But Gregory's legislation did establish finally that popes should be elected in Conclave, and his rules have remained valid with only slight changes. Modern Conclaves are not long. Leo XIII was elected after thirty-six hours; Pius X after five days; Benedict XV after four days; Pius XI after four days; Pius XII on the third round of voting after twenty hours; John XXIII was elected on the eleventh poll after three days; and Paul VI after two days. The main difficulty in the future will be to find the space inside the Vatican to accommodate the much larger number of cardinals— even in the requisite decision-making discomfort. Sixtus V set

---

* Some of the conciliar fathers, however, accepted it promptly. The Vatican archives have a solemn declaration of the English, Scottish and Irish bishops at the Council of Lyons attesting to their warm approval of Gregory's decree.

their number at seventy, a total not exceeded until John XXIII's pontificate, when the number was increased to more than one hundred. In this, John has been followed by Paul.

As soon as a pope dies, the Dean of the Sacred College is informed so that he may immediately apprise the other cardinals, summoning those not resident in Rome to the Vatican for the forthcoming election. The principal part during the inter-regnum is taken by the Chamberlain of the Church (at present Cardinal Aloisi Masella), who takes over the powers of temporal administration during the vacancy.* He immediately takes possession of the Apostolic Palace; on his entry, the Bronze Door, which opens on to Bernini's colonnade in St Peter's Square, is closed by the Swiss Guard, as are the main doors of the Lateran and the summer residence at Castelgandolfo. The Chamberlain confirms the death by withdrawing the white sheet covering the pontiff's face and calling him three times by his baptismal name. Upon receiving no answer, he says to his assistants: 'The pope is truly dead.' (The ancient ceremony of striking the pope's forehead with a silver hammer as the calls are made has been discarded.) The body is identified and the death certificate issued. The private apartments are closed and sealed until after the election of the new pope. The Chancellor takes possession of the Fisherman's Ring—the papal signet ring—and, as a sign that pontifical power is suspended, breaks off in the presence of the other cardinals the gold rim bearing the late pope's name.

The funeral of a pope is very moving. The body—vested in scarlet, the pallium and fanon draped around the shoulders and a golden mitre on the head—is brought into St Peter's for the days of lying-in-state. It is carried in solemn procession from the palace, escorted by the cardinals, the papal household, the canons of St Peter's and other clergy—all carrying lighted candles. For

* He carries a baton of office and is constantly accompanied by an escort of the Swiss Guard. His emblem is the Pavilion: a large umbrella striped in red and yellow, regarded as symbolising the temporal power of the Church. The Chamberlain of the Church can mint coins during the inter-regnum; these normally carry his personal arms surmounted by the Pavilion: a custom dating from 1521. Since 1929, the Holy See has issued special postage stamps during the *sede vacante*.

the burial, the body is placed in the first of three coffins, of cypress, lead and elm. During the funeral ceremony, a brief account of the deceased pontiff's life and deeds is read aloud and then put inside a metal container, together with gold, silver and bronze medals and coins of each year of his pontificate. The container is placed in the coffin. One by one, the cardinals approach and sprinkle the remains with holy water. The coffins are securely nailed and sealed, and either let down into the crypt on an improvised pulley, as was the case with Pius XII, or carried out of the basilica and down into the crypt, as happened with John XXIII.

Not all the activities of the Church's government are suspended. As well as the Chamberlain, the Cardinal-Major Penitentiary remains in office; so do the Cardinal-Vicar of Rome and the Cardinal-Chancellor. The Cardinal-Secretary of State gives up his duties, handing over ordinary administration to the Secretary of the Sacred College, but legates, nuncios and apostolic delegates remain at their posts and retain their authority. The essential administration of the various departments is maintained.

The inter-regnum is closely regulated by legislation drawn up in 1945 by Pius XII in his Apostolic Constitution *Vacantis Apostolicæ Sedis*,* with some details added by John XXIII, such as the ban on photographing a dying pope. (Pius XII on his death-bed had been photographed by his doctor for the benefit of newspapers.) But the great interest naturally builds up towards the Conclave and the election.

The description given by Adam of Usk, in his chronicle of the election of Innocent VII in 1404, is in principle what has still to be followed now:

> The Conclave is a close-built place, without anything to divide it, and it is set apart to the cardinals for the election of the pope; and it must be shut and walled in on all sides, so that, excepting a small wicket for entrance, which is afterwards closed, it shall remain strongly guarded. And therein is a small window for

---

* Typically, Pius laid down the detailed rules but omitted to make the necessary appointments to carry them out. Hence, at his death, the Chamberlain's duties were clear to all but there was no Chamberlain.

food to be passed in to the cardinals, at their own cost, and this window is so fitted as to open or shut as required. And the cardinals have each a small cell on different floors for sleep and rest.

A whole section of the Vatican is sealed off; sleeping accommodation is frequently roughly improvised and uncomfortable. During the Conclave which elected John XXIII, for instance, Cardinal Tisserant slept on a metal bed in a corner of the Vatican Museums. Supper was served—a plain meal, but no question of bread and water—in the Borgia apartments.

The Conclave must take place before the eighteenth day has passed since the pope's death. The right to be admitted is denied only to those cardinals who refused to enter the Conclave at the proper time or left without sufficient reason and without the approval of the majority of the College. With the cardinals, a small group of officials is admitted: the Secretary of the Sacred College, the Sacristan of the Vatican Palace, the Prefect of Ceremonies, a confessor (always drawn from a religious order), two physicians, a surgeon, a pharmacist and a few technicians. Almost all of the cardinals and officials are allowed to bring one or two personal assistants (with a third allowed as a special privilege in cases of great infirmity). All assistants are rigorously examined by a special commission appointed by the Sacred College.

On the day set for the opening of the Conclave, the Cardinal-Dean celebrates a Pontifical Votive Mass of the Holy Ghost in St Peter's. The colours are solemn; during the inter-regnum the cardinals put aside their robes of crimson watered-silk and wear trains of purple wool. Only their birettas and skullcaps are crimson, but they must be of wool, not silk. After the Mass, a distinguished preacher delivers the traditional Latin oration, *De Eligendo Pontifice*, giving an account of the qualities which they must seek in the new pope. This oration is normally taken to reflect the wishes of the curial cardinals. They return in the afternoon for the formal entry in procession into the Conclave. The assistants lead the procession, followed by a choir chanting the *Veni Creator*

Spiritus; then come the cardinals preceded by a master of ceremonies: first, the Dean and cardinal-bishops, then the cardinal-priests and cardinal-deacons. Behind them come the officials of the Conclave. They go directly to the Sistine Chapel where, after another invocation of God's light and assistance, they hear the text once again of Pius XII's Constitution, renewing their oaths to follow the rules. The Conclave is then closed.

The task of safeguarding the cardinals from outside interference is entrusted to two officials: a prelate called the Governor of the Conclave and a layman, the Marshal of Holy Church, who becomes Guardian of the Conclave—an office which for some centuries has been held by the Chigi family. In the presence of the Sacred College, they kneel before the Dean and swear to neglect nothing in the execution of their office if it would be to the harm of the Conclave, but to fulfil their duties with religious fidelity and diligence. The Cardinal-Dean orders the ringing of a bell in the courtyard of San Damaso as a final warning to those who have no right within the Conclave that they must leave the area immediately. The Chamberlain undertakes a tour of inspection; the doors at the one entrance are closed and bolted, while on the outside the Governor and the Guardian attach to them a padlock and chain.

Since 1417, when Martin V was elected during the Council of Constance, there has been only one papal election outside Rome: that of Pius VII at Venice in the Benedictine monastery of San Giorgio after his predecessor had died at Valence as Napoleon's prisoner. Until the last century, all Conclaves in Rome from the early fifteenth century took place in the Vatican except for two (Eugenius IV's election in 1431 and that of Nicholas V in 1447) that were held in the Dominican monastery adjoining the church of Santa Maria sopra Minerva. In the last century, four popes were elected in the Quirinal Palace. Presumably, since Pius XII's legislation was made with the Lateran Pacts in mind (by which the Vatican was recognised as an independent state), future Conclaves as far as can be foreseen will meet there.

The actual voting takes place in the Sistine Chapel. It is an appropriate building: plain, lofty and rectangular in shape; 133

feet long and 45 feet wide, and lit by six large windows. The design is thus simple even though the decoration assures it a place among the greatest achievements of the human mind. For the purpose of the election, purple damask thrones, each surmounted by a canopy, are placed around the walls. Before each one is a writing desk. In front of the altar is a table at which the actual voting will be carried out, and tables are placed in the centre of the chapel for the use of the officials.

A pope can be elected by one of three different methods. The first is by inspiration, the second by compromise, and the third—by far the most common—by secret ballot. Pius XII completed the most recent detailed changes in the varied methods by his Apostolic Constitution *Vacantis Apostolicæ Sedis*. Election by inspiration is deemed to have occurred when all the cardinals, moved by a common perception, declare someone to be pope, and shout out loudly to this effect and unanimously. Pius's Constitution suggests such a form of words as :'Most Reverend Lords, in view of the personal virtue and probity of ——— we consider him worthy to be elected Supreme Pontiff, and from now on for my part I elect him Pope.' For the declaration to have validity, every other cardinal, without exception, must then say in a loud clear voice, *Eligo*; and any unable to speak must hasten to write down *Eligo*. One condition is that there should be no arrangement beforehand, though how this could be known is not explained in the Constitution. As one might imagine, this rather exultant style of election happens very rarely indeed. The last occasion was in 1154, at the election of Nicholas Breakspear who, as Hadrian IV, was the only Englishman ever elected pope. It is said that an American cardinal proposed to the Conclave at which Paul VI was elected that the proceedings be by inspiration, but this was distinctly ingenuous in view of the calculations being made among the various groups.

The compromise approach occurs when the Sacred College agrees to make over the task of election to a committee. Absolute unanimity has to be achieved in the nominations to the committee, which may have as few as three members. The exact limits of the mandate must be laid down and agreed; whether, for instance, the committee's choice requires endorsement by the College as a whole, or whether a limit of time is imposed on its deliberations. The cardinals on the committee may discuss candidates with each other only in writing so that, as Pius XII ordained, 'polite and respectful words may be used without prejudice among the electors'. Presumably he was attempting to eliminate quarrels, or at least excessive wordiness.

After Gregory X's time, the ballot method required a two-thirds majority. Pius increased this total to two-thirds and one, thus obviating the possibility that the two-thirds determining vote might include the successful candidate—'for no one may elect himself or cast his vote in favour of himself, either by ballot or compromise'. John XXIII modified this rule again, making it rather more gentlemanly. In 1962, he laid down that the two-thirds and one rule applied only when the total number of votes was not exactly divisible by three.

The princes of the Church, equals of princes of the blood, sitting in the Sistine Chapel beneath Michelangelo's tortured *Last Judgment* as they cast their ballots, are kept strictly under watch when fulfilling this greatest of their duties. The process of election has become as nearly as possible a thoroughly checked secret ballot, so that this strange little world of barricaded grandeur—a microcosm of the Church's human variety, at least in its higher reaches—can follow with a just formality the unhindered and unquestionable course of its onerous task. The election is preceded by recitation of the *Veni Creator Spiritus*, followed by the Prayer to the Holy Ghost. As the cardinals go to their places the masters of ceremonies hand them each two or three voting forms. These forms have written on them:

> Eligo in Summum Pontificem
> Rev^{mum} D. meum D. Card. . . . .

(I elect as Supreme Pontiff the Most Reverend Lord, My Lord Cardinal . . . .) At the same time, the junior cardinal-deacon draws the names of nine cardinals to serve, three to each function, as scrutineers for counting votes, as infirmarians to collect the votes of the sick, and as inspectors to check the results. The

Secretary of the Sacred College and the masters of ceremonies must then withdraw, leaving the cardinals to themselves.

Each fills in his ballot form, altering his style of writing as best he can, and folds it horizontally between the two lines of Latin so as to cover the name. The cardinals, in order of seniority, then walk up to the altar, holding the ballot form between the thumb and index finger of the right hand so that it can be plainly seen. The Dean votes first; he is followed by the cardinals who have collected the ballot forms from the sick cardinals; then comes the rest of the College in order of creation. Before the altar is a table on which there stands a chalice, covered by a paten. Each cardinal approaches the altar and genuflects; then he pronounces his oath in a clear voice: 'I call to witness Christ Our Lord, Who will be my judge, that I am electing the one who, before God, I think should be elected.' He then places the ballot form on the paten and, tilting the paten, drops the form into the chalice. The method adopted for sick cardinals is that the three infirmarians go to the cells of their ailing colleagues, taking a special box with a slit in the top. Before leaving the Sistine Chapel for this purpose, the infirmarians must show the other members of the College that the box is empty. It is then locked and the key is placed on the altar. When they return, the votes are taken out of the box and counted; so long as the number of ballots is the same as the number of sick cardinals, the forms are placed individually on the paten and dropped into the chalice in the normal way. The count also has its elaborate safeguards. When every cardinal has cast his vote, the first of the three scrutineers shakes the chalice, and the third takes each form separately from the vessel and places it in a second chalice to check that the number of ballots coincides with the number of electors. If there is a discrepancy, the slips are immediately burned. If the numbers tally, the three scrutineers take their places by the table and begin the count. The first takes each form, reads the name to himself and hands it to the second. He does the same and passes the form to the third scrutineer, who clearly announces the name. The cardinals keep a tally of the voting on lists bearing the names of all members of the College. At the end of the count, the third scrutineer announces the total number of votes obtained by each cardinal. He takes the ballot forms and threads them all together, inserting the needle through the word *Eligo*, and ties a knot at each end of the thread. These forms are then examined by the three inspectors. If the two-thirds majority (or two-thirds and one) has not been reached, the cardinals immediately pass to a second round of voting. The normal number of ballots is four a day: two in the morning and two in the afternoon. When there is no decision, the results of each pair of ballots are burned by the junior cardinal-deacon. A conclusive result may, of course, mean that only one set of ballots need be burned.

The waiting crowds are informed of the main stages of the voting by that celebrated smoke-signal which has been responsible for so much confusion. Folklore has it that white smoke indicates that a pope has been elected, and black smoke an indecisive pair of votes. This is not so; it is not the colour but the consistency of the smoke that counts. Damp straw used to be placed with the papers in the event of a negative vote, emitting prolonged and thick puffs of smoke. Nowadays, since the misinterpretations at John's election, chemicals are used for the so-called 'black' smoke. When an election has been made, it is the papers alone that are burned. This means that, when a few brief, thin puffs of smoke come from the strange old chimney-stack improvised above the roof of the squarely built chapel, a pope has been elected. Once that short, thin puff has told its tale, the square before the basilica begins to fill with people and expectant curiosity: nervous excitement among chattering seminarians, grunts from large old women whose lives have been punctuated with perhaps half-a-dozen sights of a small white figure appearing on the central balcony of St Peter's to bless the crowds, to walk his allotted span in the Vatican's confines as Christ's Vicar on earth, and then lay down his tiara to be encased in a triple coffin.

The scene which the crowd does not witness is deeply impressive and moving. Once the scrutineers have announced a conclusive ballot, the Prefect of Ceremonial and the masters of ceremonies are readmitted to the Sistine Chapel. The Dean approaches the cardinal who has reached the required number of votes, and asks: 'Do you accept your election, which has been performed canonically, as Sovereign Pontiff?' As soon as the cardinal gives his *Accepto*, he is automatically pope with full sovereign authority. He is then asked by what name he wishes to be known; documents are drawn up legally testifying to his acceptance and the title he has chosen. All newly elected popes, save two, have taken a new regnal name since Sergius IV (1009–12) decided in this way to disencumber himself of an ugly nickname (*Os Porci*—Pig-Face); he may also have been more properly influenced by the fact that his baptismal name was Peter. The two exceptions since his day are Hadrian VI (1522–3) and Marcellus II (1555). Before Sergius IV, there were individual cases of a change in name, such as that of John II (533–5), whose proper name was that of a pagan god—Mercury; which is presumably why he should have been the first pope to take a new name on election. Among more than 260 popes, there are no more than eighty-one different names. Pope Lando, who died in 940, was the last pope to have a name borne by none of his successors. John is the name that has most frequently been chosen.

Once the new pope has made clear his acceptance and name, the canopies in the Sistine Chapel of all the cardinals are lowered in deference to him, only his own remaining aloft. He is led to a small room near the chapel where three white silk soutanes of different sizes are laid out; he chooses the nearest fit and exchanges this for his purple woollen soutane. He puts on the white silk sash, the lace rochet, the embroidered red silk slippers, a scarlet shoulder cape and velvet cap—almost the same clothes in which he will be dressed for his eventual lying-in-state. Newly robed, he returns to the chapel to receive the first homage of the cardinals, who kiss his hand and receive from him the kiss of peace. The Chamberlain puts the Fisherman's Ring on his finger; he returns it immediately so that his regnal name may be engraved around the rim. The homage ends with the singing of the *Te Deum*. The senior cardinal-deacon then goes to the central balcony of St Peter's to announce the 'great joy' and give the new pope's name. The pontiff himself then appears to give his first apostolic blessing *Urbi et Orbi*: to the City and the World.

The coronation takes place shortly after the election. *Sic transit gloria mundi*, he is reminded in the course of the service; wool is burned before his eyes to show the transitory nature of human life. He is reminded of something else, too. As the senior cardinal-deacon places the tiara on his head, he says to the new pope: 'Receive the tiara with the three crowns, and know that thou art the Father of kings and princes, the Pastor of the Universe and the Vicar on earth of Our Lord Jesus Christ, to Whom belong honour and glory, world without end.' St Bernard's famous stricture comes to mind: 'Wouldst thou be taken for the successor of Constantine rather than the successor of Peter?'

The crown is the symbol of temporal power. Evidence is scarce as to the precise origin of the papal crown, except that we know that popes wore a distinctive headgear from the early eighth century. The first pope said to have been crowned was Nicholas I, who ruled from 858 to 867. The mid-ninth century is an appropriate moment in papal history for the adoption of so secular a symbol. Nicholas I was a strong-minded pontiff, quite aware of the responsibilities of his position. He had a serious dispute with the Eastern Church; in the West he was forced to vigorous measures to uphold his authority. The Franks were no longer able to provide the temporal support he sought. His assuming a crown of his own was understandable. It was not yet a triple crown—this was not to appear until the early fourteenth century—but, certainly, not later than the eleventh century a coronet had appeared around the lower rim of the white Phrygian cap called a *camelaucum*, worn as a sign of the papal prerogative since at least the early eighth century. With Boniface VIII, at the end of the fifteenth century, a second coronet was added—possibly to symbolise the Papacy's two-fold authority, spiritual and temporal. Either Benedict XI (1303–4) or his successor Clement V (1305–16) added the third coronet. By the fifteenth century, it had taken on its present beehive shape. The ceremony of crowning is held on the balcony of St Peter's; but he is Supreme Pontiff from the moment of his acceptance of election in the Sistine Chapel.

* * *

The pope and the cardinals: this is the firmament from which the elements fall to the Church beneath. The pope is the creation of the Sacred College; the cardinals are the direct creation of the pope, and they go on to choose the next pope. The Sacred College is both advisory and executive.

There is no doctrinal reason for the existence of the Sacred College of Cardinals. It is the product of history and habit. Any pope could disband it or change its functions; but it is unlikely that any pope will do so, for it has become an integral and useful part of the organisation of the Holy See. The total number of the College was fixed at seventy in 1586 by the great organising pope, Sixtus V. John XXIII broke with this convention at his first consistory, and Paul VI has continued to maintain a larger College. By mid-1967, there were 118 cardinals (an unprecedented number), of whom thirty-nine were resident in Rome.

Part of its membership consists of archbishops who rule some of the most important sees. Seven diocesan archbishops in Italy have the rank of cardinal: Florence, Milan, Venice, Genoa, Bologna, Turin and Naples. Normally, Palermo can expect to have a cardinal-archbishop; in this case, however, the present incumbent was appointed to his see at the consistory of June 1967. By similar tradition—sometimes long-established and sometimes relatively recent—certain sees outside Italy are regarded as almost automatically cardinalatial: for instance, Vienna, New York, Westminster. It is true that Pius XII never made Montini a cardinal, for all that he appointed him archbishop of Milan; but Pius XII was a pope who left much undone at his death. The other part of the College's membership comprises cardinals belonging to the Roman Curia; that is, they live in Rome and take part in the administration of the Church. They are the nearest equivalent to government ministers in a secular state that the pope has in his ecclesiastical government.

THE CURIA

The Roman Curia is one of the most excoriated institutions devised by the minds of men, inspired or otherwise. It has not only incensed anti-clericals and sensationalist commentators who have found it insufferable. So did St Bernard, and so did the majority of the prelates at the last Ecumenical Council. Like so much else at the Vatican, it is the creature of historical accident, genuine piety and, humanly, quite astounding pretension.

It has three main divisions: the Sacred Congregations, the Offices and the Tribunals. Though these titles might suggest respectively a legislature, an executive and a judicial branch, so lay a categorisation would properly apply only to the third main group. Some of the Congregations, however, have judicial powers; as far as legislative and executive functions are concerned, there is no clear distinction in the government of the Roman Church. Some 3,000 clerics and laymen, all told, are employed in the day-to-day running of these administrative departments.

Congregations

The Sacred Congregations are committees of cardinals charged with the dispatch of business in a particular field of the Church's activities. Each of them has a specialised staff. The cardinal who is head of a Congregation presides at its meetings, and is known as the Prefect. The head of three Congregations, however, is the pope himself: Doctrine of the Faith, Bishops (formerly Consistorial), and Eastern Churches. Until the curial reform of 1967 the pope's 'cardinal deputy' was called Pro-Prefect, but in that year Paul VI abolished these three pro-prefectures, and the term is retained only to signify the acting head of a Congregation whose Prefect is ill or senile.

The first of these commissions of cardinals to have a permanent character was the Sacred Congregation of the Inquisition, established by Paul III on 21 July 1542 to combat heresy. Others followed, and Sixtus V, in his Apostolic Constitution *Immensa* (1587), founded the system which has survived substantially to the present day—though later popes added new features or made modifications of the basic pattern. The pre-eminence among Congregations has remained with this first commission—known also as the Holy Office—formed to protect faith and morals. It enjoyed the title of Supreme Sacred Congregation until Paul VI introduced his first reforms in late 1965, whereby its title was changed to Congregation for the Doctrine of the Faith. By changing its name, bringing in some new officials and liberalising some of its procedures, Paul did what he could to meet public opinion without going so far as to reform it radically or to abolish the chilling institution altogether—which would have been a popular measure among liberal Roman Catholics, both clerical and lay. Even so, his abolition of the office of Commissioner, or Inquisitor (which had always been held by a Dominican) reveals an awareness on his part of a strong current of thought in the Church which seeks for changes in institutional structure to reflect and guarantee the change in Catholic attitudes exemplified by the Second Vatican Council.

Quite clearly, the field of this Congregation is the most important of all to an ecclesiastical administration which for centuries has struggled to preserve and define Roman orthodoxy. Had it gone, something would have had to be put in its place; but a new body would possibly have been less forbidding than the institution whose methods of rigorous secrecy, whose private hearings of alleged misdemeanours or studies of doubtful books and teachings, allowed the accused no opportunity to answer or defend himself. Moreover, its effective leadership, until Paul brought into it a fresher element from outside, was in the hands of prelates of the most traditionalist mentality. The most authoritarian of the Church's institutions was controlled by men of the most narrowly authoritarian outlook, even though they often pleaded that, if only everyone knew the exquisite care with which every case was dealt, there would be no complaint. Authoritarianism and obscurantism, however, tend to go together in the public mind, even today when there is less ground for grim suspicion because its methods have undoubtedly been modified and improved.

The Apostolic Constitution *Regimini Ecclesiæ Universæ* of 1967 reduced the number of Congregations from eleven to nine.

1. The *Sacred Congregation for the Doctrine of the Faith* is, since 1965, the successor of the Inquisition and the Holy Office, watching over faith and morals. Its Pro-Prefect in 1967 was Cardinal Alfredo Ottaviani.

2. The *Sacred Congregation of the Bishops* is, since 1967, the successor to the *Consistorial Congregation* (founded in 1588 and charged with preparing the agenda for consistories of cardinals: the meetings at which the pope discusses business with members of the Sacred College). Its functions can be briefly summarised as the handling of matters directly touching bishops and dioceses, save in cases where mission territories or the Eastern Rite communions are involved. The creation of new dioceses and the redistribution of boundaries come within its competence. Its Pro-Prefect in 1967 was Cardinal Carlo Confalonieri.

3. The *Sacred Congregation for the Eastern Churches* (founded in 1862) deals with the special problems of the Churches of the Eastern Rite which are in communion with Rome.* These Churches, most of which are in the Middle East, North Africa and the Balkans, follow their own rites but retain loyalty to Rome, thereby distinguishing themselves from the bulk of the Churches of Eastern Christianity which, since the Great Schism of 1047, have refused to recognise the authority over them of the Roman pontiff. The Pro-Prefect in 1967 was Cardinal Gustavo Testa.

4. The *Sacred Congregation for the Sacraments* (founded in 1908) watches over the rite, the doctrines and the administration of the sacraments of the Church. Much of its work concerns the granting (by executive, not judicial, decision) of dispensations in the case of marriages which have not been consummated, and the granting of dispensations to priests who wish to leave their orders. In the case of marriages claimed to be unconsummated, the local bishop (without expressing an opinion) sends all the details—documents, testimonies and so on—to the Congregation. Here they are handled in a way that is typical of the Vatican's administrative

* These 'Uniate Churches', as they are sometimes called, comprise in the Levant; the Maronites; the Syrians of the Antioch patriarchate; the Malabarese (a branch of the Malabar Christians of south-west India); the Armenians of the Cilicia patriarchate; the Chaldeans in Turkey and Persia with a group of Malabarese following the Chaldean Rite; a branch of the Coptic Church and of the Ethiopians. Uniate Churches of the Byzantine Rite are: the Polish Ruthenians; the Hungarians; the Yugoslavs; the Podcarpathian Ruthenians; the Rumanians; the Melchites of Syria and Egypt; some Bulgars; and a large body of Ukrainians, who, however, were forcibly separated from Rome in 1946.

machinery: a kind of trial in which the two sides of the case are argued fully. Just as part of the process of declaring saints consists of hearing the Devil's advocate, so in these cases a defender of the marriage bond is heard who must produce all the reasons why the marriage should be regarded as valid. If the Congregation decides that the marriage has not been consummated, it passes its recommendation with a report to the pope, who may grant the dispensation if he thinks fit. If the Congregation considers that a judicial point is involved, it can present the case to the Sacred Roman Rota (see page 164 below). The Prefect of this Congregation in 1967 was Cardinal Aloisi Masella; the Pro-Prefect was Cardinal Francesco Carpino.

5. The *Sacred Congregation for the Clergy* was founded in 1564 to interpret and apply the decisions of the Council of Trent. 'Today', as the *Pontifical Yearbook* blandly puts it, 'the task of interpreting the canons of the celebrated Council no longer exists.' No, indeed, but the Congregation does. Though it had no part in the preparation of the Second Vatican Council, it has retained competence over certain matters which were the object of Tridentine reforms. It keeps watch over the discipline of the lower clergy and of the faithful, rather as the Consistorial Congregation deals with the higher clergy; it directs catechetical instruction, and retains the right (granted by Sixtus V) to revise the acts of provincial councils and episcopal conferences. Its Prefect in 1967 was Cardinal Jean Villot.

6. The *Sacred Congregation of the Religious* (founded in 1586) deals with questions affecting religious orders and communities, and examines the statutes of new foundations. Its Prefect in 1967 was Cardinal Ildebrando Antoniutti.

7. The *Sacred Congregation for the Propagation of the Faith* originated from a commission of cardinals set up by Gregory XIII (1572–85) to promote reconciliation with the Eastern schismatics; but under Gregory XV (1621–3) and thereafter, it assumed responsibility for the newly discovered lands. Missionary work is its main concern. It functions where there is no regularly established hierarchy and, in principle, its role ends when in a given country or area under its control an episcopal hierarchy is set up on a regular basis. Its Prefect in 1967 was Cardinal Gregory Agagianian.

8. The *Sacred Congregation of Rites* (founded in 1588) is responsible for questions of liturgy and worship, for canonisation and for anything pertaining to relics. Its Prefect in 1967 was Cardinal Arcadio Larraona.

9. The *Sacred Congregation for Catholic Teaching* (founded in 1588 and until 1967 called the Congregation for Seminaries and Studies) deals with the maintenance of standards in ecclesiastical institutions of education. Its Prefect in 1967 was Cardinal Giuseppe Pizzardo, and the Pro-Prefect was Monsignor Gabriel Gardone.

Paul VI's curial reform—the third in the Church's history—reduced the number of Congregations from eleven to nine, abolishing Ceremonies, and Extraordinary Ecclesiastical Affairs. Two other changes were potentially of far greater importance. By *Pro Comperto Sane*, a *motu proprio* of August 1967, he allowed residential bishops to come to Rome to attend the plenary sessions of Congregations when matters of great weight are being discussed. The general reform, set out in the Apostolic Constitution *Regimini Ecclesiæ Universæ*, also of August 1967, introduced a system of occasional meetings of heads of Congregations under the chairmanship of the Cardinal-Secretary of State. This innovation gave the Vatican something akin to a cabinet, or council of ministers, meeting under a prime minister. For the first time, departmental heads might be asked to agree to a decision binding on all of them—a step at least towards collective responsibility, and also a step towards devising a form of administration which could function for short periods without the pope. At the same time, he placed the financial administration of the Church on a less unwieldy basis by bringing its various departments (see page 166) under a committee of three cardinals whose first president was Cardinal Angelo Dell' Acqua. Another innovation was an office of statistics, which can be imagined as appealing to the precise mind of Paul.

This general reform was, on the whole, disappointing to those who had hoped for a modern reorganisation of the old structure. It contained some potentially important ideas, but judgement of them must await evidence of their practical implementation.

Offices

Of what are called the Offices, two are no longer important and the third has lately been abolished. The fourth, the Secretariat of State, is extremely important. To dispose of the three: the *Apostolic Chancellery* today is concerned with the preparation of official documents, but it was once, before the administrative system devised in the late sixteenth century, the main organ of papal policy. The post of Cardinal-Chancellor was vacant in 1967.

The *Apostolic Chamber* (or *Camera*) takes over the curial administration during the *sede vacante*, the period between the death of a pope and the election of his successor. It originally dealt with the revenues and property of the Holy See, but this is now in the hands of other bodies (see pages 166–9 below) and its normal administrative work is slight, except during the inter-regnum. Its present head is Cardinal Benedetto Aloisi Masella, the Chamberlain of the Church. Each of these two bodies can hardly be regarded as a major part of the central government since they do not possess powers of real decision, except for the Apostolic Chamber during the inter-regnum.

The *Apostolic Datary* was abolished under the curial reform of 1967. It was originally set up to validate official documents and end the circulation of forged papal texts; later it took on the responsibility of handling some rather special ecclesiastical appointments. It chose candidates for certain benefices in which substantial property was involved or legacies and trusts had to be administered by the priest. These appointments were reserved to the Holy See, and it was for the Cardinal-Datary to find the right men for them, usually priests with business or administrative sense. The Datary also fixed such matters as the contributions to be made to poorer parishes and the payment of pensions, often to the parents or other close relations of a priest who had died in poverty. Its last head was Cardinal Paolo Giobbè.

The *Secretariat of State* is the hub of the Curia. This Office has at its head the Cardinal-Secretary, the pope's chief minister: a man completely identified with his master's policy whether in foreign affairs or at home. (He has the immense advantage over the Congregations in that he is the only cardinal in the Secretariat.) Charged with relations with civil powers, the Cardinal-Secretary is yet more than a foreign minister; and since he may be called on to deal with almost any subject which is on the pope's mind, he is also more than a prime minister. He is, or should be, the leading personality in the Vatican after the pope himself. The Secretary of State can also have a decisive influence on the making of policy. This is clear from the contributions made by such relatively recent holders of the office as Rampolla (1887–1903), Merry del Val (1903–14) and Gasparri (1914–30). It is also clear from the fact that Pius XII kept the secretaryship in his own hands during the second half of his pontificate, no doubt because he did not want to be called on to cope with the formative influence of another mind in the course of papal business.* And Paul VI, whose long years in the Secretariat gave him a detailed knowledge of affairs, was virtually acting as his own Secretary of State during the papal diplomatic effort, inaugurated in 1964, to achieve peace in Vietnam. The Secretary of State at this time was Cardinal Cicognani, who was over eighty and had been appointed originally by John, not by Paul. The 1967 reform enhanced the Secretary's office by making him chairman of the new Council for Public Affairs.

The office of Cardinal-Secretary is usually traced to two sources: the private staff of the popes, the secretariat, handling the most delicate business; and the institution of the 'Cardinal-Nephew', which for several centuries overshadowed the private secretariat and its chief, the *Secretarius Domesticus*. A private secretariat, issuing correspondence sealed with the Fisherman's Ring instead of a bull-seal, was at work by the mid-thirteenth century. Benedict XII (1334–42) established the formal Secretariat, distinct from the Apostolic Chancellery, to look after secret correspondence. As the pope's correspondence became more heavy, other secretarial offices appeared, such as the Secret Chamber instituted by Martin V (1417–31) and the Apostolic Secretariat for official correspon-

---

* Pacelli was appointed Secretary of State in February 1930; thus, from 1930 to 1958, there were only five years (1939–44) when the same man did not hold the office.

dence in Latin. This last was given formal shape by Innocent VIII with the Apostolic Constitution *Non Debet Reprehensibile* of 31 December 1487. The Apostolic Secretariat consisted of twenty-four secretaries, the chief of whom was to serve as liaison with the other secretaries, live at the pope's residence and be constantly at his beck and call. It was this functionary whom the Venetian ambassadors in the early sixteenth century went out of their way to cultivate, since he had the ear and the confidence of the pope.

At much the same time, the institution of the 'Cardinal-Nephew' took shape, which for more than a century was to control the Secretariat and much else besides. Essentially, it meant that a pope on his election appointed a close relative to the cardinalate, placing in hands he could trust the conduct of much of the papal business. It was to this relative that the pope's diplomatic representatives abroad reported. A powerful Cardinal-Nephew would overshadow the Secretary, though this second office was to survive the Nephew's passing into a rather tainted oblivion. The move to abolish him began in 1644. The Conclave that elected Innocent X (1644–55) expressed sharp criticisms of the abuses of the post. The new pope followed the custom of making his closest relative a cardinal, but did not give him the supervision of foreign policy. This went instead to an experienced man already a member of the Sacred College, Cardinal Pancirolo. The unpopularity of the post rose to its final height in the reign of Clement X (1670–6) whose Nephew (in fact the uncle of the pope's niece's husband) aroused great resentment by his lack of adroitness. The next pope, Innocent XI (1676–89) named none of his family to the Sacred College. In 1692, Innocent XII abolished nepotism completely with his bull *Romanum Decet Pontificem*. Henceforward, formally as well as in fact, the Secretary had a clear field. He had already taken over much of the business performed earlier by the Cardinal-Nephew.

There remains, of course, the inevitable question of whether the Secretary is dealing with the Vatican's affairs because of the pope's temporal sovereignty or because of his spiritual authority. The distinction was never made, either before or after the loss of the Papal States. The confusion, as Napoleon noticed, was useful to the Holy See, which could back one aspect of papal authority with the other whenever this might prove convenient. On 11 June 1809, two French officers belonging to Napoleon's army of occupation entered the Quirinal Palace, then the pope's urban summer residence,* sealed the files of the Secretariat of State and gave the Pro-Secretary, Cardinal Gabrielli, two days to leave Rome. In his protest, Pius VII said: 'This minister is not only the political minister of a temporal prince, but also the minister of a sovereign whose primary attribute is to be the Head of the Church.' The affronted minister, the pope went on, 'is not merely responsible for the administration of the temporal concerns of this sovereign but also of the spiritual interests of the whole Catholic world.'

Even with the Papal States gone and the Papacy's claims to universal sovereignty much limited, the confusion remains. The Cardinal-Secretary deals with the diplomatic corps accredited to the Holy See, and is in contact with the nunciatures abroad. A papal diplomatic service might seem more temporal than spiritual, especially as its beginnings in the time of the Renaissance were very much identified with the pope's position as a prince. But the Vatican now regards the diplomatists accredited to it as there, not because the pontiff is head of a tiny state in Rome, but because of his spiritual position; that is why ambassadors are sent to the one religious organisation in the world that exchanges diplomatic envoys. The principal curial argument is that the Vatican does not have a foreign policy as such; it is simply that, by diplomatic means, it seeks to promote the conditions whereby souls may be saved. Talleyrand, himself an ecclesiastic though not, of course, in the Vatican's foreign service, would have had a little more difficulty than usual in preserving his composure if faced directly with an affirmation of that kind.

The Secretariat is housed on the third floor of the Apostolic Palace. Its present organisational structure dates from Pius X's Constitution *Sapienti Consilio* of 29 June 1908. (That its modern form should have emerged in the reign of a pope said to have thought of abolishing the whole system of papal diplomacy is

---

* The Quirinal was the summer palace. After 1870, the Quirinal was taken over by the monarchy of United Italy. Castelgandolfo, used since about 1623, is the pope's country house and villa.

endearingly paradoxical.) The Office has three departments: the first deals with what are called extraordinary ecclesiastical matters, and is more or less identical in staff with the Congregation of the same name; the second department handles ordinary ecclesiastical matters; and the third dispatches documents or briefs under the direction of the Chancellor for Apostolic Briefs. The staff is over one hundred strong, its members belonging to one of two categories, administrative or diplomatic. The administrators have the title either of *Minutante* or of *Attaché*. The grades of members of the diplomatic service are: attaché of nunciature, secretary of nunciature, auditor of nunciature and counsellor of nunciature. The rank of attaché is normally held for a year; the rank of secretary of nunciature is held for six years, three of which are in a major mission. Similarly, the post of auditor is held for six years, with three spent in an important mission. There is no time-limit to the post of counsellor.*

Apostolic Nuncios, the equivalent of ambassadors, go abroad not only with the prestige of belonging to a unique service—they are ambassadors of Christ's representative—but usually with the personal rank of archbishop. This is arranged by giving them one of the titular archbishoprics at the pope's disposal. It is a way of according them archiepiscopal rank without diocesan responsibilities. The practice has been criticised of late, perhaps inevitably, because the development of the responsibility of bishops in the government of the Church has made them more jealous of the dignity and meaning of episcopal orders. Hence, objections are raised against a system that offers this dignity as a form of bureaucratic convenience. The 'titular see' is, nevertheless, quite an ancient institution. The origins are traceable to the mid-fifth century, though its real development followed the expulsion of so many bishops by the Saracens during the Muslim advance in the eighth and ninth centuries, by the pagan advances in the Baltic in the thirteenth century, and by those of the Turks after the fall of the Holy Land. These bishops were accepted as auxiliaries by their

* The equivalent grades in civil diplomacy are: attaché, third and second secretary (for secretary of nunciature), first secretary (for auditor), and counsellor (for the curial title of the same name).

colleagues in the West. As they died, other bishops were consecrated to the same sees, despite the fact that these were now in territories which had become non-Christian—*in partibus infidelium* as they were called until Leo XIII ruled in 1882 that they be referred to simply as 'titular bishoprics'. These titles of non-existent sees are not limited to nuncios; they are used throughout the Curia to give rank to civil servants, and sometimes purely as a useful device. Paul VI, for instance, used it when objection was made to the presence of one of his theological advisers, Monsignor Carlo Colombo, at the meetings of the Italian episcopate during the Second Vatican Council; he made him a titular bishop.

The presence of a nuncio in a capital city can raise a delicate problem, since the Vatican insists that he be automatically accepted as the dean of the diplomatic corps, regardless of his seniority. Not all countries accept this; Britain, for example, does not. To resolve the problem, the Holy See sends to such countries, not a fully-fledged nuncio, but a representative with the rank (created in 1965) of *Pro-Nuncio*. This carries with it the full authority of ambassador but does not call for the automatic deanship of the corps. By devising this modified form of nunciate in the last few years, the Papacy has been able to follow the general international tendency of making full embassies the normal level of diplomatic relations. The two outstanding exceptions to the rule remain the United States and Britain. The first has no diplomatic mission to the Holy See, and the second maintains there a legation, not an embassy.

The Vatican's equivalent of a legation is an internunciature. The *Internuncio* is a more recent phenomenon than the nuncio, but much older than the pro-nuncio. The name goes back to the seventeenth century, when it was used to describe papal representatives dispatched to nunciatures where, for some reason or other, a nuncio could not for the moment be sent. It is now simply the equivalent of a diplomatic minister at the head of a mission. Like legations, internunciatures are gradually being eliminated; the internuncios are being replaced by pro-nuncios, and the legations by embassies.

The third kind of papal representative abroad is the *Apostolic Delegate*. Both Britain and the United States have such representatives of the Holy See. Technically speaking, they are not diplomatic representatives and are not accredited to the court or presidency of the country in which they reside. Nor are they compatible with legates, who are appointed to represent the pope for a particular purpose—as Cardinal Heenan was, for example, at the opening of the new Roman Catholic cathedral in Liverpool in May 1967. Their dealings are officially limited to the local hierarchy and the faithful. Hence, they do not claim the deanship of the diplomatic corps, like a nuncio; and their presence need not be reciprocated (there is an apostolic delegate in Washington but the United States has no mission in Rome). For all that, they are, in effect, as much the Vatican's emissaries as those who claim diplomatic status. Like nuncios and internuncios, they keep the Curia informed of affairs in the country to which they are posted, and watch over the local hierarchy. One of the tasks of nuncios and delegates is to send recommendations to Rome about candidates for vacant sees in the countries concerned.

Vatican diplomacy is widespread. There are fifty-one missions and seventeen delegations, with diplomatic status accredited to governments, as well as observers and delegates, some of a permanent character, with international organisations. These are the Vatican's principal links with international affairs. At the same time, bishops are obliged to pay periodic visits to Rome to report *ad limine apostolorum*—to the threshold of the apostles; thereby they provide another source of information about what is happening in the world.

The three departments of the Secretariat have separate functions which are not too clearly distinguishable. The first deals with relations with civil powers and business arising from concordats, unless such business falls within the competence of a Congregation. This department looks rather like a Foreign Office. It is the second department, however, which handles correspondence with the nuncios and delegates. It refers requests received from diplomatists accredited to the Holy See to the competent body in the Curia. It proposes likely candidates from among whom the pope might wish to choose nuncios or legates. Catholic Action and its affiliated organisations come within its competence. The third department deals with compiling and transcribing the final drafts of papal briefs. The Secretariat has sections divided on the basis of language: English, French, German, Italian, Portuguese and Spanish. The working language is Italian. The pope normally writes to heads of state in Latin. Preparation of these letters is one of the duties of the ancient Secretariat of Briefs to Princes which formed a separate section of the Secretariat until 1967, when its status was greatly reduced.

Almost all of the more responsible work is left in the hands of the Italians. Cardinal Tardini was said to find real Romans, not just Italians, the proper people to employ. (He was very Roman himself.) Young Anglo-Saxons are inclined to be unhappy at the Curia. A lack of responsibility can be as upsetting as too much of it, and the strain becomes intolerable after years of being left with no greater decision to make than how to end a formal letter of acknowledgment. It is often supposed that the Secretariat of State is brilliantly informed through its secret channels and its highly trained staff of devoted celibates. One's impression is that a great deal of hard work goes into the business of keeping the Papacy informed, and that a great deal less time and money is wasted than is the case with normal embassies. But there are other problems not faced by the ordinary diplomatist and civil servant. Heads of curial departments can become disastrously narrow and difficult in dealing with staff; one junior member of a diplomatic mission abroad, for instance, had to tolerate the absurd accusations of a venerable superior who had persuaded himself that his subordinate was purloining the petty cash.

The Secretariat has about it the strange air of activity combined with fustiness that is so typical of the papal palaces. Officials do not receive their visitors in their own offices but in a series of waiting rooms. Until Paul VI early in 1967 ordered a redecoration of the Secretariat in a predominantly beige-and-grey scheme, they were furnished and decorated in a unique style which combined gloom with a heavy sentimentality.* The walls were invariably

---

* Paul's characteristic colour-scheme of grey and beige has been applied throughout his official rooms and in his private apartment, as well as in the reception rooms of the Secretariat of State.

dark if not panelled or lined with ageing damask, the chairs liberally supplied with coverlets of lace made originally, perhaps, by devoted nuns. The pictures were engagingly mawkish: a piously holy face, or a rainbow over the dome of St Peter's with the world around lashed by a furious storm. It was a great-aunt's idea from hearsay of a club sitting-room, with some accessory decoration of an improving kind. There is no reason, of course, why a place with such an atmosphere should not be the collecting point of the finest intelligence in the world; but, somehow, one feels the legend to have been exaggerated.

Tribunals

The third group of curial bodies consists of the three tribunals: the Apostolic Penitentiary, the Sacred Roman Rota and the Supreme Tribunal of the Apostolic Signature. Their concern is with canon law: the written code of ecclesiastical rules governing faith, morals and discipline. The corpus of Roman canon law has grown slowly since the very early days of the alliance between Empire and Christianity, its origins being traceable to the first Councils. The Council of Nicaea, for instance, in 325 promulgated a series of twenty miscellaneous canons, which were to possess a certain primacy because of the high standing that Council enjoyed. Added to them were sets of canons devised by later Councils. There is evidence that, by the middle of the fifth century, collections of these canons were already in existence. With them were associated decrees of particularly outstanding bishops, these forming a further source of early ecclesiastical regulation. The letters of popes naturally enjoyed a special authority. The fourth and fifth centuries brought the ascription of sets of canons to fictitious authors, such as the so-called *Apostolic Canons* and those attributed to St Hippolytus. In Charlemagne's time, a start was made in standardisation, and the following generation certainly had its trained canonists. The decisive stage came in about 1140, when the jurist Gratian issued his *Decretum*. It was a private collection, not an officially sanctioned text, but such was its prestige and gradually accruing authority that it is taken to be a dividing line in the history of ecclesiastical law. Before it was the old law, *jus antiquum*; after it came the new law, *jus novum*; and what followed the sixteenth-century Council of Trent is regarded as the modern law, *ius novissimum*. The standard text of canon law is that issued in 1917. Cardinal Gasparri, then Secretary of State, had a large hand in the work, in which he was assisted by Eugenio Pacelli, the future Pius XII. It contained 2,414 canons, and came into force at Pentecost in 1918.

The *Apostolic Penitentiary* deals with problems of conscience and, since May 1917, with indulgences and with ecclesiastical sanctions reserved to the pope for punishing particularly serious crimes concerning the Host, such as its profanation in black masses. It is one of the few organs which continue to function during the vacancy between the death of one pope and the election of his successor, and the Cardinal-Penitentiary is the only member of the College with the right to remain in contact with his office during a Conclave.* Any member of the Church can apply to the Penitentiary and ask for a ruling on questions of conscience. The more usual procedure, however, is to go to one's personal confessor, who sends the details of the problem to the tribunal without revealing the name of the person seeking its advice. Fictitious names are used. The reply is sent to the confessor, but enclosed is a second, sealed envelope to be given to the penitent. It is normally opened by the confessor or by a priest on a recommended list approved by the bishop. Unlike most bodies connected with the Vatican, the Penitentiary in its dealings with matters of conscience attempts to move with all possible speed. Its head in 1967 was Cardinal Giuseppe Feretto.

The *Sacred Roman Rota* is the best known of the tribunals because much of its time is taken up by hearing requests for annulling marriages. It has twelve judges who sit in rotation under a Dean (although this is not the origin of its name). It sits *in camera*. The judges are all prelates, but lay advocates learned in canon law may plead before it. This court began as an extension of the Apostolic Chancery, being charged with the preparation of causes

---

* 'The mystery of the charity of God ... tolerates no interruption.' P. C. Van Lierde, *Dietro il Portone di Bronzo*, Rome 1961.

brought to that body. It was Innocent III who empowered it to pass sentence. John XXII gave it permanent headquarters and, in 1331, with the Constitution *Ratio Juris*, it acquired a set of special regulations. The name probably came from the circular hall in which the auditors met to hear causes. In 1472, Sixtus IV fixed the number of chaplain-auditors at twelve. Benedict XIV determined its jurisdiction definitively in his Constitution *Justitiæ et Pacis* of 1747. The appointment of auditors is reserved to the pope but their nomination used to be permitted to some nations and city-states. Thus, Spain nominated two, Germany and France one each; and Milan, Venice, Bologna, Ferrara and Perugia each nominated one. Under Gregory XVI (1831–46), with an apparent disregard for the distinction between the pope's government of the Church and his rule over papal principality, the Sacred Rota was made a tribunal of appeal for the Papal States. (It remains to this day the tribunal of appeal for the Vatican City.) Its main function now is as the tribunal of appeal for all the ecclesiastical causes in which the Roman Curia is competent and which are not reserved to other jurisdictions—the Holy Office, for instance—and it is the tribunal of first instance in cases reserved to the Holy See or which the pope reserves to himself. The only ultimate appeal from its decisions is to the Apostolic Signature. Its Dean in 1967 was Monsignor Francis Brennan.

The *Supreme Tribunal of the Apostolic Signature* derives its name from the preparation of petitions, usually relating to pardons, for the papal signature. It has existed as a permanent section of the Curia since the reign of Eugenius IV (1431–47), who expected its members to decide cases themselves, thus giving it the character of a higher court. With the setting up of the Congregations and the widening of the Rota's competence, the Signature became less important. It eventually became a court of cassation, judging whether the proper juridical forms had been observed in ecclesiastical courts: a task which Gregory XVI extended in 1834 to cover the Papal States. It owes to Pius X its present form as a committee of cardinals and its character as a supreme tribunal. It is possible to appeal to the Signature against a verdict of the Rota, and it settles differences between ecclesiastical courts of all grades.

Paul VI in 1967 gave it the task of settling conflicts of competence between curial departments. Its head in 1967 was Cardinal Francesco Roberti; the Pro-Prefect was Cardinal Dino Staffa.

SPECIAL SECRETARIATS

To these three main groups of curial institutions—Congregations, Offices and Tribunals—has been added a fourth group consisting of the Special Secretariats established by John XXIII and Paul VI. These deal, respectively, with Christian unity, with non-Christians, and with non-believers in general.

The first of them, the *Secretariat for Promoting Christian Unity*, which was set up as part of the preparatory work of the recent Council, has already made its mark on the history of Church government. From the beginning, its was presided over by Cardinal Agostino Bea, who was directly responsible to the pope. Of all branches of the Curia, it has been the one with the most consistently optimistic and forward-looking approach. The second, the *Secretariat for Non-Christians*, was established in May 1964 under the direction of Cardinal Paolo Marella; and the third, the *Secretariat for Non-Believers*, came into being in April 1965 under Cardinal Franziskus König, archbishop of Vienna, who is one of the outstanding reforming members of the Sacred College. He accepted the post on the condition that he could remain in Vienna rather than reside in Rome. He has been blamed for this by some reformers on the ground that, once again, a progressively minded senior prelate has preferred to stay away from Rome rather than abide on the spot to press through his ideas at the centre of the Church. Others, however, have praised him for setting a pattern of decentralisation.

Financial Administration

The least revealing of all the sections of the curial administration are the bodies administering the Vatican's finances. They were grouped under a committee of cardinals in 1967 into what is now called the Prefecture of the Economy.

A good many attempts have been made to procure estimates of

how much the Holy See is worth; but, apart from an occasional grumble among members of the Curia that outsiders' estimates are 'absurdly high', there is never a constructive observation from within on which any reliable calculation can be based. Why there should be this secrecy is difficult to explain, short of accepting the suggestion that either the Vatican's holdings are so vast that it is better they be not revealed, lest this prejudice the willingness of the faithful to give aid to their Church, or that they are invested in sectors of economic activity (particularly in Italy) smacking too highly of sheer speculation—and, may be, of dubious exploitation.

From its earliest days, as an adjunct of the Roman Empire, the Papacy has known what it is to have great properties. The loss of its territories ended the pope's revenues from taxation of his immediate subjects. The Papacy had never clearly distinguished between revenues and expenditure from its own temporality and those of the Church as such. One result of the financial confusion after the loss of Rome was Leo XIII's establishment in 1878 of an administration to look after what was left of the property of the Holy See. It first took the form of the pope's appointing his Secretary of State, Cardinal Nina, to carry out this work. Subsequently, he appointed a committee of cardinals to supervise both Peter's Pence and property, allowing this body wide discretionary powers. These included the liberty to conduct financial operations connected with the Holy See's assets. In 1926, Pius XI increased its competence by placing among its responsibilities the running of the Apostolic Palaces and of the administrative sections of the Congregations and Offices. This body is known as the *Administration of the Properties of the Holy See*. At the head of it is Cardinal Alberto Di Jorio.

Historically, the Administration of the Properties is the first of the main financial-administrative bodies to have been established, but a younger body, the *Special Administration*, is even more important in regard to finance. It was set up by Pius XI in 1929 after the signing of the Lateran Pacts, which had included a financial settlement with Italy. The Italian state had earlier, shortly after the taking of Rome, offered the popes an annual subsidy which they refused to accept. In 1929, as part of the establishment of the Vatican City as a sovereign state, the Italian government paid 1,500 million lire in compensation for the loss of the Papal States. This sum, worth £20 million in 1929, was to become the main financial reserve of the Church. The Special Administration was formed to handle this money. Working in complete secrecy and responsible only to the pope, this body enjoys the privileges of paying no taxes and having at its disposal the resources of diplomatic missions throughout the world. Shrewd administration of this basic capital sum has made the Vatican one of the largest financial powers in the world. No balance sheets are ever published; no direct indication is ever given of where the Vatican has placed its wealth. It can be surmised, however, that the presence on the boards of Italian companies of such persons as Count Galeazzi, and Prince Carlo Pacelli (one of Pius XII's nephews) means that the Vatican holding therein is large. It seems clear that the Holy See is closely connected with building, banking, insurance, public services and large-scale public works.

Both of these administrations were, in 1967, presided over by Cardinal Cicognani, the Secretary of State. Much of the work of the Special Administration was carried out by Cardinal Di Jorio, who was also head of the *Institute for Works of Religion* set up by Pius XII in 1942 with the aim of 'providing for the safeguarding and administration of capital destined to religious works'. This institute is, in effect, the Vatican Bank, which functions much like any other bank. It can be regarded as the third financial arm of the Holy See. A fourth financial body is the *Pontifical Commission of the Vatican City-State*.* Its functions naturally entail as much pure administrative as financial work, but a good deal of money moves within its area of activities. The presiding officer was Cardinal Cicognani, with Cardinal Di Jorio as his acting-president; and the familiar figures of Count Galeazzi (Architect of the Sacred Palaces) and Prince Carlo Pacelli (General Adviser) were prominent

---

* There are a variety of Pontifical Commissions; they deal, among other matters, with biblical studies, canon law, sacred archaeology, the Pompeii Sanctuary, with cinema, radio and television, and—most recently—peace and justice.

in this delicate side of the Holy See's activities. We are here a long way from the Golden Rose and the formal discussion in cardinalatial committees of a miracle, a relic or a claim to sanctity.

The only open scandal so far to strike these financial-administrative offices occurred in 1948, when Monsignor Eduardo Prettner Cippico, a young priest working as an archivist in the Secretariat of State, was said to be involved in a series of complicated financial arrangements which ended in disaster. He had allegedly been transferring money abroad for Italian businessmen, and critics said that he had been avoiding currency regulations by making use of the channels of the Administration of the Properties of the Holy See. He was arrested in his office and locked inside the Vatican prison, the Tower of the Four Winds. His stay here was brief, for he escaped. Caught by the civil authorities, he was placed in the city prison of Rome, the Regina Cœli (Queen of Heaven). Tried and sentenced for swindling, he was subsequently released on the Court of Appeal's reversal of the sentence.

Recruitment to the Curia

It is not easy to set out clearly the modes of recruitment to the Curia. The classic beginning is study at the Roman Seminary, which has the right formalistic atmosphere and—not to mince words—the appropriately unadventurous style of education to prepare a young priest for one of the Sacred Congregations or other of the Curia's administrative departments. Both entrance to the Curia and preferment thereafter very often depend on the recommendation of an influential prelate. The present pope, for instance, had his entry into the Curia arranged by the then Monsignor Pizzardo. The patronage system has been encouraged by the lack of collective responsibility.

* * *

Personal influence at work within a system where there is little collective responsibility affects more weighty matters than the appointment of this or that priest to such-and-such post. The lack of collective responsibility means that the more personal influence a prelate has vertically and horizontally through the curial system, the more likely he is to make his views prevail.

The route taken by a particular proposal can control its destiny. An instance of this occurred in January 1967, when plans were presented for an ecumenical service in Rome to be attended by Catholics and non-Catholics. The year before, such a service had been held in a Catholic church; for 1967, it was proposed the service be held in a non-Catholic church: the Anglican church of All Saints in the Via Babuino. Quite properly, the request to proceed was put to the local bishop. The pope, of course, is the bishop of Rome, but the routine duties of the see are carried out by a vicar, Cardinal Traglia. The cardinal referred the matter to Cardinal Ottaviani at the Holy Office, who refused to grant permission. Seemingly, the 'proper' procedure would have been to ask the pope himself, since Rome, after all, is his diocese. Genuinely interested as he is in ecumenical matters, he could have been expected to give permission. There is, it is true, some argument that can be advanced on the ground that it would have been inconsiderate to bother the pope about this matter since at the time he was suffering from influenza; but it is not very convincing. When Paul realised the bad effect of Ottaviani's action, he reversed the decision; but by then it was too late to make the pope's permission applicable for that year. Such permission is limited to one year's duration; it seems that, as with applications to enter the Royal Enclosure at Ascot, permission is hard to come by and must be made by a certain person to a certain person by a certain time; otherwise. . . .

The question is not so much whether the Vatican is serious about ecumenical relations as the sad truth that an important and salutary decision may go the wrong way and come to naught if there is a 'defect' in the line of approach in putting the proposal into the curial machinery. The present pope clearly sees the seriousness of this problem. He did what he could to rectify a wrong decision—a decision based, as usual, on the argument that 'Rome is a special case'—yet he followed up his technical reversal of it with a friendly letter to Cardinal Ottaviani.

This is the crux of the problem of dealing with the Curia. For those outside, it is a matter of knowing to whom to turn who may be disposed and powerful enough to help a proposal through the system. For those inside, this *modus operandi* blurs policy and intentions unless there is predominant over the system a vigorous leadership and clear direction from the pontiff, who alone can move the whole apparatus on recognisably consistent lines. Or perhaps—and this is something which Paul VI has gone out of his way to deny—the very weight of work and the need to delegate have made the traditional structure of the Roman Curia inoperable for a modern spiritual and moral power, which is what the Papacy is trying to be.

The problem is not simply structural, however. The papal court is essentially religious, but it has taken its style and circumstance from secular models. Structurally, it is divided into two: the Papal Chapel and the Household. The first includes the prelates and dignitaries who take part in the more important religious ceremonies attended by the pope. The second consists of courtiers with duties in the papal entourage which are quite distinct from the liturgical rites in which the prelates of the Chapel are engaged. Around them are the bodies which handle the Church's affairs: the Congregations, the Offices, the Tribunals, the Administrations, the Commissions.

The pomp is diminishing. (Rumours of greater simplification bring protests, even from the leader columns of *The Times*.) But the mental effort of adjustment involved in seeing the same man fly to New York to address the United Nations and then being carried in procession as Vicar of Christ by crimson-clad bearers of the portable throne—this is becoming more of a strain. The notes of *Tu Es Petrus* and the invocations to the Holy Ghost are very firmly associated in many minds with a baroque splendour superimposed on a theocratic dignity of ancient origin. Protests against simplification from Rome itself are understandable enough; much of the style of the city is the style imposed on it by the popes, and it might seem unfair of them to change their ways since they have made the city to suit themselves. It has the mental atmosphere of worn velvet and of gold with an ochre tinge. It is in such an environment that there sparks in the Papacy the sporadic will to be as much at home in the contemporary world as it has been in the past. The task of adjustment is desperately difficult.

6
Walls of the Vatican

THE voluntary imprisonment of the popes in the Vatican after 1870 raised walls that had not been there before. The real plight of the pope was of a different kind from that which his apologists suggested, depicting a wronged sovereign awaiting the fall of the usurpers for justice to be done; and even more different from the postcards circulated among the faithful, showing Pius IX as an actual prisoner in poverty on a bed of straw. The ill-used pope needed help, so went the message. Indeed he did, but not alms. His temporality had gone, but his supremacy and infallibility were freshly minted dogma of great power; in this emotional atmosphere, the Apostolic Palaces became a hothouse for forcing the process of institutional growth. This is the real problem of the Curia. It has had a century of unnatural increase in its powers, growing beneath the shadow of the papal supremacy inside those walls which resentment helped to build. Recent popes have found that their executive arm, which is what the Curia is supposed to be, is more and more inclined to take over the making of policy. As such power increases, successive popes have greater difficulty in curbing pretensions or in preventing abuses of the papal prerogative.

Some may feel that, the problem being identified, little more needs saying before beginning the reform: a resolute cutting back; a few stern disciplinary warnings; some spiritual exhortation to the effect that to err is human but the less of it the better when the divine interests of the one true Church are involved. Unfortunately, it can no longer be so simple as that. For one reason, the action of any pope towards his civil service must be conditioned by its standing outside the real and metaphorical walls of the Vatican. As any one familiar with a great institution will appreciate, it is far more difficult to take it in hand when attacks from outside are fierce than when there is relative tranquillity. The debates at the Second Vatican Council showed how deep-rooted was the resentment against the Curia in many parts of the Church. It was expressed in two main ways. The first was simply the feeling that the whole apparatus was overcentralised; there was too much reference to Rome, and too little sensibility there towards local and regional problems which could be dealt with far better by the local hierarchy. The second was expressed in the belief that the procedures used in certain of the Congregations and in other curial agencies were wrong in themselves and even more so in the context of the modern age.

The high point in the criticism of curial procedures came on 8 November 1963, when Cardinal Frings, archbishop of Cologne, in the second session of the Council attacked the Holy Office as being out of keeping with modern thought and a cause for scandal. He said that no one should be judged and condemned without having been heard, without knowledge of exactly what he was accused of, and without the opportunity to amend what he could reasonably be reproached with. Frings was loudly applauded. The system was being challenged. More generally, the Italian predominance in the Curia was being challenged. Suspicion of curial motives was often automatic. If two or three men of the Curia were seen gathered together, it would be generally assumed that they were conspiring over something or other. Progressives often conferred in groups, but the general assumption was that they were engaged in something exquisitely honourable. In other words, the Curia was under pressure and on the defensive from the opening of the Council. It fought back hard, often successfully. Because of the tension between the would-be reformers and the declared guardians of the *status quo*, any pope would have his difficulties of enforcing reform greatly increased. He would have to take sides and, if a reformer, he would necessarily be on the side drawn up against the people with whom he was daily and personally in contact.

Everything that is done by the Curia is done for the good of the Church. This is a motivation that should not be forgotten however hypocritical the expression of it may seem to be. It is certainly not forgotten by curial prelates themselves when evolving policy or engaged in the less dignified activities—on occasion, one can say intrigues—to which they are liable to descend. Sometimes it is a cause for marvel, sometimes of genuine sorrow, but as often as either it is just thoroughly puzzling how much they mean by these assertions of convinced, dedicated purpose, even when involved in what, from the outside, looks like unscrupulous adventure. It is not hypocrisy. It is not self-deceit. It is the natural acceptance of any reasonable means available for making a particular point prevail. They might be better civil servants if they and their methods were otherwise constituted, but they would be poorer priests in their own eyes were they to fail to defend or promote what they understand to be right. This sublime self-confidence of the Curia sets a blank wall across the path of the reformer.

Another reason why the Curia has avoided a stringent remodelling is that the three popes who have, in this generation, raised the Papacy to a high place in international esteem have not been, for one reason or another, much suited to the task of taking their civil service radically in hand—though Paul VI has attempted some improvements. Pius XII and the present pope both belonged to the Curia for years before their election, and nothing is more self-perpetuating than a civil service able to provide successive monarchs. Even John XXIII was, less directly, a civil servant. How, in these circumstances, given the acknowledged distinction of these popes, could there be anything seriously wrong with the system that produced them?

The administrative situation under Pius XII became rather curious. He had been Secretary of State before his election: one of the very few examples of a holder of that office going on to become pope. (The last to do so before him was Cardinal

Rospigliosi, elected Clement IX in 1667.) In the second half of his pontificate, Pius acted as his own Secretary of State; he saw less and less of his cardinals and cancelled the regular audiences which the heads of the Sacred Congregations and other bodies normally had with the pontiff. He was uneasy at the thought that others might disagree with him, or bring him to change his mind, or in other ways impinge on the privacy of his mental processes. Apart from a few friends and a few courtiers, 'he separated himself'— as Giuseppe Dalla Torre, the former editor of the Vatican newspaper, writes in his memoirs—'from direct contact with life, though not, unfortunately, from people who abused his confidence.' He was a great user of the telephone; the white and gold instrument was a means whereby he could reach subordinates immediately without having personal contact with them. It is said that officials of the Secretariat of State went down on their knees with the telephone in their hand when he announced who he was. As far as he could, Pius solved the problem of the Curia by having as little as possible to do with it directly. By isolating himself, as well as by an eccentric choice of friends and favourites, he encouraged an increase in curial pretensions and a worsening of its moral atmosphere.

Unlike Pius, John XXIII had had little or no direct experience of the Curia when he became pope, for his work as an apostolic delegate and then as a nuncio meant that for much of his life he had lived abroad. What personal contacts he had were not always auspicious. When Pius XII appointed him to Paris, the newly nominated nuncio saw Monsignor Tardini, head of the first division of the Secretariat of State, to whom Roncalli confided that he had not expected that he would be given the post. 'Nor did any one else', replied Tardini, the compleat curialist. When Roncalli was elected pope, Tardini—still head of the first division— was probably no less unenthusiastic. Men of his conservative stamp in the Vatican were apparently still hoping that Cardinal Ottaviani, Pro-Prefect of the Holy Office, might yet be chosen, or else the aristocratic Cardinal Aloisi Masella. The fact that he had been known to be averse to Roncalli's election may account for Tardini's unbridled action in making his way too early into the

Conclave to offer his obeisances to the new pope. He rushed in to remove any doubts about his loyal intentions to his new master, only to be told by Cardinal Tisserant, the French Dean of the Sacred College, who disliked him, that he had incurred the punishment of excommunication. John made Tardini, a man fundamentally opposed to his own outlook, his Secretary of State. It is likely, to judge from his consequent behaviour, that Tardini regarded this appointment as no less than his due.

John soon showed that, as pope, he had no intention of being a stop-gap simply to keep things going until a brainier fellow—the archbishop of Milan, for instance—should be ready to take over from him. Even so, in determinedly preparing the way for a new style of Papacy, John did not tackle the Curia. That he was well aware of what the curialists were capable of was shown in a discourse of his in 1960, after announcing the forthcoming Ecumenical Council. He pointed out that the bodies organising it were to remain distinct from the Roman Curia, which was to be responsible only for ordinary administration. However, it soon became evident that the curial cardinals had managed to get themselves appointed as heads of many of the commissions dealing with the matters which they were accustomed to handle in the Curia. In other words, despite all the pope had said, the two sets of administrations were in the hands of the same people. The pope was accused of giving way to the Curia: *Il Papa ha ceduto*.

It was not so simple as that. In fact, John felt he was being let down by his natural allies. Progressive opinion in the Church was all for his limiting the part to be played by the Curia, but to the progressive cardinals he looked in vain, it seems, for support. He was fighting their battle, ill-equipped both intellectually and in terms of his previous experience. They criticised him for giving way; they did not give him the active support he desired. The conservatives were much more consistent, much more tenacious and capable of overcoming their limited numbers by various means. They made full use of their proximity to the pope (many of the curial prelates around him were conservative) and their superior organisation which allowed them, without coming much into the public eye, to bring pressure to bear where and when it would be of most use.

Pressure was certainly exerted on Paul VI during the Council—such as warning him continually of the danger to his supremacy inherent in the idea of a College of Bishops—and also on individuals dependent in one way or another on the Curia's goodwill. This was a story to be repeated year after year as the meetings of the Council came and went. For the good of the Church, the conservatives tried to frighten the pope in an organised way, or to turn the formalities of procedure to the benefit of their cause. They were attacked in many sections of the press. Books appeared describing the conflict as though it was nothing more complicated than a Western, with the good men all on one side and the bad men all on the other. A moderate, loyal and efficient civil servant in high position in the Vatican once said, with uncharacteristic emotion, to a progressive cardinal: 'And why did you not go to see the pope?' The answer is that the progressives just did not take the trouble to organise themselves in the same efficient way as their opponents, who were much weaker in terms of numbers. They suffered, it must be said, from some serious disadvantages. Most of them had busy sees out of Italy and could not compete with the curial prelates in seeking to influence the pope or in handling the daily business of the Church's government.

Paul VI knows the Curia as well as Pius XII did, but, because of John's work, he cannot isolate himself from the mainstream of opinion in the Church. Nor can he isolate himself from his own character. He does not like hurting people's feelings. Many of the members of the central government of the Church he had known from his years in the Secretariat of State. Ottaviani, head of the Holy Office, which he was to be forced to reform, had been his superior in the Secretariat of State. As first of the Order of Deacons, it had been for Ottaviani to announce, in the traditional phrase, the 'great joy' of a papal election when Montini became pope. Ordinarily, one could have expected the joy to have been all the greater among curialists in that once again a product of the Curia was on the papal throne. Yet Montini had earlier been forced by Pius XII to leave the Curia in order to take the archbishopric of

Milan. Were he resentful or vindictive, as some popes have been,* Paul could have come back like an avenging angel. He is, however, a careful man, neither avenger nor angel. He has thought a lot about reform, but has not sought to implement radical structural changes. His method has been, with some exceptions (such as the Holy Office), to introduce a proportion of progressive-minded men into influential posts. In 1964, he set up a commission under Cardinal Roberti, the Vatican's leading jurist, to make recommendations. The commission produced some striking proposals: a retiring age for curial officials; a far greater international character for the Curia; and the obligation on any candidate for a curial post to have had pastoral experience. Paul's handling of the report throws an interesting light on his relationship with the cardinals. He invited the members of the Sacred College to a comparatively informal meeting in the autumn of 1964 at which curial reform, among other things, was due to be discussed. Cardinal Roberti gave his report. The pope evidently expected a discussion. None came: no one spoke. Awe is still reserved for popes, even by their closest associates. The cardinal who gave this account was rather critical of his colleagues. Why, then, did not he himself speak? 'Well, I felt that as I am rather junior. . . .'

Paul VI was deeply aware of the fact that his earlier relationship with many leading members of the Curia complicated matters. Some people believe that he attempted to smooth his future relations with them while the Conclave which elected him was still in progress. It seems probable that he would have reached the required number of votes on the first day of balloting; certainly, on the eve of his election it was taken for granted that he would succeed. Included in the 'opposition', however, were many of the Italian cardinals of the Curia with whom, as pope, he would have to collaborate closely. He wanted to have all their votes behind him. Some of them had already grasped the crucial point. For instance, Cardinal Micara, then Cardinal-Vicar of Rome, had told

---

* When Rodrigo Borgia became Pope Alexander VI in 1492, his bitter rival, Cardinal De La Rovere (later to be Julius II), fled from Rome in fear for his life.

them that Montini was the one Italian who could be sure of the majority because he commanded respect and support from outside the Italian ranks. It was thus in their interest, Micara argued, to vote for him. Report has it that his advice was taken and in a further round of voting the Italian cardinals who until then had been against Montini rallied to his support. Secrets of the Conclave are seldom worth retailing because too often they lack authoritative confirmation. This account, however, does have the ring of truth about it, and indicates the importance which Montini attached to good relations with the Curia.

He took it on himself quite early in his reign to address the Curia about the need for change. The confrontation between pope and administrators, courtiers, judges and other officials on whom the pope relies, as he put it, 'to govern the universal Church as well as the diocese of Rome and Vatican City' took place on 22 September 1963. He has made other pronouncements since, and also taken some reforming action, but this first discourse on the subject goes deeper than any other subsequent pronouncement so far, and it gives a clear idea of the sort of considerations which Paul VI has in mind when approaching a problem so little agreeable to his fastidious and basically rather cautious temperament. This is what he said of his own personal connection with the Curia:

> We ourselves have had the honour of serving for many years in the Roman Curia. We have met in its ranks most worthy superiors and teachers, excellent colleagues, collaborators, and unforgettable friends. We have shared the labours, the responsibilities, studies, experiences, joys and sorrows of this complex and singular organisation. We have followed, for more than thirty years, its functioning from a privileged point of observation: the Secretariat of State, that excellent, dear and faithful office which assists the pope in his personal activities. We thus have been able to appreciate better the wise composition of the Roman Curia, derived from a coherent and flexible tradition. We have heard indications concerning the new needs of this same body. We have also heard the criticisms which are directed at it, and have often made them the subject of sincere

reflection. And finally, We have come to know and appreciate the efficiency of the services which the Roman Curia renders to the pope and to the Church.

In his definition of the Curia's tasks, he reaffirmed its purely executive (though *nobilissima*) function: 'to listen to and interpret the voice of the pope and at the same time not let him lack any useful and objective information, or brotherly and pondered counsel.'

He was clearly aware of the frequent criticism that the Curia arrogated to itself the making of policy and that the information which reached the pontiff was at times filtered or slanted by some of the curial prelates. He referred to attacks on the Curia from the hierarchy: 'We must welcome the criticisms which surround Us, with humility, with reflection and with recognition. Rome does not need to defend itself by being deaf to suggestions coming from honest voices and even less if these voices are those of friends and brothers.' The situation was not as bad today as it had been in the past. 'St Bernard would no longer write his scathing pages on the Roman ecclesiastical world, nor would the sixteenth-century reformers. Papal Rome today is quite different.' Paul nevertheless accepted the necessity for change. 'That certain reforms must be introduced into the Roman Curia is not only easy to foresee but much to be desired,' and before he ended he gave a clear—embarrassingly clear to some people—summary of what the accusations were.

> The Roman Curia will not be jealous of temporal prerogatives of former times; nor of exterior forms no longer appropriate to express and apply true and lofty religious meanings; nor covetous of those of its faculties which, without damage to the universal ecclesiastical order, can be carried out better today locally by the bishops. Nor will economic aims and advantages have weight in suggesting certain reserves and tendencies on the part of organs of the Holy See, if not required by the good of the ecclesiastical order and by the well-being of souls.

Altogether, it was not entirely a pleasant occasion for the curial prelates. The pope had paid them some fine compliments in his address, but the weight of it was quite evidently in the direction of change. He had, moreover, displayed a rather disconcerting familiarity with the ways and the mentality of the Curia.

The mentality is not difficult to describe. It is formalistic, fussy, devotedly jealous. As a career institution, the Curia imposes limitations on the mind which are inclined to become more binding as the years pass. Because the approach to a career in Italy is so often through attachment to an important personality, the aspiring curialist is likely to choose a mentor; hence groups bound together by loyalty or interest are formed. This is another limiting factor. So is the fussiness: that strange sort of restless, almost exalted, delight in detail which priestly administrators are apt to suffer from—due in part, no doubt, to the perpetual bachelorhood imposed on them. The tradition of priestly celibacy has much to justify it (and is easier to manage) in the case of men actively engaged in the pastoral ministry—parish priests or diocesan bishops—but it is hard to see it as essential to pure administration. There has been, in fact, a certain demand for the greater use of laymen in the Church's civil service; and, indeed, requests were made at the Second Vatican Council that laymen should even be allowed to serve as nuncios. It is, arguably, a waste of priests to keep them dealing with matters of administrative routine when the number of vocations is falling, and certainly the rigours of the priesthood do not necessarily best adapt a man for administrative tasks.

The jealous devotion of many of the Curia's members is highly indicative of their view of its place in the Church's life. Of course, many people who are involved in the detailed work of a large institution identify themselves strongly with some part of it; a bank clerk may well feel literally a part of his bank, or a seaman of his ship. But nowhere is the strength of this kind of feeling greater than in the Vatican. Curial prelates are inclined to identify themselves, not just with the Curia, but through it with the Roman Church. The two become one. As an example of this we may cite the reported remark of one of the greatest curialists of his generation, Cardinal Ottaviani:

To those who formed me from the first hours of my priesthood, to their teaching, to their example, I owe the fact that my attachment to the Apostolic See has daily become stronger and more luminous and, so to say, more instructive and formative. Many people do not know what a great teacher of Christian life and Catholic action this Roman Curia is; it seems a contemporary of the apostles in its glory, so full of life that it seems to have been born yesterday, high and yet humble like a mother, and misunderstood only by those who do not know her.*

There is something rather splendid about views of this kind. As an outlook, it is hopelessly inadequate to modern requirements, whatever may be the truth or falsity of it. Yet every part of it can be explained by the circumstances of the formidable cardinal's career. Practically from the moment that Ottaviani was made a priest, the pressures of Rome were upon him. He was born in 1890, the son of a worker in a bakery in Trastevere: one of the rougher areas of Rome, and one which produces some of the noisier kind of anti-clericals. He went to the Roman Seminary with a scholarship. (His contemporary was Domenico Tardini, another *Romano* of a pronounced type, and destined for curial greatness.) Ottaviani has very rarely left Rome, except for occasional short visits, such as to Lourdes, the United States and Spain. He has the dogged insistence, typical of his kind of Roman, of never admitting himself to be in the wrong. When his Holy Office was under particular and effective attack at the Council, his answer was the same: criticism of it comes from ignorance of it. This was also his outlook on the Church at large. Ecumenism meant to him—and he made no secret of it—a clearer definition of where the Roman Church stands so that others, once they had looked at it, could scarce do other than join it.

As soon as the dogmatic and moral constitutions of the Church are fixed in precise terms by the Council, the Church will be able to say to all her Orthodox and Protestant brethren: 'Look at the face of the true Church of Christ; whoever wishes to recognise

* Quoted in Michael Novale (ed.), *Alfredo, Cardinal Ottaviani*, University of Notre Dame Press, Notre Dame, Ind. 1966.

in her the face of a mother of saints, the image of the celestial city, may come in; the doors of the house of this mother are open.*

Acceptance of the principle of religious liberty produces, in his view, as many problems as ecumenism itself. Of the statement in the conciliar text that 'even he who is in error is worthy of honour', Ottaviani commented: 'I do not like this and I do not understand this. An error is never worthy of honour.' Such a remark is understandable and respectable enough as coming from the Pro-Prefect of the Holy Office, expressing concern lest Catholic truth be contaminated by error; but it also betrays the intransigence, at least among the older prelates, of the curialist attitude to non-Roman Christians and to the liberalising movement in the Church. Ottaviani was a seminarian during the repression by the Vatican of the Modernist movement in the early years of this century. It was a clumsy action by Pius X, but one which not only inspired Ottaviani personally ('that pontiff who enchanted our childhood') but placed a general seal of suspicion upon the Church's intellectual ranks. Fear and distrust of new ideas were more notable in Italy than elsewhere, with Rome strongly affected by these mental inhibitions.

All the old men in the Curia grew up in the atmosphere of emergency and of condemnation which surrounded the Modernist movement. It was widespread in several countries of Europe by the turn of the century—notably in France, where Loisy was its great exemplar—and the condemnation by Pius X in 1907 had profound effects. If some of the views of the Modernists are now accepted as not only blameless but proper, the Papacy's handling of those early experimenters in the Church's relations with the modern world has served for half a century as a stern warning against anything that looks adventurous. There are no precise doctrines of Modernism that can briefly be described because the Modernists themselves differed widely in their views. Pius X pulled together a number of ideas that he disliked and condemned them under the embracing term of Modernism. However, the main

* Novale, op. cit.

strains of Modernist thought can be identified, and these clearly contain real or potential menaces to ecclesiastical authority.

The Modernists fully accepted, in the first place, the need for a critical approach to biblical studies, some of them going further to adopt a more sceptical approach to the Scriptures than many contemporary Protestants would have taken. Men such as Loisy, Blondel, Mignot, Laberthonnière in France: Murri in Italy and Tyrrell in Britain, attempted to find justification for their beliefs in Leo XIII's teachings. He had issued in 1893 an encyclical on biblical studies (*Providentissimus Deus*), the object of which was to give guidance to the clergy and others in the intellectual situation arising from archæological discoveries and from developments in textual criticism, philology and other disciplines with a direct bearing on the study of the Bible. Historically, Leo's encyclical was the first of a trilogy devoted by three different popes to the problem; it was followed by Benedict XV's *Spiritus Paraclitum* of 1920 and Pius XII's *Divino Afflante Spiritu* of 1943. The three encyclicals together represented the Roman Church's increasing concern over this period with modern approaches to biblical studies. Leo XIII, in fact, accepted the importance of new methods of intellectual inquiry, but rejected the use which some scholars were making of them. The section of opinion that came to be described as Modernist took its encouragement from the first part of this judgment. They had some justification for this, though the limited encouragement he gave was to be retracted by his successor. The second strand in Modernism was an inclination to reject the systems of scholastic theology. The Modernists preferred to place more importance on action and life than on academic formulations of doctrine and philosophy. The third—and potentially even more dangerous line of thought, from the point of view of authority in an authoritarian Church—concerned their concept of history. For all their interest in freely conducted biblical studies, the Modernists were essentially more interested in the actual product of history than in historical origins. This attitude brought them towards an advanced scepticism with regard to the beginnings of Christianity itself. For them, what was important was the developed institution—the Church spread throughout the world, the Mass as it had been shaped by history and evolving devotional experience—without placing too much weight on whether or not the historical Jesus had personally instituted it.

Pius X's condemnation of such ideas as these was outright. Modernism was 'insanity' and an 'audacious sacrilege'. He pointed out that Leo XIII had, in fact, been indicating the limits to biblical scholarship and had, at the same time, placed great importance on the scholastic philosophy of Aquinas. Pius X therefore took more stringent measures to protect the faith, including censorship, committees of vigilance in every diocese to inform on signs of Modernism, and reports from bishops every three years, on oath, about the ideas and opinions prevalent among their clergy. An anti-Modernist oath had to be taken by priests and by candidates to the priesthood.

This digression over Modernism should help to explain the propensity among cardinals of the generation which has been influential in the Curia in the last few years to fear error and favour anathema. It was in the Roman air they breathed as young men. Cardinal Ottaviani was to become head of the very department, the Holy Office, responsible for smelling out heresy, but he was far from being the only one governed by the attitude which exaggerated possible error to the extent that a liberal intellectual approach became, even in its smaller beginnings, so potentially dangerous and ugly that the heaviest hammer should be used against it. This was the attitude John XXIII was to rebel against in his famous statements that the Council would issue no condemnations, and that the 'prophets of doom' were wrong. By temperament, and in some ways by career, John was protected from the rigidity imposed on and by such curial personalities as Ottaviani and Tardini. They felt the full impact, for they were also canon lawyers. Verdicts came naturally to them. It was an influence liable to stamp a man for life. John's second Secretary of State, Cardinal Cicognani (whom Paul inherited), was of that same generation. Despite a quarter of a century spent in the United States, he came back to Rome suspicious of change; he laid himself open to accusations of slowing down the reforming process of the Council—of being, in other words, a curial reactionary.

Not everything was bad in the immediate consequences of the repression of Modernism. Pius X set up the Biblical Institute in Rome to redress the marked insufficiency of the Roman Church's biblical scholarship in its attempts to deal with the Modernists. Though Pius X is vulnerable to attack over his repression of the Modernists, he is not always given proper credit for this constructive act of establishing an institute to train scholars and put the Church's biblical scholarship on a higher level. It was to become the platform for something quite without precedent, and his initiative, though this could not be foreseen at the time, was to lead to remarkable things. From 1930 until 1949, the rector of the Biblical Institute was the Jesuit father, later Cardinal, Bea. To everyone's surprise—rather like the surprise created when Roncalli was posted to Paris—Bea was to become an extraordinarily effective spokesman of the Roman Church's ecumenical aspirations. The repression of Modernism could hardly have described a more perfect circle.

Any survey of the Roman Curia must include some mention of Bea. In the first place, like no one else before him, he became the non-Italian who really changed things. Secondly, there is his eminence as a biblical scholar exerting influence on Catholic intellectual studies from the very heart of the faith; and thirdly, there is his influence on Catholic doctrine.

The living precedents as far as concerns non-Italians in important curial posts were the Armenian Cardinal Agagianian and the French Cardinal Tisserant. The first rose to be head of the Sacred Congregation for the Propagation of the Faith—the missions—and the second held a variety of curial posts, of which the deanship of the Sacred College brought him most to the forefront of attention. The two men had little in common except that they both wore beards. The Armenian had the reputation of having become the most Roman of the entire Curia and had, indeed, lived mostly in the city since his youth. Tisserant remained impossibly French, and his part in influencing important matters of policy tended to be small. Bea was German; this did not prevent his becoming as close as possible to the centre of life in the Apostolic Palaces, where he was eventually appointed Pius XII's confessor. In his case, the man's nationality prevented his too great absorption by the curial atmosphere: the fate which overtook Agagianian.

The problem of international representation within the Curia is replete with complications. It is now fashionable to say that non-Italians must be brought into the administration at all levels. Pius XII started the process when he broke the Italian majority in the Sacred College; but, typically, he did not take it far. John carried it further by placing Bea at the head of the Secretariat for Christian Unity. Paul has been more consistent and determined than either of them. He made his intentions clear by appointing Monsignor Garrone, the highly respected archbishop of Toulouse, as acting head of the vitally important Congregation for Seminaries and Studies, which was a stronghold of curial reaction. To this French prelate he added, as Secretary to the same Congregation, Monsignor Schröffer, the bishop of Eichstadt in Germany: a prelate less identified with advanced views than Garrone, but a century or so ahead of the average curialist. To the Holy Office, Paul sent Monsignor Moeller of Belgium to serve as Under-Secretary, at the same time ejecting the Dominicans, who for centuries had monopolised the forbidding office of Inquisitor (or 'Commissioner', to use the correct title): an office which the pope abolished. Cardinal Villot went to the Consistorial Congregation, which deals with the appointment of bishops—indeed, with most matters concerning Rome's relations with the hierarchy.

These changes suggest that Paul VI genuinely believes that fresh personalities placed within the old structure will have the desired reforming effect. It is, however, not a reform but a refurbishing of the old forms. He may succeed, but it is still reasonable to have doubts. Rome in general, and the Curia in particular, have their effect on individuals. Oddly enough, it is frequently the non-Italians who have lived in the Vatican for many years who provide the outstanding cases of curial-mindedness. It is probably because they are less at home in it than are the Italians, and so subconsciously make a bigger effort to conform. By far the worst are the Americans, who lose character and gain fussiness at an alarming rate in Rome's ecclesiastical circles, becoming far more tiresome to deal with than the Italians. The Germans, except for

Bea, have so far had less opportunity to see whether they can retain their sturdiness when deprived of their native background; but they seem to have an unhappy tendency to widen their natural sentimentality in Rome. French prelates, on the whole, react badly, becoming either very curial but less engaging than their Italian counterparts, or irascibly French, like Tisserant. After Archbishop Garrone had been in Rome for a few months, he was heard to say that, had he known what it would be like, he would never have left Toulouse.

This is the typical attitude of the progressive prelate. Another of the great liberals, Cardinal König, archbishop of Vienna, undertook to set up the new Secretariat for Non-Believers only on the condition that he could remain in Vienna and not come to Rome. The progressives are very much inclined to sweep into Rome, carry out whatever business they need to transact, and sweep out again, breathing liberal indignation at the way the Curia conducts itself. The cures of most of them are a long way from Rome because the Italian hierarchy is basically conservative, even though lately it has been showing signs of fresh thought. The archbishops of Turin and of Bologna, the bishops of Leghorn and of Ravenna—each would count as a liberal prelate anywhere in the world; but it will take time for this new attitude to have its effect. For years under Pius XII, the Italian bishops were presided over by Cardinal Siri, the conservative archbishop of Genoa. Many of them are dependent on the Curia to help them administer poor dioceses. Italy, in early 1967, had 300 dioceses; with so inflated a number, many are very poor indeed. As an instance: some have relied for keeping their seminaries going on help from the Congregation of Seminaries and Studies which, until Paul VI changed matters, was extremely conservative. A bishop would thus have to follow a conservative policy to get the necessary grants.

One of the great merits of the Second Vatican Council was that Rome and the rest of the Roman Church were able to see and learn about the leading spokesmen of a more liberal Catholicism: Cardinal Alfrink, archbishop of Utrecht; Cardinal Frings, archbishop of Cologne; Cardinal Lercaro, archbishop of Bologna; Cardinal Suenens, archbishop of Mechelen-Brussels; Cardinal

Liénart, bishop of Lille. But they stayed only during the months in which the Council sat or when they were required for work on one of the commissions. The session or particular assignment done, they were glad to go home. Paul is attempting to overcome this 'homing instinct' of the liberals by appointing non-Italians, with some progressive prelates among them, to permanent posts in Rome, so that they are there on the spot when battle is joined, and do not depart until it has been won. The risk is that they will suffer from the lack of stimulus given them by their pastoral work, especially in such countries as France, Germany and Holland, where there are large and influential sections of the population which are not Catholic. This is a background to pastoral work which Italians lack, and one which they find extremely difficult to appreciate. Loss of personal contact with the faithful in communities where unbelief is strong is likely to mean that leaders of the Church will no longer be regarded as open-minded—just as Wyszynski of Poland has found, his 'advanced' views having been overtaken by John XXIII's new outlook.

Even so, such new curial appointments are at least providing a more hopeful channel of communication within the organisation at the centre of the Church. If a member of Cardinal Bea's Secretariat, for instance, has business to do with the Holy Office, he would see Monsignor Moeller, not some other prelate who might be senior but reactionary. Similarly, Bea's department has found that, in its dealings with the Secretariat of State, the best approach is through the French section, thereby avoiding both the Americans in the English section and the Italians, who are still not used to this new but influential body. Much of the value of these non-Italians in the Curia will depend on whether they can offer this more rational channel and at the same time be strong and determined enough to achieve results.

An Italianate Curia, it must be admitted, has more to be said for it than is usually allowed in circles critical of the Vatican's system. By having one nationality in all the important positions, and one language in which to work, the Vatican has sought to solve the problem of an international civil service in exactly the opposite way to that adopted by the United Nations. Italians have a refined hand in diplomacy: at the same time, they have no predominant national interests to pursue which could complicate their conduct of the affairs of the universal Church—exception always made, of course, for the internal situation in Italy which, since the war, has had great weight in decisions applied to the Church as a whole. They understand this strange machine that has gradually been formed over the centuries to rule the Church. The overlapping departments; the sinecures; the pomp; the offices which have functions quite different from those suggested by their name; the need for secrecy; the bloodless clashes which are the one way by which the monolithic structure of the Curia can be a little more flexible in practice than would appear possible—all this is second nature to many an Italian prelate.

Moreover, in spite of the criticisms of curial procedures from outside Italy, there has been a great reluctance on the part of non-Italian bishops to contribute any of their best men to the Curia's offices. They have few enough to spare; young priests of ability are hard to come by these days, and bishops cannot afford to part with promising recruits to the Church's service in their dioceses and province. Still, 'internationalisation' has provided a good watchword. It will certainly continue to be invoked; as things are going today, it will be invoked with rather more meaning. This is because the real clash is between the Italianate system and the wider concept of the Church which arose at the Council. The Curia was there seen to be impossibly narrow, obstructive, overbearing, and lamentably given to intrigue. The faults which were as much a part of history as of human failings were revealed for all to see.

The one curial official at a high level whom liberals have grown to admire is Cardinal Bea. John made him a cardinal without knowing much about him. There is a story that the pope was so unfamiliar with Bea when he began his reign that he asked if there were two Father Beas. But John evidently wished to show recognition for biblical scholarship, respect for his predecessor by promoting so intimate a servant of Pius XII, and perhaps honour towards the Jesuits by bestowing the purple on one of their number. In 1962, he made Bea the first head of the newly devised Secretariat for Promoting Christian Unity. This is the first significant point about Bea's position at the Vatican: that a German should have been appointed to this new, outward-looking department of the Curia.

The second important point about Bea is his quality as a biblical scholar. He is immensely hard-working. His bent shoulders are the mark of a man long huddled over a desk, his slender back is like some frail tree exposed to a constant gale of scholarship. His general learning makes him the equal of any of the Curia's administrators in most fields likely to arise as a result of the Council. Essentially, however, it is biblical scholarship that distinguishes him: a discipline whose approach is very different from that pursued by the great canonists, like Ottaviani and Tardini; nor is Bea's the bookish, rather arid learning of Cardinal Browne, the Irish Dominican who can always find quotations from the schoolmen to sustain the conservative cause. Bea's scholarship has brought him into contact with biblical students throughout Europe, Protestant as well as Catholic. This is why he can move so easily, and gain such respect, among the Protestants and other non-Catholics for whom his office is responsible; he is familiar with the work of their scholars and confident in his own knowledge when dealing with them. Furthermore, the time he has spent in the Sacred Palaces has made him no less confident in dealing with the Curia.

The third significant point about Bea's curial role is that a scholar, regarded as by no means wholly liberal in his theological views, has produced a marked shift of emphasis in the Roman doctrine of baptism. He argues a theory of the effect of baptism that makes all Christians to some extent brethren, and he has insisted on it until it has become a familiar part of any discussion about ecumenism. The theory was not originated by Bea, but he has applied it widely and frequently, thereby giving it a greater chance of acceptance. It is the antithesis of the classical curialist interpretation. Instead of seeking to identify what separates the Roman from the non-Roman in Christian teachings, Bea is anxious to find what they can be said to hold in common. Personal clashes over this question have sometimes been bitter. At times, Bea has been regarded by the Holy Office as little better than a heretic.

He was the victim of an unpleasant curial manœuvre to prevent his receiving an honorary doctorate from a Jesuit university in the United States. Rumours were circulated from time to time that his health was failing, presumably with the object of diminishing the importance of the work he had in hand. Apart from the nastiness, however—all done, of course, for the felicitous advance of the one true Church—it has to be said that this type of clash is the one way whereby ideas can go their course through the structural monolith at the centre of the Catholic Church. Or rather, it was the only way until Paul VI agreed to establish the international Synod of Bishops. This body should be able at its meetings to bring to the Roman pontiff and his Curia something of the currents of ideas and feelings in more distant parts of the world than Italy.

The Synod of Bishops—set up as a result of the Council and sitting for the first time in September 1967—is quintessentially Paulist. The pope has given everything and nothing; he has destroyed nothing and has added to the already thickly planted forest of curial departments. He has done two things. He accorded the bishops what they felt would be a tangible expression of the doctrine of collegiality they had elaborated during the sessions of the Second Vatican Council. However, he gave it in such a way that, in avoiding any change in the pope's prerogatives by the establishment of the Synod, he armed himself with a new instrument. This new instrument could have a double deployment. It could be used to curb the Curia; bishops would be happy to come from distant parts of the world to the Synod if they felt that by so doing they could prevent the Curia from getting out of hand. At the same time, Paul's careful preservation of the papal prerogatives won curial acceptance of his new institution, because an untrammelled Papacy means to the Curia an untrammelled executive arm. Paul is extremely sensitive about papal prerogatives, second to none of his predecessors in the concern that nothing should belittle the inheritance to be passed on to his successors. This is why he tends to refer to the dignity and responsibility of his office more often than might seem necessary. It is also the reason why one of the subtlest forms of pressure against him during the debates on the bishops' collegial powers was to advise him that, by accepting too much, he would go down in history as the pope who had surrendered some of the attributes of the greatest office on earth a man could hold.

Apart from the voluntary imprisonment of the pope after 1870, there is another form of voluntary imprisonment within the Vatican walls: that of the circle of friends on whom a pope draws for relief from isolation. The three post-war popes have all been lonely men. Pius XII became practically a recluse. John was lonely because he was in an atmosphere to which he was not accustomed, and found little support from the men outside the Vatican who shared his aims. He overcame much of it by going about to meet people far more than any other pope since the loss of the temporal power. His closest adviser, his secretary, Monsignor Loris Capovilla, was devoted to him and also to his rather radical views on the Church's place in the world and its connections with politics. The nephews of Pius XII who were deep in the financial transactions of the Vatican; the doctor who experimented with preserving the pope's body by a new method that would, if successful, have had great commercial value; the head of Catholic Action and its political inspirer—such people were seen less about the Sacred Palaces under John, or not at all. The strong whiffs of corruption grew fainter. But it was still a lonely place. Paul VI is not likely to make it less so.

The present pontiff is one of the least gregarious of men. He has no one near to him of the effectiveness of Monsignor Capovilla. Paul's secretary is little known outside the Vatican, and not much liked inside of it. Yet it is for Paul—originally so much a part of the Curia and then its victim—to preside over an attempt to change the outlook within the walls. If he is successful, the walls will gradually fall away; if unsuccessful, the number of its mental prisoners will have been increased by a handful of French, German and Belgian prelates, become indistinguishable from the rest.

7
To Treat with the Devil

For the world to look at the Vatican is a rich but confusing experience. The place itself is small, but its formalism has a series of meanings which flicker across the centuries from an almost indefinite distance, like the last reflection in a pair of opposite mirrors. The essence of it is tough and concentrated like diamond because it is microscopic and has been fired in the process of human history. In and around the tiny state, something of Constantine still remains to meet something of Hildebrand; the shade of Charlemagne weeps silently but feelingly for the death of Pope Hadrian. Somehow, the transient nature of human life in this world, on which the popes have always insisted, is belied by the pervasive presence in their own principality of a past which clings like a cloak. But if their frequent inclination is to summon the old world of tradition to help redress the balance of the new, they must still look out from their own walls, over to the world as it is. What they see is probably to them no less confusing than they are themselves to much of the world at large. Whether they are attempting to deal with the challenge of organised godlessness in the communist parts of the world, or with disorganised decadence in a number of Catholic countries, or with the challenge of the new nations, what criterion can guide their policies if not simply that of the immediately expedient? What, in other words, is the Vatican's reaction to the political and social problems of the world? What relevance do the Papacy's policies have for the modern world?

The aims of papal politics have somehow to be defined before their political usefulness to mankind can be judged. This is no ordinary power after all. To begin with, it is the only religious authority in the world which exchanges diplomatic representatives with sovereign states, entering fully, for all the greatness of its spiritual claims, into the mundane details of international diplomacy. As an instance: when the future John XXIII was appointed nuncio in Paris, he had to hurry to take up his post because, in the absence of a nuncio (always the dean of the diplomatic corps in Catholic countries), the task of delivering the New Year's message to the French head of state would have fallen by order of seniority to the Russian ambassador. And so Roncalli was speedily dispatched to deny his Russian colleague a moment of formal prominence. Papal procedure can descend with disconcerting rapidity from the sublime to the meticulous.

Because of its spiritual authority, the Vatican must be ready with any means to safeguard practice of the faith in those places where it is present and seek to extend knowledge of the faith to those countries where as yet it is weak or does not exist. 'It is of necessity to salvation', declared Boniface VIII in the bull *Unam Sanctam Ecclesiam* in 1302, 'for every human being to be subject to the Roman pontiff.' This assertion was confirmed by the Fifth Lateran Council in 1513 and has never been retracted by the Papacy. Theoretically, five hundred million people are at the moment in this necessary position—a substantial section of humanity—but maintenance and extension of the faith remain profoundly binding as the basic principles of the Vatican's policies.

In his study of the Papacy's diplomacy,* Monsignor Igino Cardinale, the apostolic delegate in London, points out that it is aimed above all at obtaining respect for the requirements of divine law and of ecclesiastical law. The organs of the State, he says, on their part must help the Papacy to assure to the Church the freedom of action that is indispensable to the accomplishment of its universal mission for the good of mankind. Monsignor Cardinale goes on to say that the indirect objective coincides in certain ways with the aims of civil diplomacy, which are the safeguarding of the

* Igino Cardinale, *Le Saint-Siège et la Diplomatie*, Paris 1962.

international balance, peace and progress among nations. What this amounts to in historical terms is that the Vatican's diplomacy is the instrument formed to continue the constant dialogue of Church and State after the rise of nations replaced the old relationship of Papacy and Empire. The papal diplomatists are the agents for dealing with a splintered world. Pius XII affirmed as much when he attempted to explain to an audience of foreign press correspondents on 12 May 1953 how he envisaged the modern problem of relations between many states on the one hand and a universal Church on the other.

> The Holy See is the supreme authority of the Catholic Church, and hence of a religious society whose goals are to be found in the supernatural and in the world beyond. Nevertheless, the Church lives in the world. Each of her sons and daughters . . . belongs to a particular state and people. It is always one of the essential tasks of the Holy See to see that, throughout the entire world, there reigns between Church and State normal and, if possible, friendly relations, in order that Catholics may live their faith in tranquillity and peace, and that the Church may, at the same time, provide for the State that solid support which it constitutes wherever it is allowed to carry on its work in freedom.

There are two links between Church and State: one is the local hierarchy which, in some cases, can go quite a long way in settling its own disputes with the secular authorities; the other is the papal diplomatic corps which can watch what the hierarchies are doing as well as study relations between the Vatican and the country of accreditation.

More than formal relationships, however, are involved in papal policy because the problem is not limited to protecting the Church's interests in a particular country. To be the one true Church does, after all, carry with it a responsibility to offer guidance at any difficult juncture in human affairs. It has a moral authority to exercise. Popes, for instance, have a certain tradition of making appeals for peace. More often than not they have gone unheeded, but this has not brought any sign of discouragement.

No recent pontiff has followed this tradition more forcibly than Paul VI, whose activities directed at ending the Vietnam war were heeded and, if sometimes resented, at least made clear for all to see that at a time of international crisis the Vatican was playing a part. If in future it might be criticised for what it had done, it could never be accused of having done nothing. That, of course, was the charge brought against Pius XII with regard to the atrocities of the Nazis. Catholic countries certainly have no better record —perhaps on balance a worse one—than the Protestant countries in listening to what the pope has to say. And communist countries are quick to grasp the significance of any papal utterance which shows the Vatican to be ahead—which in many ways it is—of much Western thinking in flexibility and objectivity on the subject of relations with the communist world. It is on that world that any glance outward from the Vatican is most liable first to alight.

DEMOCRACY AND COMMUNISM

Few confrontations are more exciting to the imagination than that of the Roman Church and communism. The two authoritarian powers have reason to hate each other. In the Marxist view, the Church is reactionary and to be dispensed with, while, from the outset, the Vatican has seen Marxism as the latest and perhaps the most dangerous challenge to the faith. A massive moral and ideological gap is there; by the mid-twentieth century, there was little between the two rock-hard monoliths but growing enmity. The blood of men and women, the destruction of many churches, the spoliation of property and the abuse of religious rights, the anathemas pronounced in retaliation, widened the gap to seemingly unbridgeable proportions. The Vatican directed its temporal and spiritual strength against powers that had rebuilt their societies on the principle that religion was to be eliminated and that the world—this world, not some hope of a heavenly future—was to be made the abode of human well-being by purely material means.

Yet, though the two forces were, and are, at opposite ends of the spectrum of human thought, it is a mistake to judge the confrontation between the Roman Church and communism as the Papacy's throwing down of the gauntlet at the feet of a predestined enemy. Rome has not regarded Marxism as necessarily and inevitably a force with which some sensible agreements cannot ever be made. Similarity has not bred contempt; inherent antagonism has not precluded belief in the possibility of an accommodation, and in our own day the two sides have shown that agreements can be made and kept. The Vatican, moreover, found itself during John's pontificate in a position which chilled many of its policy makers: that of the vanguard in a new approach to overcome the division of the world.

Popes have been outspokenly anti-communist—one thinks particularly of Pius XII—and, though relations with communist countries are now easier, the Vatican still does not condone their doctrine. In a real sense, however, the Papacy is not unmitigatedly anti-communist. It is not permanently against any political system, any more than it is permanently in favour of dictatorships, such as that of General Franco. Once it appeared to love absolute monarchy—throne and altar in comfortable combination—against the pretensions of the democrats. In our day, it has given its blessing to republican and democratic regimes, and it cannot be doubted that there is today such a thing as 'Catholic democracy'. Even so, it would be a grave error to assume that Rome is any more indissolubly linked *sub specie aeternitatis* to democracy than it was to absolute monarchy. The papal system, after all, has never been democratic, and there are limits to the extent to which even the Papacy can embrace opposing opinions, accepting elsewhere what it refused to allow in its own principality when there was one, or in the government of the Church itself. Kissing the sacred foot and casting a vote in a general election are two acts with centuries of thought dividing them. The Golden Rose will not be borne, at least in the foreseeable future, to a prophet inspired by the vision of an egalitarian structure. Marian visions, yes, but not democratic aspirations. What it all comes down to is that the Vatican is against what is against its interests, and most of all it is against a persecuting power.

At the Vatican now most people on balance would probably

favour the combination of a completely free Church functioning within a moderate democracy rather than a free Church within a dictatorship. What 'the Vatican' thinks is always inclined to be the consensus emerging from a number of conflicting opinions advanced by those who work there; that is how its ideas are developed. But the blessing of moderate democracy by Leo XIII is now of sufficient authority and proven utility to be acceptable. The democratic vine has produced tenderer grapes over the years. The heady roughness of the original vintage—of liberty, equality and fraternity, and the dreadful shocks of the French Revolution—has settled to a genial, rather dark, unintoxicating drink which is no longer noxious, not even to the idea of imperial manners surrounding an absolute spiritual ruler. The serious recognition by the Holy See of the need for a democratic exchange of ideas within the State (not within the Church, of course) came from Pius XII, often a more realistically accommodating pontiff than the current legend would suggest. In an address in February 1950 to a group of Catholic journalists, he implied that some degree of free discussion in political affairs was essential. Commenting on the behaviour of totalitarian powers, he said that to reduce citizens to silence was 'an attack on the natural rights of man, a violation of the order of the world as God had established it'. He spoke of 'public opinion in the very breast of the Church'—with the proviso, 'naturally in matters left to free discussion'. This typical example of papal reservation might seem to cancel out any real meaning to the whole address, especially as no one can be ignorant (and certainly Pius XII was not) of the heavy-handed limitation of free discussion within the Church in his time. The arrival of free discussion as a recognisedly positive force in the Church's life came with his successor's decision to call an Ecumenical Council. Discussion at Vatican II was largely free. There were attempts to clip the wings of the higher-flying supporters of new ideas; but, as an essay in the free discussion of how an absolute system should go about its mission, the Council marked a real advance. Despite his proviso, Pius had taken one important step: while refusing to endorse democracy as the proper system for meeting all eventualities, or even liberty of expression for that matter, he had clearly suggested that the basic democratic freedom was a natural part of a healthy civil structure.

There is now little fear of democracy at the Holy See. Certainly, it would be odd for it to distrust a system which brought a Catholic to the presidency of the most powerful democracy in the world. Curiously enough, the Vatican was not all that happy over what appeared so great a triumph; some prelates there were grumbling immediately after John F. Kennedy's election that the standing of Catholics at the highest pinnacle of power would now be judged by the performance of a comparatively immature politician who would not have been their first choice as paladin of the West. There may also have been the fear that, as a Catholic, Kennedy might have to take a firmer line than a non-Catholic against specifically Catholic requirements—such as financial help for Church schools—simply to show that he was first and foremost a democrat, elected by fervent anti-Catholics as well as by members of his own Church. It was clear, moreover, that Kennedy's religion would, almost *ipso facto*, prevent him from proposing the opening of diplomatic relations with the Holy See. His exercise of power, of course, brought a revision of this opinion, and his tragic death was in the full tradition of martyrdom familiar to the Church for centuries. His curial critics were then able to accept Kennedy as their own. Perhaps something remains of the uncomfortable feeling that democracies are capable of doing unexpected things, but on the whole the alien system is liked as much as it should be liked by a power more habituated to a stiffer framework of authority. And the Vatican's officials can take comfort in the thought that cohesive groups within democracies, such as Catholic organisations, can make their presence felt even if they do not command a majority.

Priests take to electioneering as to the manner born. 'What we can offer is this . . .' They were saying such things long before parliamentary candidates were heard of; and they, unlike the pleading figures with coloured rosettes and programmes for the next five years, can raise the alternatives before an undecided electorate of eventual happiness for ever in heaven or eventual pain in hell for ever if the vote should be used by the faithful in the 'wrong' way. (Of course, this is effective as a political influence only where the electorates are ignorant.) Sometimes the Church's influence is deployed with great enthusiasm, as a pure challenge, to make sure that the friends of the faith win and its foes lose, or that a particular candidate is successful. More recently, there have been signs that it is deployed with less heart, as a sad necessity because the world is as it is and because people as they are can too easily be deceived. Younger priests, particularly, are known to protest to their bishops against the conservative political outlook which they must impose —though, for the moment, most of them accept the necessity to prescribe something for their parishioners' guidance. This habit of mind belongs more to the Latin Catholic temperament. It originates in the long experience of civil administration which the priesthood has had since the days when it grappled with the task of preserving some authoritative structure after the fall of the Roman Empire. It is nourished by the undoubted attraction which political affairs—almost as if they were a hobby—have for some priests. Outside the Latin countries, it is more the element of cohesion that counts. The sense of mission is applied to the winning of places of influence; rather too openly at times, as religious quarrels in Australia, to cite but one example, show. In a word, democracy is a manageable system. Other things being equal, it is preferable to a dictatorship. But there would be nothing much for Rome to worry about if a dictatorship gave the Church what it required while showing signs of lasting so that the Vatican would not suddenly be left—as so often has happened in the past—backing the black horse which suddenly bolted at the approach of a new regime.

That is why a communist state which granted the required liberties, if such a thing were thinkable, would be quite acceptable to Rome. Few prelates there are still so ingenuous as to suppose that communism will be overturned. This is the fundamental sense in which it can be said that politics enters the Vatican's thinking only indirectly. The object is to win and to preserve the best position for the Church. Hence, as Monsignor Cardinale has indicated in rather general terms, the Vatican is in the unique position of being able to carry out, as a second or third consideration, what other powers would regard as issues demanding a first call on the attentions of the officers of state. To free the Church from limitations in communist countries means better relations with the civil authorities. A concern for closer unity with the Orthodox Church —most of whose members are in communist countries and especially in Russia—requires a relationship of some mutual trust with Moscow. The capacity to offer the underdeveloped countries —particularly the newly independent nations—the social and economic as well as the spiritual message of Catholicism entails criticism of colonialism, a tender regard for the feelings of Asian and African leaders, and a rigorous rejection of colour prejudice. The attempt to impose on some of the Latin American hierarchies the more progressive social doctrines now held by the Church will have its effect on political developments in that subcontinent. Social systems and politics for Rome are of the secondary order of things, but that does not prevent them from becoming very important indeed at times. To achieve the prime objectives of the Church it is sometimes necessary to put second things first. The Holy See's relations with communism exhibit this strategy in what is certainly its most striking form.

With the outbreak of revolution in Russia in 1917, there was no immediate need for the Vatican to declare its enmity. Indeed, it did not do so in terms of incorrigible hostility until 1930. Moreover, when the Bolsheviks came to power they were less concerned at first with the activities of the Roman Church than with those of the official Russian Orthodox Church. White Russian exiles detected in the Vatican's policies in the period immediately following the February and October Revolutions a sinister attempt to win for Catholicism a special place in Russia at the expense of the national Church. The exiles' national committee in Paris had the pope in mind when inveighing against the 'crooked paths of the base politics of our time'. Machiavelli again; or perhaps Innocent III at that bad moment in 1204 when he failed to dissociate himself from the pillage of Constantinople by the soldiers of the Fourth Crusade because the prospect of imposing a Latin patriarch on the Orthodox seemed worth the bloodshed and the disgrace.

The attack by the White Russian exiles on the pope's motives was not the first to accuse the Vatican of tricky dealing, and it would surely not be the last. What is important to note is that the guiding line of its policy, crooked or not, at this time was flexibility in seeking to exploit a new political situation. It was certainly far from a downright rejection of what later was to be denounced as an evil. 'Where there is the question of saving souls', declared Pius XI on 14 May 1929, in a colourfully exact description of the Holy See's entire approach to politics, 'or preventing greater harm to souls, We feel the courage to treat with the devil in person.' He was speaking at a time when the Church was involved with Mussolini in a dispute about education in Italy. It is a dictum as valid for communism today as it was for fascism—and, for that matter, parliamentary democracy. Devils can always change their spots, and seem to do so fairly regularly; they may be communists persecuting the faith, or they may be liberals engaged in ejecting the pope from his temporal dominions. It is not the name a political creed bears that is important, nor what its individual leaders believe in. What matters is that these latter should allow the Church to go its way without hindrance—something that was not going to happen for long in revolutionary Russia.

Not to try to treat with the new Russian leaders would have been more uncharacteristic of the Vatican than a wholesale rejection of the regime on ideological grounds. The tsars, their symbolisation of altar and throne notwithstanding, aroused little affection in Rome; they had, to put it mildly, not been helpful to the Catholic cause in Russia. A new government assuming provisional powers after Nicholas II's abdication, an administration promising religious freedom, provided an opportunity, eagerly grasped by the Vatican, of achieving what had been denied to it under the old regime. A new archbishop was appointed to the see of Mogilev, the main Catholic diocese spreading as far as Siberia and with its cathedral in St Petersburg, and two other bishoprics were filled. Negotiations opened with Kerensky's Provisional Government were going favourably for the Catholic cause, and when the Bolsheviks came to power they left the situation much as it was, except for deleting a provision about official financial assistance to religious institutions. By the beginning of 1918, the situation deteriorated, yet it was more confused than alarming. In January 1918, all ecclesiastical property was confiscated; but Catholics, like other religious groups, were still able to use their churches which were now officially the property of the state. By the end of the year, the archbishop was in prison, but he was out again within twelve months. Three bishops were sent away from their sees; yet, amidst the chaos of post-revolutionary Russia, the Vatican was able to create a vicariate apostolic in Siberia in December 1921 and other administrations for the Caucasus and for Armenian Catholics, while, in February 1923, a new diocese was set up (though soon abolished) at Vladivostok.

During the international conference at Genoa in 1922, called to settle post-war economic difficulties in Eastern and Central Europe, the Vatican was busily drawing the attention of the Soviets and other powers to the need for religious freedom in Russia. The conference produced coincidences of protocol that struck rumours like sparks from tinder, such as the seating arrangements for dinner on board the Italian battleship *Dante Alighieri* in Genoa harbour. These brought the Soviet foreign minister, Chicherin, opposite Monsignor Signori, archbishop of Genoa. This particular confrontation did not, and probably was not intended to, lead to much. However, a visit to Genoa by Monsignor Pizzardo of the Vatican's Secretariat of State,* bearing a memorandum on religious freedom, certainly meant something, though not what the Holy See hoped. It meant something which the Church was going to find a familiar problem in dealing with the Soviet Union: that the actions of the government did not bear out the official policy of freedom for conscience and for worship, nor for the use of the buildings necessary for this freedom. Communist bad faith was a bitter disappointment, but the Church for a time still preferred not to regard it as a confirmation of fundamental hostility. The Vatican would have liked two things from the Russians: freedom for Catholic worship and teaching, and the chance to develop better relations with the Orthodox. It obtained neither at the time. In the last few years, after three bad decades in relations with communist states, the Holy See has taken up the same threads once again, with a

* Pizzardo was to be the young Montini's mentor at the Secretariat.

rather less slender hope than before. For both these aims, the goodwill of the Soviet authorities is needed. The cause of greater Christian unity and the better treatment of Catholics in Eastern Europe lead to the same conclusion: a relaxed and flexible policy towards the communist powers.

This appraisal, however, cannot ignore the struggle that was waged between the first and the later attempts of Rome to reach an accommodation. The stages in the conflict were inexorable. In September 1924, the Vatican closed its relief mission to Russia. At a consistory later that year, Pius XI set aside restraint, asserting that it was his duty 'to warn and earnestly exhort all in the Lord, especially the civil leaders, that . . . they use every effort to keep far from themselves and their fellow-citizens the most serious dangers and the quite certain harm of socialism and communism'. Early in 1926, on 29 March, Monsignor Eugenio Pacelli, then nuncio in Berlin and the future Pius XII, conferred the episcopal mitre on Father d'Herbigny,* a Jesuit, whose task it would be to go to Russia and to consecrate secretly several bishops and give them formal notice of their appointments as apostolic administrators. It needs to be mentioned in this context that there had been a rising among the Catholic population of Russia as a result of the Treaty of Riga of 1921, which established a new border between Poland and Russia. More than a million and a half Catholics had ended on the Russian side of the frontier: an additional reason for the Vatican to try for as long as possible to step carefully rather than provoke conflict with the civil authorities. But Soviet religious policy was to have no need of provocation. In 1929, Stalin's power was consolidated. Laws concerning religion

---

* Michel d'Herbigny was rector of the Oriental Institute in Rome. He made three visits to the Soviet Union. The first was in October 1925 on a permit granted him as a French citizen, ostensibly going to look at ecclesiastical and other institutions sponsored by France in Russia. His second visit took him through Berlin; three days after leaving Pacelli, he was in Moscow. He carried out his mission in the course of a stay of some six weeks. The names and titles of the new bishops and administrators were not published until some years later, when it was clear that the authorities knew of them. D'Herbigny's third journey was in August 1926. In applying for permission to enter a third time, no secret was made of the fact that he was now a bishop. On this final visit, he probably consecrated one or more bishops.

were made more stringent. The practice of the ministry of the faith became well nigh impossible for all Christian groups.

In a letter of 2 February 1930 to Cardinal Pamphilj, vicar of Rome, Pius XI recalled the efforts of the Holy See for the Russian people, and made 19 March a special day for prayer and expiation. In April, he changed the Pontifical Commission for Russia into an independent body, reporting directly to him. On 27 June 1930, Stalin told the Sixteenth Congress of the Russian Communist Party of the 'clerical crusade led by the pope against the Soviet Union'. A little less than a year later, on 8 March 1931, Molotov stated that Roman Catholic priests were 'spies serving on the anti-Soviet general staff', and that the Vatican had 'in the past few years been trying to intervene actively in international affairs—to intervene, of course, in defence of capitalists and landlords, the imperialists, the incendiaries of war'. The enmity was complete and acknowledged. On 19 March 1937, Pius XI delivered his encyclical *Divini Redemptoris*. As far back as Pius IX's time, there had been papal denunciations of communism, but they were among denunciations of a lot of other things which subsequently had been seen to be more or less innocuous. There was now to be no doubt in the matter. *Divini Redemptoris*—with its 'lay' title of "On Atheistic Communism"—is the great set-piece of modern papal denunciation. 'Communism is intrinsically wrong and no one who would save Christian civilisation may collaborate with it in any field whatsoever.'

The condemnation seems absolute, unconditional. Twenty-five years only were to pass for it to be interpreted flexibly. But what, after all, is such a time-span to an institution which looks back over nearly two thousand years of continuous existence, and looks forward to eternity? On 10 February 1963, John XXIII was able publicly to express his joy at the release by the Soviet authorities of Monsignor Josef Slipyi, primate of those Ukrainian Catholics left in Russia by the Treaty of Riga who had been practically destroyed as a corporate body. Their primate had been in a labour camp for eighteen years, a victim of the post-war attempt to break up religious groups maintaining communion with Rome. On 7 March, the pope received Alexei Adzubei, son-in-law of

Khrushchev. Their talk in the private library lasted only eighteen minutes but it ended an era. On 10 April, the pope published the encyclical *Pacem in Terris* which embodied his ideas on communism and how best to approach it. At 7.49 in the evening of 3 June 1963, John XXIII died and the brief cyclone of his reign was over. Looking back, it is astonishing how concentrated were all the significant events in this radical new development in papal policy.

There were to be immediate effects of what Monsignor Loris Capovilla, John's secretary, has called the 'holy diplomacy' of the late pope. Cardinal König, archbishop of Vienna, was able to begin a series of private calls on Cardinal Mindszenty in his refuge at the American embassy in Budapest. Connected with these visits was the negotiation of a 'partial agreement' with the Hungarian government which is looked on at the Vatican as a test of whether negotiations of this kind are yet feasible with communist governments. Paul VI's list of prelates for appointment as cardinals, made public on 25 January 1964, included the name of Monsignor Josef Beran, archbishop of Prague, who for years had been imprisoned or otherwise prevented from carrying out his functions as archbishop and Czech primate. On 19 February, Beran arrived in Rome, permitted by the Czech authorities to go to the ceremonies of his creation as cardinal, though he would not be permitted to return. The release also gave the new cardinal, emotionally overcome as he was by all that had happened to him, the possibility of addressing the Ecumenical Council. He gave, on 20 September 1964, one of the most memorable addresses of the whole Council; he spoke of the need for freedom of conscience whether allowed by the civil authorities or by the Church itself.

Before all this had happened and before the Council itself had begun, a crucial event occurred which in some ways marked the watershed of the new development. From 27 September until 2 October 1962 Monsignor Jan Willebrands of the Vatican's Secretariat for Christian Unity was in Moscow. As a result of his talks there, the Russian Orthodox Church sent observers to John's Council, which opened on 11 October. The Russian authorities were persuaded it could do no harm, and might do some good, to follow the policies and activities of the Vatican at a moment of profound change. There was the added attraction for the Russian prelates that, by going as observers at the last minute while not informing the Greek Orthodox, they were able to steal a march on their rival. This they did effectively and brought about the ironical situation by which Athenagoras, the patriarch of Constantinople and spiritual head of the Greek Church, was unrepresented for all that he was known to be one of the most convinced advocates of greater Christian unity. The general feeling among Greek Christians was that the whole of the Orthodox communion should decide whether or not to go to Rome, and it caused great resentment that, while Moscow was giving Constantinople the impression that nothing new was in the wind, the decision had been taken for the Russian observers to leave for Rome. Their presence was to prove influential. There cannot be much doubt that the Vatican gave assurances of some kind that the Council would not breathe a spirit of anti-communism. Faithful to his word—and also to his own character—John opened his Council with a cheerfully firm insistence on its pastoral nature which precluded condemnations. Equally faithful to this injunction, his successor resisted in the last stages of the Council, during the autumn of 1965, the final effort by more traditionalist elements to bring the Council around to an outright condemnation of communism. Somehow that final petition went astray, apparently ending up in some convenient—and exalted—wastepaper basket instead of on the desk of the appropriate commission.

The transformation from the decades of struggle seemed complete. The seal was placed on it by the visit to Paul VI in January 1967 of N. V. Podgorny, the first Russian head of state to set foot in the Vatican since the revolution. Was it a complete reversal? Not really. Though popes are apt to overstate the element of continuity from reign to reign, John's initiative, though of immense importance, did not appear from nowhere. In this, as in other respects, Pius XII's pontificate deserves a closer attention than is usually given to it these days. Pius, as has already been suggested, was the type of man liable to arouse violent sympathies in people one way or the other; he has his fervent faithful who regard him as a saint (his canonisation has already been requested) and his detractors who regard him as a disastrous pope. The latter look upon his attitude to communism as one of blind condemnation, in keeping with the theatrical superficiality of the character which they ascribe to him. More balanced assessments are beginning to come, partly forced by Herr Hochhuth's celebrated attack on Pius XII's integrity in his play *The Representative* (which was banned in Rome), and various assertions that he was by temperament a man of the extreme right.

Pius certainly grew to be sternly uncompromising in his rejection of communism and in his later years he came extremely close to identifying the Church with that anti-Soviet crusade of which Stalin had spoken years earlier. Allegations of a bias in favour of the political right were prompted by his refusal to condemn Nazi atrocities; in addition, he had inherited a pact with Mussolini, a policy of favour towards Franco, and a hierarchy in Italy which had a substantial number of its members avowedly sympathetic towards the fascists. His formal anti-communist moves are clear, unmitigated condemnation. In July 1949, he issued his decree outlawing in the Church's sense those who voluntarily adopted communism, prescribing the penalty of excommunication. He warned the faithful of the dangers which would come from having anything to do with communism. These strictures became much harsher after the Hungarian revolt in 1956, which brought from the pope three encyclicals in three days—something no other pope had ever done—condemning the Russian action. In his Christmas message of that year, he spoke of the perils of coexistence and the idea that a discussion with communists could be maintained: 'Out of respect for the name of Christian, compliance with such tactics must cease, for, as the Apostle warns, it is inconsistent to wish to sit at the table of God and at that of His enemies.'

Nothing more anti-communist could be imagined. Yet it is wrong to simplify matters so that he appears completely intransigent towards the Soviet Union, as a matter of fundamental policy. He was proud, and had some reason to be, of the care he took, after the Germans had attacked Russia, to avoid any suggestion that a seal of papal approval accompanied this onslaught against the Church's worst tormentor. He recalled this several times. Addressing the Sacred College and the diplomatic corps accredited to the Holy See on 25 February 1946, he said: 'We took special care, notwithstanding certain tendentious pressures, not to let fall from Our lips or from Our pen one single word, one single sign, of approval or encouragement of the war against Russia in 1941.' He returned to the same theme six years later in a message addressed to the Russian people. The Christmas message of 1956, which seemed to be the height of condemnation, also contained the passage: 'We, as head of the Church, have avoided calling Christianity to a crusade, but We can understand those who suffer directly thinking in such terms.' Whatever impression other people may have had, he did not feel that he had allowed any excessive element to enter his anti-communism. The same message contained the assertion that he could not be reproached with 'wishing to harden the opposing fronts'. It could be said of the *Osservatore Romano* that no newspaper had condemned so severely the assassination in 1950 of the Belgian communist leader, Julien Lahaut. Catholic opinion in Italy was doubtful about the wisdom of Italy's joining the Atlantic alliance and, in the Catholic left, there was opposition to membership. Pius XII shared some of these misgivings, as did the then Monsignor Montini. De Gasperi was driven to do something which went against his own character: he had to convince Pius of the necessity of bringing Italy into NATO and ask for clerical influence to help him overcome the divisions of opinion within the Christian Democratic Party.

Would Pius then, in any conditions, have treated with the devil? This would be merely an academic question were it not for the fact that both of his successors have shown a readiness to attempt negotiation with the communists and to insist that the Vatican have its own direct contacts with the Russians. Paul has gone so far as to appeal for contacts with the Chinese in his Epiphany discourse of 1967. Pius almost certainly would not have taken such steps. There was, indeed, talk at the end of 1941 and at the beginning of 1942 of a possible new agreement between Russia and the Holy See; but this was the stuff of circumstance rather than of will. Pius may have thought that, with the Soviet regime hard-pressed under German attack and with the consequent signs of a relaxation of the campaign against religion, the possibility might arise for an understanding with Stalin over the Church's freer exercise of its mission. After 1945, however, Pius probably recognised that dealing with Stalin was out of the question. He went on to declare his hostility towards communism. A number of cardinals around him entered with even more alacrity into the struggle against the East on the side of the West. This policy was changed by John, who preferred flexibility and warmth to anathemas and acrimony (though he left the anathemas intact). But John was, in effect, restoring the situation from which Pius—under the heavy pressure created by communist persecution—had, one might say, diverted the traditional line of papal policy towards a powerful secular antagonist. John's own comments show this restoration to have been intentional. He spoke of the Church's 'perfect neutrality' when he received the Balzan Peace Prize. In June 1959, he told the Second World Congress of Negro Writers and Artists: 'The Church you know does not identify itself with a single culture—not even with the Western culture with which its history is so closely bound—because its mission is on another plane: that of the religious salvation of man.' In both the Vatican's immediate policy after the Bolshevik Revolution and in Pius XII's supposedly extreme handling of the Church's relations with communism, John could find substantial precedents for making a break in the black veil of the Vatican's political position.

How black was the blackness? Whatever may finally be the verdict of history on Pius's refusal publicly to condemn Nazi atrocities, there can be no doubt that he liked the Germans as a people and that in any conditions—and there could hardly have been worse conditions than those he lived to see—he would have been reluctant to look on the Germans as the leading enemies of religion. His handling of the German problem was unhappy but logical enough when the political as well as the spiritual nature of the papal office is rationally looked at; just as his condemnation of communism is explicable in such terms. Pius was a politician with a delicate awareness—unlike most politicians—of all the issues comprising a particular policy. This aptitude made his mind an accurate reflector of the varied, and sometimes contradictory, considerations which a pope must take account of even when faced with a situation which appears to require a simple denunciation. The Germans were not anti-religious in the way that their opponents, the communists, were anti-religious. Though many priests were imprisoned by the Hitlerian regime, it was only in Poland that the Germans turned to wholesale persecution of the Catholic Church. In Germany itself, priests went to prison but the hierarchy was left its physical freedom. Most of the bishops—and probably most Catholics—were willing to identify Hitler with the interests of Germany, as representative of a new national vitality and decisive anti-communism. As far as the war was concerned, they wanted a German victory even if there were some difficulties of conscience about the nature of some of Hitler's policies. On the whole, the hierarchy and German Catholicism in general still felt the scars of the struggle with Bismarck and were anxious at any cost to show their German patriotism. There were honourable exceptions. Cardinal Faulhaber in Munich defended the Jews against persecution, and the gallant Galen of Munster and Preysing in Berlin condemned the Nazi theory of racialism. Von Stauffenberg, the officer who tried to assassinate Hitler, was a practising Catholic.

In July 1933, the Holy See had signed its concordat with Nazi Germany. Pacelli was largely responsible for it, partly as a result of his time as apostolic nuncio in Germany and as Secretary of State. It represented the culmination of his own long years of work there. For that reason alone he would have had an affectionate regard for it. Equally to the point was the fact that the concordat was regarded at the Vatican not only as a notable achievement but as a favourable concordat in itself—which, on paper, it was. On paper, also, it represents Pius's primary claim to being regarded as the consummate diplomatist which his admirers affirm him to have been. Praise for him over this seems exaggerated. He knew his way about in the diplomatic world; it is not easy to see how an arrangement which brought advantages to Hitler as well as to Rome—and was, in any case, disregarded by Hitler when he felt inclined—can be regarded as a diplomatic triumph. The fact remains that it was valued in Rome. Denunciations by Pius of Nazi atrocities would almost certainly have meant the end of this prime product of his diplomacy. Whether by insight or by sheer good fortune, the Vatican was, in fact, extremely well served by its two concordats with fascist dictators. Both regimes were later to fall and leave Catholic politicians in power, while the concordats—drafted to protect Catholic interests against dictators, not sympathetic governments—remained in force. From the legalistic, diplomatic and realistic viewpoints, the argument that moral denunciations would have made the position of the Roman Church in Germany more difficult is true; and diplomacy, legality and realism have historically counted for much at the Vatican. Pius was frequently warned of the dangers which his policy entailed. Friendly powers (with certain interests of their own) pointed out these dangers. The American mission, for instance, reported in 1942 that the Vatican had been informed that the absence of any public protest by the Holy See against the Nazis was endangering the moral prestige and undermining faith in the Church 'and in the person of the Holy Father himself'. There is clear evidence, not only that the position of the Church would, in Pius's view, have been weakened by public condemnations, but also that he chose to regard Nazism as a tragic but passing aberration on the part of his beloved German people. He placed weight on the obligations of citizens to obey the civil authority. 'The conflict of conscience', as he put it, into which he would place German Catholics (anxious to assert their patriotism) by denouncing their government, carried great weight with him.

By an odd twist, the concordat of which he was so proud, unlike some other concordats, had the effect of releasing German Catholics from potential worries about second loyalties. The signing of a concordat does not mean that the Holy See approves of the policy of the government with which it is dealing; indeed, as concordats are supposed to give an agreed legal basis for its ministry, it is arguable that they are more useful when difficult governments are involved rather than friendly ones. Nevertheless, an agreement with Hitler must have meant to many Catholics that the Holy See was not unfavourable to the regime. Cardinal Döpfner, archbishop of Munich, preaching in 1964 on the anniversary of Pius's election, recalled his impressions as a student in Rome on hearing the news of the concordat: 'The Holy See could scarcely have avoided it, but it is true, as I remember very well, that many of us were bewildered and crestfallen to see it concluded.' Pius expressed with accuracy his own frame of mind, and the heart of his own dilemma, in a letter to Preysing, dated 30 April 1943:

> With regard to pronouncements by the bishops, We leave to pastors in their individual circumstances the responsibility for deciding whether and in what manner the danger of reprisals and other forms of pressure, as well maybe as other circumstances arising from the length and psychology of the war, recommend them to show reserve—in spite of the reasons there would be for intervention—for the sake of avoiding greater harm. This is one of the motives which impels Us too to set limits to our public pronouncements. . . . Christ's representative must travel an ever more difficult and rocky path if he would hold a right balance between the contradictory demands of his pastoral charge.

This last sentence is undoubtedly the crux of his attitude. While dismissing any suggestion that Pius was not shocked by the excesses of Nazism, it is fair to say that his lack of condemnation was due to the failure to recognise the one voice among all those contradictions which to most people would have been crying loudest and most true. The attacks on him for his negative attitude prompted the Vatican in 1966 to take the unusual step of publishing two volumes of selected documents from its archives in support of Pius. These documents do not, in fact, change the basic positions in the controversy. His attackers will still maintain that he failed because he was the sort of man that he was; his supporters will say, with a little more reason after the documents were published, that he did the best that could be done in extremely difficult conditions.

All this leaves unanswered the question of why Pius did not remain similarly quiet when facing communism, and bide his time until better days should come. In the past, he had shown his capacity for prudent silence and was not averse from recalling the fact. Had he been able to foresee the effects of his reticence—that a large part of Catholic Europe would fall to Soviet Russia—he might have had more to say for himself and for his Church. Two factors influenced him. One was the persecution of the Church in communist countries. With himself referring to the Catholics under communist rule as the 'Church of Silence', he would have felt that silence on his part in face of such an onslaught on the faith and its institutions—not only on the moral sense of ordinary people—would have been to fail in his duty. The second factor was the political situation in Italy.

ITALIAN POLITICS

An obvious contributory factor to the change in Vatican policies towards communism under John XXIII was the death of Stalin and the emergence of Khrushchev as Soviet leader. Less obvious, but hardly less important, is the fact that, after a lifetime abroad, John was not so absorbed in Italian internal politics as his predecessor had been. In a very real sense, Pius XII regarded himself as the defender of Italy. As well as bishop of Rome, he was primate of Italy: a recent title for popes, going back only to the unification, but it sums up a part of far more ancient claims to protection over the peninsula. During the Second World War, Pius undoubtedly looked on himself as the protector of Rome. Probably nothing gave him more pleasure than the pious tradition, much encouraged officially, that Rome escaped serious damage by air attack during the war because of the efforts of Pius XII and the miraculous intervention of the Virgin Mary. The part allegedly played by the Virgin Mary has been solemnly acknowledged by a special sanctuary on the outskirts of Rome: the Sanctuary of the Madonna of the Divine Love.

Had Italian politics been less of a passion with Pius, or the Italian Communist Party less strong, the Vatican's attitude towards communism would certainly have been more circumspect. One must never overlook the interplay between the requirements of the supreme government of the Church and the local interests of particular hierarchies in the outcome of an election or some other political event. Italy, in this respect, exercises a stronger influence than any other country. This influence derives from three factors: the geo-historical position of the Holy See; the nature of the Church-State relationship established by the Lateran Pacts; and the emergence after 1945 of the powerful Christian Democratic Party.

Italy is the home of the pope, and a small area within Rome and a few places elsewhere in the country remain his temporal sovereignty. Although his title of primate of Italy dates, in fact, only from the completion of Italian unity, from the beginnings of the Papacy in the dark times following the end of the Empire, the popes have always regarded themselves as having a special responsibility for events in the peninsula. This sense of responsibility was certainly not weakened by the concordat with Mussolini, which recognised the special position of the pope and of the Roman Church in national life. It was, however, a concordat with a dictator who kept the political activities of the Curia, no less than those of his secular opponents, within bounds of his own making. Once Mussolini had gone, and soon after him the monarchy, there was no longer a strong secular figure interested in or capable of supervising the Church-State agreement. This leads to the third and crucial factor. The end of the war saw the triumph of Christian Democracy in Italy. For the first time since the unification, the political forces of Catholicism were strong enough to govern the country. The Lateran Pacts and the concordat were reaffirmed and sanctioned in the republican constitution. From being anti-clerical liberal, and then fascist, Italy became to all intents and purposes a confessional state. In an agreement like the concordat, the framework makes a lot of difference; so does the presence of the papal court in Rome. Pius XII was to be prompt in showing how determinedly he would wield the old authority in the much greater freedom accorded the Papacy by virtue of the conditioning influence of this framework of Roman Catholic politicians.

These two events—the signing of the Lateran Pacts and the Christian Democratic predominance after the war—are the pillars of the Vatican's relations with the modern Italian state. The two men who dominated the scene in the post-war period were Pius XII and Alcide De Gasperi, who was by far the best leader the Christian Democrats have ever found.

De Gasperi was a devout Catholic; he believed, however, that a Catholic party should be left in the hands of laymen governing as Catholic politicians and, as such, adapting their policies to Catholic principles as and where possible. He did not believe in a Catholic political movement controlled by clerics. Unlike Pius, he was not born in a narrow Catholic atmosphere; in fact, he was barely Italian: an aspect of his background that gave him unusual objectivity in dealing with Italian affairs. Coming from Trent in the far north-east, he had his first political experience in the Austrian imperial assembly as a representative of the Italian minority—Trent being still, before the end of the First World War, a part of the Austria-Hungarian empire. As a result of this Austrian background, he had something else, apart from objectivity, which Pius could not be expected to have: a strong respect for and awareness of the State. This was a natural inheritance from the Habsburg empire which was, after all, the temporal arm of Catholicism at its height. A collection of mixed nationalities, as that empire was, needed a sense of the State to preserve its cohesion. Thus, De Gasperi had in mind ideas which were far from the thoughts of most of his Catholic colleagues in Italy when they were swept to power in 1948 as the first Catholic rulers of the united nation. He envisaged an autonomous political party working in the name of Catholicism; he was also motivated by a strong sense of the Italian State.

The Vatican would be unlikely to think much of the first because of the experience with Christian Democracy's predecessors. The original of these was the National Democratic League, founded at the turn of the century by Romolo Murri, who was a priest. His political Catholicism was of an advanced kind. Both his views and the whole idea of Catholic participation in Italian political life were at the time unpopular at the Vatican. In 1909, he was elected deputy and excommunicated in the same year—but for his Modernism, not his progressive politics. Another priest, Don Luigi Sturzo, founded the Popular Party (*Partito Popolare*), which is regarded as the direct ancestor of the Christian Democratic party. He brought his party on to the scene as soon as the papal ban on participation in Italian politics was lifted. It was dissolved, with the other political parties, by Mussolini, after a brief but successful career in terms of attracting popular support, but one marked by Mussolini's dislike and the Vatican's distrust. These experiences fortified the Curia's view that avowedly Catholic political parties should only be countenanced when kept under strict clerical control.

As for the State, it had come into existence at the expense of the Church. It has been said frequently enough that, to the Latin Catholic mind, the order of precedence granted to institutions is: first, the family; then the Church; and thirdly the State. It is an attitude which De Gasperi did not share, but one which he had to deal with in his everyday political life.

De Gasperi relied on the Curia to help him win elections. He was not a great administrator; during the long years in which he was leader of the Christian Democrats, he did not build a party machine. He relied for votes on the parish priests and on the 'civic committees' which are the political arm of Catholic Action. The hierarchy and the lay arm of the Church (itself controlled by the hierarchy) were thus vital to him in maintaining his majority. It appears he could see no reason why organised Catholicism should not be glad to help the Christian Democrats to power when the alternative might well be a popular front dominated by the communists. Though constantly accused by the left of subservience to the Vatican, De Gasperi was far from being so. He had worked at the Vatican during the fascist period when he was unable to continue his political activities in the Popular Party. (He had a minor post in the library.) There were people at the Curia who were never to grasp, after he had become prime minister, why it was that their former employee was not more obedient. His votes, however, came through the Church. Catholic Democracy and the Catholic Church in Italy were driven together by the fear in the immediate post-war years—an exaggerated fear, one may think, in the light of the overwhelming victory of Christian Democracy —that Italy might go over to communism. So emerged the partnership which was ideological and electoral. Anti-communism was an immensely appealing slogan. It guaranteed American help on a full scale: help from abroad and help from on high. The confrontation with Italian communists, adherents of the political force that was crushing political and religious liberties in Eastern Europe, lent itself to dramatisation; and Italians are masters at dramatising any situation. The Christian Democrats have never forgotten that period. The Vatican of today has. This is one of the principal sources of Christian Democratic discontent ever since John's accession.

The Church by its nature is capillary. Its organisation in Italy runs up through all levels of life: schools, parish halls (which still have an important place in Italian life), hospitals, professional associations, newspapers; and everywhere there is the presence and influence of priests. A priest is often in the best position to help in any one of a highly varied set of circumstances—or not to help. In many places, for instance, particularly when unemployment was at its height, it would have been impossible for a man to find a job without the goodwill of the priest. As far as the employer was concerned, a recommendation from the priest would mean that the man was not likely to be an agitator, that he would have voted for the governing party and taken notice of the reminders hanging in the confession boxes about the serious consequences of voting for the extreme left or belonging to its organisations. A contractor in Rome would not expect his tender to be accepted unless accompanied by a letter from a cardinal. Such things were the commonplaces of Italian life. They are made fun of in films but are still a serious reality. In the south, people remember the days after the war when to be a socialist was to place one's self outside the ranks of organised society. Socialists who abjured their Marxism were ordered by the bishop to do so publicly, like Albigensians abjuring their heresy. The old sense of enclosure, of the fortress, had not had time to wither away before the new challenge arose in new conditions strongly favouring the Church's political activities.

At a higher level, the effect of making the Catholic religion the established faith was sure to mean that Italian politicians would at times be treated as if they were in ecclesiastical tutelage, just as the future Emperor Frederick II had been ward of Innocent III. In the case of Italy, the tutelage is more specific because the historical basis is more profound and the republican constitution so explicit. This is why the post-war years have been studded with examples of the Vatican's attachment to Italian policy. A cardinal (Ottaviani) could publicly upbraid the president (Gronchi) for visiting Russia. The Christian Democrats could not, without the Vatican's connivance, join the socialists in a centre-left alliance (and, having eventually done so, would see two consecutive coalitions fall on the schools issue). Before the centre-left was sanctioned, a prime minister-designate (Segni) would throw in his hand when his study of the prospects of such a coalition looked set for success. The Vatican would call for the withdrawal of a leading Christian Democrat (Fanfani) from the presidential campaign in the interests of Catholic unity, and he would obey. The economic holdings of the Vatican in Italy and its business would be vast but it would not pay a dividend tax. Certain subjects would be tacitly kept out of programmes for the coalitions. A bishop (Fiordelli of Prato) would refuse to appear in court when indicted over referring to civil marriages as concubinage. And the marriage in question, needless to say, went badly; the man's business failed and he had a stroke which left him partially paralysed. What clearer indication could one have of the advisability of leaving protests to fools or martyrs, of not challenging so deeply rooted a system?

In April 1952, between the nineteenth and twenty-third days of that month, there occurred in Rome what is perhaps the most thorough-going example ever to be exposed to the light of day of the limits to which the Christian Democrats and the Vatican—both behaving at their worst—were prepared to go in discreditable intrigue. It concerns an attempt by Pius XII to impose on the prime minister, De Gasperi, an alliance between his party and the neo-fascists in the city's local elections: an attempt, by this device, to avoid the possibility of a communist mayor in the sacred city. Even now, fifteen years later, it is worth recounting in some detail if only to show how bad things could be on both sides (there is little to be said for the behaviour of the Christian Democratic leadership, De Gasperi apart) before they began to get better. A full account was given in an article published in the summer of 1965 by Giulio Andreotti,* minister of defence when the article appeared, and a right-wing Christian Democrat normally regarded as having close personal contact with conservative elements in the Curia. There are a number of accounts; his is the full one, bringing out with remarkable blandness the way in which a governing party could become involved in such an intrigue.

Municipal elections were due in Rome. There appeared to be a fairly even battle with Nenni socialists and communists on one side and the parties of De Gasperi's centre coalition on the other (his party, social-democrats and liberals). The prime minister had insisted, from the beginning of his attaining office, on bringing into positions of responsibility as many as possible of the genuinely democratic parties, while leaving to one side the extremes both of left and right. This maintenance of the 'democratic centre' was fundamental to his whole policy. At the time of the approaching local election in Rome in 1952, the Christian Democrats were passing through one of their periodic bouts of disunity. In the secretaryship—then held by Guido Gonella, who earlier had written political articles for the Vatican's newspaper, *L'Osservatore Romano*—there was no great confidence that Rome would be retained. And so the problem, in Andreotti's words, was 'taken directly to the pope as bishop of Rome'. He gives a defence of what, even to him, appears to have been questionable conduct. It seemed to him undeniable that a bishop had the rightful duty, within the legal constitutional methods and limits, to work to prevent positions of power—such as the Roman municipality—from being controlled by people who were not only adversaries of Christian Democracy, but enemies of the Church and, indeed, of every religious value. (These events occurred, be it recalled, about a decade, no more, before Khrushchev's son-in-law was received by John XXIII.) In 1952, it was not regarded by senior personalities in the government of Italy as in any way trespassing on the rights of the civil power, or being a confusion of the sacred and the profane, for them to take their problems to the pope. When

* *Concretezza*, August 1965: a periodical edited by Andreotti.

it was convenient to them, Andreotti has pointed out, all in the governing party recognised the competence of the bishop of Rome to deal with any of the city's problems, from military security to feeding the populace.

Pius XII's idea was that the Christian Democrats should make an alliance with the neo-fascists (Rome has always had, and still has, a substantial right-wing vote), so that the non-communist forces could enter the battle undivided. Behind them would be the big battalions of Catholic Action, led by its president, Professor Luigi Gedda, who was a fervent supporter (and probably the originator) of the plan. De Gasperi, however, was utterly opposed to it, for it made nonsense of his national policy. It appeared to be an expression of wilting confidence in his powers of organising an election. He also had to bear in mind the anti-fascist feelings of some of his coalition partners—social-democrats and liberals—who would be aghast at this 'sacred union'.

Great pressure was put on him. On 19 April, he was so taken up with the question that he missed a cabinet meeting. At one a.m. he had telephoned Andreotti, then his secretary, and told him to report to him at the start of the day's work, after having called on the party secretary. Andreotti learned from Gonella that the Vatican intended forming, in the event of the failure of the Christian Democrats to make the alliance with the neo-fascists, a second list of Catholic candidates drawn from outside the ranks of the governing party. This body of candidates would have the support of the Vatican's newspaper and of Gedda's cohorts. Such a development would have meant the Vatican's abandoning of the Christian Democratic Party. No one knew better than De Gasperi that, without the priests and Catholic Action to bring in the votes, his party would be in a hopeless position.

On the morning of 19 April, a Jesuit called on the prime minister's wife—'inopportunely', as Andreotti admits—to persuade her to change her husband's mind. In answer to the Jesuit's request, Signora De Gasperi said: 'Mussolini must not be brought back.' 'Better Mussolini than Stalin', answered the priest. He got the retort he deserved: 'Better neither one nor the other.' More details of this odd interview have been given in an account of the affair by De Gasperi's daughter Maria.* She says that the Jesuit, Father Lombardi, was with her mother for an hour and a half, mixing praise and threats in recommending the wisdom of agreeing to a common list with the extreme right. 'The pope would prefer', the priest affirmed, 'Stalin and his Cossacks in St Peter's Square to a communist electoral conquest of the Campidoglio.' Of the prime minister, he said that, should the election go badly, 'we shall make him resign'. And who was 'we'? Father Lombardi, like Professor Gedda, was in the circle of Pius's intimates, and he was obviously intending to convey that papal wrath was involved.

It was an instructive intrigue because national considerations were ignored. The fact that a right-wing alliance in Rome would probably bring down the coalition of the democratic centre and would, thereby, be a betrayal of the prime minister's whole policy —this seems scarcely to have entered the clericalist calculations. Andreotti himself was beginning to dislike the idea. He called on Monsignor Tardini at the Curia and asked if the second list of Catholic candidates could be withdrawn. Perhaps... *in extremis*... he was told; what was wanted was unity. The future Secretary of State to John XXIII at least admitted some doubts on his own part and on the part of the next pope but one: 'Even we, who are servants of the pope and your friends (both I and Monsignor Montini, who these days, poor fellow, is reduced to a rag) feel the same worries.' There were to be some more anxious hours. After what Andreotti calls a Babel-like confusion, the plan was abandoned. Don Sturzo, the Sicilian priest and founder of the Popular Party, who had been placed in charge of the project (presumably because his long years as an anti-fascist exile would make more acceptable the idea of an alliance with fascism's heirs), gave it up in the early afternoon of 23 April. Once the failure was known, says Andreotti, there was 'great concern at all Vatican and para-Vatican levels to be freed of any responsibility or suspicion in the eyes of the pope'. But Pius understood the situation, and the proofs of the second list of Catholic candidates remained on his desk.

It was a discreditable business. It was also understandable in terms of history and of personalities. For Pius XII to have seen

* Maria Catti De Gasperi, *De Gasperi: Uomo Solo*, Rome 1964.

Rome freely vote the communists into power would have been the humiliating climax to the loss of the temporal power. If no local election in Italy took place without a detailed analysis of the results by him, it was still more true of Rome.

There is another side to the constant controversy about the limits of Church and State in Italy. John reduced the Church's direct hand in political affairs, but he could not in so short a time do much that would last. During his pontificate Professor Gedda lost the presidency of Catholic Action, though retaining that of the National Civic Committee, which is the admittedly political section of the movement. He was seldom seen at the Vatican after the death of Pius. Paul VI astounded liberal opinion by granting an official audience to Gedda and his colleagues, as if to reinstate him in favour and re-establish the hold of the hierarchy on internal Italian affairs. What he did, however, was to read a discourse which clearly laid down the limits of competence of Gedda's organisation. After enjoying high favour, Gedda knew disfavour, and then an exactly defined and circumscribed account of what he could do.

John's move responded to the feelings of many priests. It is wrong to suppose that all priests with a hand in politics are blackly reactionary. There is a fairly constant element of paternalism in what they do and teach—how could it be otherwise, after all?— but many of them feel indignation about the state of affairs. Better than most people, they know how ordinary Italians live. They are frequently too tied to local interests, but they have not by any means all lost the power of reacting spontaneously to social injustice. Particularly in central Italy, the younger priests are inclined to be advanced in their social views and have let their bishops know as much. Hence, from the Church's point of view, the original support of the Christian Democratic shift leftward of centre had much to recommend it. More than that, it meant that, as a result of the socialist alliance with the Christian Democrats, the traditional socialist anti-clericalism was likely to be diminished —as indeed it has been.

In continuing the process of allowing more space for political Italy to breathe, Paul VI reorganised the balance of power inside the Italian hierarchy. Pius XII's nominee as chairman of the episcopacy was Cardinal Siri, the conservative and political archbishop of Genoa. He was a declared opponent of the centre-left and an uncompromising advocate of condemning communism openly when the occasion arose—to the extent that, on one occasion, he appears deliberately to have gone against the present pontiff's wishes in bringing out a condemnation of communism as such. He belonged to the group of Italian conservatives—all personalities, incidentally, on a fascinatingly grand scale—which included Cardinal Ottaviani, head of the Holy Office, and Cardinal Ruffini, archbishop of Palermo, who was as openly right-wing in political sympathies at home as he was self-confessedly impressed by what he felt were General Franco's achievements in Spain. Substantial importance was thus attached to the decisive way in which Paul VI in August 1965 accepted the Genoese cardinal's resignation from the chairmanship of the episcopacy—proffered as a formality—and replaced him temporarily by a triumvirate of moderate cardinals. This triumvirate gave way to the appointment as chairman of one of its number, Cardinal Urbani, who had succeeded John XXIII as patriarch of Venice. New appointments to leading sees were indicative of Paul's desire to freshen the outlook of his Italian hierarchy. In his old see of Milan he established Cardinal Colombo*: another man of Urbani's cautiously moderate stamp. To Turin, the third of the four great northern sees (Siri was still entrenched in Genoa), he appointed Monsignor Pellegrino, whose approachable ways made clerics and laity alike familiar with his determined views on keeping religion and politics apart (he has appeared on television to say so), and on freedom for scholars. His 'style' is revealed in apparently small—but, in such a country as Italy, very significant—requests that he should not be addressed as *Eccellenza*: the normal form of address for a bishop or archbishop.† He was introduced at one press conference as

* Not the Colombo referred to on p. 160.
† The small republic of San Marino in central Italy claims to be the oldest in the world. It is ruled by two captains-regent: joint heads of state who are elected every six months. The republic falls under two dioceses, but neither bishop lives in the town. This is because the official form of address of the captains-regent is *Eccellenza* and, according to local lore, the San Marinese

having 'conceded' that no one need address him as *Eccellenza*. Monsignor Pelligrino promptly called the chairman to order, pointing out that he had asked for the dropping of the title as a favour to himself. (He was made a cardinal in 1967.)

The effects of the work of John and Paul have been quite quickly felt on the Italian scene. As the Vatican's outlook on the world at large becomes broader, the last pope and his successor have not felt the same compulsive attraction for Italian national politics. John, indeed, by nature was little concerned with the local political situation. Paul is more interested but, with the broader horizons opened up to papal action, it seems that the days are over when pontiffs would spend so much of their time poring over the results of municipal elections in Sicily or Lombardy. In the meantime, the Christian Democrats have been slowly building up their own party machine, so that their reliance on priests and on Catholic Action and its civic committees has grown less.

The motivations for the party's autonomy have changed in a curious way. Under Pius, and before the effects of John's pontificate were fully felt, the *autonomisti* in the party looked for greater independence because they were disturbed at the rightward pull of the Curia, at the constant pressure towards conservatism. But in recent years, those in the party seeking autonomy have done so because disturbed at the thought of their being swept too far to the left by the radical social attitudes of the post-conciliar Church. Had the Christian Democrats, for instance, adopted the Vatican's latest approach to communism as their own, they would have had to forfeit that anti-communist appeal which is the basis of their electoral support. The present situation is not a happy one for them. It has given their opponents the opportunity to portray them as politically archaic by comparison with their Vatican masters. But anti-clericals would presumably have even more to complain about if the Christian Democrats openly changed their Italian policies in conformity with changes in the Vatican's international policies. It is no bad thing if the Curia is thinking so much more widely that it can allow the Catholic party in Italy to go more

have ever abominated the idea of according the same title to the representative among them of another power.

its own way, instead of watching and controlling from the Apostolic Palaces the intricate patterns of political *chinoiserie* and applying peculiarly Italian experiences to the international stage.

POLAND AND WYSZYNSKI

Under Pius XII, a Golden Rose, the proofs to correct of an electoral list, the Cossacks in St Peter's Square, the red and the black—all were elements in an atmosphere made by him and history. It is this atmosphere of a rather virulent involvement in anti-communism, expressed in an ornate delicacy, which explains why the Vatican in his time did not care to underwrite the agreements made by the Polish bishops with the Polish state. The first agreement was signed in April 1950, and in December 1956 was renewed with certain modifications. This understanding between the hierarchy of Church and the hierarchy of party in Poland was the exact reverse of Rome's political position in Italy. The comparison is instructive. The Italian situation had not been allowed to remain wholly Italian. Whether by the *non expedit* denying Catholics a political part in Italian national life after 1870, or the Holy Office decree against communism, the Vatican had sought to control political affairs. For years, it was difficult for an Italian to reconcile a strong patriotic feeling with religious obligations. The opposite was true in Poland. To be Catholic and Polish was to be doubly patriotic because the faith and the nation, to the majority of Poles, were identical. An agreement of the kind made by the Polish hierarchy was only thinkable to Pius XII—and then thought of with reluctance—if the principle were firmly established that it applied only to Poland and could in no way be used as a precedent for experiments elsewhere in negotiating with communists.

It can be argued that one reason for this difference is that the pope is primate of Italy and not of Poland; or that he is an Italian and not a Pole, and so sees these things differently. John was to disprove both points. He was very Italian, yet he did not see the world through the sights of the Italian political situation. Or perhaps it is that he was influenced by the gentler elements of the

Italian political scene: the communist mayor on agreeably friendly terms with the parish priest; communist villagers acting in the annual Passion Play. ('All left-wing, our cast', it was said at one of these traditional performances in the countryside near Rome, 'except for Jesus, who's a fascist . . .') All seemingly rather cosy. But it is doubtful whether John, with his countryman's good sense and background, would have missed what most people miss in these cases: the viciousness from both sides that is often the dominant note at the local level after twenty or so years of rivalry at all levels. Certainly, there is a kind of Don Camillo element; but there is also a sharper, meaner and far less human side to these rivalries, and something of John's application of human warmth to the whole field of relations with communism may have been derived from an awareness of this fact. He carried out during his short reign many of the things which advocates of a non-Italian pope have always said would have to await the end of the long Italian monopoly of the Holy See—a monopoly which has lasted since the early sixteenth century.

The significant point about the Polish agreement was that both party and hierarchy wished to be seen as the embodiment of Polish patriotism. In so far as the nation existed, it did so through Catholicism. At the same time, Catholics felt a loyalty to their national government, albeit a communist government. This is a phenomenon difficult to understand in the mental background of a nation such as Italy, which came into being as a state by expelling the pope from his territories. Politically, the Catholic Church has rarely stood for nationality. The worst political challenge and the most damaging development to its imperial position came from the growth of national states. While it was strong enough, until the sixteenth century, to nullify the disruptive effects of heresy on spiritual unity, it could not dominate nationalities once papal authority declined from the summit reached by Innocent III. There are, indeed, a few areas where it has managed to settle easily into the national consciousness—Ireland and Poland come readily to mind: both cases, significantly, of ethnic combined with religious oppression. But, in general, resurgent nationalism—whether of the young nations of the Renaissance, or of the enlightened despots of the eighteenth century, or of the liberals of the nineteenth century—has been among Rome's most taxing problems, doubly lethal to its basic ideals when allied with a heresy. A concordat can be negotiated to give legal safeguard to what the Church believes to be vital to its mission; but this, and any other device of practical convenience, carries the risk of seeming to undermine, in however limited a field, the feelings of Catholic citizens for their own nation. This is an inevitable dilemma when a certain part of a citizen's rights are affirmed and upheld from outside, the forms being that of another power. A tendency to devalue the State as such is one of the explanations given for the lack of impulse to vigorous government in some countries long regarded as Catholic.

Right or wrong, it is still possible in Poland to appeal to these long-standing contentions and yet to have both parties arguing with a certain reserve, both arguing fundamentally as Poles. On 18 March 1961, for instance, Wladyslaw Gomulka, the Polish party leader, accused the Church in Poland of looking for conflict with the Polish state on the instructions of the Vatican, which needed, he alleged, persecutions and martyrs for its own ends. His outburst brought a reply from Cardinal Wyszynski, the Polish primate, who solemnly affirmed that in his thirteen years of office no pope or Secretary of State had ever tried to give the Polish bishops instructions on how to conduct themselves. Indeed, had the cardinal been still more frank, he might have referred to the cloud of doubt which afflicted the minds of some people in the Vatican at what the Polish bishops had done by their agreements. It was not until John XXII's reign that Wyszynski was publicly shown to be in favour. And by that time the Polish primate, feared earlier as too ready a pioneer, had already been left behind by the pace and efforts of the Vatican itself in revising its policy towards communist governments.

The Polish agreements merit attention because they give some idea of what a determinedly led episcopacy will, at worst, accept from a regime which, at best, should not exist. The Church had two things for which to thank the Polish authorities. The first was that, by occupying the Oder-Neisse territories and resettling them, the communists had replaced largely Protestant German populations with wholly Catholic Poles. It was a long time since the Church had won so large an increase in its territories. Secondly, the government showed respect for the Church in the immediate post-war years until 1949, more or less until the time of Gomulka's fall and the imposition of Stalinism, and the thoroughly bad times did not last long. The communists would have had an impossible task if they had tried to do away with the Church in Poland or attack it frontally; its popular following was far too great for that. The first agreement was reached on 14 April 1950. It came as a surprise, but it need not have done. With the Church in so strong a position, the best that a devoted communist could hope for—and probably what Gomulka had in mind when he renewed his arrangement with the cardinal on his return to power six years later—was that the Church would gradually diminish in popular appeal as socialist ideals took root. It would, in other words, precede the State in withering away.

The cardinal had no intention of allowing any such thought to be given currency. Wyszynski is a leader who sums up much of the peculiar character of the Polish Church. He is not a politician in the strict sense—not, for instance, in the way that the Hungarian primate, Cardinal Mindszenty, was a politician. In his first pastoral letter after being consecrated bishop of Lublin in 1946, he said of himself: 'I am no politician, no diplomatist, and no reformer.' That sums him up rather well. He is shrewd: his narrow, light eyes say as much; and he is introspective, somewhat mystical, with rather a lonely look. He can be unpredictable, as men with mystical streaks so often are. He is no easy enemy, nor is he an easy representative for the Vatican in a socialist country. The faith and Poland are what matter to him; he cannot—and, indeed, who could?—envisage a Poland which was not utterly Catholic. Though regarded as somewhat to the left in social views during his younger days in Poland, he showed in his performance at the Ecumenical Council that he is of a fundamentally conservative frame of mind. He did not want the liturgy in the vernacular (had he not said years before, 'I am no reformer'?), and preferred medieval Latin even to Ciceronian as nearer the traditions of the Polish people.

He spoke out against certain progressive Catholics 'who defame the Church as if it neglected the lot of the workers'. The Polish episcopate under his leadership at the Council's third session, for all its reputation in the past among some people as containing an advanced species of prelate, made a good many jaws drop by its urgent request that the Council proclaim the Motherhood of Mary as embracing the whole of humanity. Their proposal was fully supported only by the Mexican, Spanish and Sicilian bishops. Equally indicative of Wyszynski's mentality was his dignified appeal to the Council that it should fully present the spiritual nature of the Church. He pointed out, during the debates on the document *De Ecclesia*, that the term 'Church Militant' ran the risk of supplanting a more essential aspect of the Church: namely, its mission as an instrument of sanctification and a well-spring of spiritual life. Men trusted the Church, he said, because the Church offered them hope which gave them life and sanctified them inwardly.

Here one is faced by the somewhat mystifying phenomenon of prelates with reputations for daring or for advanced thinking who then reveal that such intellectual liberalism affects only a part of their outlook, and that elsewhere in their thinking they are traditionalist. The Polish primate is nothing if not Polish. Like Latin Catholicism, the Polish form is marked by Marian devotion and a mystical quality. Unlike Latin Catholicism, however, it cannot properly be accused of having tended to erode regard for the State; rather has it strengthened the idea of Poland by religious zeal so that, in its turn, patriotic feeling has reinforced the respect in which the Church is held. It was this combination which allowed the primate to make his agreement in 1950 and then to renew it when Gomulka came back to power. The terms are of interest for what they show of the primate's essential requirements from the Polish authorities.

A joint commission of representatives of government and hierarchy, convened to review the position at Gomulka's return to power, issued its communiqué on 7 December 1956:

> The Joint Commission of representatives of the government and the episcopate discussed a number of unresolved questions

concerning relations between the state and the church. In the course of the conversations, the representatives of the government emphasised their readiness to remove the remaining obstacles to the realisation of the principle of full freedom for religious life.

The representatives of the episcopate stated that, as a result of changes in public life aimed at the consolidation of legality, justice, peaceful coexistence, the raising of social morality and the righting of wrongs, the government and the state authorities would find in the church hierarchy and clergy full understanding for these aims.

The representatives of the episcopate expressed full support for the work undertaken by the government aiming at the strengthening and developing of People's Poland, at concentrating the efforts of all citizens in harmonious work for the good of the country, for the conscientious observance of the laws of People's Poland and for the implementation by the citizens of their responsibilities towards the state.

The document then went on to discuss the detailed matters on which agreement had been reached: the arrangements for the appointment of bishops; the question of religious instruction in schools; religious care for the sick and for prisoners; and some particular arrangements for the former German territories in the west. The first two points are crucial to any arrangement by representatives of the Church with the Polish government. On the question of bishops the agreement stated: 'The new legal act regulating these matters will guarantee the influence of the state in the appointment of archbishops, diocesan bishops and co-adjutors with right of succession, as well as parish priests, preserving at the same time the requirements of church jurisdiction.' On education it said:

> Full freedom is assured and the voluntary character guaranteed of religious instruction in elementary and secondary schools for children whose parents express such a wish. Religious instruction will be conducted in schools as an extracurricular subject.

The school authorities are to make it possible for religious instruction to be followed through a properly drafted syllabus of lessons.

Teachers of religion will be appointed by the school authorities in agreement with the church authorities. The teachers of religion will be paid from the budget of the Ministry of Education. The programmes of religious instruction as well as the religious instruction manuals must be approved by the church and the educational authorities.

Inspections of religious instruction will be carried out by the church and educational authorities. The school authorities will endeavour to enable the children and youth to participate freely in religious practices outside the school.

The school authorities and the clergy will ensure complete freedom and tolerance both to believers and to non-believers and will firmly counteract all manifestations of violation of freedom of conscience.

The Vatican, as we have noted, has never given its formal approval to this agreement or to its predecessor. This is not only because Pius XII was unhappy about it (showing his feelings by keeping the cardinal waiting for several days in Rome before receiving him). It is also, and more significantly, because the Vatican wants to avoid any suggestion that similar agreements elsewhere are to be encouraged. By giving no sanction, the Holy See —the supreme spiritual authority—is in no way bound. The Vatican likes to be in a position of being able to disavow what it dislikes.

An example of this outlook is the ill-defined status of its newspaper, *L'Osservatore Romano*. It is generally known by those who have any dealings with such things that the leading articles are written only after consultation with members of the Secretariat of State. The newspaper staff, for that matter, is administratively dependent on the Secretariat of State. What it says is authorised. It is not, however, an official publication of the Holy See. That title is reserved for the *Acta Apostolicæ Sedis*, the Vatican's equivalent of an official gazette. The newspaper's views, authorised at the time or not, are not binding. This is that strange almost-never, sometimes-however land over which the prelates and the shades of the Vatican drift insubstantially, always ready with a half-denial, and always prepared to issue a part retraction of what someone nearly said. The American Jesuit, Father Robert Graham, places the following footnote in his study of Vatican diplomacy: '... denials issued by Vatican spokesmen also complicate the problem of the historian. These denials are sometimes diplomatic in nature, designed to put the brake on premature speculation. Their real force needs close scrutiny in each case.'* Italian newspapers complain that a fact retailed to them one day by someone at the Vatican and published the next day will be denied by someone else there on the third day. But not an official denial, of course—not the Vatican rising to its feet and saying 'No' for all to hear. Instead, a news agency will report that 'authoritative sources at the Vatican describe the assertions given in an Italian newspaper of the north this morning as devoid of all foundation'. And that is that. Next week the 'assertions' may be true again. Sometimes this method is used for questions of high policy, and the next step in the Polish situation contained such a purposeful blurring of intentions.

In general, John XXIII brought a cheerful freshness by actions aimed at removing doubts. No one, for instance, quite knew the exact standing of Cardinal Wyszynski at the Vatican, given Pius XII's misgivings about his negotiations. John made his own feelings clear when, at one of his regular mid-day blessings of the crowd in St Peter's Square, he presented to the onlookers the Polish primate, who was visiting him. And privately he left no doubt that he approved of what the cardinal was doing and gave him a wide measure of freedom of action in conducting relations with the Polish authorities. (Application of the agreement was constantly punctuated by disputes.) But John did more, far more, and this was where the subtle hand of experienced diplomacy was used to striking effect. On 8 October 1962, the pope received the Polish bishops attending the Ecumenical Council. He had a habit

* Robert A. Graham, *Vatican Diplomacy*, Princeton University Press, Princeton, N.J., 1959, p. 349.

of receiving national hierarchies. Included in what he said to the Poles was this:

> I am told that in distant Poland, in the defence of your country's freedom, our compatriot from Bergamo by the name of Francesco Nullo, sacrificed his life. You tell me that resurrected Poland has set up a monument to this noble colonel, that streets bear his name—how this happened in Wroclaw, in the western territories which have now been recovered after centuries...

It was already enough. The Poles had what they wanted. The reference to the 'recovered' territories was balm to the ear of Polish Catholic and Polish Marxist alike.

Inevitably it brought a perturbed request for elucidation from the West Germans. What appeared to be affirmed was the Vatican's *de facto* acceptance of Poland's western frontier. Officially, the Vatican takes the view that, until a definitive international agreement is reached on such issues, it must remain apart from the affair, not taking sides. In the Oder-Neisse question, it has skilfully managed to remain clear of offending the Germans (who do not accept the frontier as final) by appointing Polish bishops to these sees without calling them bishops of the places concerned. They are formally made titular bishops—of some non-existent see in Asia Minor—and put in charge of an Oder-Neisse bishopric. This device carefully avoids taking sides and as carefully avoids breaking the concordat with Germany, which states that appointments of bishops to German sees must be looked at first by the German government. This was the reason why the Germans were worried by John's reported words and why the Poles were elated. The Germans were given an assurance to the effect that policy had not changed and that the words used by His Holiness in a private talk with bishops could not be made public or commented on—the second remark coming somewhat lamely after the text had been made readily available by the happy Poles. The delegation of sixteen bishops that had accompanied the cardinal to Rome was shortly afterwards raised to the full twenty-five which the primate had first requested of the Polish authorities. This was taken as a sign both of the Polish government's satisfaction and of the cardinal's confidence that he could now have so large a number of bishops out of Poland without the fear that the government would not allow them in again. He would be able to go home speaking with his usual firmness about the Church's rights, the national feelings of the Poles, the queenship of the Virgin Mary, and his confidence that the faith would conquer the enemies of religion.

Before leaving the Council, however, the Polish bishops provided the material for the next dispute with their government. They addressed letters to other hierarchies inviting them to Poland for the celebration in May 1966 of the millennium of Polish Christianity, to be held at the Marian sanctuary of Czestochowa. In the letter to the German hierarchy, they touched on the Oder-Neisse frontier issue and, in what was presumably intended to be a plea to let bygones be bygones and for Germans and Poles to forget their differences, they implied that Poland's western territories helped to counter-balance what the Russians had taken away in the east. Whether the Warsaw government's reaction was spontaneous or prompted by the Russians is not clear; certainly, it was some days in coming. The bishops were accused of political meddling; personal attacks were resumed on the cardinal, alleging that his anti-communism had made him weak towards fascism. A clash was probably inevitable, for May 1966 was to be marked, not only by a religious celebration, but also by a commemoration of the founding of the nation. Thus, each side was straining hard to show symbolically the weight of its contribution to national life.

Despite the renewed quarrel with the secular power, Cardinal Wyszynski still hoped that Paul would come to Czestochowa, 'if', as he put it in one of his sermons, 'God permits'—which was a shorthand way of expressing the difficulties. They proved to be too great. The Polish government informed the Vatican that the moment was 'not opportune', though leaving open the possibility of a visit some time later. Paul was extremely upset, expressing his 'keen regret' at a ceremony in St Peter's on 15 May 1966. Speaking with unusual directness, he rejected the reasons given by the Polish authorities as not only unjustified but unlikely to have the support of the Polish people. His words were:

> We had wanted to bring in person, by accepting the invitation of Cardinal Wyszynski, primate of Poland and archbishop of Warsaw, Our paternal greetings to the people of Poland and Our devout homage to the Most Holy Madonna honoured at Czestochowa, to celebrate with the entire people this fateful day. But this pilgrimage was not permitted to Us.
>
> We have naturally felt keen regret. We are convinced that the reasons given for opposing Our pilgrimage, and ascribed to the actions and attitude of Cardinal Wyszynski, are not justified and We cannot believe that they are supported by the common will of a nation so noble and so deferential to the Church as is Poland.

It was a harsh discourse, with the implication openly expressed that government and people were far from being at one over the issue. The pope was aware then, and was to grow increasingly cognisant, of the demands which the Polish government was making on the Vatican. Certainly, Cardinal Wyszynski was scarcely diplomatic in his dealings with the secular authorities, and his attitude towards them no longer accorded with the Holy See's more flexible approach to communist authorities in general. But the Polish government required far more of the Vatican than could be given.

It was understood that Warsaw was still pressing for papal recognition of the Oder-Neisse frontier. A concession on this point would have transgressed the Vatican's policy of not recognising new frontiers until they had been sanctioned by an international treaty. Moreover, acceptance of Warsaw's requirement that the Polish administrators of the former German dioceses be appointed full diocesan bishops would have broken the Holy See's concordat with the German Federal Republic, which gives the German government in Bonn the right to approve episcopal nominations. Appointments of Poles to these dioceses in eastern Poland could have been carried out only against strong German protest. Gomulka and his colleagues, it seems certain, also made strong complaints about Wyszynski's intransigence. There was a Polish suggestion that the pope might meet the government halfway by appointing a second cardinal for Poland, thereby diminishing Wyszynski's pre-eminence. Paul could hardly have been expected to listen to criticisms of Wyszynski; he would have felt morally bound to support the primate (as in his discourse of May 1966) against complaints from the Polish government. (Even so, the archbishop of Cracow was made a cardinal in 1967.)

In the months following the rebuff over the Czestochowa pilgrimage, relations between the Vatican and Warsaw deteriorated further. By March 1967, Paul had on his desk the report of a member of the Secretariat of State, Monsignor Agostino Casaroli,* who had just returned from his second tour of the Polish bishoprics with the impression that the government was unwilling to show any degree of accommodation. The differences were too great. Just how much the Polish government set by its demands on the Vatican became explicit less than a year after Paul's discourse on Czestochowa, when Edward Ochab, the president of Poland, in .... 1967 visited Italy as guest of the Italian government and left with the distinction of being the only foreign head of state not to call at the Vatican since Hitler's visit to Rome in 1938. Only a few weeks had passed since the Russian president had called on the pope.

Before Ochab left for Rome, the central committee of the Polish Communist Party had thoroughly debated the question of whether he should ask to see the pope. On balance—though it was apparently a fine balance—opinion was that he should not do so. This enabled the Polish government to state officially that there had never been any intention of the president's asking for an audience. The party and government came to their decision in the face of pressure from the Italian Communist Party in favour of Ochab's meeting Paul. The Italian party's view was that visits to the pope

---

* Monsignor Casaroli has proved to be the Secretariat of State's most experienced negotiator with communist countries. He was responsible for the agreement with Yugoslavia in June 1966: the only complete agreement made by the Vatican with a communist government since the war. It ended a break of fourteen years in relations, and established an exchange of non-diplomatic envoys.

by leading communist figures prove electorally advantageous for it. This urging from a fraternal party apparently irritated the Polish communists.

The pope was undoubtedly ready to receive President Ochab. The *Osservatore Romano*, either purposely or by accident, did not help the situation by printing, during the visit, a photograph of a church in the Oder-Neisse territories to which they gave its old German name instead of its new Polish name.* But Paul had before him Casaroli's report, as if in readiness to discuss the Polish situation with the president, and would not have rejected a request for a discussion with him. The encounter was so near to happening that members of the Polish delegation, after leaving Rome for a private tour of Italy, were still saying that there was time for the president to return to Rome and see the pope—presumably if the initiative were to come from the Vatican.

It was an historic non-event, and hardly offered much hope of a change for the better in relations between the Holy See and the communist rulers of a predominantly Catholic country. Significantly, Ochab was at pains to rebut the rather fulsome welcome given him by his Italian hosts, who were inclined to hail him as the representative of an Eastern European country that is culturally a part of the Western world. He was quick to point out that Poland's place is between East and West. One of its greatest links with the West is, of course, its Catholicism; by making this point, he was undoubtedly seeking to depreciate as much as possible a religious adherence which, in many Polish minds, embodies their patriotism and turns it westward. This combination of religion and patriotism provides the reason—and, indeed, some justification—for Paul's desire to go to Czestochowa and his bitter resentment at being refused the pilgrimage.

MINDSZENTY AND BERAN

Cardinal Wyszynski has at least been free to speak his mind in Poland; and, from the Vatican's point of view, he could be left to a large extent to his own devices in the full knowledge that his

* A correction was printed later.

arrangements with the Polish communists could be disowned if his independence proved too embarrassing to the Holy See. Such was not the position in regard to the primates of Hungary and Czechoslovakia.

As the years went by, Cardinal Mindszenty was becoming a relic of the past as he sat in his two-roomed refuge in the American embassy in Budapest. He had not been a Church leader of Wyszynski's contemplative outlook; he was harder and fiercely conservative: as typical of a strong strain among his countrymen as Wyszynski is of the Polish national character. Arrested in 1949, he was sentenced to life imprisonment. He was released in 1956 during the revolt, only to be compelled to seek asylum with the Americans when Russia suppressed the rising. As he talked only textbook English, his reluctant hosts often had trouble in understanding what he was saying. Spiritually, and physically, he remained in good order; intellectually, less so. His contacts with the outside world were few, and he relied a good deal on the regular visits of his confessor: a priest of extremely conservative views who strengthened his belief that the Hungarian government was failing and would not be long in falling. He would have had a more realistic appraisal from Cardinal König, archbishop of Vienna, who was sent first by John XXIII to explore Mindszenty's frame of mind; then by Paul VI, with the gift of a chalice to mark the fiftieth anniversary of his ordination. König paid a third visit, in 1966, to take to him some documents of the Second Vatican Council.

In Mindszenty's case, there was a problem both of policy and personality. He was adamant about staying in his refuge, within the country if not among his flock, until he had been accorded full reinstatement by the Hungarian authorities. It seems that the government would have been happy for him to leave the country, so long as this meant that he would go to Rome and stay there. The primate felt that the dignity of the Church required more of him than that. To Wyszynski, Poland and the Church are indistinguishable; to Mindszenty, the dignity of the Church is identified with his own. From the Vatican's point of view, he has been an asset—but a wasting one. Paul, like John earlier, does not want to force the cardinal to leave Hungary for this would humiliate him. But both popes have sought more sensible relations with the Hungarian government, especially after its allowing three bishops to attend the Council: the Vatican's first formal contact with the Church in Hungary since the communists seized power.

Unlike the Hungarian primate, Monsignor (now Cardinal) Beran, archbishop of Prague, agreed to leave his country—though it seems he was not aware that he would be unable to return. He had been imprisoned first by the Nazis and then by the communists. He knew of the effect of persecution, both on persecutor and persecuted, and rejected the theory that harsh treatment is salutary for the Church.

It is an odd reflection of how things have developed in a decade or so. The Vatican, at the time of the Council, was actively negotiating with governments which it had formerly execrated as tormentors of Mindszenty and gaolers of Beran. Paul could contemplate a visit to Poland. Mindszenty, by the mid-1960s, no longer had a hero's status; though treated with respect, he could hardly have helped feeling that everything had changed around him except himself. Beran, in his milder way, drew from his own privations the lesson that, however wrong these persecuting governments were, the Church was not free from blame, and might well be atoning for faults committed in the past. Respect was accorded him at the Council, but not many liked the tone of some of the passages from his address to it:

> From the very moment that freedom of conscience was radically restricted in my country, I witnessed the grave temptations which, under such conditions, confront so many. In my whole flock, even among the priests, I have observed not only grave dangers to faith but also grave temptations to lying, hypocrisy and other moral vices, which easily corrupt people who lack true freedom of conscience.
>
> If this repression of conscience is knowingly directed against true religion, the gravity of such a scandal is evident to every Christian. However, experience shows us also that such procedures against liberty of conscience are pernicious, morally

speaking, even if through them the good of the true faith is intended or pretended. . . .

So, in my country, the Catholic Church at this time seems to be suffering expiation for defects and sins committed in her name against religious liberty in times gone by, such as in the fifteenth century, with the burning of the priest John Huss, and in the seventeenth century, with the forced reconversion of a great part of the Czech people to the Catholic faith. . . .

By such acts, the secular arm, wishing or pretending to serve the Catholic Church, in reality left a hidden wound in the hearts of the people. This trauma was an obstacle to religious progress and offered—and offers still—easy material for agitation to the enemies of the Church.

Beran's answer was liberty for all, granted willingly by all.

GOODNESS AND PEACE

Mutual interests bring flexibility. Help for Catholics in Eastern Europe, and the hope for better relations with the Russian Orthodox Church, are two of the most important motives of Vatican policy. Oddly enough (though it is small credit to the kind of men we are, Roman or non-Roman), love enters into all this. Only the silliest of sceptics would suppose that John's attitude—or Paul's, for that matter—was just political. John's warmth helped to melt the accretions of cold distrust and pure enmity that had interposed for so long between communists and the West, between the antagonists of religion and the Church. John was the same to all men. He was unhappy that they were communists or unbelievers, but this did not alter his basic attitude to them. He wanted to see the best in everyone. He saw the best in communism, refusing to accept the thesis of its totally evil nature, asserting instead that, mistaken as it was, it might still arrive at some good results. It appears that he genuinely believed in a beginning of the end to the sterile conflict and that God was drawing back the curtains of enmity so that each side would gradually see the virtues of the other. In his talk with Alexei Adzubei, he replied to his visitor's question about how East and West might come together with the following words:

> You are a journalist. You certainly know the Holy Bible. The Bible states that God created the world in six days. The days certainly were epochs, an infinite space of time. On the first day the Lord said 'let there be light'. Today we are at the first hour. It is God who is giving us light. He, do not doubt it, my son, will give us the rest.

This account was given by his private secretary, Monsignor Loris Capovilla, who also added an explanation of why John received a not particularly agreeable Russian. The first reason was that the Russian members of the jury of the Balzan Peace Prize were in favour of awarding it to the pope and he in his turn wished to show his appreciation. The second reason was more characteristic, and goes back to the time when he was leaving his diplomatic post in Eastern Europe. He publicly stated that if a Bulgarian, or Turk, or Slav—Catholic or otherwise—should knock on the door, he could enter because the door would be open. And how could he refuse the request of the editor of *Izvestia*? The conclusion for John was simple. The secrecy and frequent deviousness surrounding the Vatican's international policy; the sometimes suspect devices used to maintain the spiritual authority intact in appearance; the impression of shifting from one foot to another—it could all be transmuted by warmth and by goodness.

For Paul VI, the new approach opened fields which he could not have cleared without John's help. He more or less espoused John's view that communist systems could evolve into something better. This is how he expressed his outlook in *Ecclesiam Suam*, the first encyclical of his pontificate:

> ... bearing in mind the words of Our predecessor of venerable memory, Pope John XXIII, in his encyclical *Pacem in Terris*, to the effect that the doctrines of such movements [*sc.* communism], once elaborated and defined, remain always the same, whereas the movements themselves cannot help but evolve and undergo changes, even of a profound nature: We do not despair that they

may one day be able to enter into a more positive dialogue with the Church than the present one which We now of necessity deplore and lament.

It is a cautious acceptance of an outlook which Paul would not have evolved of himself. He does not have John's instinctive assurance. For him, 'the apostle's art', to repeat his phrase, 'is a risky one'.

The dispersing by John of the heavily acrid clouds of unrelenting ideological conflict freed his successor for a form of appeal much more suited to his character: the appeal for peace. It has been the plea of many popes. Some have uttered it while preparing to go to war themselves or to incite others to take up arms. This century has seen the notable, but unavailing, efforts of Benedict XV and of Pius XII to use their influence to stop the outbreak of the two world wars. It was often said that Pius's reluctance to condemn the Nazis in stronger terms sprang from his continuing hope of being the mediator in the conflict. In his case, it is arguable that the pursuit of the phantom of a mediator's chair contributed to his failure to call open evil by its proper name and to issue the necessary condemnations which, though it is unlikely that they would have shortened the Second World War, would have clarified the issues and kept the Church's ethical majesty unimpugned. It is manifestly difficult to be both pastor and diplomatist, unless so much emphasis is placed on the first task that the second is fulfilled in the natural course of events. The pretensions of peace-maker can muffle the obligation of interpreting the Christian outlook in the life of ordinary people. John and Paul have not made this mistake. Their various appeals for peace—mainly over Cuba and Vietnam when not more generalised—have been less diplomatic than admonitory, and have succeeded in expressing the feeling of a wide range of public opinion in the world.

John appealed for peace at the height of the Cuban crisis of 1962. He did so with his customary effectiveness. On the day after the opening of his Council, he invited the eighty-six diplomatic missions present at the ceremony to an audience in the Sistine Chapel. With these representatives from most countries of the world present, he drew their attention to Michelangelo's fresco of the *Last Judgment*, warning them that one day they would have to give an account of themselves to the Supreme Being.

> Let all who bear the responsibility of government hear the anguished cry which, from every part of the world, from innocent children to old men, from individuals and communities, rises to heaven: peace, peace. May the thought that [leaders of nations] will have to render their own account prevent them from ever neglecting any opportunity to achieve that good which for the human family is the highest good of all.

As the crisis grew more serious, John repeated his appeal, speaking on the radio in a solemn reminder of what he had told the diplomatists, carefully maintaining his neutrality as far as the issue itself was concerned. Did his appeal have much effect? Probably not. It was his successor who was to add the new dimension to appeals for peace: a detailed political knowledge which transformed them from the generic to the specifically practical.

The sincere way in which Paul VI addressed the General Assembly of the United Nations on 4 October 1965 made his speech there a moving as well as an historic occasion.

> Many words are not needed to proclaim this loftiest aim of your institution. It suffices to remember that the blood of millions of men, that numberless and unheard-of sufferings, useless slaughter and frightful ruin, are the sanction of the pact which unites you, with an oath which must change the future history of the world: No more war; war never again!

Paul was already at work to add to this appeal the knowledge of events learned from his years in the Secretariat of State. Vietnam weighed on his mind. Ever since his accession, he seems to have been gripped by the potential dangers of this conflict. Long before he made his worries public, visitors to the Holy See were impressed by his detailed knowledge of the problem and by his real fear that it would be exacerbated into a tragedy of the widest proportions. Paul also had a genuine feeling that simple people should not have their homes bombed and their crops destroyed in the name of freedom, of equality, of social justice, or any other slogan, however much (as he pointed out) it might be acceptable enough to those who understood the meaning of what the politicians were saying, and also had the good fortune to live a long way from the fighting.

Paul fully revealed his hand at mid-day on 19 December 1965 to the fairly large crowd gathered for his blessing in St Peter's Square. He appealed for a truce at Christmas as the minimum relaxation of conflict the politicians should agree to. These words were certainly intended for a larger audience than the whole of St Peter's Square could hold. The style is very much of his own. With popes, the style does not necessarily show the man because papal utterances are always studded with formal phrases which are common to pontiffs over the centuries, and they are frequently set forth in a kind of formalised sentimentality. But whenever some trait of personality penetrates this stiffness, a strong impression is given of what is really deeply preoccupying a particular pontiff's mind. There was no escaping the anguish in Paul VI's rather grating tones:

> Dear children, the word which comes to Our lips for this weekly salutation is the hope of a good Christmas: a good Christmas for the city of Rome; a good Christmas for the whole Church, for the whole world. But We must tell you that Our mind is full of sadness because of the very many divisions and struggles and antagonisms which disturb humanity and which in various places incite conflicts between peoples. Among them is Vietnam, a country which is very dear to Us and which has its own place in civilisation. The war in Vietnam is becoming more serious and more bloody; the numbers of combatants grow, as do the numbers of victims, the piteous mass of refugees, and the danger of wider conflagrations.
>
> Where is peace? Where is the human and Christian Christmas? We have heard mention of negotiations to resolve the conflict. We know of certain proposals for a truce at least for the blessed day of Christmas. And We know of many statesmen of good will who are seeking to resolve the difficult situation. But, in particular, We know that millions of hearts tremble,

suffer and wait for the return of peace. We applaud therefore those who are working loyally to end the menacing conflict. We would desire that, at least—at least!—the proposal for a truce be heard and applied, so that Christmas may be for all of us a day sacred to peace.

We recommend it to the wisdom and to the hearts of the responsible leaders. We hope that, after the truce, will come reflection; then a negotiation; then finally balance, concord and peace. Unite, dear children, prayer to hope: that Mary, with Christ, the centre of Christmas, is seen as Mother and Queen of Peace.

There was a truce. Before it was assured, the Vatican made quite clear that its diplomacy was working at full stretch. That the pope should have taken a direct hand in the efforts to end the conflict— though without taking sides—was not surprising. He said as much to the Vietnamese bishops. In a letter to them of 13 February 1966 he explained that he would be active behind the scenes in trying to bring peace.

We are making efforts in a confidential way to approach personalities representative of various governments to ask them with insistence to contribute towards an honourable and pacific solution of the various international differences which cannot but worry Us gravely. We readily assure you that We shall continue to do everything in Our power both to obtain peace for your dear country and to favour peace in the whole world.

It seems that for some time Paul was confident that secret diplomacy, in the form he explained to the Vietnamese hierarchy, would bring about a truce. He then, so it was said at the Vatican, heard rumours that Haiphong was to be bombed. He was also concerned about the effects of a controversy then approaching its height in Italy following the revelation that a semi-private attempt had been made to persuade Ho Chi Minh into negotiating. And so he made his public appeal.

The critical outposts of the Vatican's diplomacy were—apart from Washington—the apostolic delegation in London (Monsignor

Cardinale is an experienced diplomatist enjoying the pope's confidence), the newly appointed apostolic delegate in Cambodia, Monsignor Pedroni, and Monsignor Giovanetti, the observer at the United Nations. (As a matter of interest, none of these prelates held a real diplomatic post; all were delegates and not nuncios, except for Monsignor Giovanetti who was an observer.) It seems reasonable to suppose that the Vatican also made use of its friends within the diplomatic corps of other countries. There are some Italian diplomatists with strong connections of family and sentiment with the Papacy, and trusted by the Vatican, who can be called upon informally in posts where it has no representative.

On 1 January 1966, Paul published his letters to the heads of state of North and South Vietnam, and of Russia, and to Mao Tse Tung. This last letter was of particular interest. The pope signed it personally, which is unusual with letters to persons other than heads of state or sovereigns (Mao was chairman of the party); and the tone was deliberately respectful. 'The prestige', he wrote, 'which China now rightly enjoys draws to it the attention of the world . . . an intervention on your part would resound to your honour in the eyes of the world and permit a people sorely tried to resume in peace the work of reconstruction which is rendered impossible by the continuation of the war.' There were some criticisms. Was the pope not going too far? Was he not using all the resources of the Vatican—its spiritual authority no less than its diplomatic connections—in a crisis not of the first dimension? If something more serious happened in world affairs, of more peril, what resources would he have left? Paul had, in fact, already reached as far as his secular and religious arms could stretch. In September 1966, he had sent forth both in the shape of Monsignor Sergio Pignedoli's burly frame. This Vatican diplomatist, officially the apostolic delegate to Canada, was sent to Saigon to preside over a special meeting of the Vietnamese Catholic hierarchy.

Paul claimed, justifiably, a share in the credit for the Vietnamese Christmas truce and for the American peace initiative which followed it, and he sought to resolve the problem on the international level while the bombers were grounded. President Johnson, as part of the United States' initiative, sent Arthur Goldberg, his permanent delegate at the United Nations, to see the pope on 29 December 1965. What was surprising for some people—and perhaps the most important factor of all—was the lack of public hostility in America to the papal hand in international affairs. That President Johnson—a thoroughly professional politician—should not be loath to hear what the pope had to say is reasonable enough; that no one of note attacked him for doing so is more surprising.

Criticisms of the kind outlined above probably mistake Paul's aims. He is deeply worried about Vietnam. He may have exaggerated the crisis; that remains to be seen. He wishes to show the Holy See fully functioning in a crisis so that no one can say that more should, and could, be done. To spiritual exhortation he has added what seems to have become an efficiently devised plan of diplomatic activity and moral pressure. He is also credited with something of great potential importance: by remaining neutral in his appeals, he has helped prevent uncritical acceptance of the Vietnam war by American public opinion. He will not allow the conflict to become a 'holy war' of West versus the communist East, as envisaged by Cardinal Spellman in a sermon to United States servicemen in Vietnam on Christmas Day 1966. Paul could not silence Spellman; but he could—to use a word distasteful to the cardinal—'neutralise' him.

The second way in which Paul has made John's inheritance of neutrality and peace more really his own is in his approaches to the newly emerging nations. With these goes his regard for the United Nations as the natural forum for solving problems and for keeping the peace.

The latter point can more directly be dealt with. He went to the United Nations on 4 October 1965. He would not have done so, would not have made his speech there the centre-piece of the first visit ever paid by a reigning pope to the New World, if he had not wished to seek the right forum for his words and for the future application of his ideas. Of the United Nations as an institution, he said:

Gentlemen, you have performed and continue to perform a great work: the education of mankind in the ways of peace. The

United Nations is the great school where that education is imparted, and we are today in the assembly hall of that school. Everyone taking his place here becomes a pupil and also a teacher in the art of building peace. When you leave this hall, the world looks upon you as the architects and constructors of peace.

Peace, as you know, is not built by means of politics, by the balance of forces and of interests. It is constructed with the mind, with ideas, with works of peace. You labour in that great construction. But you are still at the beginning of your task. Will the world ever succeed in changing that selfish and bellicose mentality which, up to now, has been interwoven with so much of its history? It is hard to foresee. But it is easy to affirm that it is toward that new history—a peaceful, truly human history, as promised by God to men of good will—that we must resolutely march. The roads thereto are already well marked out for you; and the first is that of disarmament.

If you would be brothers, let the weapons fall from your hands. One cannot love while holding offensive weapons. These armaments, especially the terrible arms which modern science has given you, long before they produce victims and ruins, nourish bad feelings, create nightmares, distrust and sombre resolutions. They demand enormous expenditure; they falsify the very psychology of peoples. As long as man remains that weak, changeable and even wicked being that he often shows himself to be, defensive arms will, unhappily, be necessary. You, however, in your courage and valour, are studying the ways of guaranteeing the security of international life, without having recourse to arms. This is a most noble aim; this the peoples expect of you; this must be achieved.

Let unanimous trust in this institution grow, let its authority increase, and this aim, We believe, will be secured. . . .

He implied support for the entry of the Chinese People's Republic, evidently wishing the organisation to be fully comprehensive.

In some ways, it might seem that the United Nations is being looked upon at the Vatican as the modern development of the temporal, imperial power (imperial, but anti-imperialistic, of course) that has been lacking since Napoleon imposed his caricature of it, or since the desires were not fully realised of some post-war prelates who looked eagerly towards the United States in the hope of its fulfilling this role.

NEW NATIONS

Praise for the United Nations; neutrality; a special regard for the conflict in Asia; India as the first country to be visited by Paul after the Holy Land; respect for China—it is logical that the new nations should be entering heavily into the Vatican's calculations.

From the beginning of his reign, Paul VI has shown a special attachment to the young countries of Africa and Asia. It may seem strange to envisage the ancient formalities, the ascetic celibacy and luxuriant subterfuge, face to face with boisterous hopes of young nations. It was John who brought the first African-born bishop into the Sacred College (Cardinal Rugambwa of Tanzania: perhaps its first member to have been born a pagan), and the late pope had much to say in his encyclicals about Afro-Asian problems, criticising traditional colonialism and speaking as a champion of the underprivileged.

Whether moved by his travels in Africa before his election, by the teachings of his predecessor, or by some other feelings and calculations, Paul has taken this element in papal policy far forward. His canonisation of the Uganda martyrs, for instance, gave the Church in East Africa that touch of sanctity through martyrdom which is regarded as an essential part of the process of Catholic growth. He insisted on baptising with great ceremony and by his own hand a group of African converts. His encyclical *Progressio Populorum*, issued at Easter 1967, deals fully with the social questions involved in developing countries. It all suggests a deliberate development, one combining religious aims with a political concept in a way that is typical of the Papacy's outlook.

The present pontiff has made it clear that he believes the Church to have in the new nations an important field for expansion. This is not just a form of latter-day imperialism, though historically it has similarities with the Church's dealings with the Franks and other new peoples after the collapse of the Roman Empire of the West. Obviously, granted the claims which the Roman Church makes for itself, the obligation to expand is incumbent upon it. This is a constant factor. What, in addition, seems to have struck Paul with some force is that countries suddenly coming to nationhood—trying desperately, as most of them are, to catch up with the centuries in the space of two five-year plans; needing some sort of over-all philosophy (for nationalism, as any pope knows, is not enough; indeed, may be already far less than enough)—could well be ready to accept a faith, complete with social theories and long experience, such as Rome can offer. It could attenuate their boisterous nationalism because Catholicism and nationalism have seldom gone together. It could give moral and psychological stamina to peoples arriving swiftly to full autonomy. It could also bring a genuine feeling that the poor and underprivileged should have a better life and better treatment from the rich, including the richer nations. And, not less important in the Church's thinking, if such benefits should not come their way before they die, they would have the saving message of the after-life.

Such thinking is logical enough. It also accords with the feeling now widespread that Europe cannot predominate in the Church for much longer. Having adapted and systematised in Europe an oriental faith, investing it with secular power and organisation and with intellectual brilliance, and spreading its influence to all corners of the earth, the Church must now look to pastures new for a fresh spirit. Throughout the Second Vatican Council, there were complaints that the bias of its work was too European, that too much of the talk about the Church in the modern world meant the Church in the Western world. The Western bishops present, moreover, were not allowed to forget—and this is one of the great obstacles to the faith today in Asia and Africa—that the Church in the past was associated with the colonial powers, with repression and authoritarian methods of implanting the gospel of love. It is still very much identified with Western attitudes and interests, but it is trying hard to reduce that impression.

The Pope's plea in the *Progressio Populorum* for more resolution in helping the young nations may seem a long way removed from papal opposition to the rise of nationalism in the sixteenth and nineteenth centuries. But the Holy See may be reckoning that the beneficent influence of the Church, exercised early in the life of the new nations of the twentieth century, could diminish any latent anti-clericalism and curb the excesses of nationalism. The majority of the new states, controlling the United Nations, could at some future date—so might the dream of some prelates go—become the Frankish kings of the new era, taught by priests how to manage their affairs and where to look for help, to say nothing of salvation. This could be no more than a dream, but the outlines of a policy are there. Young nations without a destructive form of nationalism could be good friends of the Papacy at a time when old nations are suffering from a process of dechristianisation. Industrial civilisation has encouraged the attitude that religion is irrelevant. The pursuit of prosperity consumes time and mental energies. The fall in the number of candidates for the priesthood has been sharp in most European countries of advanced social and economic development. Western society is moving fast, and formal religion is not keeping pace with it.

There have been attempts to face this problem. The most famous is that of the worker-priest movement in France (discussed in the next section of this chapter). It is in connection with such attempts to grapple with the problems of modern society that Paul expressed in *Ecclesiam Suam* the 'great principle enunciated by Christ... to be in the world but not of the world'. His words here convey the seriousness of the difficulties encountered in using the means necessary—or judged to be necessary—to be 'in the world' and in employing worldly institutions for purposes greater in their assumptions than any others in human history. The Vicar of Christ —the 'Servant of the Servants of God', to cite another of his titles (adopted by Gregory the Great twelve centuries ago, when he heard that the bishop of Constantinople had taken the title of 'Universal Patriarch')—brought the whole legacy of imperial rule to bear on organising the Church. When the protection of the Roman Empire was no more, he turned to simpler, devout people who were ready to hear his message and sometimes to take up arms on his behalf, wielding a sword held from his authority. It did not need St Augustine to tell them that Christianity should not be blamed for the fall of Rome and its civilisation. In giving their loyalty to the pope, they asked no difficult questions about why all that grandeur should have declined and fallen in spite of the presence of Christ's Vicar and of the one true Church. It is consistent with its history for the Vatican today to seek for new 'daughters of the Church' when earlier members of the family have fallen from grace.

OLD CATHOLIC COUNTRIES

Complementary to the problem of the new, non-Catholic countries is that of those old, nominally Catholic countries which are faced, after centuries of Western civilisation, with the same economic and social obstacles as the rising nations. And parallel with both problems of 'underdevelopment' is the problem of the erosion of the influence of religion in the more prosperous Western nations which have hitherto been the stronghold of Christianity.

The *locus classicus* of the Roman Catholic response to this last problem is the worker-priest movement in France: an endeavour to give the Church a more vital relationship with the day-to-day lives of men and women in urban, industrialised societies. The worker-priests were both heralds of the Ecumenical Council and one of the reasons why it was necessary. Their movement and its fate formed one of a number of forces prompting several leading French bishops to head the attack on the Roman Curia.

The worker-priest movement was an attempt by priests to shake off the historical burdens of their Church, including its identification with established social orders, and to meet the uncomfortable reality of modern life. The basic concept was not to bring industrial workers into the traditional pattern of the Church, but to bring the Church to the factory benches and to the faithless confusion of the workers' movement in France.* Its origins go back

---

* A similar, though not identical, endeavour had been essayed by the Anglican Church in Britain, in the form of diocesan industrial missions. Perhaps because of its very different constitutional character, the Church of

two decades before the Second Vatican Council. It is now mainly remembered for its suppression by the Vatican, but its failure is no more eloquent than its aspirations. This is all the truer since John XXIII, who was pope when the experiment was finally abandoned, and Paul, who was attracted by it when working at the Secretariat of State, have both sought to bring the Church and the modern world closer together.

The self-questioning in France after the collapse in 1940 affected the Church as it did other sections of French society. In 1941, Father Augros, a Sulpician priest, began an inquiry into seminary training. A year later, he became rector of a new kind of training centre for priests: the *Mission de France* in Lisieux. Fathers Godin and Daniel, two chaplains belonging to the *Jeunesse Ouvrière Chrétienne* —a workers' social movement begun by Canon (later Cardinal) Cardijn of Belgium—studied there and produced a now famous report for Cardinal Suhard, then archbishop of Paris, called *France: A Missionary Country?* They proposed that specially trained priests be freed from conventional duties for work in missions of a new kind. Another centre, the *Mission de Paris*, was established in 1944: the year following the decision to send priests secretly as civilian workers to German labour camps. In his Lenten pastoral of 1949, Cardinal Suhard explained what the worker-priests were trying to do:

> In too many so-called Christian countries, particularly in France, the Church—in spite of the presence of many ecclesiastical buildings and many priests—has ceased to exist for the majority of people. They no longer have the chance of deciding for or against Christ. A vast accumulation of prejudice has completely distorted the face of the Church in their eyes. The priesthood is still less accessible to them. Therefore it is a good thing that

---

England has not so far experienced the same tensions and agonies as have afflicted the social *aggiornamento* of the Catholic Church in France; and the differing state of labour and trade-union relations in the two countries also is of importance. Even so, all has not been plain sailing for the Anglican industrial missions, as certain clashes of opinion on purpose and method between bishop and mission priest—notably in the Sheffield diocese in 1966 —have shown.

priests become witnesses again, less to conquer than to be a sign. . . . This means so to live that one's life would be inexplicable if God did not exist.

The movement right from the start ran into opposition from Rome. In June 1945, Suhard received a communication expressing anxiety at the activities of the worker-priests. In February 1947, at Rome's request, he submitted the first of his annual reports on their activities.

The worker-priests found that their mission led them into paths so far unexplored by men of their cloth. Many of them decided that identification with the workers virtually meant identification with the labour movement as a whole. They thus became involved in left-wing political action. The year 1949 brought the death of Cardinal Suhard and the Holy Office's decree against communism. The French bishops' intention was to interpret the decree broadly, but they found that the worker-priests were giving them no assistance in this softening of the impact of the decree. Many of the worker-priests in 1950 joined the campaign against French policy in Indochina, and one of them was wounded in a clash with police during a demonstration in Limoges organised by the communist-directed World Peace Movement. In July of that year, Monsignor Feltin, the new archbishop of Paris, was asked to submit another report. Pius XII was evidently not at all comforted by its contents. In an apostolic exhortation in the autumn of 1950, he said: 'We are sure that you are well aware that among certain priests, not distinguished for learning or austerity of life, there has been an alarming spread of revolutionary ideas.' It was clear to whom he was referring. In 1952, two worker-priests were arrested for taking part in demonstrations against General Ridgway on his arrival in Paris to assume the supreme command of NATO forces. The Catholic workers' organisation in France, ACO, was angry at the confusion caused by worker priests who held offices in left-wing unions. Some of the French hierarchy became dismayed; by no means all of the pressure against the movement was generated in Rome.

In January 1953, Feltin was made a cardinal; so was Roncalli, the nuncio in Paris, whose promotion was interpreted as evidence of the Vatican's conviction that he was incapable of dealing firmly enough with the situation and needed to be withdrawn from Paris. He was succeeded by Monsignor, now Cardinal, Marella. In August, Rome issued the order that the worker-priests be disbanded. The time limit for submission was 1 March 1954. Many of the worker-priests left the Church rather than submit. Under strong pressure from Cardinal Feltin and several of his colleagues, Pius XII issued a set of conditions under which the movement might continue, including the restriction of a priest's 'factory labour' to part-time work and the carrying out of the traditional priestly obligations. But, in effect, this mitigation ended the movement as effectively as maintaining an outright ban on it. One of Pius's last acts before his death was to suppress the *Témoignage Chrétien*, which had published a defence of the worker-priests.

Roncalli's election promised better things. The new pope was especially welcomed in France, where he was regarded as a 'French' pontiff succeeding to a 'German'. Yet, even if he had wanted to do something to revive the worker-priest movement, it was by then probably too late; and, in any case, the first months of his pontificate were marked by curial predominance. It took John XXIII some time to learn how to exert himself. Feltin decided to bring a report in person to the pope. He fell ill, and his report went instead to the Holy Office. He eventually arrived in Rome only to be told that the final—and adverse—decision had already been taken. On his return to Paris, he received a letter from Cardinal Pizzardo, Secretary of the Congregation for Seminaries, confirming the movement's demise. In this letter, which caused much ill-feeling, Pizzardo expressed views which denied the basic concept of the worker-priests: '. . . it is surely difficult to regard as completely dechristianised a mass of people that still includes a very large proportion who have received the indelible seal of baptism.' Cardinal Liénart of Belgium gave his answer to this in an address to the *Mission de France*: 'The plain fact of dechristianisation is very widespread in France, particularly among the workers.'

The endeavour was over, but not the problem. This particular solution foundered amid the lack of understanding in Rome, the lack of resolute support from the French hierarchy as a whole, and the extreme situations in which the worker-priests involved themselves. But mainly it foundered in the huge gap between Church and contemporary industrial society in France.

Paul, as we have noted, is believed to have supported the first experiment when he was in the Curia, and he is still clearly interested in the idea despite John's confirming of Pius's closure of the venture. But it is a cautious interest. In *Ecclesiam Suam*, he observed:

> Is it not perhaps true that often the young clergy, or indeed even some zealous religious, moved by the good intention of penetrating the masses or particular groups, tend to get mixed up with them instead of remaining apart, thus sacrificing the true efficacy of their apostolate to some sort of useless imitation? The great principle enunciated by Christ presents itself again both in its actuality and in its difficulty: to be in the world but not of the world.

It is too early to say if this analysis of the difficulty is to be Paul's last word on the worker-priest endeavour. What can be hazarded is that, should he seek to institutionalise priestly efforts to penetrate the unleavened mass of dechristianised communities in economically advanced states, it is highly unlikely that he will allow it to take the same form as that developed by the worker-priests in France.

In many ways, the problems experienced by the Roman Church in less developed countries of Catholic tradition are more crucial to its reputation in the world than those in advanced societies, for it is extremely vulnerable to the charge of being, in part, responsible for much of the social, economic and political backwardness in Southern Europe and Latin America.

Latin America is largely an undeveloped area. Within it live about a third of the world's Roman Catholics. The faith was brought there and imposed by the Spaniards and Portuguese. The population is rising at an intense rate; by the end of the century, according to present forecasts, there will be some five hundred million people living in the subcontinent—which is the total Catholic population of the world in the mid-sixties.

Just as the Christian Church, of all denominations, in Africa and Asia is handicapped by the 'colonialist' taint of its Western origin, so in Latin America it has long been associated with unpopular institutions of one kind or another: with the old imperial authority of Spain or Portugal; with the landowning class; with the forces of reaction when the nineteenth-century nationalist movements were shaping the national frontiers of the subcontinent. The end of the metropolitan connection of Spain and Portugal with Latin America was accepted only with reluctance by the Papacy. The instability of politics there since independence has meant that the Church has all along been inclined to be closely involved in political affairs, either in support of a particular dictator or in suffering oppression at the hands of another. It has to contend with much anti-clericalism among the educated class. Illiteracy is widespread among the lower class. Hence, neither class can supply the lack of priests: one because it does not wish to, and the other because it is incapable of doing so. The result is a disastrous shortage of priests. This situation tends to keep the Church more and more apart from the masses. The ecclesiastical authorities, moreover, are experiencing a strong threat from communism.

In some countries, it is true, there are signs of improvement. In Mexico, for instance, there is an encouraging number of vocations: the effect, perhaps, of the twenty or so years of oppression suffered there by the Church earlier in this century. Some bishops —in Chile, for example—have grasped the fact that landowning does them little good financially and much harm in public repute; they have made over some of the Church's possessions to the movement for land reform. The over-all situation, however, is very grave for the Church. There is occasion for some rueful nods in the Vatican when the field seems promising in the new nations where Rome is still a newcomer, and the situation is catastrophic in countries which have for long been nominally Catholic.

That things are critical in Latin America is fully recognised by the Holy See. Some steps have been taken there in an attempt at organising combined action to offer some hope of rescue. Two special bodies have been set up. The first in order of age is the Latin American Episcopal Council, established in 1956 to co-ordinate the activities of the hierarchy in the subcontinent. The second is the Pontifical Commission for Latin America, which sits at the Vatican and includes in its work the co-ordination of help for Latin America from elsewhere and promotes such initiatives. By coincidence, the second of these two bodies celebrated the first five years of its existence shortly after Paul VI began his reign, so that its members were among the earliest papal bodies to be received in a celebratory audience. The Council also enjoyed an anniversary, reaching the tenth year of its existence while the Vatican Council was sitting, which made it possible for the pope's meeting with the Latin American hierarchy to be used for reviewing its work.

In his address to the Pontifical Commission, Paul seemed reasonably unruffled at the extent of the problem, though in no way inclined to make light of it. He pointed out that an approach to social problems was an essential part of the work of priests in Latin America: 'It will be an extension of the priestly ministry in the true sense.' He went on: 'We are happy to know that Our venerable brothers and Our beloved sons of Latin America have this pastoral sensitivity which urges them to have care for the bodies as well as the good of the souls, while bearing in mind man's final destiny.' He had heard something of the Commission's five years of work from the report delivered by Cardinal Confalonieri who is its chairman. Its resources, the cardinal said, had been devoted to three main lines of policy: encouraging vocations by building, restoring and extending seminaries both in Latin America and in Europe in order to train priests to work in Latin America, and distributing scholarships; increasing religious instruction; and, finally, undertaking social work, such as the development on a subcontinental scale of enterprises like the training of specialised workers and of experts who would be able to take an active part in schemes of economic development and plans for social reform. Outside Latin America the Commission's activities are mainly twofold: seeking priests to go there and raising money to pay for the Church's work there. It has encouraged the formation of episcopal committees for Latin America, and these already exist in Canada, the United States, Italy, Spain, Belgium, France and Germany. The United States has its ties with the Commission's work as the good—and rich—neighbour, though the task of paymaster is not by any means the most comfortable. Spain and Portugal have the ties of former empire and of a common language.

In his discourse to the Latin American hierarchy, Paul offered a full and frank analysis. Apart from the facts he presented, the whole tone of this discourse revealed two general problems of papal policy. The first is to what extent can, or should, the Vatican impose a certain outlook on local hierarchies. It is well enough to say that Latin America has had the good fortune to have been Catholic for so long; it has also suffered the ill-fortune of a Church which in general has fallen far below the needs of the people. Bishops, however lamentable in performance, can hardly in these days be peremptorily instructed by Rome what to do. The second problem is whether the Church should be thinking first of putting its own house in order or of enlarging its field; which means, should Latin America or the newer nations be given priority? Is it enough, when countries are nominally Catholic, to hope that their difficulties will be resolved? The pope drew attention to signs of progress—such as the decisions of several hierarchies to make over their holdings to land reform—'encouraged and authorised by this Apostolic See'. He felt that the Church was still the most substantial social force in the continent, and capable of saving it; if the Church moves, he said, 'she is largely followed'. The problem is to make the Church move in the proper direction. Calling for the need to encourage a Christian social conscience, the pope gave the Latin American bishops this advice:

> It is necessary in all ways that the position of the Church towards the social changes in motion in Latin America be clear and defined. We have said that it is the duty of the pastor to know social conditions; it is not however sufficient to recall the Church's social doctrine and teach it in the abstract; it is necessary to promote its application in actual situations as they

present themselves and translate it into definite rules of action, defining opportunely the responsibilities of the hierarchy and the laity.

Despite the daunting size of the problem, Paul is trying to place the Church on the side of social progress. It is easier to say this in Rome than to get it done in Latin America. And there is so much else to say of countries elsewhere with much the same problems, all demanding the Vatican's attention and resources.

* * *

The various activities of the Papacy we have been examining have two sides to them. Either they are concerned with defending or improving the Church's position in a particular country or region so that it can carry out its work with more freedom; or they present the pope as the 'conscience of the world', calling on rulers to press forward with right-minded energy towards the solution of mankind's problems. Altogether, they constitute the Roman Church's claim to play a constructive part in temporal affairs, to be an influence on contemporary life and thought. This influence would, naturally, be regarded by the Church as of secondary consideration in comparison with the main purpose of ministering to souls. Its active pursuit of influence, nevertheless, forms a vast and varied corpus of 'works'.

The Vatican is resilient and resourceful. After suffering intense persecution at the hands of communist powers, it has been able to attempt with caution and surprising success a fresh approach to dealing with communist authorities. It has had its rebuffs, it cannot be denied. The Polish problem, made complicated by the triangle of government, primate and pope, stubbornly has eluded solution. So, in the wider field of international affairs, has the war in Vietnam, despite the pope's personal and urgent efforts. But on this issue, he has succeeded in one, very important, respect: his appeals for peace have summed up the feelings of large sections of international public opinion; and, to some extent, they have helped to form it.

Paul VI is clearly fascinated by diplomacy, and likes to regale informal gatherings with the latest trend in events. ('Better news', he once informed a crowd awaiting his blessing in St Peter's Square, 'from San Domingo last night.') He has also reaped the wilder winds which occasionally sweep the chanceries of the world. By going to India in 1964, he annoyed Portugal, still smarting from Nehru's seizure of Goa. In return, or partly, he went to Portugal in May 1967, to find himself subjected to accusations that he was favouring obscurantist politics by going to Salazar's country, and an obscurantist aspect of Catholicism by making the shrine of the Madonna of Fatima the object of his pilgrimage. While conducting an objective neutrality in the Vietnam war, he found his policy contradicted by a subordinate in the shape of Cardinal Spellman of New York, who matched the pope's appeal for peace with an exhortation to American troops to press on to total victory. The encyclical on the problem of development was a genuine urging to action; his strictures on colonialism have been in keeping with the outlook he is seeking to give to the Church in contemporary affairs, and are consistent with the radical strain in his social thinking. But his harsh words on liberal capitalism and the naked profit-motive have laid him open to bitter counter-attack from the political right, with lampoons of a nineteenth-century acridity pointing out that the Vatican is one of the world's greatest capitalists. These brick-bats have been thrown with all the greater force in knowledge of the fact that the Vatican refuses to pay dividend tax on its Italian holdings.

There is, however, a unifying common factor to all these varied activities: they largely represent the political side of the Church. They reveal its style and comportment when it is trying to preserve or enlarge the basis for its spiritual labours. 'The Church must exercise its government over men who live in the world', writes Monsignor Van Lierde, 'but with the aim of directing them towards Heaven.'* From concordats to calls for an investment of some part of the money spent on armaments in measures for helping the poor, the Roman Church is trying to act according to its own teachings in the midst of the world. Those teachings themselves, with one exception, are not what is at stake, however. They

* Van Lierde, op. cit.

stand behind the active front of temporal diplomacy, unmoved and unmoving as the negotiators come and go. Only in one case is the Church's teaching directly in collision with the day-to-day factors of the twentieth-century world. Rome's doctrine here may prove to be neither unmoved nor unmoving. That doctrine is the condemnation of birth-control by artificial means.

8
Guests at the Banquet

No other problem of the many facing the Roman Church has been so much publicised as birth-control. No other has so profoundly rent the pastoral life of the Church, at the same time placing it in an untenable position in that arena of international life where it seeks to deploy its full influence on human affairs. It has found two of the three popes since the Second World War unprepared to meet the challenge. John did not wish to take it up; Paul, though forced to face it, has clearly brought himself to the question with much anguish. Neither of them, unprompted, would have made the advance that Pius XII's acceptance of the rhythm method represented. For Paul, the birth-control issue has all the makings of a nightmare. It is urgent. Only he can decide. The eyes of the world are on him. It involves the well-being of the Church itself and its claim to a formative role in contemporary society. More ominously still, it involves the very authority of the Church, for a change in the appreciation of the problem would entail changing a doctrine of the Church that has been declared time and again to be an essential of the faith. Can a pope, in so crucial a matter, undo what another pope had solemnly enunciated and the Church has taught for centuries?

And yet, a pope can scarcely watch inactively the process by which the Roman Catholic faithful are abandoning in large numbers any attempt to live by the traditional teaching in the very heart of religious and social life: the family. This teaching has been challenged by new ideas about the nature of marriage, by the development of new contraceptive techniques, and by what can only be called the demands of the age on individuals and nations alike as the menace grows of too great an increase of population in relation to the estimated supply of food. Overpopulation and underdevelopment both lead inevitably to the question of birth-control. As part of its international aspirations, the Church has set itself to contribute to solving the problems of poor and developing nations. Yet, with this contribution, it brings a teaching that condemns millions to poverty in backward countries, and millions in advanced countries to nervous breakdown or to plain rejection of that teaching, whatever the cost to the individual conscience and whatever the peril in incurring the 'grave and mortal fault' of such rejection. The Church is already suspected of caring too little about social progress in this life because of its insistence on the priority to be given to eternity. Rome's teaching on birth-control adds substance to these accusations; it also sends people to eternity quicker. The unpopularity of the teaching is widespread. So much so that one cannot withhold respect from Paul VI for stating clearly at the United Nations his Church's view on birth-control, disliked though it is outside the Church and already discredited as it is in some sections of Catholic opinion. Nowhere, perhaps, is it more disliked than in such a body as the United Nations General Assembly. The relevant passage runs:

> ... the life of man is sacred; no one may dare offend it. Respect for life, even with regard to the great problem of the birth-rate, must find here in your Assembly its highest affirmation and its most reasoned defence. You must strive to multiply bread so that it suffices for the tables of mankind, rather than to favour an artificial control of birth, which would be irrational, in order to diminish the number of guests at the banquet of life.

These were brave but unfortunate words, for they gave some people the impression that the pope had finally made up his mind against any change in traditional teaching. Moreover, they carried an undertone of unintentional bitterness for anyone reading them a few months after their delivery, when the Vatican was well forward in the activity of raising donations to help millions destined not to the banquet of life but to death from sheer starvation in India.

There is a precedent that could help Paul move away from traditional teaching. Pius XII had managed to deduce, out of his odd mental mixture of mysticism and precision, that sexual intercourse sought for to achieve pleasure without the intention of procreation could yet be regarded as licit in the Church's eyes. This is the great importance of his approval of the rhythm method. He did go on, however, to reiterate the condemnation of artificial means of contraception which 'holds good today' (i.e., 1951) 'as it did yesterday. It will hold good tomorrow and always, for it is not a mere precept of human law but the expression of a natural and divine law.' Around Paul, from the beginning of his pontificate, new ideas have been burgeoning about responsible parenthood and the rights of the individual conscience. But behind him, in the avenues of the Church's history, the sight is daunting. Throughout the centuries, the Roman Church and the world at large have danced their strange *paso doble*, grotesquely pulling each other in different directions as they move in the shadow of doctrine and utility around the obelisk of contraception.

For about two thousand years, that dance has been performed to a music which has mixed in its parts a reaction to the enemies of Christendom; a rationalisation of scriptural values, such as the respect shown in the New Testament for virginity, and in the Old Testament for the patriarchal family; preoccupation with a falling birth-rate in Catholic countries, especially in France until fairly recently; and horror at the alliance of non-belief with contraception, as in the advocacy of the latter by such rationalists as Jeremy Bentham and James Mill. The callers of the Church's steps in the dance make an odd company: Onan, whose condemnation in Genesis for refusing to raise children by his deceased brother's wife has been taken by the Church as indicating God's wrath at the prevention of conception, in all circumstances; the Stoic philosophers, whose stern view of life, in which marriage was regarded as simply a means for the creation of children, enabled the early Christians to synthesise marriage and virginity in a faith-easing way, for by giving the first this sole, if vital, aim, they could maintain the second in splendid superiority of status; St Augustine, who evolved a doctrine giving honour to child-bearing as the sole end of sexual congress, herein opposing the Manichees, who dissociated sexual activity from procreation (as, apparently, did the saint himself in his earlier Manichean days); Pius XI, who denounced the decision of the Lambeth Conference of 1930, by which the Anglicans eased their opposition to contraception, as part of the 'moral ruin' of the time. Not so many years before that pope's famous encyclical against birth-control (*Casti Connubii*, 1930) occurred the advances in the mass-manufacture of contraceptives that brought the first significant change in techniques in this field since the ancient Egyptians mixed pulverised crocodile dung with fermented mucilage, nearly two thousand years before the birth of Christ.

These are the main lines in the formation of the Church's teaching. From the Jews came the idea of the large, patriarchal family system, in which plenty of progeny and the survival of the name were in high regard. The texts taken to epitomise this outlook were the condemnation of Onan, whose name was forever to be associated with the first known instance of birth-control—in his case *coitus interruptus*—just as Cain was to become the archetype of murderers; and the divine command to 'increase and multiply; fill the earth and subdue it'. (The second part of the command seems likely to be carried out effectively in the next decades.) Such passages as these can be interpreted in different ways, particularly the nature of Onan's offence (was it mainly disobedience, for instance?), but there can be no doubt that the Old Testament is rich in references to the blessings of fecundity. It contains at the same time warnings about the dangers from sexuality. Sexually attractive women, for instance, as Samson or Adam himself discovered, lead to sin and trouble. This outlook in its turn led to the Christian view that sexuality should not be confused with the high purpose of producing children. In the New Testament there is no great weight placed on the idea of procreation as the aim of marriage. Christ himself called for a higher sexual morality than did the Old Testament authors, because lustful thoughts amounted to adultery in the heart. St Paul commended virginity but saw marriage as a sensible institution to prevent moral lapses ('it is better to marry', he said, 'than to burn'). But already by the time of the Early Fathers, the conflict was developing which would, as an outside influence, shape the Church's teachings from this rather mixed collection of *dicta*. The doctrine developed by stages.

The first was the threat from the Gnostics, which lasted until about the first quarter of the third century. As it disappeared it was replaced in the fourth century by the Manichean challenge to orthodox Christianity. What these two faiths had in common was repugnance towards procreation and its separation from sexual activity. Christianity was thus faced in its comparatively early years with a long and constant threat from rivals who were regarded as immoral but also dangerous and so required answering. The possible case that could be argued from the New Testament in favour of celibacy gave more force to the argument that marriage should have a high purpose, and, if not, one should be found for it. The obvious answer was procreation. Behind the New Testament considerations was the Stoic theory of marriage, which viewed procreation as the only factor distinguishing sexual activity from lust. It is curious that the first known Christian reference in writing to contraception entailed an attack on a pope for favouring it indirectly. The writer of the *Elenchos*, or *Refutation of all the Heresies*, dated between 220 and 230, accuses St Calixtus (bishop of Rome from 202 to 218) not only of having usurped the throne of Peter but also of having been responsible for 'concubinage' between Christian free women and their slaves. It is probable that the bishop did little more, in fact, than allow Christian marriage to a free woman and a slave, the union of whom was not recognised in Roman civil law. The result, according to Calixtus's critic (probably St Hippolytus, the rival of Calixtus for the see of Rome), is that women, frequently with property or of prominent family, 'want no children from slaves or low-born commoners, and use sterility-producing drugs or bind themselves tightly in order to expel a foetus which has already been engendered'. The relationship is described as adultery, and contraception as murder, along with abortion.

It is interesting to note that, among Christians in these early days of the faith, there appears to be no strong feeling that procreation should be encouraged because of the falling birth-rate, though this might have been a sound socio-religious argument in the light of the shortage of manpower in the late Empire. St Basil the Great (c. 300–79) interpreted the text 'increase and multiply' in a manner proper to so strong an advocate of the monastic life, seeing it as a command for man to increase from infancy to maturity and govern the world by reason. Tertullian, writing in 200, found the world to be full enough of people already: 'We are burdensome to the world. The elements are scarcely sufficient for us.' What he said was not true, but it suggests a Christian lack of regard for or understanding of the contemporary problem of a falling population. On 31 January 320, Constantine introduced a decree ending some of the Augustan laws intended to encourage procreation. He did so, it seems, out of deference to the Christian respect for virginity (celibates, both male and female, were given status in law equal to that of married persons), and without regard for one of the most serious problems of the Empire. Today, the Roman Church finds itself in precisely the opposite position: under accusation for contributing to the dangerous increase in the world's population.

Twice more in the Church's history, its reaction against major challenges to its doctrine—the internal threat of the Albigensian movement and the external threat of 'technological secularism' in the nineteenth century—was to influence substantially its teaching in sexual matters. The nineteenth-century challenge came with the diffusion of theories and techniques of birth-control aimed, not against procreation as such, but against unplanned procreation. The great challenge of the Albigensian heresy in the twelfth century constituted, among other things, an onslaught on the Church's views of sexual morality. At much the same time, but at the level of the sophisticated minority, the troubadors of the Provençal school were propounding in their verses an ideal of sexual love quite distinct from any notion of procreation. Before the Albigensian heresy's massive and complete suppression, the countering of the sexual tenets ascribed to its adherents—

the hostility to procreation in the belief that pregnancy was the devil's work, but the acceptance of sexual activity outside marriage*—was powerfully to reaffirm the Church's traditional teaching.

Operating upon the doctrinal 'residue' (to employ Pareto's term) formed by opposition to the Gnostics and Manichees, the Albigensian crisis had two important effects. In the first place, indirectly it may be, it led to the embodiment in canon law of absolute assertions defining a *necessary* link between sexual congress and procreation, and imposing child-bearing as an obligation on the faithful that must not be avoided. The second effect arose from the association of the Albigensians with the Manichees in the public mind of Christendom. This, promoting a revival of interest in St Augustine's rejection of the earlier heretics' views on marriage, incidentally served to stimulate Marian devotion as the popular version of the teaching in the canons. In the twelfth century the *Ave Maria*—with its double benediction of Mary as Maid and Mother, embracing in one act of devotion the Church's reverence both for dedicated virginity and dedicated parenthood —became the most popular invocation in Catholic Europe. At a Council held in 1254 at Albi, the town from which the heresy took its name, the *Ave Maria* was prescribed as one of the three prayers, along with the *Pater Noster* and the Creed, to be taught to every child above the age of seven. 'Hail Mary, full of grace; the Lord is with you. Blessed are you among women, and blessed is the fruit of your womb, Jesus.' What clearer refutation could there be, in terms of prayer, of Albigensian doctrine?

The elaboration of doctrine thus went ahead fast and forcefully up to the thirteenth century, gathering strength from the countering of heresy—and also, it may well be, from the Church's struggle against the brutalised laxity of much of medieval life in communities where men were prone to treat women without respect. If traditional Roman doctrine imposes on women what now seems

* They were also sometimes accused of unnatural vice: a frequent indictment in ecclesiastical disputes. Their Cathar tenets came from the Bogomils, who antecedently were identified with a Bulgarian origin. This association gave English and other European languages a new word—bugger, bougre, buggaro—originally intended to apply to a wide field of sexual deviation.

to many a cruelly undiscriminating burden of obligatory child-bearing, it must not be forgotten that its stress on the marriage bond and on the responsibilities of parenthood gave a dignity and status to women not readily accorded in many parts of medieval Europe, and still far to seek in many non-Christian societies today. This said, it must be recognised that the explicit spelling out of the doctrine in the *summae* for the use of confessors was to impose on Catholic thinking for centuries to come an outlook that was largely juridical. An essential point in the development of Church teaching from the early years was the argument that contraception was evil because unnatural. Reference to natural law affected other aspects of sexual behaviour. Aquinas believed that natural coitus was of divine institution and unalterable without sin by man. Sinning against nature included deviations from what he called 'the fit way' for sexual intercourse, by which he meant that the man must be on top of the woman. 'Sins against nature' continued to worry prelates and saints. St Catherine of Siena, for instance, in a vision of Hell, referred particularly to only one type of damned soul: 'those who sinned in the married state'. Chaucer gives an account of sinful practices in connection with procreation in his "Parson's Tale". This episode in the *Canterbury Tales* deals with the seven deadly sins, and under the sin of wrath treats of manslaughter; among the species of manslaughter is a woman's 'drynkynge venenouse herbes thurgh which she may nat concevve'. Another form is when a woman puts 'certeine material thynges in hire secree places to slee the child'.

With all this background of teaching, it is not surprising to find that Pope Sixtus V (1585–90), the most extreme applier of the laws of morality in the atmosphere of the Counter-Reformation, should have interpreted literally as homicide the practice of contraception as defined by canonical theory. His bull *Effraenatam* of 1588 dealt specifically with abortion and contraception. Both for the purposes of canon law and for the laws governing the Papal States, the giving or taking of contraceptives—those 'cursed medicines' for impeding conception and child-bearing—was regarded as murder. Sixtus V's view was that of an extremist. It was he, after all, who prescribed hanging for adultery in Rome. The bull was in effect for only two and a half years. His successor, Gregory XIV (1590–1591), was clear-minded enough to see that it simply drove people to ignore even so great a sanction as excommunication.

The real confrontation between the Church's teaching and individual behaviour would come only when contraception ceased to be practised by individuals—however many of them—still using methods dating from remote antiquity, and became an organised and technically advanced movement, promoted for rational reasons as socially beneficial. The first effects of the practice of birth-control on a wide scale, as yet without social reasoning, were seen in France in the late eighteenth and early nineteenth centuries and were an advance-guard of what was to come. It was at that time easy to condemn. There was not as yet any coherent theory behind it, and the methods were not yet properly scientific, though none the less effective for that. It was irreligious in the sense that it was a matter of convenience, not of principle: 'irreligious, calculating, egotistic', in Professor Noonan's words.* To the ease with which it could be attacked on traditional grounds a new factor was added with the French defeat in the Franco-Prussian war: the patriotic reason that France was simply not producing enough soldiers. But if the French experience looked vulnerable, the more formidable movement had already begun, first in England, embodying reasoned economic and social theories for contraception. With the writings of Malthus at hand after 1798, such philosophers as Bentham and James Mill began looking at the problem without reference to traditional Christian beliefs—those 'superstitions of the nursery' as Mill called them. They were followed by Francis Place, who was more outspoken in his advocacy of contraception, if anonymous in his writing. The discovery in 1843 of the process for the vulcanisation of rubber meant that industrial methods could be adapted to making and distributing a simple type of contraceptive, and soon it was to become a highly profitable business.

The Church is generally regarded as having been rather poorly equipped to meet these various challenges. Intellectually it did

* John T. Noonan, *Contraception*, Harvard University Press, New Haven, Mass., 1965.

not have available men who could lead it successfully through the mounting difficulties. Gradually the reaction of traditional teaching became discernible, first to the French situation, then to the more organised movement. The anxieties immediately before and, even more, immediately after the First World War, with its massive losses in manpower, enabled the national hierarchies to mix patriotic and moral motives. In 1913, the German Catholic bishops condemned contraception as 'a very serious sin', asserting that the aim of Christian marriage was 'to secure the continuation of the Church and the State'. In May 1919, the French bishops stated that 'the theories and practices which teach or encourage the restriction of birth are as disastrous as they are criminal. The war has forcibly impressed on us the danger to which we expose our country.' That was one way of looking at it even if it was a trifle strange in strictly moral terms. The answer of the advocates of birth-control was that overpopulation itself led to war. It is significant that legislation opposing contraception came to Italy and to Germany during chauvinist dictatorships. The organised advocacy of contraception in the United States began in 1913, when Margaret Sanger founded her movement. Her first national birth-control conference was closed in New York in 1921 because, she recounts, of the objection of the Catholic archbishop. The hierarchy in the United States ever since has been consistent in its opposition.

In the midst of such confusion, it was for Rome to provide the authentic teaching for the Roman faithful. Pius XI did so in his encyclical *Casti Connubii*, promulgated on 31 December 1930. It was the most powerful statement against contraception since the bull of Sixtus V, and it was destined to be effective for much longer. It brought together the whole medley of opposition to birth-control; and no one could doubt that it was a solemn papal document.

Of the several causes for the promulgation of *Casti Connubii*, the change in Anglican teaching was the most immediate. At the Lambeth Conference in August 1930, the Anglican bishops issued their famous statement which moved their communion away from absolute condemnation of contraception. Some sections of German

Catholic opinion were calling for a rethinking of the Roman Church's teaching, and there was an unhappy awareness in national hierarchies and at the Holy See that its injunctions as they stood were not being properly obeyed. The essential passage in the encyclical, however, takes as its point of departure the decision of the Lambeth Conference. 'Certain persons have openly withdrawn from the Christian doctrine as it has been transmitted from the beginning and always faithfully kept.' This leads logically to the fundamental statement:

> The Catholic Church, to which God Himself has committed the integrity and decency of morals, now standing in this ruin of morals, raises her voice aloud through Our mouth, in sign of her divine mission, in order to keep the chastity of the nuptial bond from this foul lapse, and again promulgates:
> Any use whatever of marriage, in the exercise of which the act by human effort is deprived of its natural power of procreating life, violates the law of God and nature, and those who do such a thing are stained by a grave and mortal fault.

There are various views on the precise implication of this encyclical and also its exact weight. Can it be looked upon as infallible papal teaching? There is no doubt that it is very weighty indeed, and though its scope does not include everything, it embraces a wide area. All the same, many theologians now argue that it is not an *ex cathedra* statement for which infallibility can be claimed. Perhaps no encyclical letter can have such authority.* Pius XI, moreover, could legislate only for what he knew about, and there have been important discoveries in the field of contraception since his day. His encyclical gave what was the complete Catholic answer at that time to the latest developments in birth-control. It did so in a language that the advocates of birth-control would, on the whole, not begin to understand. Social reformers looking on contraception as a rational social practice would have as much

---

* The only pronouncement issued indisputably under the seal of infallibility since the doctrine was promulgated in 1870 is Pius XII's *Munificentissimus Deus* of 1950, declaring the Assumption of the Virgin Mary to be a revealed dogma of the faith.

difficulty in understanding the Church's view as the Church appeared to have in accepting contraception as more than the mere pursuit of erotic pleasure. The drawbridge looked to be drawn up and bolted, if unwarrantably so. Three developments, however, were soon to suggest that even *Casti Connubii* was far from invulnerable: the Holy See's endorsement of the rhythm method; the growth of a new concept of marriage; and the argument that earlier papal pronouncements on this subject were not necessarily binding for all times and occasions.

On 29 October 1951, Pius XII gave his approval, at an audience for a group of Italian Catholic midwives, to the use of the rhythm method by all Catholic couples with serious motives for avoiding procreation. The independent researches of Kyusaku Ogino and of Hermann Knaus—the first Japanese and the second Austrian—had reached the same conclusion. Demonstrating that ovulation occurred sixteen to twelve days before the anticipated first day of the next menstrual period, they predicted that a woman with a regular menstrual cycle could avoid conception by abstaining from intercourse at the time when fecundation of the ovum might be expected to occur. The pope spoke both of economic and social considerations as reasons for following this method. A month later, he described what he told the midwives as affirming the lawfulness and at the same time the limits—'in truth, quite broad' —of the regulation of offspring.

The second development was the growth of a new outlook on morality in marriage. For couples faithfully to abide by the traditional teaching of the Church, there was nothing for it but to carry out their sexual intercourse without any artificial method of contraception, and with the 'natural' position approved by the patristic authorities: a position both symbolic of the traditional notion of the male as the superior partner, and also physiologically conducive to conception. Procreation was the final cause of the sexual activity of the devout couple; just procreation; otherwise they would not, except for the 'safe period' (and then only for serious motives), be doing such things at all. This teaching would have been difficult to follow at any time, and the number that have rejected it in any given age is probably high, though there is no way of determining this. In modern conditions, certainly, it is untenable. This is not to say that it is right or wrong; there are times when right and wrong begin to look irrelevant labels, and this is a case in point.

The traditional view ignores—how could it do otherwise?—the changed status of women. They can no longer be regarded in the way the Early Fathers judged them: inferior by nature and even more so in an age of slavery and concubinage. Today, they do not require the paternalist 'protection' of their dignity which the Church gradually vouchsafed them as its civilising influence overcame social barbarism during the Middle Ages. A large number of children has become financially crippling, physically and mentally exhausting. Overpopulation is becoming a problem of frightening magnitude; from preoccupation with redressing the flagging birth-rate in Europe intellectual concern has moved to the advocacy of a reduction of the birth-rate throughout the whole world. Little more than a single generation has seen so radical a reversal in general attitudes. Until the middle of the seventeenth century, the population of the world, it is reckoned, was around 500 million, with an annual rate of increase of about 0·1 per cent. The annual rate of increase then became greater until, by 1850, the total world population was of the order of 1,000 million. By 1900, the rate of increase was one per cent a year and, by 1930, the total population was 2,000 million. In 1964, the annual rate was 1·75 per cent, double that of 1880, and the world looked set to have 4,000 million inhabitants by 1980. Parallel with these demographic trends there were signs by the middle of the twentieth century that higher educational standards among Catholic men and women, recovering from the period when both Modernism and birth-control received such heavy handling by the Church, were having a 'dedoctrinising' effect on marital relations generally. In other words, the context of the traditional doctrine was changing and, as a result, the doctrine itself was seen to be highly questionable. Even what Pius XI had had to say in the matter now appeared to be of less than final authority.

At least as important as all this was the ground gained by new ideas of the purpose of marriage. The idea was being more thoroughly discussed that physical love within marriage had great importance in itself. As far as children were concerned, the conviction gradually began to emerge that responsible parenthood could justifiably be interpreted as entailing the limitation of the size of the family, and that Christian parents exercising their responsibility in this sense could be instruments, not abjurors, of Divine Providence. No greater number of children need be brought into the world than could be properly educated and cared for. When the traditional injunctions were introduced, neither responsible parenthood in this sense nor the value of sexuality itself had ever been seriously considered as possibly acceptable to Christian life and practice. The traditional teaching was becoming less easy to argue without embarrassment, appearing more than ever remote from common—and natural—thinking.

'As we produce our arguments', said Father Gregory Baum, a much publicised theologian, 'we feel strangely uncomfortable. The awful thought comes to mind that we may be pushing millions of people into conditions of misery just because we do not want to admit that we were wrong.'* Such a comment throws a piercing light on the Church's crisis of conscience. Spiritual pride, it could be argued, and not spiritual authority, was sustaining the strict enforcement of Church teaching; and perhaps spiritual pride was no less operative at the time when the teaching was formulated. Certainly, one of the main objections of the traditionalists to any change in doctrine arose from their unwillingness —horror even—to grant that the Church's teaching, however inconvenient, could be other than eternal and incontrovertible. The Church—and let us make no modest assessment of what that word means in the way of claims and pretensions—might have to be made to admit that in the past it had been wrong. Only sixty years after papal infallibility had been proclaimed, Pius XI had issued his *Casti Connubii*, and some people were now—within a mere generation of its promulgation—already saying that it might have to be changed. What, then, would such a doctrinal change make of the great and infallible spiritual authority of the Papacy?

* Gregory Baum, O.S.A., in *Contraception and Holiness*, Herder and Herder, New York 1964.

Thus, the third great development in modifying the Church's doctrine sprang precisely from this anxious, at times anguished, debate over the binding force of earlier papal pronouncements. Paul VI has, indeed, implied that the work of earlier popes could be disregarded or modified if the necessity arose. In June 1964, he said that the rules as left by Pius XII remained, but not necessarily for all time: 'Consequently, these norms should be considered valid at least until We feel obliged in conscience to change them.' The debate was taken up in a manner quite unprecedented in the history of the Church. This was not the defence of an inherited and sacrosanct ideology against the onslaughts of nonbelievers. It was an honest reappraisal within the Church, with the pontiff reluctantly having to do the same: a reappraisal taking implicit advantage of the Church's boast that it thought in centuries, not in years. In that case, to have been mistaken for a few centuries on this subject might not seem so great a reflection on Rome's wisdom. There were now advocates of the use of the progesterone pill, another weapon in the armoury of reasons why change could be possible, to say nothing of desirable. The chemical action of this type of pill could not have been known at the time of the bans because it had not been invented. Moreover, if it could be argued that it did not stop natural processes but simply regularised them, then this surely cut the ground away from theological objections? If there was no exact precedent for the scope of such a debate, arguably analogous precedents were found to show that on major socio-religious questions the Church had altered its attitudes between one age and another. An eminent theologian, Father Bernard Haering, for instance, cited usury as a practice at one time subject to the Church's complete ban, and then later admitted to be acceptable. The feudal society of the Middle Ages, which sustained the idea of usury as a religious and social offence, was replaced after some centuries by a capitalist form of society. The Council of Vienne, which met in 1311 and 1312, as Father Haering pointed out, 'threatened theologians who might dare to justify loans against interest with chains and imprisonment'. But thereafter, a long process of development led to the *Quadrigesimo Anno* of Pius XI, which concedes, in the modern economic structure, the right to a reasonable rate of interest. Father Haering observed that something similar has occurred in the case of conjugal morality. Does this mean that accepting the inevitable is another way of carrying out Divine Providence? No less so, it would seem, than trusting in Divine Providence, unseconded by human reason, for the right number, spacing and education of children.

By the time the Second Vatican Council came to discuss birth-control in 1964, a clear division was evident over the mode of interpreting the Church's traditional teaching. If the pope's statement of June 1964 seemed to give encouragement to the reformers, it also seems to have been intended to mitigate the anxiety of those who feared lest the Church, in adjusting to new conditions, should tamper with essential truths of the faith. An example of these fears had been provided, a month before the pope spoke, in a statement issued in the name of the English and Welsh hierarchies by the archbishop of Westminster in which he said: 'It has even been suggested that the Church could approve the practice of contraception. But the Church, while free to revise her own positive laws, has no power of any kind to alter the laws of God. . . . Contraception is not an open question, for it is against the law of God.' The difference in outlook between this and the pope's statement of June 1964 is marked and eloquent. Monsignor (later Cardinal) Heenan regarded contraception, not as a matter of Rome's positive law, but contrary to the very law of God. It should be added that he felt provoked to write some uncompromising statement because of an article published in April 1964 by the Jesuit archbishop, Thomas Roberts, questioning the entire Catholic position on birth-control. Heenan seems to have been driven to a traditional statement of the traditional position for local reasons.

Paul VI endeavoured to find what in politics would be called a 'statesmanlike solution', for he was by now aware of the dangers of the situation. The stance he took was ambiguous. Traditional teaching had to be respected; but it was reviewable if the pope thought fit. He was worried about a division in the Church. That is why he gave both opinions. His handling of the problem was from then on to be tied to his wider problem of authority. He would not permit the Ecumenical Council to debate the issue which, like clerical celibacy, he kept to himself.

Even so, there were several speeches on the subject at the Council, most of them outstanding in their matter and presentation. Three prelates in particular argued the need for change with remarkable force. Cardinal Léger, archbishop of Montreal, said that the final document (they were dealing at the time with the subject of the Church in the modern world) 'should clearly present human conjugal love—I stress human love, which involves both the soul and the body—as a true end of marriage, as something good in itself, with its own characteristics and laws'. They should proclaim two ends of marriage (human conjugal love and procreation) as equally good and holy. 'Once that is done, the moral theologians, doctors, psychologists and other experts can much more easily determine for particular cases the duties both of procreation and love.' The Melchite Patriarch Maximos IV Saigh of Antioch referred to the pastoral dilemma caused by the fact that some of the faithful 'find themselves driven to live in breach of the law of the Church, far from the sacraments, in constant anguish, for want of being able to find the viable solution between two contradictory imperatives: conscience and normal conjugal life.' And Cardinal Suenens, archbishop of Malines-Brussels, declared that 'God's first demand of the act of love is that it be based on love'.

These and like-minded prelates were all calling for a re-examination of the Church's teaching. The subject was more open perhaps than at any time in Christian history. It was of absorbing and widespread concern whether one considers, rightly or wrongly, popular opinion as the real test of what the Church should do to make itself relevant to the modern world, or whether one's criterion be the engagement in the problem of some of the best minds the Church could boast. The pleas of the modifiers did not go unchallenged. Cardinal Ottaviani made the point during the Council that he was the eleventh of twelve children whose parents would never have thought of questioning the ways of Divine Providence. He was shocked that there should be people who called in question the inerrancy of the Church. Other bishops stated that large families were the best restocking grounds for the priesthood.

The Council did, in fact, adopt the formulation of responsible parenthood and the dual ends of marriage, though with fairly pointed references to the integrity of existing doctrine. Paul VI insisted that Pius XI's and Pius XII's teachings should be included in the final document; his somewhat peremptorily expressed wishes were granted in the form of footnotes, with a reminder added that it was for the pope to make a clearer definition of the Church's position. This formulation at least prevented doors from being closed. To that extent, the outcome was not bad.

But it was only not bad because it was negative, leaving the main question still to be answered by the pope himself. It was certainly not good. Paul's ultimate commitment in the matter was still uncertain. There was a feeling among experienced observers that, by nature, he would have preferred to abide by the traditional teaching as left by Pius XII. But he was worried at keeping it unaltered because he had been left in no doubt that, for most of the world at large, a change by the Church on birth-control was essential evidence for the genuineness of its intention to catch up with modern thought. The issue seemed to depend on two possible motivating factors, neither wholly determinative but each in its way capable of conditioning the pope's decision. The first was the possibility that, in one of his moments of deep pessimism, and under pressure from his conservative advisers, Paul would be governed, to the exclusion of other considerations, by the cares of office and the need to preserve the good name of the teaching authority—indeed, of ecclesiastical authority in general—and would rally to the traditional point of view, reiterating it as he had done at the United Nations, and leaving the controversy at that. The second possibility was that he would realise he must act against his own nature and convictions. There seemed some ground for believing that this might be the case. On the whole, the pope is inclined to work best in what might be called an anti-Montini way. His outstanding achievements, such as his journeys, have gone against his own cautious character and the effect of his training and earlier career.

Paul himself was awaiting the report of a special commission of six members set up by John to review the problem. Paul had enlarged it to fifty-two by March 1965, when it held its first plenary session.

Paul's commission was an international body: nine members from the United States, seven from France, six from Germany, five each from Belgium and Italy, two each from Canada, England, India, Japan, the Netherlands and Spain, and one each from Brazil, Chile, Jamaica, Madagascar, the Philippines, Senegal, Switzerland and Tunisia. Nineteen were theologians, fifteen were demographers or economists, twelve were doctors and six were married representatives of the laity. There were five women members of the commission. Above this advisory body the pope placed a committee of bishops, presided over by Cardinal Ottaviani, which was to look at the commission's report before passing it on to the pope. The commission was later enlarged so that, at its final session, held in the Spanish College in Rome from 18 April to 9 June 1966 (the longest meeting of its short life), sixty-four persons took part, though not all were present at every session.

Proceedings were secret. It was common knowledge, however, when the commission's majority and minority reports, having passed through the episcopal committee, were presented to the pope in June 1966, that a large majority was in favour of change. A majority, but a comparatively small one, of the episcopal committee also favoured change. One account gives nine bishops as having voted in favour of change and five against, with one abstention and one absentee. Accompanying the majority report, moreover, were recommendations as to how the change could be announced without giving the impression that the Church's teaching had been in error in the past. The pope was advised by the nine bishops to make his first step towards relaxation on 29 October 1966 when he was due to receive a group of gynæcologists in audience.

In the event, he did nothing of the kind. He virtually rejected the majority report as unsatisfactory, asserting that more studies would be required. Until further notice, he stated, traditional teaching remained in force and could not be regarded as in doubt. This greatly encouraged the conservatives. Paul, in effect, had made nonsense of the famous doctrine of episcopal collegiality.

Having appointed a group of eminent bishops to look at his commission's recommendations, he then rejected the results of their work as inadequate. In a normal organisation, men of this eminence would have handed in their resignations. His statement that the traditional teaching was not in doubt showed how far he had travelled rightward since June 1964, when he had at least implied that sufficient doubt existed for the position to be reviewed. Moreover, by his statement of October 1966 he was deliberately closing the doors to a possible compromise solution. He could tacitly have accepted the state of doubt which existed about the authenticity of traditional teaching. This is a device to which popes have had recourse in the past, calling on both sides to refrain from attacking the other until such time as the generally accepted truth emerged. His refusal to make up his own mind (partly, it seems, because he expected his commission to arrive at a unanimous report) and the harshness of the statement's tone, which seemed to show a grim unconcern for the sufferings of conscience of ordinary Catholics—this required all the justificatory support it could get from the Vatican's press. The *Osservatore Romano* found in his decision to delay 'a nobility that faithfully expresses the weight of responsibility not only to God, but towards the human race'. The newspaper continued in some detail with a reiteration of traditional teaching. This was the pope's low point. In *Populorum Progressio*, his social encyclical of March 1967, he was less categoric—and was thereupon criticised for confusing the issue.

Paul's dilemma could quite clearly be seen when the *National Catholic Reporter* of Kansas City in May 1967 published in full the majority and minority reports of the special commission. This move was apparently taken to force the pope's hand. Impatient with his refusal to settle the matter one way or the other, some members of the commission decided to show to the world the excellence of the reasoning by which an undoubtedly large majority of their colleagues favoured change. In fact, publication may have harmed the progressive cause. The present pontiff is not the kind of man to be bullied into a decision; he is more liable to be bullied out of one. Moreover, the documents showed something which, though it might have been suspected before, had not been effectively demonstrated: the conservative minority had a very good case. There was worse, from the pope's point of view: publication of the reports revealed that it was a question of one thing or the other. There could be no reconciling of the two documents, as the commission itself had found despite the pope's impatience over its failure to achieve unanimity. Both documents are long. Passages taken from each will show the breadth of the gap between the minority and the majority positions on the commission.

The conservative minority report sets out to show that the 'constant and perennial' response of the Church to birth-control has been one of opposition. 'Therefore, it is not a question of a teaching proposed in 1930 which, because of new physiological facts and new theological perspectives, ought to be changed. It is a question rather of a teaching which, until the present decade, was constantly and authentically taught by the Church.' It was taught, moreover, for one reason and one reason only: it was true.

> The Church could not have erred through so many centuries, even through one century, by imposing under serious obligation very grave burdens in the Name of Jesus Christ, if Jesus Christ did not actually impose those burdens. The Catholic Church could not have furnished, in the Name of Jesus Christ, to so many of the faithful everywhere in the world, through so many centuries, the occasion for formal sin and spiritual ruin, because of a false doctrine promulgated in the Name of Jesus Christ.

Whether or not this position seems inappropriate and ill-measured in the contemporary world, it is at least one which abides by the claims which the Roman Church has been making down the centuries. The minority report is equally open and consistent about the Church's claim to Divine guidance:

> If the Church should now admit that the teaching passed on is no longer of value, teaching which has been preached and stated with ever more insistent solemnity until very recent years, it must be feared greatly that its authority in almost all moral and dogmatic matters will be seriously harmed. For there are few

moral truths so constantly, solemnly and, as it has appeared, definitively stated as this one for which it is now so quickly proposed that it be changed to the contrary.

What is more, however, this change would inflict a grave blow on the teaching about the assistance of the Holy Spirit, promised to the Church to lead the faithful on the right way toward their salvation. For, as a matter of fact, the teaching of *Casti Connubii* was solemnly proposed in opposition to the doctrine of the Lambeth Conference of 1930, by the Church 'to whom God has entrusted the defence of the integrity and purity of morals . . . in token of her divine ambassadorship . . . and through Our mouth.' It is, nevertheless, now to be admitted that the Church erred in this her work, and that the Holy Spirit rather assists the Anglican Church!

This was too much, according to the conservative minority, for the ordinary faithful to grasp:

> Some who fight for a change say that the teaching of the Church was not false for those times. Now, however, it must be changed because of changed historical conditions. But this seems to be something one cannot propose, for the Anglican Church was teaching precisely that and for the very reasons which the Catholic Church solemnly denied, but which it would now admit. Certainly, such a manner of speaking would be unintelligible to the people and would seem to be a specious pretext.

The majority report naturally enough presents a far broader vision. It recounts how a part of the Church's teaching has been shaped in the course of controversy with heretics:

> The tradition of the Church which is concerned with the morality of conjugal relations began with the beginning of the Church. It should be observed, however, that the tradition developed in the argument and conflict with heretics—such as the Gnostics, the Manichees and later the Cathari—all of whom condemned procreation or the transmission of life as something evil, and nonetheless indulged in moral vices. Consequently, this tradition always, albeit with various words, intended to protect two

fundamental values: the good of procreation and the rectitude of marital intercourse. Moreover, the Church always taught another truth equally fundamental, although hidden in a mystery, namely original sin. This had wounded man in his various faculties, including sexuality. Man could only be healed of this wound by the grace of a Saviour. This is one of the reasons why Christ took marriage and raised it to a sacrament of the New Law.

It is not surprising that, in the course of the centuries, this tradition was always interpreted in expressions and formulas proper to the times and that the words with which it was expressed and the reasons on which it was based were changed by knowledge which is now obsolete. Nor was there maintained always a right equilibrium of all the elements. Some authors even used expressions which depreciated the matrimonial state. But what is of real importance is that the same values are again and again reaffirmed. Consequently, an egotistical, hedonistic and contraceptive way which turns the practice of married life in an arbitrary fashion from its ordination to a human, generous, and prudent fecundity is always against the nature of man, and can never be justified.

The large amount of knowledge and facts which throw light on today's world suggest that it is not to contradict the genuine sense of this tradition and the purpose of the previous doctrinal condemnations if we speak of the regulation of conception by using means, human and decent, ordered to favouring fecundity in the totality of married life and towards the realisation of the authentic values of a fruitful matrimonial community.

The authors of the majority report go on to give the reasons prompting them to arrive at their conclusions:

> ... social changes in matrimony and the family, especially in the role of the woman; lowering of the infant mortality rate; new bodies of knowledge in biology, psychology, sexuality and demography; a changed estimation of the value and meaning of human sexuality and of conjugal relations; most of all, a better grasp of the duty of man to humanise and to bring to greater perfection for the life of man what is given in nature.

Then must be considered the sense of the faithful; according to it, condemnation of a couple to a long and often heroic abstinence as the means to regulate conception cannot be founded on the truth.

There, on the pope's desk, are two completely opposing views of the Church's authority, its obligations to its past and its obligations to the present and future. Superimposed on this dilemma is the sure knowledge that Paul's failure to come out promptly on one side or another—or think of something else which is neither one side nor the other—is judged to be the Roman Church's most massive weakness in asserting that it wishes to come closer to the modern world.

9
Light the Weary Vessel

IN October 1962, the great nave of St Peter's was transformed into the Council Chamber of the Church. Between then and December 1965, the twenty-first General Council in the Roman reckoning held its four sessions. These sessions produced sixteen documents, some 27,000 pages of records, and filled about 138 miles of recording tape. Historically, it was the religious event of the century. It could have been, still could be, perhaps, much more even than that. It gave a new impetus and a new opportunity: the immediate aftermath, however, was unhappily confused and uncertain.

Tiers of seats for some 3,000 prelates banked the massive nave. St Peter's is the biggest church in Christendom and Roman pride has recorded this aspect of its glory in lines marked on the pavement, giving the lengths of other famous churches and showing clearly how far short they fall of this most imposing of basilicas. Rome has the measure of them all is the message. For centuries, such pride and self-confidence have been exclusive and not a little contemptuous when not actively hostile to other branches of Christendom. The Second Vatican Council witnessed something unique at least since the Reformation: the splendour of Rome exhibited in charity to the 'separated brethren'. The Vatican invited observers from other Christian communions to follow the Council's proceedings. They were given generous facilities—better in some ways than those enjoyed by the actual members of the Council, for Rome's guests were briefed on what was happening as well as being supplied with running translations of the debates, which were all conducted in Latin.

Their presence was described by some people as 'a miracle'; it was certainly a marvel, but miracle is perhaps too strong a word for a gesture that was motivated, not only by a new generosity of spirit, but also by a realistic awareness of the vulnerability and growing isolation of all Christian denominations—Rome no less than the others—in an age marked by increasing indifference to religious beliefs and sanctions. Miraculous or not, the presence of these observers did the Roman Church a great service. They helped to prevent its bid for self-awareness from degenerating into that vein of narcissism which so readily afflicts aged ecclesiastical authorities.

Then the Council dispersed, its work done—or so some of the participants thought. The seats and special tribunes, the computers for counting votes (the Council held 500 ballots during its four sessions), were all removed. The cleared nave seemed to soar upwards in greater triumph at being freed from these tiresome obstructions. There was space to move again—or not to move, as one wished. With the bishops' departure went the grand sweep of purple down the steps of the basilica each day as the Council fathers adjourned for lunch: a sight as impressive in its way, and no less essential for the visitor to Rome, as the Colosseum or Via Veneto on a summer's night. Left behind by the ebbing of the purple wave was the same basilica, that ornate exemplar of apostolic rock made tremendous by its sheer exaggeration. Also left behind was the blueprint, in the form of the Council's documents and the spirit of its debates, for a new approach to the modern problems of religion. The Roman Church had turned back to look at the world. Some of the problems were fumbled; one of the most urgent—birth control—was left open, in every sense of the term, so that the failure was negative, not positive. Above all, by turning back, the Roman Church had, unlike Lot's wife, regained its mobility. The crucial issue was whether the old structure could provide the leadership and the stamina to make use of this fresh freedom.

THE ECUMENICAL COUNCIL

Like no other event in recent history, this Council—officially designated the Second Vatican Council—made religion a subject of popular interest. At one time or another during its sessions, 3,000 journalists were accredited to the Vatican expressly to cover the Council. There were about as many journalists as prelates, and a good number of the former had a clearer and wider idea of what was happening than many of the latter. Journalists grew used to the uncanny experience of being awakened by telephone calls from the editorial staff at home asking plaintively for something more about Divine Revelation ('the agencies are saying there's deadlock . . .'). The popularity of the two popes, particularly of John, had done much to stimulate this absorbed interest; so had the fascination of seeing the Roman Church in the process of self-examination: a proud, corpulent, experienced, elderly, slightly musty, scented, silk-clad figure in red and black and purple, venerable and suddenly vulnerable, appraising itself in a mirror. It was as if the floodlights which regularly light St Peter's square had been mentally turned inward so that priestly hearts and minds and intentions could be read by the world at large. Whatever was said and done at the Council, its success in arousing an irreligious age to take an interest in a religious event was its most impressive achievement. For a while, at least, people cared whether the Roman Church was on the verge of a new and better era; whether the figure which for so long had posed as Europe itself could unstiffen its bones to meet a changing world; or whether what was being witnessed was a desperate and finally vain attempt at introducing change to stave off collapse, as Constantine had done in his effort to save the faltering Empire.

John must have been anxious, in his own way, about having called it in the first place; and Paul was to be torn by his own anxieties at having to deal, not only with its most crucial three sessions, but also with the application of its decisions. The calling of it was John's great act and Paul's great opportunity—possibly a greater opportunity than any accorded a pope in modern history. It was no light matter to summon a Council. No Council had sat for nearly a century and, before the First Vatican Council which closed in 1870, there had been none since the Council of Trent in the sixteenth century which met to face the Protestant Reformation. It was different from all others because it was not brought together to deal with a specific threat, such as a heresy or a challenge to Rome's authority. John made clear in his address at the opening ceremony on 11 October 1962 that condemnations were not to be the order of the day. The Church had always opposed errors, he said, but nowadays it preferred to make use of the 'medicine of mercy rather than that of severity'. Nor were the habitual contemners of contemporary life to be allowed to set its course. John rejected the narrow, curialist outlook of some of the eminent but conservative prelates who surrounded him in Rome. In the daily exercise of his pastoral office, he told the Council, he had to listen, much to his regret, to the opinions of persons who, though burning with zeal, were not endowed with too much sense of discretion or measure. In these modern times they could see nothing but prevarication and ruin; they said that our era by comparison with others was getting worse, as though everything at the time of former Councils was a full triumph for the Christian idea and life. 'We feel We must disagree with these prophets of gloom who are always forecasting disaster, as though the end of the world was at hand.'

It was an odd formulation of the Church's problems, but a significant one. The trouble, John was implying, was more to be found around the pope than out in the world at large. He had grasped the curial mentality and disliked it. He had decided that the only way to give it an airing was to summon the outside world, in the shape of the bishops, to redress the balance in Christendom's old centre. But how? That was for the Council itself to decide, following the general lines laid down by the pope himself. John intended his Council to be pastoral. In delineating its aims rather broadly, he spoke of the spiritual riches of the Church, of the need for new energies, for renewal and for fresh strength in order to face the future without fear.

It was a momentous occasion. The entire Roman Catholic hierarchy—far larger in number than at any other time in the history of General Councils—was called together to do something about itself and about the Church as a whole. Or try to. With the sense of men conscious that they must move in order to avoid a stagnant confusion, they flexed their intellectual and spiritual muscles at the very opening of the first session, by challenging the Curia's attempt to dominate the proceedings. (On this occasion, the challenge was successful.) They went on to define the powers of the bishops in governing the Church. Then they attempted, painfully and uncertainly, to draw up a design for the Roman Church's relations with the contemporary world, including relations with other Christians. Around these three central issues, the Council hammered out a series of other statements, documents and declarations, all intended one way or another either to correct some of the impressions of the Church's behaviour in the past—the Declaration on Religious Liberty falls into this category, as does the exoneration of the Jews from the accusation of deicide—or to modify institutions, like religious orders and seminaries, in the light of modern requirements.

If John had no markedly radical intentions in mind, he was certainly concerned about the state of the world and the state of the Church. He intended his Council to put right the latter in order to correct the former. The problems in the world at large varied from the continued disunity of Christians to the threat of war; the inequality of nations which might lead to conflict; the sterile point reached in relations between the communist and non-communist camps; the need to assert a religious presence, and one no more to be suspected of ties with political interests; above all, to go to the world with a series of propositions on such questions as the reasons for man's existence and, if not to persuade the world, at least to put before it the challenge of answering such fundamental questions as the meaning of life.

To imagine a kind of choral unanimity in presenting the claims of Christian goodness and the special claims of Rome to speak in its name would be ridiculous. The years of the Council were marked by sharp practice, by bitterness and by intrigue. In the name of goodness, conspiracies were frequent; under the pressure of national politics, the purely spiritual idea of the Council took some sharp blows. For some English and American bishops, for instance, Christian pacifism could not be reconciled with stocks of nuclear bombs, and the nuclear policies of their governments were allowed to impinge on the final wording of the Council's statements on modern warfare. The conflict between Israel and the Arab countries had its effect—though in the end not disastrously—on the document dealing with the Church's relations with the Jews. On several issues, the Council could not rise to its full height as a spiritual body. The burden of history was too heavy.

CURIA AND PROGRESS

The first sitting of the Council after its ceremonial opening lasted for about a quarter of an hour. It ended because the majority of bishops, led by the French and Germans, refused to have their minds made up for them about whom they should elect to the various conciliar committees. The task of these ten committees was to be the modification or redrafting of documents in the light of the Council's debates. It was thus important that they should be broadly representative. The chairmen of these committees, moreover, were all curial cardinals appointed by the pope. One third of the members were papal nominees and the remainder elected by the Council. The more liberal-minded bishops insisted on time to choose their candidates. They demanded and received an adjournment so that the national hierarchies could meet to discuss the matter among themselves before going ahead with the voting. The postponement was called for by Cardinal Frings; the tone of this first meeting was such that his request could not be denied. At that time, all members of the Council were bound by a strict oath of secrecy. One of the English Council fathers, who took his oath literally, wrote a letter to a friend after that sitting, carefully avoiding saying any more than that the first sitting had been a short one. When he bought the Rome evening papers, he found that they contained detailed reports of proceedings. From that day—13 October 1962—the world knew that the prelates who had crowded into Rome really took their Council seriously. That first, vital meeting broadened the whole horizon. They went to vote on 16 October. The following day, John was able to say at a general audience: 'We are now on our way.' And so it seemed.

The Curia had been the first target. In part, this was John's own fault. As has been mentioned earlier, he had placed the work of preparing the Council largely in the hands of curial men. They controlled the various preparatory commissions. The result was that a number of documents were immediately attacked on the grounds that they were too bound to the traditionalist outlook and remote from modern thinking; changes were insisted on and achieved. Few people bothered to conceal the fact that they regarded the Curia as the stronghold of this outlook. The Curia resented criticisms, just as it resented the claims that the bishops were to make for a share in responsibility in governing the Church. As the pope's executive, the Curia's members had grown used to basking in the sun of papal power, while identifying much of their own activities, by an easy sleight of mind, as virtually blessed with papal prerogative. The curial atmosphere was exotic and close, reflecting little awareness of what was happening outside those sacred walls. Thus, the lines of battle were traced, inevitably, before the great pageant began. This was unfortunate. As events have shown, the Curia is left untouched by frontal assault. Only in the most glaring instances, such as over the procedures of the old Holy Office, did angry protests from the Council floor against the structure and customs of the Curia bring change, and this was scarcely radical reform.

The pope alone could put the matter right if he felt so inclined. A papal decision could, in fact, have saved the wearisome *guerrilla* that lasted throughout the whole Council. When successive popes refuse to give their executive arm a thorough transformation, they invite bitterness because no one who has not lived in Rome can understand the mentality of the papal civil service, and those living outside Rome are inclined to place all of the faults of the Church on the Curia. This antagonism resulted in unnecessary strife during the Council and in shameless, if understandable, attempts by members of the Curia to slow down the application of the Council's work once the bishops had departed. But, basically, it was an artificial struggle. This is a fundamental point which few people,

Catholics and non-Catholics alike, seem able to grasp. It became real as it developed because, like so much else in the Church's growth, reality grew from circumstances.

Why the original artificiality should have passed unnoticed is largely because the pattern of the Council's debates was so frequently one setting the Curia against most of the others. The bishops appeared to be demanding no more than reasonable, recognisably democratic, rights against an overbearing executive. But the Curia is simply the extreme expression of the Roman Church's structure. It is the essence of self-protective self-assertion: authoritarianism gone to ground and taken deep root. Much of this character is due to the Church's history in the last century, and the Curia is a faithful, if extreme, reflection of that history. It is quite impossible to believe that some of the bishops who were so ready to attack the Curia did not do so because they knew very well that the Curia was not an untypical distortion but a typical expression of the Church's nature allowed to blossom in an overluxurious way. And if the bishops did not grasp this point, there certainly were parish priests who did so. The great battle was not at all so well received at what might be called the sub-episcopal level, at least in Anglo-Saxon Catholicism. The Church is an authoritarian structure; this characteristic is not reserved only to the pope and the curialists. The thought of greater powers for the hierarchy, and thus a diocesan centralisation instead of a Roman centralisation, looked less attractive than the course of the Council's debates would have suggested. 'God save us from our bishops!' is an irreverent but accurate description of this feeling.

It should not be forgotten that a bishop has to be very advanced to be regarded as liberal among his own people. Cardinal Alfrink, the archbishop of Utrecht, put the matter frankly: 'In Holland, my position sometimes compels me to warn against exaggeration. On the other hand, it can and must speak a different language outside the country where the thinking of people has lagged behind.' In other words, a whip for Rome and a rein for Utrecht. Other bishops were not as perceptive as Alfrink. Many of them left the Council genuinely thinking that the problem was how to bring the message of change to those poor priests and laymen who had not been vouchsafed the experience of the Council. Instead, they found that they would be applying the brake, not offering stimulus to new thought.

As for the claim that the struggle against the Curia was essential in order to change the Church's outlook, the answer is that such a claim can be no more than half true. Of course, the civil service had to be harried into accepting fresh formulations. It nevertheless survived virtually unscathed, and, as the embodiment of conservative interests as a whole, it saw to it that the final documents had their fair measure of safeguards. This has meant that the Curia has still been able to make a substantial amount of the running since the Council closed. The more progressive-minded bishops slowed down their efforts too soon and at the same time misjudged the staying power of their opponents. They still have a long campaign in front of them. The material is there in the documents for their use, for the Council certainly was, on paper, a victory, if not a complete one, for the moderately liberal attitude. But, as one official observer put it, the liberals who have shown as champions at the sprint have still to show their prowess at the marathon.

The first severe clash on a conciliar document came over the subject of Divine Revelation. This immediately brought out the essence of the quarrel with the Curia: the juxtaposition of a traditional, official view, desperately trying to insist on teaching the ways of truth from the old textbooks, with the fresher view from the outside, which wanted new thinking on the presentation of the Church's teaching. The debate on Revelation opened on 14 November 1962. The draft prepared for discussion was introduced by Cardinal Ottaviani, head of what was then still known as the Holy Office, and the curial personality possessing, by common consent, the most rigid outlook and the most influential position to make this outlook effective. As he introduced the document, drawn up under his supervision, he said that he knew of the existence of alternative drafts, prepared quite obviously by people who disagreed with the official text. This, he declared, was against the rules of procedure. The presentation of documents belonged solely to the pope; hence, such a way of doing this was hardly respectful of the papal prerogative. His attitude summed up much of what the reforming bishops found obnoxious in curial tactics: when under attack, take cover behind talk of papal prerogative.

Ottaviani's document came under attack for two reasons. It was intransigent in its insistence on the traditional schoolbook distinction between Scripture and tradition as the two sources of Revelation. At the same time, its tone imperilled the cause of ecumenism since it paid no heed to the Protestant concern for the superiority of Scripture as the prime source of Divine Revelation as distinct from tradition, which Rome for long had argued to be of equal, and at times of greater, authority. By tradition, the conservatives meant a lot of things: the study of the works of the Early Fathers, for example, and the papal pronouncements on dogma. The later teaching of the Roman Church on Mary is an example of 'traditional' authority seen as a source of Revelation; and it is precisely this kind of example which worries Protestants, who assert (with justification) that the Scriptures contain nothing of such matters as the Bodily Assumption. Tradition is suspect, as one Roman Catholic prelate, the then Abbot of Downside, put it, because it is regarded as a kind of lucky-dip from which Romans can draw out whatever they want whenever they want it. Interpretations of what the Council of Trent had to say on the subject of Revelation—a Council, be it noted, that was called specifically to deal with the problems of Protestant rebellion—had built up over the centuries a rigid teaching which suggested that Revelation had two sources, both of which, so long as in the hands of Catholic wisdom, were equally valid. What was needed now, according to the more progressive bishops at the Council, was a less scholastic and more deeply thought presentation of teaching on the subject. 'We should be thinking', as Cardinal Liénart, bishop of Lille, said, 'more along the lines of our separated brothers who have such a love and veneration for the word of God.' The majority of bishops voted in favour of rejecting altogether Ottaviani's quite clearly inadequate document.

They did not, however, command a two-thirds majority. By the rules of procedure, a simple majority was not enough to force the withdrawal of a document. The general feeling was manifestly in favour of withdrawal, particularly because of the apparently deliberate attempt to confuse the voting. The prelates were asked, not to vote for or against the draft, but to vote in favour if they wanted a rejection. This method undoubtedly caused a lot of confusion and was probably meant to; the result of the voting was that 1,368 voted for the withdrawal of the document against 822, with 19 invalid votes. It was then announced that 1,473 votes were required for a two-thirds majority; it had not been reached and thus debate on the draft would begin. This moment was the high point of bitterness, unruly tempers and recrimination in the first session. Moderates were outraged; there was talk of sharp practice and of lying. On the following day, 21 November, John intervened. He ordered that the draft be withdrawn and that a new one be drawn up by a committee under Cardinal Ottaviani and Cardinal Bea as joint presidents.

The revised text was passed at the fourth session in 1965. Only twenty-seven prelates out of more than two thousand voted against the document as a whole. The text was comparatively short, explicit and worded in terms of broad but confident affirmation. This is a summary drawn from the text:

> Sacred tradition and sacred Scripture form one sacred deposit of the word of God, committed to the Church. Holding fast to this deposit, the entire holy people united with their shepherds remain always steadfast in the teaching of the Apostles, in the common life, in the breaking of the bread and in prayers, so that holding to, practising and professing the heritage of the faith, it becomes on the part of the bishops and faithful a single common effort.
>
> But the task of authentically interpreting the Word of God, whether written or handed on, has been entrusted exclusively to the living teaching office of the Church, whose authority is exercised in the Name of Jesus Christ. This teaching office is not above the Word of God, but serves it, teaching only what has been handed on, listening to it devoutly, guarding it scrupulously and explaining it faithfully in accord with a divine commission and with the help of the Holy Spirit; it draws from

this one deposit of faith everything which it presents for belief as divinely revealed.

It is clear, therefore, that sacred tradition, sacred Scripture and the teaching authority of the Church, in accordance with God's most wise design, are so linked and joined together that one cannot stand without the others, and that all together and each in its own way, under the action of the one Holy Spirit, contribute effectively to the salvation of souls.

John's action had brought excellent results. It was a simple intervention and none the less brilliant for that. It took the sting from the wounds, giving encouragement to moderate reform while curbing the pretensions of the Curia. It is surprising how, sometimes, a simple but authoritative action can put an end to the interminable clatter of priestly wrangling. It rather makes one wonder if so straightforward a method could not be used with greater frequency.

BISHOPS AND THEIR POWERS

The great theme of the Council was the power of the bishops. What the majority claimed and won was recognition of the episcopacy's right and responsibility to govern the Church with the pope. The idea had its fullest expression in the document *De Ecclesia*, dealing with the nature of the Church, but it pervades almost all the Council's work. The basic assumption is that the bishops, as descendants through consecration of the apostles, are a college and govern the Church together with the pope. The conservative minority fought hard against acceptance of this theory —a sure sign that the theory was to mean in its application a lot more than it actually said. The more intelligent conservatives were always quick to detect the threat of change. In some ways, they were more honest than the progressive majority, even if more inclined to be conspiratorial. They saw that progress would change the Church and probably damage its authority; for them, no amount of talking around the question would alter this fact. As things have gone since the Council, they were undoubtedly correct; at the same time, their position was a false one, not simply because their opponents outnumbered them, but because the majority had at least an inkling of what had to be done to refit the Church for life in the modern world. The 'reformers' in this issue, too, were almost all conservatives, but the majority of them managed to avoid giving this impression.

The definition of the powers of the bishops was a completion of the work of the First Vatican Council which, in 1870, had defined the Papal Supremacy. The most tortuous efforts were made at the modern Council to avoid any idea that the theory of the episcopal college impinged on the concept of Papal Supremacy. The conservatives, of course, quickly pointed out that it did do so. On the whole, the arguments that the papal office was in no way diminished were well formulated. Their advocates could not, however, argue away the principal point that many things can be subject to changes of environment—suffering a sea-change—even if the thing itself is not explicitly modified, except by the reflection of its immediate surroundings. Before the days of collegiality, the Papacy was surrounded by the Curia. The more lofty, the more theocratic and the more extreme the claims made for the Papacy, the more the Curia prospered, growing in an exotic greenhouse. With a college of bishops at hand, neither the Supremacy nor the Curia would look quite the same.

The practical expression of collegiality was the establishment of the Synod of Bishops, to meet when summoned by the pope and to discuss subjects on which he called for advice.* If it meets regularly, this body—with a large part of its membership elected by national episcopal conferences—will keep the Papacy far more closely in touch than hitherto with what the hierarchy throughout the world is thinking. These exchanges, moreover, will no longer need to pass through the notorious sieving processes of the Roman Curia. Existing episcopal conferences emerged strengthened—and the creation of such bodies, where they were lacking, was encouraged—as a result of the Council's elaboration of collegiality.

* Its functions are mainly advisory, but it may on occasion have deliberative powers, though the pope would have to ratify its decisions. The pope decides where and when it meets, and draws up the agenda.

Collegiality is a theoretical way by which a certain amount of decentralisation can be permitted; national and regional episcopal conferences will now be able to make decisions which previously would have had to be referred to Rome, such as the detailed application of liturgical reform. The Council turned to the document on the liturgy—important among other things for its endorsement of the vernacular Mass—as the first draft to be substantially debated. There is no doubt that John put reform of the liturgy first because this led naturally to many other things he wanted in the way of pastoral change; and one of them was a greater degree of responsibility for the bishops.

Finally, collegiality has an ecumenical importance. For Protestants, it makes the Papal Supremacy look less objectionable. At least, it is now framed within a broader structure and is no longer a naked assertion. This apparent modification of the doctrine has been welcomed by all other Christian bodies, but particularly by the Protestants. The Eastern Orthodox Churches like the idea of a Synod. They are used to a deliberative system in which patriarchs sit down with their bishops and together arrive at a decision binding on the Church or a given patriarchate.

THE ECUMENICAL APPROACH

The ideal of Christian unity is one that has aroused warm aspirations, petty conflicts and full-blooded war for centuries. It has been both an ideal and a torment during the 900 years in which Eastern and Western Christianity have been irreconcilably divided, and during the 400 years since Protestantism turned away from Rome. John XXIII died with thoughts of unity uppermost in his mind. Its ultimate achievement was one of the principal aims in his decision to call a Council. He mentioned it on the very day when he astonished his group of cardinals by announcing his Council, at St Paul's Without the Walls. John, however, was not an inspired leader in the field, unless one bears in mind that Christians of different Churches felt at one with him in his presence. There is the story of his remark to a Methodist bishop attending the Council as an observer who asked him when he thought unity might be achieved: 'You and I, bishop, have achieved it already.' But he was not personally adventurous in the ecumenical jungle; far less than Paul VI. What he did was to make the prayer of Christ *ut omnes unum sint*—that all should be one—seem possible (perhaps too close for reality) in his own presence. In some ways this was a disservice because it glided over the difficulties. It aroused hopes based, not on the actual situation, but on sentiment. John did something else, however; he established under Cardinal Bea at the Vatican the Secretariat for Christian Unity, which is now a permanent part of the Curia but not, as yet, sharing the Curia's ancient prejudices. Of all the Vatican bodies, it is the best staffed and the most open-minded, and its services in keeping the Council's eyes on the non-Catholic world as it debated Rome's internal problems were invaluable. John's outlook was to think less of the difficulties and more of the similarities. He had personally got on well with the Orthodox when stationed in the Balkans; he must have dreamed his dreams of unity while patriarch of Venice, for there is no Italian city so evocative of the East as Venice, and its monuments are decorated with trophies robbed by the crusaders from Christian Byzantium.

Basically, John thought in terms of converting other Christians to the Roman faith. We have it on the authority of his devoted private secretary, Monsignor Capovilla, that the pope told him— to be precise, on 26 December 1962—that after long meditation he had 'consecrated his whole self to God for that great enterprise of the conversion of all Russia to the Catholic Church'. Fundamentally, any serious Catholic, whether the great enterprise in mind is the Armada or the winning over of an atheist state, must think in terms of conversion. If not, Rome's historical claim as the repository of the one true faith is made pointless.

History, where Christian unity is concerned, is an old source of contention. It has usually been found deepening the gap, multiplying faiths and sharpening differences. No organisation has been more determined than the Catholic Church to maintain its unity; but it lost Eastern and part of Western Christendom. Its sense of authority was not sufficiently shared. Both Orthodox and Protestants must have known the gravity, in Roman terms, of the act of severing their loyalties with the leading Christian see. Why did they do it? The answer, in a word, must be that, though Rome may have had a vital hand in shaping Europe, it exceeded reality by its claims *to be* European civilisation. There has been an element of masquerade in its posing as the heir of the Caesars. This factor played into the hands of Christians who, at various times, have consciously rejected Rome's insistence on jurisdictional authority. It is as much a cause of disunity as the real differences on doctrine. The problem is to seek unity without trying to base it on the imperial concept of authority.

THE ORTHODOX

The rejection of the full papal authority is one of the principal differences between the Orthodox Churches and Rome. The other is that the Eastern Christians have their own doctrine on the Holy Spirit.

Much of the original cause of the break was genuinely doctrinal, but political factors were of great importance. Constantine set the seeds by moving the political capital from Rome to Byzantium. A century later, the Council of Chalcedon gave Constantinople equal privileges with Rome, though ranking after it. The political prestige of the bishopric of Constantinople was thus a rival to the historical prestige of Rome. Up to the fifth century, the two were united under the same emperor. In name they would continue to be so associated for some time to come, but as the invasions of Italy succeeded one another, the two cities grew wider apart. The emperor retained territories in Italy and administered them, not from Rome, but from Ravenna. In 751, Ravenna was captured by the Lombards. The popes had already appealed to the emperors for help; none had been forthcoming. With the old imperial power proved ineffectual, the Papacy had to look elsewhere for protection and that was why, in 754, Stephen made his unprecedented journey across the Alps to negotiate with Pepin their treaty of mutual assistance. After 757, no pope turned to Constantinople for the customary confirmation by the emperor of a papal election. The coronation in Rome at Christmas 800 of Charlemagne, Pepin's son, was regarded in Constantinople as an outrage. The Eastern Empire never recognised the Holy Roman Emperors of the West who were to follow Charlemagne. The two cities were even more isolated by the loss to Islam of the African Church and by the Arab command of the seas. Byzantium was inclined to despise the Western Empire as its cultural inferior. Its own sense of authority grew as it continued to live close to the imperial power. This gave it a sense of equality of authority towards Rome, if not superiority.

The religious difference, apart from the Roman pontiff's authority, concerned the relation of the Holy Spirit to the other persons of the Trinity. In this celebrated controversy, the Eastern Church looked on the Latin Church's insistence on the *filioque* clause in the creed as heretical. The crucial point is simple enough, and probably only the fine minds of ecclesiastics could have transformed it into the cause of a spiritual tragedy. The Western Church taught that the Holy Spirit 'proceeds from the Father and the Son'. The Eastern Church adopted the teachings of Photius, who maintained that the Holy Spirit proceeds from the Father alone.

This is the type of controversy which Rome in its halcyon days would no doubt have happily taken in hand. In the vital years, however, at the beginning of the tenth century, Rome was weak. From 901 to 1059 there were forty popes, most of them creatures of the Roman families and many of them either evicted or killed to make way for a rival. The Eastern Empire, on the other hand, was flourishing at this time. Basil II had conquered much of Asia Minor, Bulgaria and a part of Italy. It was Constantinople which brought Christianity to Russia, not Rome. The emperor suggested to the pope that Constantinople be given a place equal in the East to that which Rome held in the West, except that the Papacy should keep its universal primacy. The pope refused. On 16 July 1054, the papal emissaries in Constantinople solemnly placed on the altar of Santa Sophia a bull of excommunication directed against Michael Cerularius, the patriarch of Constantinople, referring to him as worse than previous heretics (the most outstanding of whom were contained in an attached list). The patriarch replied with an excommunication of Leo IX (1049–54), burning the latter's bull (though only a copy of it because the original was prized as evidence of Rome's overweening pretensions). It was these excommunications which were mutually rescinded by Pope Paul VI and Patriarch Athenagoras as the end of the final session of the Second Vatican Council.

The effect of the Crusades was to widen the gap between the two Churches, especially the Fourth Crusade of 1204, which never reached the Holy Land but pillaged Constantinople instead. The result of that sortie was a short-lived Latin Empire of the East and the imposition of a Latin patriarch. Subsequent political pressure of the strongest kind could not bring about genuine reunion. This pressure took two forms. One was the fear of another attack on Constantinople from the West; the emperors saw union as a logical means for staving off such a threat. Fear of the Turks was the second factor; this did bring about a decree of union in July 1439, but it did not last. In 1444, an army organised by the pope to drive the Turks from Europe was defeated. Constantinople itself fell into their hands in 1453. Five years earlier, in 1448, the Russians had elected and consecrated their own metropolitan in Moscow (patriarch of the 'Third Rome') without bothering to refer to Constantinople.

There are now some 100 million Orthodox Christians. Their historical tendency has been to gather round the temporal power, continuing to a greater or less degree the Byzantine tradition of caesaro-papism. This tendency helped the formation of national Churches within the Ottoman Empire, whose rulers chose, as a matter of political and religious convenience, to work through the religious leaders of the ethnic communities under the Sublime Porte. The religion-centred nationalism that this encouraged was eventually to be the basis of the struggle for independence of the Sultan's Christian subjects. In doctrine, the Orthodox Christians are closer to the Catholics than to the Protestants. They accept tradition as a source of Revelation; they have a powerful Marian devotion; their sacraments and priesthood are considered valid by Rome. They believe they are the true Church in the way that Catholics do. They have, however, no equivalent of the pope; the patriarch of Constantinople has spiritual pre-eminence but cannot impose any policy on the separate national churches who owe him theoretical allegiance. Moscow is still going its own way, as was shown at the opening of John's Council when, at the last minute, the Russians sent observers after having given the impression to Constantinople that they would not do so. One of the difficulties in achieving unity with the Orthodox Churches is that they more often exhibit rivalry than unity among themselves. Even so, despite this, the Eastern Christians had their effect on the Council.

The presence of the Russian observers was important, for all that it was at the cost of humiliating the other Orthodox. Of the 100 million Eastern Christians, some 50 million are in Russia, with 30 million in other communist countries. The Russian acceptance of the pope's invitation was to have an effect on the Vatican's international diplomacy as well as on its ecumenical thinking, for John from the outset made it clear that the Council was not to be identified with attacks on Russia or its regime. The East made remarkably high contributions to conciliar debate. These did not come from the Orthodox representatives, who attended as observers only, but from the representatives of the Eastern Churches in communion with Rome. These comparatively small groups within the Orthodox tradition that have never given up the connection with Rome, or have resumed it, are still regarded with deep suspicion by the Orthodox. Moreover, until recently, they were treated by Rome as rather tiresome kinsmen in need of some Roman discipline. Yet no one at the Council was listened to with more attention than Patriarch Maximos IV Saigh of the Melchite Church, one of the commanding figures in the debates. In terms of wisdom, the two outstanding elements at the Council were, first, the splendid theologians whom the bishops of Western Europe brought with them as *periti* (advisers); and, secondly, the good sense and frankness brought from the East.

THE PROTESTANTS

There is no Protestant enclave within Catholicism to compare with that of the Eastern groups maintaining communion with

Rome. Yet it is not improper to speak of a 'Protestant temper' in modern Roman Catholicism. Cardinal Liénart was right in pointing out that the process of dealing with such subjects as Divine Revelation owed much to the spirit among Catholic scholars of greater critical attention to the Scriptures: an outlook closer to Protestantism than to the traditionalist Catholic view. At the same time, according to Catholic scholars, Protestants have lately been showing more interest in the theme of Revelation through tradition.

It is probably only now that the Reformation and the Counter-Reformation can be seen with accuracy as the smoke of old battles settles on ageing vestments. These movements were doctrinal and political. They were something else besides, which is still worth thinking about as the differences grow less. The Church's imperial inheritance could not survive the sixteenth century for two reasons: it was unable to meet the rise of national states; and it had failed to develop a sufficiently comprehensive consensus of ideas to support the Papacy. In the fifteenth century, the Conciliar movement and the popes were unable to reach a reasonable understanding so that, for dissidents, rebellion was the only other course to take. There was no way of containing the ideas which were later to be known as Protestantism within some machinery of discussion. The Renaissance popes met the classical revival and the growth of the state by joining both. The Renaissance popes were Renaissance rulers. Worldly, princely, their conduct was not much removed from the conduct of other rulers who laid no claim to be Christ's Vicar. Revolt was touched off by the campaign to raise money for the new St Peter's. The Church did not have the spiritual competence to meet it, nor the platform from which dissent could be expressed, discussed and eventually reconciled. Rome suffered its wounds and then, at Trent, between 1545 and 1563, attempted to put its own house in order. Inevitably, it did so in a spirit that breathed anti-Protestantism; both doctrinally and politically, the Protestants were now enemies. This spirit distorted some of the Council of Trent's work. It also followed that the reorganisation of the Roman Curia by Sixtus V (1585-90) was done on strictly centralised lines.

The Second Vatican Council immensely improved the atmosphere between Catholics and Protestants. By calling for an international synod of bishops, it produced the kind of body which the Roman Church, to its enormous loss, had never been able to evolve in the past. The two documents of the Council setting the new course of Rome's relations with other Christians (and, for that matter, with other religions) were the decree on ecumenism itself and the declaration on religious liberty. The first represented a conscious change in policy: Rome was now involved in the ecumenical movement. The second was intended to show a change of heart: to free Roman Catholics from the stigma of appearing to favour religious liberty only when they are a struggling minority and of snuffing it out once they get hold of the levers of power. The majority in the Council carried both documents with enthusiasm. Each, however, bears the marks of none too happy a birth. Liberty and discussions with other faiths as equals of Rome are obviously difficult concepts for a Church which has stridden through history as intolerant in belief as authoritarian in method. It seemed at times that Paul VI had misgivings or was unenthusiastic about these two crucial documents. As finally accepted, they paid marked attention to the claim of Rome to be the one true Church. In so doing, they went some way to mollify fearful traditionalists and certain sections of Catholic opinion suddenly dislodged from simple security by Rome's countenancing other Christians in terms of apparent equality. Yet, despite these worries, the Council could be said to have subscribed to the remark by Cardinal Heenan that the goal of ecumenism is now 'part of the normal outlook of intelligent Christians everywhere'.

Yet a document of the Council could not overcome the essential differences or disperse the centuries of suspicion. The real importance of the movement for Christian unity was a lot for anyone to grasp. Like the Council itself, it was partly a product of a wide fear that religion itself—not just one faith or another—was in danger because of the indifference and materialism of the age. For the Roman Church, the defence of institutional religion meant two other things besides. It meant a deliberate effort, and a huge one for many Catholics, to turn round towards other Christians, speaking of them and to them with a new respect while collaborating with them to an unprecedented extent. It was also an aspect of the Church's decision to look outward, the end of that enraptured, enclosed narcissism which John XXIII was elected to dispel.

The present pope has sometimes appeared cold towards the cause of unity. He aroused resentment by making alterations at the last moment to the Council's document on ecumenism. The changes he required were small, but they were chosen as if to whittle down slightly the substance of the document and substantially detract from the warmth of its tone. The rather authoritarian way in which they were imposed accounted for much of the resentment. Paul VI is quite frequently liable to say things and do things which show how disconcertingly fallible he is in misjudging the effects of what he does on public opinion. This was one such case. He is also exact by nature, which at times makes him seem to be far less than expansive. But he is genuinely interested in the movement towards unity, with a combination of calculated adventurousness and honesty. He refuses to be forced into underestimating the difficulties, but he is willing to go a long way to chart the common ground.

Two Meetings

He has done so personally with the patriarch of Constantinople, who still claims spiritual authority over the Orthodox, and with the archbishop of Canterbury in his capacity as leader of the Anglican communion throughout the world. The first he met in Palestine and later (in 1967) in Constantinople; the second in the Sistine Chapel—all sites with associations that might make the stiffest prelates weep. In fact, on both occasions, a good deal of weeping and emotion accompanied the embraces.

Paul met Athenagoras in January 1964 as a pilgrim to the Holy Land, the first pope to return to the geographical source of the faith, and the first pope to meet an Orthodox patriarch of Constantinople. They met twice in Palestine. Paul was moved, but refused to allow himself to give ground through emotion. In between the two encounters, he spoke at Bethleham and said, among other things:

> Even on this very special occasion, We must say that such a result [Christian union] is not to be obtained at the expense of the truths of the faith. We cannot be false to Christ's heritage; it is not Ours but His; We are no more than stewards, teachers and interpreters. Yet We declare once again that We are ready to consider every reasonable possibility by which mutual understanding, respect and charity may be fostered so as to smooth the way to a future—and, please God, not too distant—meeting with Our Christian brothers still separated from Us.

All very steady and balanced; and honest. The embrace of the burly, bearded patriarch and the slender pontiff expressed the will of both for greater unity. Only the pope, however, is in much of a position to bring his Church behind him along the path which he has mapped. The patriarch still retains his primacy *inter pares* of the Orthodox Church, but notice is taken of him by the other patriarchs only when they feel inclined. His own following is small, since his base is in a non-Christian country. His relations with the Turkish authorities are not good, and every now and then the alarm is raised that the patriarch may finally have to abandon the see given him by Constantine, and settle elsewhere— in Greece, perhaps. In contrast with the earlier experiences of the Roman Church, the Eastern communion did not find that the end of Christian Constantinople and the onset of Ottoman rule left it to fend for itself in a world of simple, unlettered men. The conquerors of Constantinople were confident in the God-endorsed superiority of their religion; they were a more cohesive force and much more sophisticated than the barbarian invaders of Italy had been. The Church was not to be tried by much persecution, while the political responsibilities required from it by the Turks were not such as to give it a centralised aggrandisement on the Roman pattern. The process of liberation from Turkish rule was highly nationalistic. As the Orthodox Church played a vital role in this process, the emergence of new nations meant the emergence of new national Orthodox churches, with only the spiritual pre-eminence of Constantinople—and that much weakened—to give them a semblance of unity.

The pontiff and the patriarch embraced across the centuries, across two totally different historical experiences and two contrasting views of ecclesiastical leadership, to say nothing of the theological questions involved. Nevertheless, this embrace also symbolised the revaluation on the part of the Papacy of the Greek religious heritage. This is an aspect of ecumenism that is particularly important to the Roman Church after its long period of self-defence and self-satisfaction. Among the things made patent to Rome in its looking outward was the realisation that the Orthodox Church, albeit shaped by a different history and constantly opposed to Rome's pretensions, still possessed a great spiritual heritage.

When Paul returned from his meeting with Athenagoras, Rome gave him a hero's welcome. Flaming torches and thousands of people lined the streets that evening. The pope responded with weary, proud happiness. It was like the triumph of an imperator who had taken the East. It was also the first time that Montini had been accorded a fervent accolade by the Roman crowds, which do not readily rise to him.

The meeting with the archbishop of Canterbury was more audacious from the papal point of view. Athenagoras is, after all, acknowledged to be a priest by the Roman Church. Anglican orders are not recognised. The Anglican Church is not regarded as being in the true apostolic succession; it has rejected vital doctrine, such as the Papal Supremacy; it has gone ahead on its own to become a universal communion, for centuries a bulwark of anti-Romanism. Historically, there are two factors that matter. In the first place, Canterbury was founded as an archiepiscopal see directly from Rome, the key centre for the latter's revivification of Christianity in Britain after the disruption of the faith by the pagan invasions. The visitor to Rome can walk from the church of St Gregory the Great, supposed to mark the site of that pope's house on the Cœlian Hill, to the ruins of the Forum below, where he polished his famous epigram about Angels and Angles. Gregory's decision to send Augustine to Canterbury was in the grand imperial manner. The second factor is that, following the break four hundred years ago, the two Churches were both deadly enemies and yet also, seemingly, not so different from each other. Henry VIII and Elizabeth I had encouraged the growth of a patriotic Church of England, but had largely guarded it from the more radical influences of the Geneva-style reformers. While Protestant interpretations of doctrine were made part of Anglican belief in certain important particulars, its institutional structure and a good deal of its devotional temper continued to be markedly Catholic. For Rome, the *Via Media Anglicana* was the worst of abominations. Not only had schismatics and heretics broken away with impunity—indeed, with triumphant success: here was also an uncomfortable rival, affirming itself to be both Catholic and Reformed.

The first formal meeting between a pope and an archbishop of Canterbury could not be an easy or a light matter. What there was of precedent was hardly encouraging. Archbishop Fisher, Dr Michael Ramsey's predecessor, had visited John XXIII unofficially in 1960. On this occasion, all of John's warmth could not change the attitude of the Vatican as a whole, where the visit was treated like a guilty secret. No photograph was permitted and every effort was made for the event to pass as unobtrusively as possible. It was happily to be otherwise when Dr Ramsey and Paul VI met on 23 March 1966. They embraced beneath Michelangelo's fresco of the *Last Judgment* in the Sistine Chapel, and in their mutual salutation spoke of the hopeful prospects as well as of the difficulties of unity. On the following day, they went to a public service of prayer in the basilica of St Paul Without the Walls, where a solemn reading took place of their joint declaration. False hopes were raised on neither side. The archbishop thought that progress would be made in his generation, but not until the next generation would results be strongly seen. Nevertheless, the pope had shown that, ecumenically, he was a more adventurous man than his predecessor.

The practical outcome was the decision to set up a joint commission of theologians to examine the differences between the Roman and Anglican Churches. The preparatory work of this commission was outlined at a meeting at Gazzada in northern Italy in January 1967. The commission is independent of the two hierarchies, reporting directly to the pope and to the archbishop. This device answers a common complaint of Anglicans that in the past they have had to go abroad to discuss ecumenical matters with Roman Catholics because they could make no headway with the local hierarchy. The latter's attitude is understandable enough. In a largely Protestant country, the Roman Catholic hierarchy is reluctant to allow any relaxation that might appear to be a weakening of its position in relation to that of the Established Church. Herein lies a major reason for Britain's being one of the few countries in which Roman Catholics have expressed substantial opposition to the introduction of the vernacular Mass, another of the Council's innovations. It looks too much like following what the Anglicans did four centuries ago.

Mixed marriages is another such problem. Essentially, it is very simple; if a couple wish to marry and one is Catholic and the other non-Catholic, their love for each other collides with the Roman Church's claim to be the one true Church. Thus, the Catholic is advised not to marry a non-Catholic. If, however, the marriage takes place, it must be before a Catholic priest, and the non-Catholic must undertake to have the children baptised and educated as Catholics. Where difficulties arise, according to the latest instruction on the matter, a local bishop may waive the obligation to put this promise in writing. By this slight relaxation, incorporated into a document issued shortly before the archbishop of Canterbury arrived in Rome, fears were revived of the Vatican's 'double morality'. A promise made verbally between Christians at an occasion as important as a marriage might well be considered as binding as a written promise, but the tone of the document is that the obligation is less onerous if not put down on paper. This whole instruction was a strange misjudgment. It far from satisfied the Church of England's requirements, as Dr Ramsey made clear. The pope issued it just before the archbishop's arrival because he had been given to understand that it would satisfy the Anglicans: a sign of how isolated a pope can be. It is easy enough to agree with Cardinal Bea in his view that mixed marriages is one of those problems which will not be completely solved until unity has been restored. And how to do that? Mixed commissions are clearly not enough. For the cardinal, whose contribution to the ecumenical movement has been of colossal importance, the breaks in the past have only happened because Christians did not follow at all costs the precepts of loving one another. The point at which to start repairing the damage is to seek to love one another.

Bea's position is in the tradition of John. Paul has added the requirement that the separated Churches should come to know each other and, with the will to unity accepted, should carefully work towards the elimination of differences. It raises the point of how far the Roman Church can go in playing its full—and recent —part in the ecumenical movement. The answer is that, once the genuine will is there and widespread, the means of doing something need not require much more than intellectual ingenuity. Already Rome has come a long way. The pressure of failing religion has brought greater charity and greater clarity from all sides. So much of Catholic doctrine has been the offspring of history; history has constantly shaped the attitudes and behaviour of the Church. History now demands an effort to place religion back in the centre of the lives of people who call themselves Christian. The process was begun at the Council. That is why the Council passed such documents as the declaration on religious liberty, the exoneration of the Jews and the decree on ecumenism itself. It explains why at so many points in the debates, eyes were turned towards the non-Catholic observers. On theological matters—such as the sources of Revelation; on the whole emotional, twilit, rather haunted subject of Marian devotion; on biblical scholarship; on the college of bishops—there were always speakers to plead an attitude which would lessen the gap between Catholicism and other Christians. At every turn there was someone to draw attention to the 'separated brethren'.

There were some with no interest in these matters. Most of the curial cardinals have no time for ecumenism. Bishops from the solidly Catholic countries were less progressive on this issue than those from countries such as France, Germany and Holland, where Catholics and Protestants have grown used to living together. In general, the move of the tide was outward. In calling a Council, John had instinctively grasped a point that too many people miss. It is hard to make single individuals progressive. Bring them together and their outlook changes. A bishop is usually a conservative individual; with a few thousand other bishops around him, he is all for progress, attacks the central administration as the root of troubles which earlier he did not realise existed, and takes the blessed moment to call authority into question.

THE MODERN WORLD

No other Council in the Church's history has attempted to look so directly at the contemporary world and to define so precisely the Catholic approach to general and detailed problems. An entire document—The Church in the Modern World—was devoted to this approach to contemporary life. It was the only document of the Council to be addressed 'to all mankind'. The text was drawn up in French because of a feeling that only a modern language could clearly express modern thinking. To many people, the whole idea was a mistake; to others, the basic idea was not bad but the drafts put to the Council (there were to be four in all) were unsatisfactory. Monsignor (now Cardinal) Heenan, archbishop of Westminster, dismissed the penultimate draft as 'a set of platitudes' unworthy of a general council of the Church. The final document, it is true, is not very striking, but for three reasons it is important: in its significance for the Church's emergence from isolation; in its attempt to grapple with specifically modern problems; and in its eschewing both a condemnation of the Church's secular rivals and also an immediate radical revision of Catholic thinking on secular matters.

Very marked is the document's character as a milestone along the road away from the isolated fortress. The drafting was done by a subcommittee under Monsignor Guano, bishop of Leghorn: a slight, smiling figure whose physique belies his resilience in the cause of a more modern outlook. He is looked upon as one of the leading figures in the more progressive tendency in the Italian hierarchy. When Monsignor Guano introduced the draft of *The*

Church in the Modern World, he appealed for understanding of the style and content that differentiated it from other conciliar documents. It was not a definitive statement but the beginning of a discussion of contemporary problems and the Church's reaction to them. Then he said: 'The Church cannot remain closed up within herself, as in a fortress, intent only on defending her own interests and members. The Church recognises that she is living in the world, sharing the life of men in order to give them the life of God, existing among men and for men.' The whole *raison d'être* of the Council could not have been better expressed.

The document's second importance is to be found in the best of the contributions to the debate which it aroused. This may seem irrelevant. It is not. The problems of most urgent concern dealt with, in fact, were those relating to marriage, nuclear war and the Church's outlook on atheism. In its final version, *The Church in the Modern World* is muted on all these questions—for different reasons—but the debates were much clearer in the demand for thorough rethinking in all three areas of Roman teaching.

An attempt to define the moral outlook towards family life and problems was certain to be indecisive without some definite statement about birth-control. This statement could not be made. As has been explained in Chapter 8, the matter had been made over to the pope, and he was only at the early stage of an agonising reappraisal of whether there should be a reappraisal. The Council has been heavily criticised for having so little to offer on birth-control. The archbishop of Westminster, anticipating this criticism, at one point proposed that the section on marital morality be simply cancelled from the document as it could not be complete without the pope's decision on birth-control. The world is right to place immense significance on what is done about birth-control; it is unfair, however, to suppose that the Council should have produced its solution. What it did, in effect, was to sketch a fresh way of looking at the problem while offering, in a number of speeches, the fundamental reasons why birth-control, divorce and the aims of marriage must be reconsidered, not just as opportunism might suggest—or even because of the growing pastoral crisis caused by these problems—but because of the possibility that the

Church may have been misguided, indeed wrong, in the past. This was what so much worried, and still worries, the authoritarians. It should be worried about.

The final wording avoided both a prejudgment on the issue of birth-control—this largely satisfied traditionalist opinion—and any attempt to insist that procreation was the one aim of marriage. 'Marriage', it stated, 'to be sure, is not instituted solely for procreation; rather its very nature as an unbreakable compact between persons, and the welfare of the children, both demand that the mutual love of the spouses be embodied in a rightly ordered manner, that it grow and ripen.' Dealing with the consequences of a need to limit the size of a family, the document stated:

> To these problems there are those who presume to offer dishonourable solutions. Indeed, they do not recoil even from the taking of life. But the Church issues the reminder that a true contradiction cannot exist between the divine laws pertaining to the transmission of life and those pertaining to authentic conjugal love . . . sons of the Church may not undertake methods of birth-control which are found blameworthy by the teaching authority of the Church in its unfolding of the divine law.

The text was the stretcher to hold the canvas taut; the debates provided the pigments with which the picture could be painted once the pope felt it opportune for him to take brush in hand. How the picture has taken shape since the Council ended was described in the last chapter.

Much the same processes occurred with the passages dealing with war and peace. In theory, it ought not to be difficult for a Christian to condemn nuclear weapons. But clerical responsibility has to take in its purview the realities of fear and suspicion among states. There was talk of just wars and unjust wars, of whether a condemnation of the nuclear deterrent might not appear a political commitment of Rome to an anti-American, anti-Western position. Such arguments as these found their way into the compromise whereby the document eventually expressed the Church's views on these problems. But, at least, there was a moment or two of exalted talk, as if purely spiritual considerations were going to be given precedence over political and other secular anxieties. English prelates led the attack on passages in the draft apparently condoning the possession of nuclear arms, or looking on the conscientious objector in a censorious manner. The abbot of Downside, Dom Christopher Butler (now auxiliary bishop of Westminster), acquitted himself best. Conscientious objectors, he thought, might really, in some cases, be the prophets of a truly Christian morality. This was his final appeal to the Council on warfare in general:

> Let us take this opportunity of saying clearly that the Church, the people of God, does not seek protection from its enemies—whoever these may be—in war, and especially not in war of the modern type.
>
> We are the mystical body, and Christ is our head. He refused to defend Himself and His mission by the swords of His disciples, or even by legions of angels, the ministers of God's justice and love. The weapons of the Gospel are not nuclear but spiritual; it wins its victories not by war but by suffering.
>
> Let us, indeed, show all sympathy for statesmen in their immense difficulties; let us gratefully acknowledge their good intentions. But let us add a word of reminder that good ends do not justify immoral means; nor do they even justify a conditional intention of meeting immoral attack with immoral defence.

Dom Christopher Butler's outright Christian pacifism was supported, though with less ardour, by two other English prelates in the Council, Monsignor Charles Grant and Monsignor Gordon Wheeler. It was also supported by the controversial Jesuit, Monsignor Roberts, titular archbishop of Sugdea, who made his views known at a press conference because he had not been allowed to speak in St Peter's. Such an unorthodox approach has a mixed effect. Monsignor Roberts' attacks on officially held opinions are sometimes inclined to make officialdom close its ranks. His claim that the individual Christian conscience is the highest authority has brought a public attack on him for alleged heresy. The views on war and peace he pronounced outside the Council chamber were not shocking; the shocking thing is that they should have been regarded as nonconformist. Perhaps the greatest scandal of the Church, he said, for too many centuries had been that almost every national hierarchy in almost every war had allowed itself to become the moral arm of its government, even in wars recognised later to have been palpably unjust. He proposed that the Council break with this 'tragic past' by making a clear affirmation of the right and obligation of every Christian to obey the voice of his informed conscience before and during a time of war.

The passage in the final draft on nuclear weapons was noncommittal about the value and the morality of the deterrent. 'Whatever may be the facts about this method of deterrence'—there is rather a resigned note here—'men should be convinced that the arms race, in which an already considerable number of countries are engaged, is not a safe way to preserve a steady peace, nor is the so-called balance resulting from this race a sure and authentic peace'. There must have been times, during this debate, when Constantine turned a little uneasily in his grave, as if what he had done so well might be on the verge of reversal. But relief would soon come to him in the hesitations marking the final debates.

The one place in which a refusal to be specific can be said to have had positive value was the absence of any direct condemnation of communism. Paul VI's decision to abide by John XXIII's policy of no condemnations had to be defended towards the end of the Council against a powerful effort, largely from conservative bishops, to reiterate in clear language the Church's condemnation of the old enemy. A petition urging such a reiteration, said to have been signed by 450 bishops, was sent to the drafting commission. It was ignored. Does the whole thing look half-hearted? This is the third significant element in this sometimes stimulating, sometimes mystifying debate: the Church without an enemy, yet still attached to the armed strength of its temporal friends; the Church for the first time in its history rising to an appreciation of poverty in the world that is above the level of alms and prayer, yet unable to take a clear look at the control of population. The great ferment of ideas—and no one should doubt the breadth of the views expressed in and about the Council during its four sessions—was not in itself enough.

Edmund Spenser lampooned the Roman Church in the *Faerie Queene*. Yet there are some moving lines of his which can be sympathetically transversed to convey the atmosphere of the final session of what may prove to be the last full Council of the Roman Catholic Church:

> For we be come unto a quiet rode,
> Where we must land some of our passengers,
> And light this wearie vessell of her lode.
> Here she awhile may make her safe abode,
> Till she repaired haue her tackles spent,
> And wants supplide. And then againe abroad
> On the long voyage whereto she is bent;
> Well may she speede and fairly finish her intent.

Few prominent passengers have so far been landed. In Britain, the theologian Charles Davis is the best-known among those who, after the excitement of the Council, have found the aftermath too disillusioning or authoritarian, and have left the Church. The vessel still bears its full load, mainly a historical burden. The pope drew attention to this in one of his characteristic misjudgments of public opinion. As an inducement for attending sermons and lectures on the Council's work, he offered indulgences. The mere mention of the word is still enough to shake the ecumenical fervour of many Protestants, while modern-minded Catholic prelates are hardly less pained by this echo from an unhappy past.

The Roman Church would not be the Roman Church, though, if there were not some occasion for doubts about it; some suggestion, however slight, that not only the greatness of the past, but also the distortions of the past, would still somewhere protrude from crevices of that ancient rock. For the Council's work to penetrate the strata of the Church that have not directly experienced the conciliar soil-movement—parish priests, the lay faithful—firm leadership is vital. And firm leadership is the opposite of what is connoted by the institution and the meaning of indulgences. On the Roman Church the onus remains to 'fairly finish her intent'.

10
Alone Once More

EVERY age seeks authority; herein is one of the principal reasons why the Roman Church throughout the centuries has maintained its strength. The present age puts authority in question, and yet, paradoxical as this may seem, still seeks it. Only, the authority must justify itself. The temper of our age rejects pretension. This rejection is all the more determined because of the anxiety of modern man. Surely, it is the most anxious age since the twilight of the Roman Empire; and, like the pagan world then, it has bad dreams. That troubled emperor, Marcus Aurelius, spoke as much for our times as for his own when he rejected the element of life made up of 'stage plays and the vain pomp of processions'. To the religious man, the problem is why the faith, which reputedly moves mountains, cannot dislodge the encrustations with which the rock is so elaborately covered. To the man who has no religious commitment, the question is whether the system can stand the strain. Both can be sensible of the danger that the whole may gradually fade into irrelevance before the leadership emerges that is capable of dispensing with those inessentials—but enduringly dominating inessentials—that have adhered to it in the course of history. The crux is whether the Roman Church is suffering the pangs of growth or the strains of excessive rigidity.

To talk of our age as one of anxiety is, admittedly, as commonplace as to call Rome a baroque city. Baroque was the style devised to express exuberant confidence; anxiety had no part in it. But anxiety is no more a respecter of styles than of persons. Beneath the soaring assertiveness of that triumphal architecture, anxiety, like a creeping lichen, is discolouring the patina of the Vatican, robbing it of its dazzling magic. Amid the fantastic show of assertion, there is the feeling that the Roman Church is not sure about what it should do.

Despite John XXIII, despite the Council, the Roman Church is still tied to the totality of its history. There has been a change of attitude, an effort to look outward; but the impression remains of someone looking forward and over his shoulder at the same time. This is Paul VI exactly. But what else can he do?

If I were a Roman Catholic, I would feel more deeply for Paul VI than for any other pope of our century. I would also fear for him, invoking God's blessing on him with an urgent, almost desperate hope. He has accepted the historical burden of his office; he has also accepted the burden of the *aggiornamento*. He is a martyr for both causes because he has shown them to be incompatible; martyrdom is the ultimate demonstration of the incompatible. What has been revealed in his anxious bid to walk abroad in modern life still vested with the trappings of old empire, to engage in the desire and pursuit of the whole of both the ancient and the contemporary worlds, is the condition summed up in the phrase 'crisis of authority'. The Catholic faithful—and all Christians, for that matter—should be grateful, and therein chastened, that this epochal condition is also the personal crisis of the man who can truly be termed the 'modern pope' of the twentieth century. A man's anguish, and assuredly when that man is Supreme Pontiff, is more eloquent than all the shrewd disquisitions on the tensions and tribulations of the age. Rome is extreme, peculiar in its very universality, and the heaviness of Paul's burden is peculiarly Roman. Yet is it not in essence the burden of every priest, presbyter or minister of the Gospel who strives to relate the transcendent to the transitory? He is faced with the burden that has been with Christianity—as it was, indeed, with the Hebrew prophets—since acceptance of the responsibility of religion's promoting role in human society.

ALONE ONCE MORE

Paul VI is the least secretive of popes. His worries, at times, are disclosed with a disarming simplicity. In his farewell address to the non-Catholic observers in St Paul's Without the Walls on 4 December 1965, he said:

> Each is about to take the road of return to his own home, and We shall be alone once more. Allow Us to confide to you this intimate impression: your departure produces a solitude around Us unknown to Us before the Council, and which now saddens Us.

Loneliness he certainly knows. At times, the cares of his office seem to hang on him like robes of iron. In September 1966, at a time when he was known to be borne down by one of his bouts of depression over the ferment of dangerous ideas in the Church, he visited the tomb of St Celestine V (1294), who is famous for having abdicated St Peter's throne. This has made him infamous to those who hold, with Dante, that he cowardly abandoned his sacred trust, making *per viltate il gran rifiuto*; but the Church reveres him as having acted for the highest spiritual motives, worthy of canonisation. Paul's was a curious gesture and a significant one, for it was certainly not made without forethought. He expresses a good deal in his choice of gestures. Some people took it as a reminder to elderly prelates of the pope's recent urging that they should resign once they had reached the age of seventy-five. Others had a different interpretation. So, it seemed, had Paul himself, to judge from a poignant remark he made about Celestine at the saint's tomb: 'He knew that he was being deceived by those around him'; and so he left the papal throne. The deceivers are still there; and far from impotent are those deceptive voices of the past, the medieval shades, the imperial ghosts, who whisper the same message that the Silveri trumpets blare out beneath St Peter's dome to a modern pope treading the paths of the modern world.

On 7 December 1965, as the pope addressed the Council's final session in St Peter's he summed up the effect of its work in these words:

> Never before perhaps, so much as on this occasion, has the Church felt the need to know, to draw to, to understand, to

penetrate, serve and evangelise the society in which she lives; and to get to grips with it, almost to run after it, in its rapid and continuous change.

When he visited workers in a Rome suburb, he said: 'I am here because of the Council.' It was one of many instances demonstrating how seriously he regarded the Council's aim of bringing the Church into the world, 'almost to run after it'. Whatever may be said of his handling of the post-conciliar Church, Paul has never sought to make people forget what the Council did, and he has constantly kept the Council in the forefront of his public utterances. This is the spirit in which he undertook his journeys to the Holy Land, to India and to New York; the same spirit governs his diplomatic adventures. These two initiatives—travel and his personal diplomacy—have already assured him an important place in the history of the Church and, combined with his sensible approach to ecumenism, provide his best claim to be regarded as an innovator. The first of them—his travels—is potentially by far the more significant as the foundation for a new role for the Papacy in the modern world. The idea of a 'pilgrim pope' has since lost much of its force but, as Paul originally devised it, remains a blueprint of much promise. It is an attractive notion and not without its historical precedents.

One of its greatest attractions is that a pope who spent a substantial amount of his time outside Rome would contribute to the advances a modern pontiff needs must have at heart. He would be away from the dank formalities of the Curia. He would be able to see problems for himself instead of studying his world through the Curia's mirror. Paul gave lavish testimony to the merits of travel in the encyclical *Progressio Populorum* when he spoke of his visits to the Holy Land and to India, where he was able 'to see and virtually to touch the very grave difficulties besetting the peoples of long-standing civilisations who are at grips with the problem of development'. The use of the phrase 'and virtually to touch' makes the difference between a general acknowledgment of the benefits of travel and a genuine experience gained from being able to come close to the real issues. The pilgrim pope would have—

as India and New York showed—new platforms from which to pronounce his message, and new and vaster audiences to judge him on the merits of what they actually saw and heard of him. Though Paul in Italy is accounted a rather unremarkable speaker, he is, in fact, superior as a public figure to the statesmen of the contemporary world in the impression he can convey of real moral sincerity combined with a highly professional knowledge of affairs.

His occasional naïveté can make him more attractive, for it shows him to be touchingly human: a trait which does not readily emerge from the formal transactions of his office. His appeal, for instance (when archbishop of Milan) to Franco not to execute students accused of sedition received the tart answer that, beside other points of the question, the changes were not punishable by death. In January 1967, he elected to call for better relations between the Church and the Chinese communist leaders just when the leaders themselves were going through a period of extremely bad relations (to say the least) with each other. But this strain of ingenuousness is less important than his undoubted ability to express himself on international issues in a way that ordinary people accept because it expresses what they also are thinking. Strangely, he is less successful in winning sympathy when dealing with ecclesiastical matters. This notwithstanding, the potential significance of his travels is equally great from the point of view of his Church's own specifically ecclesiastical requirements.

The Council had shown the diversity of Roman Catholicism: a diversity largely drawn along national lines. This was recognised by the Council's encouragement of national episcopal conferences. The strongest feeling of all was for less centralisation. A travelling pope could conceivably supply an imaginative answer to the twin requirements of greater local autonomy and ultimate papal authority. There seems really no earthly reason why a pope should be immured in Rome, and plenty of spiritual and practical reasons why he should not be. Time and again, when someone asks in tones of despair: 'Why has the Holy Father done this?', or 'Why has he not done that?', the answer comes: 'Don't forget, he's an Italian bishop, and in Italy they simply don't know, or care, about these things.' This was all very well as an argument when popes were content to keep themselves inside the Vatican, but now that they have chosen to come out into the world they are expected to look beyond all frontiers, mental as well as geographical.

Rome would naturally have to remain the basic centre of papal activity, but it would no longer have the exclusive rights to the papal presence. Such an innovation would cut across everything that the more conservative elements in the Curia stand for. Quite apart from losing a decisive share in the briefings of the pope, the Curia would no longer be able to deploy the papal aura to lend authority to its own pretensions. There would, of course, be difficulties, particularly of a formal kind; and the men of the Curia could make sure that these prevailed with a weak or hesitant pope. But problems of this kind would not be insuperable for a pope who was resolutely determined on a mobile exercise of authority. It would be ridiculous to argue that, in a world of improving communications, the pope would be technically inhibited from far-ranging visitations as a regular feature of his rule, and even more ridiculous to assert that formalities depending entirely on the temporal side of his rule should in any way inhibit such a development. Probably the greatest difficulty would be in keeping the papal style simple, befitting a 'pilgrim pope' rather than a supreme pontiff; and it would be for the pope himself to insist on simplicity. If Paul could succeed in this, he would be carrying out the wishes of many members of the Ecumenical Council who strongly felt the need for less pomp and spectacle in all of the Church's affairs. The more hysterical and glorifying aspects of his receptions, moreover, would diminish and the purely practical effect of his presence be facilitated.

Of course, some of the mystery would go, and Rome itself would lose a part of its special relationship to the rest of Christianity. But this would probably reflect changes occurring inevitably in historical relationships. Rome grew quickly into pre-eminence for a reason almost as important as its connection with the two great apostles: in the East, the great Christian sees—like Alexandria, Antioch and Constantinople—each had its own respectable, and sometimes rival, claims to eminence. In the West, Rome was alone, set amidst a troubled half-continent wherein was no city that could look at Roma Eterna with any possible murmur of civic equality, quite apart from spiritual associations. This is not so now; it has not been so for centuries. And, in any case, Catholicism is now spread far beyond its original European home— so much so that demands have grown recently for reducing the specifically European element in its organisational structure. For the sake of collegiality, it would be no bad thing for the pope to go and sit down with his bishops summoned to meet outside Rome in some area with a particularly urgent problem; or, indeed, to preside over a national episcopal conference when local problems called for authoritative decisions with the special weight that only the Supreme Pontiff could provide.

The notion of a pilgrim pope was sustained by Paul's description of his journey to Palestine. Of all his journeys, that was the most dramatic. He was going back to the origins of the faith to see, as he put it, 'that blessed land where St Peter set forth and where not one of his successors has returned'. At last, after all those centuries, a pontiff had symbolically gone back beyond Constantine, beyond Domitian. It was a brilliant start to his pontificate. But it seems it may prove to have been a master-stroke without a follow-through. Rome still prevails over the pope as well as over the Church. The pilgrim pope is still only an idea. He is still wandering in the visionary landscape of what might be, sadly leaning on his staff as he stops to survey the desert places, hoping that someone might emerge from a conclave who would embrace the vision, give the idea flesh and make it his own.

In so many ways, it looked a promising idea. What became of it? Did the idea never really take decisive shape in Paul's mind? Or did his will to impose it, against the wishes of his entourage, fail him?

These questions may seem unfair, given that Paul followed his Asian and American journeys with others, to Portugal and Turkey, and was believed at that time to have in mind a number of projected visits to be chosen from the many invitations received following his breaking of the papal aversion to travel. The fact remains that the Fatima pilgrimage is an entirely different type of journey, with entirely different aims. In no way does it discount the view—rather the opposite—that the original idea of papal travels has lost its vigour. More than anything else, probably, the development of the pilgrim pope concept has been stunted by the refusal of the Polish government to allow him to attend the millennary celebrations at Czestochowa in 1966. As a son of the Church and as Holy Father, Paul keenly desired to take part in Catholic Poland's great act of national and religious devotion, and with good reason felt that he was asking no more than should have been granted to him. He very likely felt, moreover, that the work of John and his own endeavours for peace and better international relations had given the papal office a respect and acceptability as would disengage it, for such an occasion, from the antagonisms and distrust arising from ideological conflicts and quarrels between Church and State. The Polish government may have suspected a 'political' motivation on Paul's part; it was certainly politically motivated itself in denying him entry, however understandable its reasons. No doubt, also, it reckoned that the presence of the pope in so devout a country would mean that the regime's contribution to the celebrations would be overwhelmed by the magic of the papal presence; and that magic, or some of it, would remain with the regime's old enemy, the Polish primate. But Paul's mind must have suffered a very painful disillusionment. The whole world, communist states included, was ready, it seemed, to welcome a pilgrim pope travelling on the world's business: calling for peace in Vietnam, for war against hunger and poverty, and identifying himself generally with received progressive ideas in the field of economic and industrial relations. But a pope who sought to be a pilgrim on the faith's business was evidently destined to knock in vain at many closed doors. This seems to have cut Paul to the heart and dispirited him.

The reaction to the visit to Fatima in May 1967 can hardly have cheered him, in view of the politically-based attacks on him for visiting a Portuguese shrine, and the hardly less sharp censure on him for visiting a Marian shrine which is not one that inspires the greatest confidence in many Catholics, let alone non-Catholics. Yet it is perhaps, all things considered, the most instructive of his journeys up to that time. It represents his first attempt since the visit to the Holy Land (itself mainly devotional in character) to fulfil a purely religious aim. This purpose was so strongly operative that he felt it important the visit be free of any political overtones. As a trained diplomatist, he accordingly called for a report on the likely reactions in Africa. The advice given was that he should not go. But, as a man disappointed but determined to hold to his original intention, he rejected the advice. Sadly, the visit and its aftermath showed that, whatever the pontiff may say or do, his steps are watched for every political relevance they may suggest. A millennium and a half of papal political activity and a few years of the renewed policy of involvement in the world mean that a religious gesture is likely first to be judged politically.

The religious motive is very simple. It seems that, among the pope's growing anxieties, is the current trend in theology towards the 'naturalisation' of religion: the idea that, in a scientific age, the beliefs of the Church must be adjusted to the human intellect's rejection of mystery. He is oppressed by awareness that many clerics throughout Christendom—from the *nouvelle vague* diocese of Woolwich to some of the quieter reaches of Rome itself—have discarded the concept of the supernatural operating alongside the natural. Before the visit to Fatima, he had expressed his concern to the Jesuits about this trend, which was one of the reasons he gave for the anxieties the Society of Jesus was causing him.* His seeking to resist this trend should not be considered stubbornly conservative in the retrograde sense; unfashionable, perhaps, but not retrograde. Other Christian communions are encountering the same problem, evangelical Protestants among them. Rome's problem is probably the greater in that, generally speaking, Catholic doctrine until fairly recently has been insulated from the intellectual revisionism which has been part of the theological experience of many of the Reformed Churches for nigh on a century. But Paul's response differs very little in substance, albeit expressed in forms particular to Rome, from that of intelligent Christian pastors everywhere who seek to maintain the essential belief of the faith in a personal God and in the immanence of the divine. Moreover, Paul is constantly being taxed with the responsibility of following

*See p. 338 below.

the lead given by John. Consciously or unconsciously, people everywhere are wanting him to be 'like John'. If ever there was a man who said his prayers to individual saints and angels with a profound faith in the direct inspiration and intervention of God in human affairs, it was Angelo Roncalli. And did not John, on one of his most ambitious visits outside Rome, offer his devotion at the sanctuary of Loreto?—that sanctuary where is venerated the house in which Mary lived in the Holy Land, reputedly brought by angels, first to Dalmatia, and then to Italy.

John's pilgrimage to Loreto was seen as the simple act of faith of a good man. Paul's gesture of Marian devotion could have been similarly regarded, but not from the moment when he made known the particular shrine where he hoped—with his propensity for significant gesture—to demonstrate his affirmation of a basic tenet of the faith. The ecclesiastical calendar showed that the sanctuary at Fatima was about to celebrate the fiftieth anniversary of the first of the alleged appearances of the 'White Lady'—the Madonna of Fatima—to three shepherd children. It was also the twenty-fifth anniversary of Pius XII's consecration of the world to the Immaculate Heart of Mary: an action taken as a direct consequence of what the Madonna is reputed to have ordained, in an instruction to the children, as a means of bringing about the conversion of Russia. In spite of the advice to the contrary given him by his apostolic delegate in the Congo, and thereby accepting the political risk, Paul decided to visit a shrine reprehensible in other ways to enlightened opinion for its association with the darker side of popular devotion, and there to pray for peace in Vietnam and to honour, as he put it, the Madonna. That no one should fail to understand the mystical import of his decision, he declared at a general audience in St Peter's a few days before his departure that the pilgrimage had been 'suggested by the Madonna Herself'. This seemed clearly to indicate his belief that he had a direct, supernatural bidding to go. It seemed rather overwrought and rarefied for people expecting the Roman Church to show clear signs of that modern, pragmatic approach which, it is thought, is appropriate to contemporary needs.

He ignored such evident hazards as the exploitation of the visit by the extreme right, which happily interpreted it as an endorsement of the extremer forms of the Marian devotion and as a return to the policy of intransigent anti-communism. He put aside the criticism (from intelligent supporters of American policy no less than from its opponents) that, with the Portuguese fighting a colonial power's war in Angola, Portugal was scarcely the place in which to pray for peace in Vietnam. He either overlooked or wished to placate the strong protest made by the Portuguese government against his visit to India on the ground that India had seized Goa. (The government's annoyance at the time was such that it forbade newspapers and radio to report the visit.) Immediately after publication of *Progressio Populorum*, the encyclical on development and peace containing an outspoken criticism of colonialism, he honoured with his presence a country which, more than any other in African minds, represents the worst in surviving colonialism. He went nevertheless.

The world's reaction must have dispirited him at least as much as the Czestochowa rebuff, because the essential meaning of the gesture for him was inevitably swamped by angry controversy. It is a sad irony that Paul won more sympathy in general public opinion by his inability to go to honour the 'Black Madonna' of Czestochowa than by his going to honour the 'White Lady' of Fatima. There can be no more poignant example of the obstacles which political considerations present to the mission of a supreme pontiff of the Church. The Polish jilting almost surely has sapped Paul's ardour for travelling in the manner set by India and New York; the Portuguese embrace can hardly have encouraged him in thinking that he is on the right path as a pilgrim pope, for all the change it represents in devotional intention from the pioneering political journeys.

The alternative to not going to places is to read about them; and for heads of state this means diplomatic dispatches and confidential reports. Paul has shown clearly that he sees diplomacy as one of the ways—probably, for him, the most important way—of making the Church's presence felt in the modern world. His international design is imaginative. It is unique in world affairs in its combination of moral weight and practical policy. It is also personally congenial to him, for, having spent most of his pre-pontifical career in the Secretariat of State, the ground is familiar to him. An active papal diplomacy would deploy to good effect the traditional machinery of the Vatican—Secretariat, nuncios, delegates—in which he is an expert. It would, moreover, place the Vatican in the midst of the issues of peace and war.

It has its disadvantages, however. Fundamentally, the pope does not carry the kind of weight in international affairs that secular powers possess. He can force an issue only if he can ally the Vatican's moral authority with a dominant movement in international opinion. (At one time, it seemed that Paul might achieve such an alliance over Vietnam. He did not succeed, but the possibility of an effective papal intervention was demonstrated.) Moreover, the pope does not have anything like the control that popular opinion thinks he has over his subordinates. Defective control at the centre can be disastrous in diplomacy. For instance, had Paul been deeply engaged as a major party in negotiations over Vietnam at the turn of 1966, his status as a negotiator would have been gravely impaired by Cardinal Spellman's Christmas sermon in South Vietnam calling for total victory against Hanoi. A strong pope might have resorted to older methods and stripped the offending cardinal of his diocese, sending him into exile to purge his offence. But this would have brought him up against a no less parlous situation. Spellman was speaking to American servicemen as Catholic Vicar to the forces. It was a purely American occasion, and it is not unreasonable to assume that the administration in Washington found the cardinal's views acceptable and in the national interest. The discomfiture of the cardinal by the pope in such a matter would have reawakened the old antagonism between clerical and civil powers. What right could an Italian pope have in punishing an American prelate speaking, in his official capacity, to American troops? Diplomacy is full of pitfalls for all engaged in it; the pitfalls are certainly not fewer when a pope treads its paths. This said, it should not be thought that Paul's diplomatic initiative was valueless; if it achieved nothing else, it convincingly demonstrated the Vatican's sincere identification with the sufferers in the Vietnamese war.

Like card-playing, with which it is often (usually wrongly) compared, diplomacy's main characteristic is that it is time-consuming. For those engaged in it, it fills the mind. Some question whether there is much to be said for it. Going abroad to chatter for one's country is not everybody's idea of a worthwhile vocation. An exaggerated view, of course, but the point of it is not irrelevant in this context. The pope has been criticised for filling his mind with telegrams from the nunciatures instead of taking the lead in settling the Church's vital internal problems. The complaint may be well-based, but it is rather like criticising a leopard for having spots. Popes are individuals. The system of papal election, though having immense merits, has the defect that the successful candidate is usually of advanced years. He has very little time in which to do what he wants, and he has no knowledge of who will follow him; and so he acts in a determinedly individual way. This is a result of the system. Catholics can hardly complain if, when a trained diplomatist of long experience is elected pope, diplomacy occupies a prominent place in pontifical activity.

In any case, this personal factor apart, there is a direct connection between papal diplomacy and the Vatican's moral position in the world. In this field, John showed what goodness, plain goodness, could do; Paul is seeking to apply his sincerity and goodness through the Vatican's machinery of state. What is sifted out through that fine mesh has added lustre because it emerges in spite of everything that historical and bureaucratic obstructions can do to confine it.

It is easy enough to say that, when the conventions and shibboleths of tradition and institutional procedures impede the new role sought by the Papacy, these should be over-ridden or abolished. Easy, but scarcely intelligent. The system has been shaped by history and by the personalities of popes. If it is grotesquely wrong, as some progressive Catholics assert, it has been wrong for centuries. It has also been accepted for centuries, albeit not always willingly and not without attacks. But the type of attack it now has to face—the attack on institutional religion as such—is not of the kind that can be met by making a correction or so here, putting a different man there, allowing concelebration, saying the Mass in the vernacular, or removing the crosses from St Peter's shoes. The sword of attack is too long for such parrying. Paul seems to sense this. It constitutes an assault on authority.

But, in facing the problem, he seems reluctant to arrive at the final conclusion. The idea of authority in the Christian religion—maintained in all its fullness only in the Roman Church—originated in a situation that was the exact opposite of the present situation. The Church's partnership with the late Empire was derived from the strength of Christianity as a spiritual force and in contrast to the weakness of the civil structure and its morale. It is now institutional religion that is weak, and authority cannot be resorted to in the same way to produce, in reverse, the sustenance-yielding relationship of the classic Church-Empire alliance.

At the end of the Council, Cardinal Heenan stated that the Roman Church was on the threshold of a great era. The statement seemed justified at the time, and may still be. The debates had produced among Catholics a remarkable euphoria; at last, they were really on the move. It was like experiencing the atmosphere of one of those emotive evenings in the concert-hall or opera-house when a great conductor relieves the long siege of mediocre performances. Hats were thrown in the air. The best man in the Sacred College was on St Peter's throne. Because of his known outward-looking tendencies, Paul's very name was a policy. He was only waiting for the Council to end in order to begin a glorious era in the history of the Church. But, though the Council proposes, the pope disposes; and Paul has to deal with the hard realities of a Church that, albeit possessing a new temper, is unchanged in basic structure. Shortly after the Council closed, his warnings began. The innovators were not to go too far. Dangerous doctrines were being voiced. The ferment of the Council had gone to people's heads. If he had had secret fears, these were now taking tangible shape. Throughout the Council, vague rumours ran that the alarmist warnings were being whispered in his ear: episcopal collegiality would endanger the Papal Supremacy; authority as such was being imperilled. These promptings have not lessened since then.

Paul is very vulnerable to pressures of this kind. He is prone to spells of intense depression. Concern over this influences curial procedures. Reports prepared for him will be returned to the originating officials for rewriting before they reach the papal desk if the first draft is not hopeful enough in tone. His anxiety is not relieved by such consideration, which seems to be prompted more by bureaucratic sagacity than real sympathy. He receives very little warmth from his immediate staff, many of whom, one must say, are rather unattractive people. Occasionally, he perceives that efforts are being made to keep certain things and certain people away from him. This is undoubtedly not all done for the sake of kindness. He works in a chill atmosphere, hardly conducive to quick, instinctive decisions. His anger, though it can be very real, is short-lived. He once wrote to his Maestro di Camera (the official who arranges audiences) to complain that the people he did not want to see were sent to him and those whom he wanted to see were not given audiences. It was a just complaint, but he virtually negated it within a matter of hours by writing a letter to the Maestro full of regard. It was much the same story when he indicated to the Roman nobility that its days were numbered; his strong words were followed by a kindly letter to the leader of the outraged black aristocrats. In the spring of 1967, Cardinal Ottaviani forbade Catholics in Rome to attend services for unity in non-Catholic churches. The pope countermanded this unforgivable instruction (too late to have effect), but followed it with another of his kindly letters to the cardinal.

Paul's acutely anxious state of mind clearly accounts for some of the more extreme instances of his warnings against innovation. They also owe something to the habits of mind of a diplomatist. The broad areas of peace and goodwill do not perturb a diplomatist; what most worries him are the small incidents which may grow into a perilous crisis, the early signs of revolt, the threat of future trouble. Thus, if the Dutch Catholics are being a worry and the French rather difficult—or groups of them—all the resources of the papal mind are concentrated on them. In an organisation so dependent on complete obedience, it is those who will not conform, whether progressives or conservatives, who command the pope's attentions and impose priorities. This situation contributes to the crisis of authority that is felt in one or other of its forms throughout much of the Church. No successful general is so worried by skirmishes on the flanks that he fails to attend to the main threat from the enemy. The enemy is non-belief, scepticism, materialism. It is not unruly clerics.

Paul's anxiety is understandable, given the gravity of the situation. Decisions are required, and almost any decision could be calamitously wrong. He knows for himself that clear decisions are essential; and if he did not, he was told it enough times during the Council to become aware of it. The other horn of the dilemma, the danger of a calamity through a wrong decision, has no less firmly been pointed out to him by his entourage. This is a major contributor to his anxiety: to do what many sections of the Roman Church at large want him to do brings him straight up against the predominantly conservative Curia. Yet the crucial factor is not this but his own difficulty in reconciling the two opposing forces in the Church. He wants to correct a number of things; he wants to conserve far more. He patently seeks to do what is necessary for the Church's well-being, slowly perhaps, waveringly at times, but with deliberation. And the scope of the problem does not admit the attitude of a trimmer.

The ensuing crisis of authority is real, yet it surely was not unexpected. It is not possible to allow a Council to debate for years in great freedom and then, suddenly, expect the debate to stop. Moreover, authority is being called in question everywhere; it is not just the Papacy that is suffering in this way. The Council recognised this, hence its endorsement of the theory of collegiality. It remains to be seen whether the practical outcome of this theory —the Synod of Bishops—can do much to evolve a new form of Catholic authority.

Authority is an unwelcome subject for discussion to those who have it and must use it. So much was shown by the fascinating clash between Paul VI and the Jesuits in the summer and autumn of 1966. This was brought to the attention of an amazed public on 16 November, when the pope rebuked the leading members of the order on this specific point of obedience. It sounded like a somewhat perfunctory plea against change: 'If you continue to be what you were', he told them, 'you will not lack Our esteem and confidence.' This was said after the Jesuits had been meeting in their General Congregation to discuss what changes were necessary in the order to allow it to maintain its position as the intellectual bulwark of the post-conciliar Church. The Society of Jesus is the largest and most active of all the Roman Catholic religious orders, and one which has had since its foundation a special tie of loyalty to the Holy See. Some Catholic apologists have tried to gloss over a clash which needs to be understood in its full import. To pretend that it was nothing exceptional (some writers have pointed out that Pius XII had also been stern with the Jesuits) suggests a monumental lack of confidence, or else the stretching of *savoir faire* to the point of ridiculousness. The differences were about the exercise of authority, and there is no greater question before the Roman Church.

The audience was given in the Sistine Chapel. This in itself was very remarkable because it was the first time that the members of the governing body of an order had been received in such historically sumptuous surroundings (a 'sacred and tremendous place', the pope reminded them), and it was evidently meant as an honour. It might also have occurred to some of the Jesuits, who are normally well-versed in the interpretation of papal gestures, that Paul VI wanted an awe-inspiring background, as John had wanted when he made one of his peace appeals during the Cuban crisis. What followed mystified many of the 226 Jesuits present. The discourse was a mixture of what seemed like excessive rebuke and excessive praise. Paul told them that it was an historic moment and that the audience provided the opportunity for a definition of the relations between the Society of Jesus and the Church. He asked them whether they wished to continue to be what, since their foundation, they had been to the Church and the Holy See.

> There would be no reason for this Our question if information and rumours had not come to Our ear regarding your Society—and other religious orders—for which We cannot conceal Our astonishment and, to some extent, Our pain.

Certain strange and sinister suggestions have caused the doubt to appear in some corners of your capacious Society as to whether it should continue to exist as the Saint, who devised and founded it, described in very wise and very firm rules . . .

Perhaps, he continued, some among them adopted the principle of the absolute historical nature (*storicità*) of human affairs, as if Catholicism did not contain a charisma of permanent truth and invincible stability, 'of which this rock of the Apostolic See is the symbol and foundation'. It seemed that some were implying that the austere and virile obedience which had always characterised the Jesuits should be diminished as hostile to the personality and an obstacle to vitality of action, therein forgetting what Christ, the Church and the spiritual school of Loyola himself had taught about this virtue. Perhaps some among them there nurtured the illusion that, in order to spread the Gospel, it was necessary to adopt the outlook and mentality of the modern world, with its naturalistic approach. These clouds in the sky, the pope went on, had been dispersed to some extent by the decisions of the current meeting of the General Congregation. (But only, be it noted, 'to some extent'.)

What was worrying him? The variety of views within the Society of Jesus makes it a microcosm of Catholic thinking; conservatives it has, and also some of the foremost advocates of fresh thinking in the Church. It is also facing up to the task, entrusted to it by Paul himself, of countering atheism and materialism.

Father Pedro Arrupe, a modern-minded prelate, was elected General of this most powerful of religious orders in June 1965. A Spaniard and a former medical student, Arrupe was in charge of Jesuit novices in Hiroshima when the atomic bomb was dropped. The Jesuit house was in the blast area. He was immediately in the midst of its appalling effects, treating victims of the disaster. Arrupe has a deep respect for the oriental mind and for oriental stoicism. He recounts with admiration that, as he cut away flesh from unanæsthetised victims, no one screamed. He relates readily— and did so at the dinner organised by Anglo-American journalists after the papal audience—another experience of those calamitous days which has clearly had a profound effect on him: the Emperor Hirohito's frank admission to his people that he was not, after all, divine. He had had to offer his hitherto invincible country's unconditional surrender. This was the spiritual equivalent of the physical upheaval of the atomic bomb. For untold years, the Japanese had accepted imperial divinity as an unquestioned article of faith. Arrupe found the Japanese emperor's statement deeply moving. Supernatural authority had suddenly gone.

The General of the order is not proposing, of course, that something similar might happen in St Peter's square, that the rëigning pontiff should announce from the balcony *urbi et orbi* that he and all his predecessors and the whole Roman Church had been wrong. But his experience at Hiroshima has given him a new idea of authority which it is extraordinarily difficult for a Roman pontiff, surrounded by the city's religious and historical associations, to grasp. Father Arrupe is still an authoritarian. How could he be otherwise at the head of what is still the most disciplined of the great Catholic religious orders? But he has perceived that authority can no longer be applied in the old way. In some of its aspects, held in the past to be essential, authority must be diminished. He has accepted the idea, which the pope does not seem to have grasped, that discussion is essential as a prelude to any decision. Once made, the decision must be firmly established.

After the papal audience, Father Arrupe called a press conference—in itself unprecedented—to explain the decisions taken by the Jesuits at their General Congregation. He admitted that the order had had some failures, as well as splendid successes, in carrying out the Ecumenical Council's mandate of adaptation and renewal. It was evident, he said, that some delegates at the General Congregation were inclined to attach great importance to retaining what was of value in the traditional ways, while others tended to lay more stress on the values inherent in adaptation. At times during the discussions, audacity had exceeded prudence. But all were agreed on the basic principles to be safeguarded. It was not a conflict between conservatives and progressives but, rather, a common desire for fidelity to the original spirit of the Society.

This led the order to reflect on its own nature and on the fundamental importance of obedience to the pope. There was never any question of disputing the teaching on obedience, although the exercise of authority had to be reconciled with the modern Superior's need for information and advice. Decision-making, to some degree, had to include all members of the Society. The theological principles underlying ecclesiastical and religious authority remained unchanged, but its supernatural character had to be insisted on more strongly. The modern Superior, Arrupe observed in a highly significant remark, could no longer live a life apart; he needed to be on close terms at all times with the members of his community. The decrees approved at the General Congregation recognised the advisability of wide regional adaptation because of the order's need to permit Jesuits of different cultures to find their own ways of developing and working in the apostolate. He was undoubtedly going a long way beyond what the mood at the Vatican would accept for the Roman Church as a whole. It may be added that the General Congregation had to deal with the order's own internal problems, one of the most important of which is the fall in vocations and the difficulty of convincing young men that the traditional training is suitable for a modern apostolate.

Father Arrupe was at pains to point out that the pope's rebuke had been uttered in terms of 'paternal worry' and should not be regarded as condemnation or castigation. What he did not enlarge on was the two meetings which he had had with the pope before the audience. One was at Castelgandolfo in August 1966, shortly before the General Congregation settled to its task of meeting the needs of adaptation and renewal. Paul was in one of his anxious moods. He had on his desk a bulky file. Many of the passages in the pages he turned over were underlined. It was a report on the alleged misdoings of certain Jesuits who had gone too far in pursuing renewal and a modern approach. Arrupe was new to Rome and did not recognise the arms on the cover of the cardinal who had prepared the dossier.* He was not allowed to see these reports,

---

* Opinion within the Society ascribed it to Cardinal Antoniutti, one of the most conservative of curialists and Prefect of the Sacred Congregation for the Religious. The material was supposed to have been sent in by

only to hear of the pope's anxieties. He saw Paul a second time in the autumn of 1966, to report to him about the General Congregation then meeting in Rome, principally to apply to the Society of Jesus the decisions of the Council on the organisation and work of all religious orders. The pope was in an easier frame of mind. He raised no objections to the subjects of discussion.

The November discourse in the Sistine Chapel was thus a combination of these two papal moods: praise of the order, and concern over some of its members. After the allocution was ended, Father Arrupe approached the pope, and prepared to kneel before him and thank him for his words. But Paul forestalled him and insisted on embracing him. The General of the Jesuits admitted afterwards to being very moved. In true Jesuit style, he added: '. . . but the Holy Father was even more moved than I was'.

It is not to be wondered at that, since November 1966, Jesuits have been rather frank in private about the present pontiff and his shortcomings. What does arouse wonder is that Paul, a diplomatist by training and, some would say, by nature, should so forthrightly have offended an order that is his most valuable instrument in terms of intellectual stamina, of pastoral vigour and of obedience to the Holy See. He had recognised its importance by giving it the special task of opposing materialism. The pope confused his finest militia at a time when the march forward had begun and then been halted by uncertainty at the centre. Historical circumstances, as any student of the Church will grant, may modify the meaning of what is said and done. They do not help to explain Paul's dealings with the Jesuits, unless it be to say that, unusually for a pope, he has found historical circumstances too much for him. The Jesuits have not, and that is the basic difference between the élite and its leader.

The fear that widening the basis of authority, or placing it in any way in question, may mean that authority will crumble, this is what is at the heart of Paul's most striking hesitations. The

---

conservative bishops, certain Vatican diplomatists—led, it was thought, by Monsignor Vagnozzi, then apostolic delegate in Washington—and some conservative members of the Society itself.

birth-control issue is the most outstanding case. He has laid a tremendous emphasis on the difficulties inherent in this problem. There is only one difficulty of over-riding importance. It is simply that a decision allowing change would inevitably be looked on as an admission that, for centuries, the Church had been wrong in an important aspect of its teaching. Some conservative advisers are constantly assuring him that change would be a 'mortal blow' to the Church's teaching authority in all spheres. This, for Paul, is the vital issue. This is why he fights shy of accepting the implications of that other hard reality: the fact that the Church's teaching is widely looked on as not only in doubt but as completely impossible. In his famous rejection, on 29 October 1966, of the report of the special commission, he insisted that Catholic teaching on birth-control was not in doubt. For all the effect that statement could have on what countless Catholics think and do, he might as well have tried to straighten, personally, every baroque curve in the churches of Rome. Paul probably realised this. But what was important for him was that he was 'keeping the papal faith', that he was defending authority.

There are those who insist that the answer to this crisis of authority is more and more democracy. This ingenuous proposal comes mainly from troubled or enthusiastic Catholics, unwilling or unable to see their Church sufficiently clearly to judge what its nature is. Theirs is a fundamental misconception because the whole structure is a pyramid rising to a single spiritual apex. The Roman Church simply would not function on democratic lines. Many a good prelate would be non-plussed at the idea of a democratic choice. This is not what priests take the cloth for; and, in many cases, it is not what they teach either by word or example to their flocks in matters of secular life. Some people have tried to argue that the Ecumenical Council was a great working example of democracy in the Church. It was nothing of the kind. It was certainly a reasonably free forum for the expression of ideas (though some subjects, such as birth-control, were forbidden), but the whole purpose in elaborating drafts was to reach unanimity, or near-unanimity. Had the Council taken straight majority-voting as the principle for reaching decisions, it would have accomplished far more sweeping changes—provided, of course, that the pope were in agreement with them, which in many cases he would not have been. Where modifications required to satisfy conservative opinion did not come from the floor, they were imposed by the pope himself. The essential claim of the system is that it is an autocracy guided by the Holy Spirit. Where does democracy enter into such a system? Nowhere. (It could be argued that, if it did, the result—for the faithful, at least—would be the same since the Holy Spirit would presumably be guiding a democracy as it had been guiding an autocracy.) The word 'democratisation' in its strict constitutional sense does not bear examination in the papal context. No one with any perception of what the Roman Church is about would countenance it. The Vatican is inherently authoritarian or it is nothing.

Yet developments are taking place at the Vatican which, seeking to enhance papal authority by popularising the person of the pontiff, distort the nature of his authority, detract from the reverence due to it from believers, and flatly contradict what the Council had to say on the point.

In any system of personal absolutism, the man who embodies authority will inevitably be the cynosure of obedient and curious eyes alike. The danger is that overfamiliarisation of the person may eventually undermine respect for the authority. Certain great princes—one thinks of Henry VIII and Louis XIV—have been able to combine the reality of absolute power with an almost embarrassing accessibility (to the modern mind) as a 'public show'. Yet the reverent awe inspired in those seeing the one play tennis in an open-necked shirt, yeomanlike in his bluffness, and the other eat his supper alone at a table before a motley cluster of sightseers, wearing hired swords to gain entry, would not have survived the tourist guide-book and the systematised camera-clicking and neck-stretching of our day. There is a limit to the familiarisation of personal authority if it is to remain charismatic. If this is true for secular dignitaries, it is far truer for a man of power who is also the earthly embodiment of a religious mystery. While the accommodation was being prepared at the Vatican in 1967 for the first meeting of the Synod of Bishops, work was also in hand there on a new, vast audience-hall in which the pope would be on show to pilgrims, to visitors ... to tourists. It has been designed to hold 24,000 people.* Is it irrational, perverse, of those who deplore the resentful self-immurement of the 'prisoners of the Vatican' after 1870 to be concerned at the prospect of a pontiff as a routine spectacle? And what does this make, one may ask, of the idea of collegiality? Or is a pope one thing to his Synod, and something quite other to the trippers?

There is already one of these vast audience-halls at Castelgandolfo, built in Pius XII's time and redolent of the public style of his pontificate. The old reception arrangements for the few hundred who used to go to see the pope in his retirement from the Roman heat proved inadequate for the thousands who now flock there. Not so very long ago, visitors used to foregather in the courtyard of the palace, and the pope appeared on a small balcony to bless them. Pius XII did this with great charm. And so might Paul VI, for the smaller the gathering, the more natural he is; the goodness of the man shines through the ceremonial, and sweetness overcomes his anguish. But the place of assembly at Castelgandolfo is now a huge, cinema-like construction, erected specifically to show off the pope to large crowds brought by motor-coaches. The atmosphere of these exhibitions of the pope is quite devoid of any element of a great spiritual occasion—which, surely, it should be. The building of another such audience-hall in the Vatican seems a negation of dignity erected into a system of advertisement. It certainly does not indicate an intelligent appreciation of what the modern crisis of authority is about: it is, rather, the exact opposite.

The deliberate fostering of a papal 'personality cult' (though originating, it may be, in a cult of the office rather than of the person) is likely to put a papal audience on the same level in the visitor's mind as all the other sights of Italy: the Bay of Naples or the Leaning Tower of Pisa—more exotic, perchance, more emotionally stirring, but that is all. Constantine would feel at home; Marcus Aurelius would groan in spirit: yet more 'stage

* The architect is Nervi; it will be the first modern building of interest in the Vatican.

plays and the vain pomp of processions'. The first Christian emperor invoked new techniques—a new religion—to counteract the decay of the civil power. The modern Vatican, in an age marked by the near-collapse of institutional religion, is deploying its traditional imperial pomp in the style of the public relations expert.* It has even lost its elegance.

Rome is the most cynical of cities. It destroys illusions and nurtures false hopes. The greatest achievement of John was that he made it the seat of goodness. This is not to say that the element of goodness had been lacking in the Church, or that it is particularly lacking now. The present pope is quite certainly a good and holy man. It is just that goodness has been, and is, but an element, not the whole matter. The main talking-point in Rome in early 1967, let us say, would not have been a spiritual or philanthropic matter. It would have been the public controversy as to whether the Italian government was justified in acceding to the Vatican's somewhat peremptory demand that it continue to be exempted from paying dividend tax on its industrial holdings in Italy.

Most of the priests one meets in Rome seek to justify this exemption. The money is destined for good works: charities, for instance, and Catholic schools. Suggest that in some cases an example of accepting communal obligations borne by every one else might be no less constructive than charity; suggest that the voluntary isolation of Catholic schools from other schools is a questionable policy in the contemporary world: the answer is certain to be a solid defence of the existing system. Defending one's own can be a virtuous trait, up to a point. For a religious organisation, most things connected with it have to be shown in a good light, otherwise the beliefs themselves might be impaired in the minds of the faithful by association with corruption. But this determination to give no ground, or seeming to give it but not, in fact,

* One smiled patronisingly at business-man's *gaucherie* when Jackson Martinelli, called on in the mid-fifties to advise the Curia on modern methods of administration and 'promotion', declared: 'There is not much difference between Standard Oil of New Jersey and the Catholic Church's operations. The only difference is that Standard produces oil, and the Catholic Church produces a way of life and thought.' (*Manchester Guardian*, 23 January 1956.) Today one is inclined to treat Mr Martinelli's appraisal with greater respect.

moving, can cost an irreplaceable amount of respect. In Rome, the Vatican's financial dealings are known to be vast and profitable. Some of the enterprises in which it is known to be involved are a safe distance away, to judge by their behaviour, from any observable operation of the Holy Spirit. The Roman saying on the subject is a mordant play on words:

> *A Roma Dio non è trino*
> *Ma quattrino*

Quattrino is an old coin, a colloquialism for 'money'. The couplet cannot be neatly translated. Perhaps the best rendering would be something like:

> In Rome God is not One in Three,
> Four-square cash is He.

Defence of the traditional authority and of its claims, at whatever cost, is dispiriting. There have been plenty of suggestions, usually from disgruntled Catholics, for a better course; there is the impossible idea of transforming the system into a decent working democracy. Or a foreign pope. These are catchwords, scarcely constructive ideas.

Not that a foreign pope is an impossibility. He would have to be from a small, preferably neutral country, such as Austria: or one associated with peace-making without national claims, such as Canada. Both these countries happen to have cardinals of the calibre for election. It might be difficult to round up votes for them. (It will be recalled that Montini was elected partly because some of his conservative colleagues, opposed to him, faced up to the fact that he was the only Italian acceptable to a majority of the non-Italians.) But it is no longer hard to envisage a foreign pope. It is just that a seemingly radical change of this kind would probably make little difference. John XXIII showed that the best 'foreign' pope was a real Italian.

The constitutional structure is not the problem. At any rate, the changing of it would have less effect than enthusiastic reformers believe. The popular vision of the Roman Church is hierarchical, with the topmost pinnacle in close proximity to supernatural authority, whence it receives its own authority. Change must begin at the top, if necessary helped by pressure from below; but such pressure can hardly expect to be predominant at all times.

Certain of the changes introduced, mainly in the type of individual appointed to influential offices, will have notable effects in the future. Progressive personalities have been placed in some key posts, like Monsignor Moeller at the Holy Office and Monsignor Garrone, the former archbishop of Toulouse, who now directs the Congregation for Catholic Teaching, which previously had been a preserve of militant conservatism. They will influence one or two generations, and then the younger men will be criticising these reforming spirits of the 1960s as out of date and out of touch. They are almost certain to become so if they remain at the Vatican. The outlook in the Curia is still one of extraordinary inflexibility. This outlook would change only if, for long periods, the real executive were away from Rome. The city's associations are with lost grandeur and with nothing closer to the touch of real life than the ritual tip of a finger thrust forward to be kissed.

Here is one of the reasons why the Vatican appears heartless. It might seem impossible that a man of priestly goodness should be intent on opposing the divorce of utterly miserable and misery-making couples, should condemn sharply all talk of birth-control and raise his hands in horror at the thought of a non-celibate clergy. These are the issues that are hurting the minds and hearts of millions of people throughout the world. The total of human suffering and human distortion they cause is unmeasurable but manifestly immense. But this tribulation does not touch to anything like the same degree the great prelates in Rome. If it did, they might do something about it other than keep such problems at arm's length. These men in authority are, in the first place, members of an older school; secondly, they do not experience such personal suffering in their own lives or in their own families. The cousin or niece, for instance, of a prelate at the Vatican would have a much easier time than an ordinary individual in obtaining an annulment or some dispensation. Birth-control, or rather, the real agony of it as a problem, does not confront them in anything like the starkness which it presents to priests in the parishes. In

Rome, matters of conscience are liable to be silenced by empty religious gestures. Non-Italian prelates who take confession in Rome are struck by the stereotyped level to which many confessions have been reduced, often with little evidence, or requirement, of genuine pangs of conscience. Curial prelates, moreover, may well not have even this limited experience of grim reality. Their pastoral work generally does not amount to very much, and they are frequently attached as confessors or spiritual advisers to religious houses where they have their board and lodging. In a word, they are enclosed from the world.

As for celibacy: the continuation of this custom of the Church—it does not have scriptural authority—has less to do with Rome than the other issues, but it does depend to a large extent on the Vatican's refusal to admit weaknesses to be weaknesses and to change old instructions. The demand for the relaxation of the rule of celibacy is based on the sound evidence that many men are simply not suited to a celibate life, though they would be good priests, and that many of those on whom it is enforced are under too great a strain. Moreover, it is a great obstacle to missionary work. In Africa, for instance, Catholic missionaries find that the search for vocations is hard indeed if matrimony is forbidden. The Council reintroduced an order of married deacons, but it is not a solution for men who wish to be priests. This is an age in which pretence is not much valued. There need be nothing wrong in admitting that the institution of celibacy has, in fact, had its element of hypocrisy; many priests have not managed to live up to it and their conduct has been condoned. The logical, human solution would be to relax the law with the proviso, as a salute to the past, that celibacy would still be thought of as a particular virtue, a great distinguishing merit, in a priest.

Rome likes things to be the same for everybody. This is, again, a part of the imperial heritage. The instruction from Rome must be followed throughout the Catholic world. This is beginning to be recognised as a weakness, and an unnecessary one. The Catholic world itself is becoming increasingly complex. Centralisation has two defects. The first is that the instructions emanating from the centre are likely to be conditioned by the environment in which it is established. That is to say, with Italian affairs dominating the thinking of the Curia, instructions will tend to be issued because of what Italians may or may not be doing. This has undoubtedly occurred. The second disadvantage is that the centre will react to something that is happening in one part of the periphery, and will make its reaction applicable to the whole Catholic sphere, not just to the segment from which the disturbance came.

The week-end before the fourth session of the Council opened, the pope published *Mysterium Fidei*, his encyclical on the Eucharist. It was an attempt to redefine teaching because of some controversies among Belgian, French and, particularly, Dutch theologians. The pope had become convinced that these controversies amounted to a threat to the integrity of the faith. Some priests and doctors of divinity, it seems, were questioning basic doctrine. However, what they were actually arguing is not the main point in question here, which is the Vatican's disproportionate reaction to a disturbance in a strictly limited part of the universal Church. It called forth a papal document filled once more with expressions of anxiety and with restatements of familiar positions, and this at a time when many Council fathers were still looking hopefully for papal leadership after the depressing end to the previous session. They found *Mysterium Fidei* a discouraging document: exaggerated in its fears, old-fashioned in its content. It was taken for granted that his disciplinary words were aimed at certain definable geographical areas. As the prelates were gathering for what was to be the last session of the Council, Dutch bishops were able to read in the Italian press that the pope 'condemns' Holland. Thus, an encyclical addressed to the bishops and clergy of the entire Roman Catholic world manifestly applied only to some Dutch and, to a lesser extent, to some Belgian and French scholars. It was no less obvious that these newspapers' interpretation of the pope's statement was inspired by prelates who wanted precisely that impression conveyed. The all-embracing instruction looked a little foolish in its inflation.

What if nothing very substantial emerges in the way of profound change? To intelligent progressives in the Church, this is a forecast of despair which has as yet no justification. They believe that patience is needed until the Church emerges with a new stature from the pangs of development. They may be unduly optimistic. Like many people, they have perhaps been influenced by the many accounts of the Roman Church's affairs written during the last few years in a highly prejudiced way. These accounts have presented the recent history of Papacy and Council as if it consisted simply of the interaction of two bodies of men: a group of honest and honourable priests on one side, called liberals or progressives; and a set of obscurantist bullies on the other, called conservatives, of whom the prime examples are to be found in the Curia. No reader who has borne with me so far can be in doubt as to the strong representation of conservatism in the Curia. But it has too readily been taken for granted that the sensible and obvious thing to do is to retire Cardinal Ottaviani and his like, and to promote any number of Dutchmen, Frenchmen and Germans, with some Englishmen, to influential offices in a reformed Curia, where choirs of modern-minded *capellani* and prelates would daily sing the praises of liberty, democracy, Galileo, Teilhard and Cardinal Bea.

Most people have overlooked the fact that the conservatives—some clumsily and insensitively, it may be, but almost all sincerely—are seeking to retain many of the elements in Roman doctrine and practice which the Church has found both useful and attractive: the security of established authority; the sense of exultation that inspires an institution long tried by its enemies but still able by coherent discipline to keep them at bay. To be narrow is frequently to increase the pressure of faith; and that might be, in the absence of decisive liberal leadership, a reasonable alternative policy. It is the intransigent, the inflexible believers, those confident that what has been done for so many centuries is the right thing to do now and in the future—it is these, not the equivocators, who continue to hand down through the generations the trust bequeathed by history.

The liberal prelates at the Council were easier to get on with than the generality of conservatives. Their outlook was more modern, which meant (among other things) that they could find a far easier relationship with representatives of the press and television, and were sociable in a way that the hide-bound can never be. The ingredients of their faith seemed to be more broadly Christian, less exclusively Roman, than those of their opponents. They liked committee rule, as exemplified in their pressing for a greater participation by the bishops in the government of the Church. They were willing, on the whole, to have scientific methods received into biblical scholarship, going further in this than Pius XII. They wanted their brethren and their flocks to be modern Catholics, not just Catholics in the modern world. That was their most important distinguishing characteristic. It is not surprising that they gained widespread sympathy, particularly among people who had come surprisedly to the conclusion that the Roman Church might have something significant to say and do in the future, after all.

Their conservative opponents cherished a supreme and infallible pope, untrammelled by the advice of bishops residing who knows how remotely from Rome. What more could a pope want, surely, than the Curia and the Holy Spirit to guide him? They revered tradition as much as Scripture, and possibly more. They distrusted the concept of religious liberty, supported providence against contraception, and were far more thoroughly authoritarian than the most tradition-respecting among the reformers. They suspected every innovation as being of damage to some part of the Church's life, law or teaching particularly dear to them. They had real power but avoided publicity. They knew that, though relatively weak in numbers at the Council, they had only to maintain a coherent opposition and they would attain a position in which they could dominate the implementation of the Council's proposals. Hence, they worked harder than the liberals, with the result that they gained some important changes in the texts of conciliar documents and a few hundred contrary votes—against 2,000-odd—in vital ballots. It was not their voting strength in debate that mattered; it was the strength of their position, in attitude and in function. Many of them are in influential posts in Rome and in national hierarchies. They have effectively prevented the more thorough transformation that was confidently expected, by liberals within the Church and most people outside it, in the post-conciliar period.

They are wrong, of course. They are not contemporary. They are obscurantist. They are not even romantic. But the fortress mentality they represent is consistent with the Church's history. There is something to be said for consistency in an uncertain age. It has been Rome's successful rallying cry in the past. It could be so again.

If the danger of the prevalence of the conservative outlook is ossification, that of a liberal dominance could be a flabby process of osmosis between faith and secularity leading to the disintegration of the former. To be successful in its aims, a process of change needs to be strongly controlled. It needs more strength to direct the forces of change than to inspire a fortress garrison. For the conservatives to appear as possible steerers of the sounder course would be a great disillusionment for countless people within the Church and outside it. Moreover, a reversion to a conservative policy would, in every sense, be a second-best solution: one forced by circumstance from a general reluctance to follow the consequences of the liberal victory at the Council. Even so, the conservatives' effort then and since offers a valuable term of reference in that it is based on views which, in the very recent past, were regarded as essential tenets of the Roman Church. So much has to be said in justice to the conservatives. It also has to be noted as the basis for a forecast of the possible future line of development if the present courageous attempt to turn the Church's face towards the contemporary world should fail. The success of this *aggiornamento* depends on many things, not least of which is the Church's ability or otherwise to overcome its structural inelasticity and adhesion to the ideas of authority which have been shaped, like its institutions, by the process of history. It is certainly too early yet to say that the conservatives have been defeated. The marathon is still being run, though its pace is hardly what it was when the contenders leapt forward from the starting-block.

What would be the solution to the problem, consistent with the declared resolve of majority opinion in the Church to succeed in the *aggiornamento*? It is to be found, I think, in following the implication, in intellectual terms, of Paul's journey to the Holy Land. He spoke of returning to the origins. This would require a survey of every aspect of the Church's life, from the papal office itself to the officials of the Holy See who want payment for giving cameramen the best positions for filming a papal funeral. It would need to be conducted with ruthless honesty, inspired by the Council's debates but going beyond them where necessary. Everything would need to be re-examined with the aim of dispensing with what is superfluous, mistaken, or simply imposed by history, pride or plain supposition. The Council did not conduct its work in this way. It has, nevertheless, left behind it a number of indications which—if followed by a resolute mind and one determined to pay as little heed as possible to the safeguards for pride and institutional prerogative with which the conciliar documents are fairly heavily studded—could lead to the transformation of the Church into what it desires to be: the keeper, and the exerter, of the conscience of the modern world.

John and the Council between them left the Vatican and Catholicism in general on a pinnacle of public esteem unparalleled in modern history. Some of the interest and sympathy has already been eroded. It is a grief for the world, not only for the Roman Church, that the anxieties of an anxious age should so deeply mark a body which, to judge from its claims, ought uniquely to be in a position to cope effectively with these anxieties. Paul VI has nevertheless made the immense contribution, for which he has had little credit so far, of having laid before the world the problems besetting his Church at a moment when new forces and old doubts (or new doubts and old forces: both expressions are valid) are causing its venerable framework to tremble. In this, he is the true successor to John XXIII, because he has revealed the other side of the new-minted papal medal. He has shown the travail that accompanies attempts to impose a new pattern by ancient forms. Roncalli breathed into them a new spirit; Montini is grappling with the mind and body of a Church thus reanimated, enduring in his person the strain which his predecessor would have had to endure if he had lived to preside over the Church throughout the Council and in its aftermath. The present pontiff is confronted by an historic moment, but cannot cast off his historic burden.

Of all the moments of self-realisation offered to Christianity since its becoming a world religion, this may be the greatest. To meet the moment, Paul has shown that some of the burden of history must be removed. It is true that, by offering his ear to conservative voices, he has aroused fears that the character of the Roman Church may, in the end, retain a heavily traditionalist impress. This would be a profound misfortune because it would imply the missing of the great opportunity to achieve something far greater than the preservation of tradition. But it would not be the disaster some people assume it would be. Consistency is a refuge; yet a refuge is better than extinction on the slopes of higher endeavour. But it is premature, to say the least, to assume that, in redressing to some extent the balance between the liberal and the traditionalist forces, the pope has committed himself to the position of the latter. In areas where the initiative is wholly his own, not circumscribed by the contending schools of change and conservatism, he has taken radical steps. By his journeys, he has essayed an indication of how the new Papacy might become a vital part of contemporary life without losing its essential spiritual function. In particular, his pilgrimage to the Holy Land represents a radically fresh approach to the whole life of the Church.

How will he fare in steering St Peter's barque? Again and again one wonders if, in the interaction of necessity, personality and environment, the last has not the best chance of prevailing. John was the charmed, instinctive inspirer, responding almost gladly to the world and its difficulties, and evoking in return its warm affection. Paul, both intentionally and unintentionally, is the demonstrator, the delineator and the worrier. In his pursuit of the world and its difficulties, the world marks the strain of a heavily burdened runner. It is divided between regret and indignation when he stumbles. He was probably fated to have his person accompanied by a shade of disillusionment in the world's regard.

And against John and Paul alike there stands Rome: the great preserver, the weaver of the glorious garment of papal dignity and also the winding-sheet of many a papal intention. There is no apparent will in Rome to begin again at the beginning. The mental shudders still start as soon as questioning goes deep, as if doctrine, institutions, ritual, shareholding, musty privileges and trite vested interests—all must be defended with undiscriminating vigour.

Christianity may, like other religions, be experiencing great troubles, but it has more freedom than ever before to operate in the forms it wishes. To be a Christian now is of vital importance simply because it is no longer important socially or politically or for the satisfaction of conventional ambition. The potential of the Christian Churches for doing good is greater than their performance. This is one of the reasons why so many more people now are interested in what the Roman Church is doing, including its 'stage-plays and processions'. Few people, especially after any close experience of it, would fail to appreciate the extraordinary power of an organisation able still to provide spiritual comfort to millions by giving them simply a sense of belonging to a body possessing the truth, and bringing together on this basis in prayer and discipline a substantial part of mankind. The vision remains a beautiful one and, in such passages as the opening of the Council's decree *De Ecclesia*, can still be defined in moving terms:

> [God] planned to assemble in the holy Church all those who would believe in Christ. Already from the beginning of the world the foreshadowing of the Church took place. It was prepared in a remarkable way throughout the history of the people of Israel and by means of the Old Covenant. In the present era of time the Church was constituted and, by the outpouring of the Spirit, was made manifest. At the end of time it will gloriously achieve completion when, as is read in the Fathers, all the just, from Adam and 'from Abel, the just one, to the last of the elect', will be gathered together with the Father in the universal Church.

This teleology is not only sublime, it also diminishes in the mind of the faithful any fear that historical circumstances have made too deep a mark on the visible Church. The sceptic is rather overcome by the grandeur, and the pretensions, of the prospect. He cannot deny that, if the Church has to live in this world and accept its historical conditions, so has everybody else. Yet the feeling that, somewhere, under an elaborate, irrelevant but immovable superstructure, unfathomable good is struggling endlessly to emerge—this, in the short human term, can be plain saddening.

11
Even from Within

ON September 29, 1967, shortly before ten o'clock in the morning Paul VI took his private lift down to St Peter's for the first time since his illness the month before. He had come to open the international Synod of Bishops, meeting for the first time. His face was pale and showed the weariness brought on by discomfort. There was a brief moment of unsteadiness when he took his seat in preparation for his concelebration of mass with fourteen of the bishops attending the Synod; but physically he managed the morning well. The pope's voice, huskier than usual when he began his discourse, warmed as he insisted on his great preoccupation with dangers to doctrinal purity. In sombre terms, he told the bishops that their objective was to be the preservation and strengthening of the Catholic faith—its integrity, vigour and development, its doctrinal and historical coherence—and the acknowledgement of the faith as the foundation of the Church and its *raison d'être*. Solicitude for doctrinal fidelity, he said, should direct the work of the post-conciliar Church.

Paul spoke of the immense dangers caused by the irreligious orientation of modern thinking. Among these was the insidious tendency to adapt the dogma of the faith to secular thought and language. Even from within the Church ideas were being uttered by teachers and writers who, sincerely desirous as they were of giving new expression to Catholic doctrine, were frequently intent on secularising it rather than of abiding by the Church's teaching authority.

Paul had earlier, in June 1967, strongly confirmed celibacy as a rule of the priesthood, and his address to the Synod was likewise essentially conservative, in the proper sense of the term. The progressive mind might have found some comfort in the fact that, for the first time, the pope had come to a great ceremony in St Peter's with no members of the Noble Guard in uniform, no courtiers in ruffs with swords at their sides. It was taken to be the beginning of changes at the papal court.

There, under the dome in perhaps the most theatrically majestic place on earth, the ancient institution of the synod, of the patriarch as first among equals, was revived, and the pope shared the altar with his fellow-bishops. Before the Mass he did something else. He walked to the bronze statue of St Peter, attributed to Arnolfo di Cambio, placed a candle before it and bent to kiss the statue's foot in a mist of incense.

Index

Acta Apostolicæ Sedis, 234
Adam of Usk, 140
Administration of the Properties of the Holy See, 167
Adzubei, Alexis, 122, 207–8, 243
African Church, early, 33–5, 41
Afro-Asian problems, 252–4
Agagianian, Cardinal Gregory, 115–16, 153, 187–8
Alaric, 40
Albi, Council at, 272
Albigensian heresy, 62, 65–6, 72, 220, 271–2
Alcuin, 47
Alexander VI, Pope, 71, 179n.
Alexander Severus, 13, 15
Alexandria, 30, 36, 38, 63, 329
Alfrink, Cardinal, archbishop of Utrecht, 189, 297
Ambrose, St, 27–8
Andreotti, Giulio, 222–4
Angola, 333
Antioch, 14, 30, 38, 63, 136n., 328
Antonelli, Cardinal, 86n., 104
Antoniutti, Cardinal Ildebrando, 153, 342n.
Apostolic Canons, 163
Apostolic Chamber (Camera), 155
Apostolic Chancellery, 155–6
Apostolic Constitution, 157
Apostolic Datary, 155
Apostolic Delegate, 160–1
Apostolic Nuncios, 159–60
Apostolic Penitentiary, 163–4
Apostolic Secretariat, 156–7
Apostolic Signature, Supreme Tribunal of, 165–6
Aquinas, St Thomas, 186, 273
Arabs, 35, 41, 46, 72, 295, 306
Arianism, 27, 33, 35, 37–8, 40, 42–43
Arius, 35–7
Arnolfo di Cambio, 357
Arles, Council of, 35
Arrupe, Fr Pedro, 340–3
Athanasius, 37
Athenagoras, 65, 209, 307, 311–13
Athens, 25, 113, 117
Attila, 41
Augros, Fr, 256
Augustine, St, 40, 42, 47, 255, 269, 272, 313
Aurelian, Emperor, 12
Australia, 202
Austria-Hungary, 88, 218
Avars, 46
Ave Maria, 272
Avignon, 31, 65n., 69–70
Azeglio, Massimo d', 84

361

INDEX

Balzan Peace Prize, 122, 212, 244
Baptism, doctrine of, 192
Basil the Great, St, 271
Basil II, Emperor, 306
Baum, Fr Gregory, 279
Bea, Cardinal Agostino, 112, 166, 187–93, 300, 304, 315–16, 352
Becket, St Thomas, 33
Belgians, 53, 77, 351
Benedict XI, Pope, 69, 148
Benedict XII, Pope, 156
Benedict XIV, Pope, 165
Benedict XV, Pope, 82, 90, 185, 245
Benevento, duchy of, 44, 64
Bentham, Jeremy, 268, 274
Beran, Cardinal Josef, Archbishop of Prague, 112, 208, 242–3
Bernard, St, 148, 150
Bernini, Giovanni, 139
Bethlehem, Paul VI at, 312
Bevin, Ernest, 110
Biblical Institute, 187
Biblical studies, encyclicals on, 185
Birth-control, 6, 66, 126, 265–89, 291, 318–19; Special Commission on, 283–9, 344
Bishops: Congregation of, 152; French collaborators, problem of, 113; under Holy Roman Empire, 58–9; Italian, 189; powers of, discussed at Council, 294, 301–3; in Russia, 206; 'titular', 159–60, 236; at Vatican Council, 189, 295–8; *see also* Synod of Bishops, *and* Episcopal collegiality
Bismarck, Prince Otto von, 79–80, 88
Bologna, 70, 149, 165, 189
Boniface, St, 42–3
Boniface VII, Pope, 56, 69

Boniface VIII, Pope, 138, 148, 196
Bonomelli, Emilio, 94
Borgia, Rodrigo (Pope Alexander VI), 71, 179n.
Boris, King, of Bulgaria, 114
Bossuet, Jacques, 83–4
Bramante, 71
Brennan, Mgr Francis, 165
Browne, Cardinal Michael, 132–3, 192
Butler, Bishop Christopher, 299, 320
Byzantium, 10, 15, 17, 38, 47, 304–306; Byzantine emperors, 55

Calixtus, St, 270
Cambodia, 249
Canon law, Roman, 163–4
Canossa, 60, 64, 75
Canterbury, archbishop of: *see* Fisher *and* Ramsey
Capovilla, Mgr Loris, 115, 132, 194, 208, 244, 304
Cardijn, Cardinal, 256
Cardinal-archbishops, 149
Cardinal-bishops, 135–6
Cardinale, Mgr Igino, 196, 202, 249
Cardinal-Nephew, 156–7
Cardinals, 134–49; national characteristics of, 188–9; numbers increased, 139, 149; *see also* Sacred College
Cardinal-Secretary, office of, 154–158
Carpentras, conclave at, 138
Carpino, Cardinal Francesco, 153
Casaroli, Mgr Agostino, 239
Caspar, 57
Castelgandolfo, papal villa, 15, 86, 94, 96, 139, 158n., 342; audience-hall, 346
Casti Connubii, 269, 275–9, 287

362

INDEX

Cathari, 272n., 287
Catherine of Siena, St, 273
Catholic Action, 92–5, 161, 194, 219, 223, 225, 227
Cathulf, 47
Cavour, Camillo Benso di, 85–6
Celibacy, of priesthood, 56, 58, 114, 282, 349–50, 356; respect for, 270–1
Celestine V, Pope, 325
Chalcedon, Council of, 305
Chamberlain of the Church, office of, 139–40, 155
Charlemagne, Emperor, 45–51, 59, 64, 72, 195, 305; memorial poem to Pope Hadrian, 49; theory of royal authority of, 47–48
Charles V, Emperor, 70, 76
Chateaubriand, François René de, 77
Chaucer, Geoffrey, 273
Chigi family, 142
Chile, 260
Chinese People's Republic, 101, 211, 249, 251, 327
Christian Democrats, 81, 87, 93–6, 211, 217–27
Christian unity: Secretariat for, 304; theme of, 129–30, 166, 191, 206, 208–9, 303ff.
Church in the Modern World, The, 317–18
Ciappi, Fr Luigi, 132
Cicognani, Cardinal Amleto, 117–118, 156, 168, 186
Cippico, Eduardo Prettner, 169
Clare, St, 70
Clement, St, 29–30
Clement IV, Pope, 137
Clement V, Pope, 69, 148
Clement IX, Pope, 176
Clement, X, Pope, 157

Clement XIV, Pope, 75
Clericos Laicos, 69
Clovis, King, 40, 42–3
Cluny monastery, 56
Colombo, Cardinal, bishop of Milan, 226
Colombo, Mgr Carlo, 132, 160
Colonna family, 69, 133
Communism: Holy Office decree against, 102–3, 257; methods of, 25; papacy's attitude to, 2–3, 26, 34, 72, 100–2, 119, 123–4, 129, 198–216, 263; in Poland, 228–40; Vatican Council ignores petition on, 321
Conclave, 10, 108, 115, 138; arrangements for, 140–2; Governor and Guardian of, 142
Confalonieri, Cardinal Carlo, 152, 261
Congregations, Sacred, 150–4, 187–8
Constans, Emperor, 27n., 37
Constantine the Great, Emperor, 2, 70, 83, 148, 271, 305, 346; attitude to Christianity, 10–28, 30–1, 33–9, 43–5, 47, 55, 63–4; builds St Peter's, 8, 30–1, 49; death of, 37; statue of, 50
Constantine II, Emperor, 37
Constantinople, 30, 38–9, 42, 47, 113, 254, 305, 311, 312, 313, 328; controversies with Rome, 41, 65, 306–7; Council of, 38; sacked by Crusaders, 63, 203, 307
Constantius II, Emperor, 21, 27, 37
Corinth, 29
Coronation of pope, 147–8
Council for Public Affairs, 156
Crusades, 62, 65–6, 72, 307
Cuba, 245, 339

363

INDEX

Curia, Roman, 149–71; Americans in, 190, 295; conservatism of, 105, 118–19, 227, 352–3; criticism and reform of, 53, 96, 174–191, 255, 294–301; recruitment to, 169; three main divisions, 150; *see also* Congregations
Czechoslovakia, 101, 208, 241
Czestochowa celebrations, 237–240, 330, 333

Dalla Torre, Guiseppe, 176
Daniel, Fr, 256
Dante, 325
Davis, Charles, 322
De Ecclesia, 232
Defrocked priests, 91–2
De Gasperi, Alcide, 94–5, 211, 218–19, 221–4
De Gasperi, Maria Catti, 224
De Gaulle, General Charles, 116n.
D'Herbigny, Fr Michel, 206
Dell' Acqua, Cardinal Angelo, 154
Democracy and the Church, 198ff.
Diocletian, Emperor, persecutions of, 13–15, 18–20, 28, 33–4, 135
Di Jorio, Cardinal Alberto, 167–168
Diplomatic service: Dean of corps, 160–1; delegates, embassies and legations, 160–1; grades, 159; privileges, 86
Divini Redemptoris, 207
Divino Afflante Spiritu, 185
Divorce, 91, 318, 349
Dodds, Prof. E. R., 25
Dogmas, new: *see under* Virgin Mary
Döllinger, Dr Johann, 6n.
Dominic, St, 66
Donation of Constantine, 63–4, 83
Donatists, 33–5, 113
Don Bosco, 87

Döpfner, Cardinal, 214
Downside, Abbot of: *see* Butler, Bishop Christopher
Dutch, at Vatican Council, 53, 351

Eastern Churches, 152, 305–8; Congregation of, 150, 152; *see also* Orthodox Church *and* Uniate Churches
Ecclesiam Suam, 129, 244, 254, 259
Ecumenical Council: *see* Vatican Council, Second
Ecumenism, decree on, 310, 316
Edward I, King, of England, 69
Elections, papal, 107, 115–16, 124, 128, 136; Gregory X's rules for, 137–8; smoke-signals, 146; three methods for, 143; voting at, 144–6
Elizabeth I, Queen, 74, 100, 314
England: contraception movement in, 274; early Church, 42–43; English pope, 143; industrial missions, 255–6n.; overlordship of Innocent III, 62–3; resists papal authority, 68–9; Roman Church in, 77, 315
Enlightenment, 65n., 75–6
Episcopal collegiality, 133, 193, 301–2, 336, 338
Eugenius IV, Pope, 165
Eusebius of Caesarea, 27–8
Extraordinary Ecclesiastical Affairs, Congregation for, 154, 159

Fanfani, Amintore, 221
Fascism, 81, 91–4, 96, 204, 210, 223–4
Fatima, shrine of, 264, 329–33
Faulhaber, Cardinal, 213
Felix of Aptunga, 33
Feltin, Archbishop, 257–8
Feretto, Cardinal Giuseppe, 164

INDEX

Financial administration, 154, 166–9
Fiordello, Bishop, 98n., 221
Fisher, Archbishop Geoffrey, 314
Fourth Crusade, 62, 203, 307
France: birth-control movement in, 268, 274–5; bishops of, 53, 56–7, 60; French Revolution, 75, 154, 200; resists papal claims, 31, 68–9; worker-priests, 254–9
Franks, 40, 43–52, 55
Francis, St, 66, 70
Francis Joseph, Emperor, 88
Franco, General, 199, 210, 226, 327
Franco-Prussian war, 274
Frederick II, Emperor, 64, 68, 221
Frings, Cardinal, archbishop of Cologne, 174, 189, 295
Funerals, papal, 139–40, 355

Gabrielli, Cardinal, 158
Galeazzi, Count, 168
Galen, Bishop, 213
Galileo, 352
Gardone, Mgr Gabriel, 154
Garibaldi, Giuseppe, 85
Garrone, Archbishop, 188, 189, 349
Gasparri, Pietro, 156, 164
Gasperi: *see* De Gasperi
Gazzada, commission at, 315
Gedda, Prof. Luigi, 94, 97, 223–5
Genoa, conference at, 205
Germany: Church established, 42; emperors, 51–6, 68; modern, 88, 212–16, 275; relations with Poland, 233, 236–8
Gibbon, Edward, 17, 25, 40
Giobbè, Cardinal Paolo, 155
Giovanetti, Mgr, 249

Gladstone, W. E., 79–80
Gnostics, 270, 272, 287
Goa, 264, 333
Godin, Fr, 256
Goldberg, Arthur, 249
Gomulka, Wladyslaw, 17, 230–2, 238
Gonella, Guido, 222–3
Gorresio, Vittorio, 116n.
Graham, Fr Robert, 235
Grant, Mgr Charles, 320
Gratian, Emperor, 10, 163
Great Schism, 136, 152n.: *see also* Avignon
Gregory the Great, Pope, 41–2, 44, 71–2, 104, 254, 313
Gregory III, Pope, 143
Gregory VII, Pope, 30, 56–61
Gregory IX, Pope, 66
Gregory X, Pope, 137–8, 144
Gregory XIII, Pope, 153
Gregory XIV, Pope, 274
Gregory XV, Pope, 153
Gregory XVI, Pope, 165
Gronchi, President, 221
Guano, Mgr, 317
Guiscard, Robert, 64

Hadrian I, Pope, 49
Hadrian III, Pope, 51
Hadrian IV, Pope, 143
Hadrian VI, Pope, 147
Haering, Fr Bernard, 280–1
Haiphong, 248
Hales, E. E., 102
Heenan, Cardinal, 118, 135, 161, 281, 310, 317, 336
Henry III, Emperor, 55, 68
Henry IV, Emperor, 60, 62
Henry VIII, King, 314, 345
Heresy, suppression of, 65–6, 150, 186
Hilary, St, 21, 27–8

INDEX

Hildebrand, Cardinal: *see* Gregory VII
Hippolytus, St, 163, 270
Hiroshima, 340–1
Hitler, Adolf, 213–14, 239
Hirohito, Emperor, 341
Hochhuth: *The Representative*, 210
Ho Chi Minh, 248
Holland, Roman Church restored in, 77
Holy Land (Palestine), 130, 252, 311–13, 329, 331, 354, 356
Holy Office, 150-1, 165, 178–9, 186
Holy Spirit controversy, 306
Homoousin, 36–7
Honorius III, Pope, 132
Hosius, bishop of Cordoba, 27–8, 36
Hungary, 34, 101, 208, 210, 240–2

Immaculate Conception: *see under* Virgin Mary
India, 2, 130, 252, 264, 268, 326–7, 333
Indochina, 257
Indulgences, sale of, 71, 322
Innocent III, Pope, 27, 61–6, 68–71, 164, 203, 221, 229
Innocent VII, Pope, 140
Innocent VIII, Pope, 156
Innocent X, Pope, 157
Innocent XI, Pope, 157
Innocent XII, Pope, 108, 157
Inquisition, 66, 150–1, 188
Investiture controversy, 58–61, 68
Ireland, 77, 229
Irenaeus, St, 33
Italy: Communist Party, 2, 216, 220–5; modern politics, 216–28; papal political ban, 90, 219, 228

Japan, 340–1

Jerusalem, 63
Jesuits: at Hiroshima, 340; Paul VI's clash with, 331, 338–43; suppression and restoration, 75
Jews, relations with, 294–5, 316
John, King, of England, 62–3
John II, Pope, 147
John XIII, Pope, 56
John XXII, Pope, 138, 165
John XXIII, Pope: as papal nuncio, 34, 114, 115, 176, 196, 257–258; as patriarch of Venice, 113–15, 304; attitude to birth-control, 266; attitude to communism, 3, 26, 122–4, 207–9, 212, 216, 228–9, 243; attitude to Curia, 118, 177; character and aims, 4–6, 97, 101, 110, 112–14, 117–19, 194, 347, 356; diary— *Journal of a Soul*, 114; election of, 115–16, 128, 138–9, 146, 176–7; encyclicals, 23, 120, 123, 129, 244; Hungarian policy, 241–2; illness and death, 121, 124, 140; Loreto pilgrimage, 332; origins of, 113; peace appeals, 243–6; Polish policy, 228–9, 235–6; popularity of, 96, 107, 109, 332; progressive outlook, 57–8, 79, 186, 190, 194, 199, 227; three main contributions of, 119–21; Vatican Council called by, 119, 292ff.
Johnson, President Lyndon B., 249–50
Joseph II, Emperor, 75
Julian, Emperor, 12, 25, 37
Julius II, Pope, 71, 179n.

Kennedy, President John F., 32, 123, 201

INDEX

Kerensky, Alexander, 204
Khrushchev, Nikitas, 122–3, 208, 216, 222
Knaus, Hermann, 277
König, Cardinal Franziskus, 166, 189, 208, 241

Laberthonnière, Lucien, 185
Lahaut, Julien, 211
Lambeth Conference (1930), 269, 275–6, 287
Lamennais, F. R. de, 76
Lando, Pope, 147
Langton, Archbishop Stephen, 63
Larrona, Cardinal Arcadio, 154
Lateran Councils, 30, 66, 136, 196
Lateran Pacts (1929), 85, 91–2, 95, 142, 167; reaffirmed, 217
Lateran Palace, 55, 86, 139
Latin America, 259–63
Law of Guarantees, 85–6, 91
Léger, Cardinal, 282
Leo III, Emperor (the Isaurian), 41
Leo I, Pope, 41
Leo III, Pope, 45–7, 50–1
Leo IX, Pope, 64, 306
Leo XIII, Pope, 88–90, 121, 138, 160, 167, 185–6, 200
Lercaro, Cardinal, 189
Licinius, Emperor, 14n., 18, 36
Liénart, Cardinal, 190, 258, 299, 309
Lincoln, Abraham, 104
Lisi, Dr Galeazzi, 97, 194
Liturgy, reform of, 303
Liutprand, King, 43
Liverpool: new cathedral, 161
Loisy, Alfred Firmin, 184–5
Lombardi, Fr, 224
Lombards, 41–6, 50, 305
Loreto, John XXIII at, 332
Louis VIII, King, 62

Louis XIV, King, 345
Lourdes, 78, 183
Loyola, Ignatius, 340
Luther, Martin, 70–1
Lyons, Second Council of, 137–8

Macaulay, T. B. (Lord), 65, 75
MacCloskey, Cardinal, archbishop of New York, 104
Machiavelli, 72, 203
Magnentius, Emperor, 37
Malthus, Thomas, 274
Manichees, 269–70, 272, 287
Manning, Cardinal Henry, 77n.
Mao Tse-tung, 249
Marcellus II, Pope, 147
Marcus Aurelius, 25, 323, 346
Marella, Cardinal Paolo, 166, 258
Marjorinus, bishop of Carthage, 34
Mark, St, 38
Marriage, 66, 91, 152–3, 164, 221, 268–70, 273, 277, 282–3, 288, 318–19; mixed marriages, 315–316
Martel, Charles, 41, 43
Martin IV, Pope, 138
Martin V, Pope, 142, 156
Martin of Tours, St, 48
Martinelli, Jackson, 347n.
Masella, Cardinal Aloisi, 112, 115–116, 139, 153, 155, 176
Mass, in vernacular, 303, 315
Massimo family, 133
Mater et Magistra, 23, 120–1
Mathilda, Countess of Tuscany, 64
Maximinus, Emperor, 14n.
Maximos IV Saigh, patriarch, 136n., 282, 308
Meouchi, Paul Pierre, patriarch, 136n.
Merovech, 43
Merry del Val, Rafael, 156

INDEX

Mexico, 260
Micara, Cardinal, 179-80
Michael Cerularius, patriarch, 65, 306
Michelangelo, 71, 99, 144, 246
Milan, 30, 127, 149, 165, 179; Edict of, 18-19, 21, 23
Mill, James, 268, 274
Mill, John Stuart, 78
Miltiades, Pope, 34, 113
Mindszenty, Cardinal, 34, 101, 208, 231, 240-2
Missions, 153, 187, 256, 350
Modernist movement, 184-7, 278
Moeller, Mgr, 188, 190, 349
Mogilev, see of, 204
Mohammed, 41
Molotov, 207
Montfort, Simon de (elder), 66
Montini, Giovanni Battista: see Paul VI
Montini family, 125-6, 134n.
Mozart, 116
Murri, Romolo, 185, 218
Mussolini, Benito, 81, 86-7, 91-3, 204, 210, 217, 219, 223
Mysterium Fidei, 351

Napoleon I, Emperor, 9, 75, 142, 157-8, 252
National Civic Committees, 94, 225
National Democratic League, 218
Nazi atrocities, 198, 210, 212, 214-215
Nehru, Pundit, 264
Nenni, Pietro, 222
Neoplatonism, 25, 36
Nervi, architect, 346n.
New York, 104, 149, 275, 326-7; Paul VI in, 2, 32, 58, 130
Nicaea, Council of, 36-7, 163; Nicene creed, 37-8

Nicholas Breakspear: *see* Hadrian IV
Nicholas I, Pope, 148
Nicholas III, Pope, 64, 138
Nicholas IV, Pope, 138
Nicholas II, Tsar, 204
Nicomedia, bishop of, 37
Nina, Cardinal, 167
Non-Believers, Secretariat for, 166, 189
Non Expedit, 92, 228
Noonan, Prof. John T., 274
North Atlantic Treaty Organisation, 211, 257
Nuclear weapons, 3, 295, 318-21

Ochab, President Edward, 239-40
Oder-Neisse territories, 230, 236-238, 240
Ogino, Kyusaku, 277
Old Catholics, 6n.
Oran, 268-9
Orsini family, 133
Orthodox Church: Greek, 63, 114, 209, 303, 305-8, 311-13; Russian, 203, 208-9
Osservatore Romano, 211, 222, 234, 240, 285
Ostia, diocese of, 135-6
Ostrogoths, 40, 42
Ottaviani, Cardinal Alfredo, 103-104, 133n., 192, 221, 284; conservatism of, 182-4, 186, 226; Vatican appointments of, 124, 151, 170, 176, 178; at Vatican Council, 282, 298-300
Otto the Great, Emperor, 51, 54-55, 56, 59, 108
Otto III, Emperor, 55

Pacelli, Prince Carlo, 168
Pacelli, Cardinal Eugenio: *see* Pius XII

INDEX

Pacelli family, 101, 125
Pacem in Terris, 123, 208, 244
Pamphilj, Cardinal, 207
Pancirolo, Cardinal, 157
Papacy: claims over civil authorities, 16–17, 27, 45, 47–8, 62–4; coinage of, 44, 139n.; crisis of authority, 338–47; coronation, 147–8; death of pope, procedure at, 139; elections, *q.v.*; general audiences, 31, 346; industrial holdings, 17, 21–2, 44, 167–8, 264, 347; inter-regnum, 139–41, 155; in Italian politics, 96, 216–28; 'pilgrim pope' notion, 326–34; political involvement, reasons for (resumé), 71–2; robes, 147; temporal power, beginnings and loss of, 44–6, 85; titles of pope, 30, 62, 216–217, 223, 254; *see also* Vatican
Papal Court: chapel, 171; household, 171; posts and titles at, 132–4, 140
Papal Infallibility, dogma of, 5–6, 78–80, 279
Papal Supremacy, concept of, 79, 302–3
Papal States, 53, 64, 76–7, 81–6, 96, 157–8, 167–8
Paris, 78, 256–8; Roncalli as nuncio in, 113, 115, 176, 187, 203
Passaglia, Fr, 86n.
Patrimony of St Peter, 64
Paul, St, 11, 29, 270
Paul I, Pope, 45
Paul III, Pope, 150
Paul VI, Pope: 26, 65, 94, 96, 118, 123–30, 160, 166, 170, 241; as archbishop of Milan and at Curia, 96, 102n., 110–13, 116, 121, 124–5, 211, 224; addresses Latin-American bishops, 261–263; addresses Synod of Bishops, 356; administration and reforms, 54, 57, 82, 97, 150–151, 154, 175, 178–9, 188–90, 193–4, 225–7, 259, 280; assessment of, 5–6, 31–2, 107, 126, 128, 178–9, 324–8, 355–6; attitude on birth-control, 266–8, 281–6, 289, 344, 349; attitude to communism, 211, 244–5; ecumenical outlook, 304, 307, 311–314; election of, 111–12, 124, 138, 143, 179–80, 348; encyclicals, 58, 129, 252, 285, 326, 333, 351; interest in young countries, 252–5; international affairs, 326ff.; John's appraisal of, 126; journeys of, 2, 32, 128, 130, 252, 264, 311–13, 326, 329–33, 354; peace efforts, 156, 198, 245–51, 330; personal connection with Curia, 178–82; Polish visit projected, 2–3, 237–40; relations with Hungary, 241–2
Peace, efforts for, 245–52
Pedroni, Monsignor, 249
Pelligrino, Archbishop, 226–7
Pepin the Short, 43–5, 47, 51, 64, 305
Pétain, Marshal, 34
Peter, St, 11, 29, 38, 45–6, 50, 52, 55, 130; burial place, 30–1
Photius, 306
Philip I, King, of France, 60
Philip the Fair, King, of France, 69, 76
Piedmont: monasteries dissolved, 87
Pignedoli, Mgr Sergio, 249
Pius VI, Pope, 75
Pius VII, Pope, 75, 142, 158
Pius IX, Pope, 78–81, 83, 86–8, 104, 173

INDEX

Pius X, Pope, 90–1, 138, 158, 165, 184, 186–7

Pius XI, Pope, 91–3, 97, 114, 127, 138, 167, 204, 206–7; views on birth-control, 269, 275–9

Pius XII, Pope, 80, 94, 113, 115, 117–21, 125–8, 149, 168, 194; as cardinal, 156n., 164, 206, 213; administration of, 156, 175–6, 178, 188; assessment of, 96–106, 140; attitude to birth-control, 266, 268, 277, 280, 283; attitude to communism, 3, 209–12, 215–216, 228; attitude to Germany, 212–15, 245; death of, 96–7; election, 138; encyclicals, 185; politics and modern problems of, 197–200, 216–17, 221–5, 257–8; rules for inter-regnum, 140, 142–4; Tardini's criticism of, 105, 110–11

Pizzardo, Cardinal Giuseppe, 127, 154, 169, 205, 258

Place, Francis, 274

Podgorny, N. V., 209

Poland, 3, 17, 75, 77, 206, 228–40, 263, 330; joint commission's communiqué, 232–4; Pope receives bishops, 235–6

Popular Party, 218–19, 224

Population, world, 278

Portugal, 131, 260, 262, 264, 329, 333

Prato case, 98–9, 221

Preysing, 213, 215

Prince Assistant, office of, 133

Pro Comperto Sane, 154

Progressio Populorum, 252–3, 285, 326, 333

Pro-Nuncios, 160

Protestantism, emergence of, 70, 309–10

Providentissimus Deus, 185

Quadrigesimo Anno, 280

Quirinal Palace, 142, 158

Radini-Tedeschi, Bishop, 113

Rampolla, Cardinal, 111, 156

Ramsey, Dr Michael, archbishop of Canterbury, 32, 311, 313–15

Raphael, 71

Ravenna, 42, 44, 64n., 189, 305

Reformation, 53, 65n., 74–5, 293, 309

Refutation of all the Heresies, 270

Regimini Ecclesiæ Universæ, 151, 154

Religious Liberty, Declaration on, 294, 310, 316

Rerum Novarum, 89, 121

Revelation, 298–301, 307, 309

Rheims, Council of, 66

Ridgway, General, 257

Riga, Treaty of, 206–7

Risorgimento, 76, 81, 84–5

Roberti, Cardinal Francesco, 166, 179

Roberts, archbishop of Sugdea, 320

Roman and Anglican joint commission, 314–15

Roman Empire, 10–24, 40, 48

Roman Rota, Sacred, 153, 163–5

Rome: beautified by Julius II, 71; centre of Christendom, 52; ecumenical services in, 170; Italian troops take city from pope, 67, 76, 78, 80, 85; municipal elections, 221–5; primacy of (concept), 28–32; titular churches, 135

Roncalli, Cardinal Angelo Giuseppe: *see* John XXIII

Rospigliosi, Cardinal, 176

Royal Chapel, 48

Rudolf of Habsburg, 64

INDEX

Ruffini, Cardinal, 226
Rugambwa, Cardinal, 252
Ruspoli family, 133
Russia, 196, 203-12, 216, 221, 237, 241, 304, 307-8, 332

Sacred College of Cardinals, 19, 57, 99, 104, 108, 112, 115, 124, 128, 135ff.; dean of, 154; membership of, 149; organisation of, 135-6; right to elect popes, 136; *see also* Elections
Sacred Hospice, Master of, 133
Saint-Basle de Verzy, Council of, 56
St Peter's (Rome), 45, 49-50, 74, 126, 128, 141; audiences in, 31-32, 98-9; balcony, 147-8; building of, 8, 21, 30-1, 71; as Council Chamber, 290; lying-in-state in, 139; statue of St Peter, 92
Sanctuary of Madonna of Divine Love, 216
Sanger, Margaret, 275
San Marino, 226n.
Sapienti Concilio, 158
Schröffer, Bishop, 188
Secretariat of State, 5, 96, 109-10, 127, 155-63; departments, 161-162
Secretariats, Special, 166
Secret Chamber, 156
Segni, Antonio, 221
Sergius IV, Pope, 147
Sheffield, Anglican *see* 256n.
Siberia, 204-5
Sicily, 64, 68
Simony, 56, 71, 108
Siri, Cardinal, 112, 125, 189, 226
Sistine Chapel, 32, 124, 142-8, 245, 311, 339, 343
Sixtus IV, Pope, 165

Sixtus V, Pope, 138, 149-50, 273, 309
Slipyi, Mgr Josef, 207
Socialism, 89, 90, 220, 222, 225
Society of Jesus: *see* Jesuits
Sofia, 113-14, 117
Spain, 41, 43, 260, 262, 327
Spanish College, 284
Special Administration, 167-8
Spellman, Cardinal, 250, 264
Spenser, Edmund, 322
Spiritus Paracletum, 185
Spoleto, duchy of, 44, 64
Staffa, Cardinal Dino, 166
Stalin, 206-7, 210, 212, 216, 223-4
Stephanos I Sidarouss, patriarch, 136n.
Stephen II, Pope, 44, 305
Stoics, 268, 270
Sturzo, Luigi, 218, 224
Suburbicarian dioceses, 135
Suenens, Cardinal, 189, 282
Suhard, Cardinal, 102, 256-7
Supreme Pontiff, title of, 10, 16, 148
Swiss Guard, 86, 139
Syllabus of Errors, 78
Sylvester I, Pope, 63
Synod of Bishops, 67, 193, 302, 310, 338, 345-6, 356
Synod of Sutri, 55

Talleyrand, 158
Tappouni, Cardinal, 136n.
Tardini, Cardinal Domenico, 105, 109-10, 117-19, 127, 162, 176-177, 183, 186, 192, 224
Tertullian, 10, 16, 21, 271
Testa, Cardinal Gustavo, 152
The Hague, conferences (1899 and 1907), 87
Theodoric, 40
Theodosius I, Emperor, 10, 27, 38

371

INDEX

Thessalonica, 38
The Times, 98, 171
Tisserant, Cardinal Eugène, 116, 136, 141, 154, 177, 187, 189
Togliatti, Palmiro, 2, 21
Torlonia family, 133n.
Toulouse, 188–9
Tours, 47, 49
Traglia, Cardinal, 170
Trent, Council of, 67, 74, 153, 164, 293, 299, 309
Tribunals, 163–6
Triple Alliance, 88
Troubadours, 271
Turin, 189, 226
Turkey, 329
Tyrrell, George, 185

Ubi Arcano, 92
Ubi Periculum Maius, 138
Uganda, 252
Unam Sanctam Ecclesiam, 196
Underdeveloped countries, 2, 9, 24, 58, 129, 252
Uniate Churches, 136 and n., 150, 152 and n.
United Nations: Paul VI's address to, 129–30, 171, 246, 250–1, 267, 283
United States, 117, 183, 186, 193, 220, 262; birth-control movement in, 275; bishops at Vatican Council, 188, 295; Roman Catholicism in, 77, 103–4
Urban VI, Pope, 136
Urbani, Cardinal, 226
Usury, 280–1

Vacantis Apostolicæ Sedis, 140, 143
Vagnozzi, Mgr, 343
Valence, 142
Valeri, Cardinal, 116n.
Vandals, 41

Van Lierde, Pietro Canisio, 264
Vatican: administration, 131, 140, 167; armed forces, 86; audience hall, new, 346; ceremonial, 6–7, 11, 14–15, 98, 128, 133, 154, 171, 328; Conclave arrangements, 140ff.; decoration of, 11, 162; finances, 166–9; hereditary titles at, 133; popes as 'prisoners' in, 76, 86, 88, 173; pope's roof garden, 126; pope's study, 4–5; prison, 169; Sacred Apostolic Palaces, 5, 133, 139, 158, 167, 173, 187; Secretariat offices, 158, 162–3; see also Papacy
Vatican City, 45, 85, 87, 91, 165, 168
Vatican Council, First, 67, 80, 293, 302
Vatican Council, Second, 290–322; appointment of committees, 295; Beran's address to, 208, 242; conservative prelates at, 353–4; end of, 325, 336; free discussion at, 200; Hungarian bishops at, 242; liberal prelates at, 352–3; opening of, 245, 290; origin of, 119; Polish delegates, 232, 235–7; reasons and aims of, 22, 292–5, 326, 344; results of, 355; Russian observers at, 208–209, 308

Some subjects discussed at: Birth-control, 281–3, 318–19; Catholic Action, 95; Communism, 321–322, 325; Episcopal conferences, 24, 193–4, 301, 327; Greater simplicity, 22; Lay participation, 182; Nuclear deterrent, 3; Priests' clothing, 39n.; Privileges of temporal rulers, 61; Religious liberty, 23–4, 310; War, 295, 319–21

Venerabilem, 62
Venice, 113–15, 117, 123, 142, 149, 165, 226, 304
Verona, Council of, 66
Victor Emmanuel II, King, 85
Vienna, 75–6, 111, 149, 166, 189
Vienne, Council of, 280
Vietnam, 2, 9, 156, 198, 245–50, 263–4, 330, 332–4
Villot, Cardinal Jean, 153, 188
Virgil, 40
Virgin Mary: Bodily Assumption, doctrine of, 6, 105, 276n. 299; Immaculate Conception, dogma of, 78; Madonna of Divine Love, sanctuary of, 216; Madonna of Fatima, *see* Fatima; Motherhood concept, 232
Viterbo, Conclave at, 137
Vladivostok, 205
Von Stauffenberg, 213

Warsaw, 127

Washington, 161, 248, 343n.
Westminster, see of, 135, 149, 320
Wheeler, Mgr Gordon, 320
White Russians, 203
Willebrands, Mgr Jan, 208
William the Conqueror, 60
William the Pious, duke of Anjou, 56
Woolwich, Anglican diocese of, 331
Worker-priest movement, 254–9
World Congress of Negro Writers and Artists, Second, 212
World Peace Movement, 257
Worms: Concordat of, 68; Council of, 60–1
Wyszynski, Cardinal, 17, 34, 190, 230–41

Yugoslavia: Vatican's agreement with, 239n.

Zacharias, Pope, 43–4